Chess Openings for Black, Explained

A Complete Repertoire

2nd Edition, Revised and Updated

by Lev Alburt, Roman Dzindzichashvili,
and Eugene Perelshteyn

with Al Lawrence

Published by:
Chess Information and Research Center
P.O. Box 534, Gracie Station, New York, New York 10028
Telephone: 212.794.8706

For ordering information, please see page 552.

Distribution to the book trade by:
W.W. Norton, 500 Fifth Avenue, New York, New York

Staff:

Editing & Design	Al Lawrence, OutExcel! Corp
	Email: al@outexcel.com
Creative Director	Jami L. Anson, Jadesign
	Email: jadandesign@aol.com
Editorial Consultants	Gary Colvin
	Michelle March
	Peter Kurzdorfer
	Daphne Lawrence
Technical Assistant	Igor Yagolnitser
Cover Design	Jami L. Anson, Jadesign
Illustrations	Kathleen Merz, Jadesign
Photo Credits	Jami L. Anson
	Nigel Eddis
	Brian Killigrew
	U.S. Chess Federation

ISBN: 978-1-889323-18-3
Library of Congress Control Number: 2008938050
10 9 8 7 6 5 4 3 2 1

Second Edition, Fully Revised and Updated. The first edition of this work was published in 2005, and reprinted with updates in 2006 and 2007.
Printed in the United States of America.

Preface to the 2nd, revised edition

This is the second, updated and fully revised edition of *Chess Openings for Black, Explained*. This new edition incorporates literally hundreds of changes, reflecting all relevant opening novelties and the authors' ongoing research in the three and a half years since the publication of the first edition. The vast majority of the recommendations in the 2005 edition fully stood the test of time. The few that didn't have been improved or replaced in this 2009 work. What's more, we give you a number of interesting alternatives not discussed in earlier editions.

Here are just some major examples: In the Accelerated Dragon, we make some important corrections regarding the move 7. f3 (p. 61). Also, after 9. 0-0 (p. 64), we discuss White's recent successes in the 9. ... d6 10. Ndb5 line—and two promising alternatives for Black to 9. ... d6. In "Defending against 4. Qxd4" (p. 110), we introduce a new, more promising line for Black. We fine-tune a number of our recommendations against the Maroczy Bind. We take note of White's improvements in the Alapin (p. 223)—and ways to counter it. We discuss how to play after 1. d4 Nf6 2. c4 e6 against rare (but tricky) third moves, such as 3. g3 and 3. a3. And there are many more updates!

You'll be able to read this book without squinting, without flipping pages back and forth to find the relevant diagram, and without trying to keep a 12-move variation in your head. More than 1,400 diagrams allow you to follow the action, even without a board and set. And whenever possible, we make sure that diagrams on a page-spread relate to the moves on that spread, reducing the need for back-and-forth page-turning. Moreover, we use color to emphasize important points and to give your eyes some variety. Importantly, we employ proven instructional techniques—such as forecasting important ideas in a chapter and ending each chapter with brief "memory markers"—to make following along and learning easier and more fun.

Look for **blue** diagrams and **blue** boxes that call your attention to the most important positions and most interesting ideas. This highlighted information will be especially worth revisiting and, sometimes, even committing to memory. The most important, or "main" lines are clearly set off in **bold** type. Diagrams related to main lines are larger than analysis and side-line diagrams, which are clearly labeled "ANALYSIS."

Table of Contents
Chess Openings for Black, Explained
A Complete Repertoire

Part IV: Defending against 1. c4 and other first moves   429

Part V: Illustrative Games   489

Chess Notation

Chess players around the world use "notation," a universal system for reading and writing chess. It's easy to learn, and once you know it, you'll be able to decipher quickly any book or newspaper article on chess.

The vertical columns of squares that run up and down the board are called *files* and are lettered. The horizontal rows of squares that run sideways are called *ranks* and are numbered. The intersection of a file and rank gives a square its name. Let's look at a board that gives the "address" of every square:

a8	b8	c8	d8	e8	f8	g8	h8
a7	b7	c7	d7	e7	f7	g7	h7
a6	b6	c6	d6	e6	f6	g6	h6
a5	b5	c5	d5	e5	f5	g5	h5
a4	b4	c4	d4	e4	f4	g4	h4
a3	b3	c3	d3	e3	f3	g3	h3
a2	b2	c2	d2	e2	f2	g2	h2
a1	b1	c1	d1	e1	f1	g1	h1

To make writing and reading fast, each piece is assigned a single letter. In English, we use these:

King =	K	Knight =	N
Queen =	Q	Rook =	R
Bishop =	B	Pawn =	the file it's on

So, the move "Qe5" means that the queen moves to the e5-square. Captures are marked with an "x," as in "axb5," which means that a pawn on a4 captures a pawn or a piece on b5.

Another special convention: Although the word "exchange" means to trade, "Exchange" (with a capital "E") means the trade of knight or bishop for a rook. A player who manages this trade "wins the Exchange."

PART ONE

ABOUT THIS BOOK

BY GM LEV ALBURT

Chapter 1
The Authors & the Book

This book provides you with a complete repertoire for Black, no matter what reasonable first move White makes. Two of your three authors are international grandmasters and repeat winners of the U.S. Championship. The third and youngest of us, Eugene Perelshteyn, was an IM when we wrote the original work in 2005; now he is a strong grandmaster.

This volume contains every secret the authors have compiled over decades of research in the recommended openings, and are still constantly digging for. No theoretical novelty (**TN**) will be withheld from you.

Such information is normally revealed only to world championship contenders, who hire top theoreticians, like Roman Dzindzichashvili, for that purpose. But shared TNs are only one of this book's unusual offerings.

Eugene Perelshteyn

To derive the most benefit, you should first understand what the book is designed to do. Part I of our five-part volume makes this point clear.

It helps if you understand who the authors are and what they bring to you that's unique. I'm a three-time U.S. Champion turned chess instructor. My books, including the *Compre-*

Roman Dzindzichashvili

hensive Chess Course: from beginner to master, which I co-authored and published, are among the best received chess instruction in the U.S.

GM Roman Dzindzichashvili ("Dzindzi" to his many fans) has been one of the prime movers and creators of modern opening theory for the past 40 years. His advice and help has been sought, with rewarding results, by such greats as Boris Spassky, Victor Korchnoi, Anatoly Karpov and Gata Kamsky.

In fact, Roman's revolutionary reassessment of the main line of the Scandinavian Opening allowed American Gata Kamsky to win a game (with Black) and then the match against world championship contender Vishy Anand. At that time, Gata was losing by two points with two games to go in a match played in Anand's home turf, India, for the right to play the world champion.

Roman is extremely generous in sharing his ideas. Perhaps that's because he knows he can always create new, equally important ones! In the 1984 U.S. Championship, Roman gave me a tool to handle the "Anti-Benko" move order: 1. d4 Nf6 2. Nf3. He suggested 2. ... e6 3. c4 a6!?.

This paradoxical move (later christened the "Dzindzi-Indian") remains unrefuted, and can be very useful in the hands of devoted Benko/Benoni players. It took me less than an hour to grasp the ideas behind this amazing system—and 90% of the credit goes to Roman's innate ability to single out and emphasize essentials, and to convey his knowledge of moves and ideas in a logical, easy-to-learn, easy-to-remember and practical way.

Every chess player should know how good it feels to go into a game completely confident in his opening repertoire, and it's even better when you have an important novelty or two up your sleeve. Not surprisingly, I played very well in this tournament. And with 3. ... a6 (first looked upon as completely ridiculous), I scored 2$\frac{1}{2}$ out of 3 versus Jim Tarjan, Larry Christiansen and Yasser Seirawan—all top GMs.

Such a result (with Black!) couldn't help but catapult me into clear first place—my first U.S. Championship crown.

Importantly, the Dzindzi-Indian wasn't a surprise novelty for one game (or one tournament) only. A year later, in another U.S. Championship, Christiansen tried to smash my position with a homemade, aggressive line. But Dzindzi's and my analyses held. I got an equal position (but one that was very sharp, and very familiar to me), eventually winning. Many opponents soon gave up trying to deal with Dzindzi's innovation and switched to other openings!

Roman's teaching talents aren't limited to GM chess—as the enormous popularity of his "Roman's Forums" and "Labs" videos attests. Dzindzi's TNs, ideas and, crucially, the convincing way he presents them, should help readers of this book feel as confident as I did during the 1984 U.S. Championship. As a result, you'll win many important games—whether you're playing a friend at home or competing in the U.S. Masters!

You'll find in this book many games played by Roman's student and our co-author, Eugene Perelshteyn. He helped Roman with opening research, checked their co-discoveries with computer programs and tested some of them, with success, against top GM opponents.

Putting it all together

Just the Facts!, the seventh and final book in the *Comprehensive Chess Course*, is one of the fastest-selling endgame books of all time. It was selected by the Chess Journalists of America as the best book of 2000-2001.

Comprehensive Chess Course Executive Editor Al Lawrence built special features into that series—and now into this book. These features make these books especially easy to learn from. Al is a former teacher with advanced degrees in curriculum and instruction. Additionally, Al is a former Executive Director of the U.S. Chess Federation and then served as volunteer Executive Director of the World Chess Hall of Fame in Miami. He is presi-

Al Lawrence

dent of OutExcel! Corp, a marketing and publishing firm.

Al is the author of more than a dozen books and scores of articles of his own on a variety of subjects. He writes on chess with great style and unique perspective. In fact, he was voted 2000-2001 Chess Journalist of the Year.

The new series: Alburt's Chess Openings

After Nikolay Krogius and I completed the endgame book *Just the Facts!*, only one part of the game, the opening, remained to be explained. (It wasn't within the scope of the *Course* to tackle opening theory in detail.)

Many of you are already familiar with *Pirc Alert!: A Complete Defense against 1. e4*, which I co-authored with the Pirc's number one practitioner, GM Alex Chernin. In *Chess Openings for Black, Explained* and its *White* companion volume, Roman, Eugene and I provide you with a solid, effective and interconnected repertoire for *both* White and Black—plus reviews of all other openings from both sides' points of view.

Following in the tradition of *Pirc Alert!*, our goal was:

• To convey the overall understanding of openings in such a way that it makes its readers self-reliant;

• To reveal all the theoretical secrets, often five to 10 years before they get into the opening reference books;

• To do all this with respect for the other demands on the reader's time.

How we selected these openings

The criteria we used to select an opening for the repertoire are:

• It's completely sound, even up to the super-GM level;

• It rewards ideas rather than rote memorization—thus its theory can be reduced to a relatively small and completely understandable portion;

• We gave preference to openings rich in our TNs!

Who should read this book?

Players of all strengths, from beginners to super-GMs, will profit from this book. Here are some who will benefit most:

• Anyone who already plays some of the recommended openings—for you this book will be like having the personal opening notebook you always wanted;

• Anyone who has to play against these lines;

• Anyone who wants to develop a comprehensive, coherent and completely modern, competitive repertoire for Black, without

Lev Alburt

gaps in his understanding;

• Anyone who wants to acquire back-up openings to understand on a very high level;

• Any player who wants to know what it means to master openings like top professionals do.

Structure and content

In *Chess Openings for Black, Explained*, we provide you with a complete repertoire for Black. The companion volume does the same thing for White—based on 1. e4.

Part II of this book deals with defending against 1. e4, discussing various replies to it, and then concentrating on our chosen line, the Hyper-Accelerated Dragon. Roman and Eugene have contributed greatly to the theory of this opening. Much of their analysis has never been published previously, nor even played. We also provide you with reliable, yet in some cases little-known, systems to counter more and more frequent Anti-Sicilians.

Part III provides readers with a "five-star" defense against 1. d4. We offer the venerable Nimzo-Bogo complex, the most popular choice among the world's elite for more than half a century. But even there you'll find numerous new and bold ideas!

Part IV deals with 1. c4 and the rest of White's first moves. Again, we review all of Black's main options. Our recommendation: 1. ... c5, followed by the king's bishop fianchetto. This line shows how inter-connection works—positions we seek are the same Maroczy-Binds we've studied in depth in Part II.

Part V consists of carefully chosen and instructively annotated sample games.

Your repertoire will indeed be coherent—and complete!

Some Chess Symbols

n chess literature, the assessment of an entire position is frequently expressed with one of a number of symbols. Here are the most common:

+–	**White has a decisive advantage.**
±	**White has a clear advantage.**
⩲	**White has a slight advantage.**
=	**The chances are equal.**
⩱	**Black has a slight advantage.**
∓	**Black has a clear advantage.**
–+	**Black has a decisive advantage.**

Individual moves of a game can also be assessed with symbols:

!!	**A very good move**
!	**A good move**
?	**A weak move**
??	**A blunder**
!?	**An interesting or provocative move, often involving some risk**
?!	**A dubious move**

Our thanks to the U.S. Chess Federation
for the use of the photos throughout this book.
The U.S. Chess Federation is the membership organization for chess
players of all levels, from beginner to grandmaster.
For information on USCF membership, please go to www.uschess.org.

Thanks also to the World Chess Hall of Fame.
For information on Hall membership, please go to www.worldchesshalloffame.org.

For DVDs on playing better chess, go to chessondvd.com
or call 877-chessdvd (243-7738).

Chapter 2
How to Use This Book
Making the most of your time

You can count on this book as your primary source of chess opening knowledge for a very long time. It will guide you through the moves, ideas and surprises of a recommended network of related openings—defenses that have never been refuted and that offer you a rich source of creative resources.

Besides making the book rich in chess knowledge, including previously secret theoretical novelties, we wanted to make it easy to learn from—and to help you remember and apply what you learned.

You'll learn and understand the typical positions, the key ideas, and the relative value of the pieces in each line.

You can read and study this book sequentially, as it is laid out. Or you can take the chapters out of order, studying first a variation that you have reason to be interested in immediately. (Perhaps you are preparing for a tournament or a special game.) Or if you're researching from White's point of view, you may want to go to a chapter on a specific variation. Taking the material out of order shouldn't make any difference in the benefits you derive, as long as you ultimately read the whole book, and as long as you do read each chapter itself in sequence. The reasons will become clear as you take a look at the special features we've built in to help you learn and remember.

Special features and how to use them

• On the left-hand page before each chapter, you'll find "Some Important Points to Look For"—a very short preview of the chapter to put the upcoming information in context. Then you'll see a series of briefly explained diagrams, touchstones for the most important ideas you're about to study. Previewing the most important ideas will prepare you to better understand them when you meet them in the context of the chapter—and will increase your ability to remember them. Additionally, there will be an index of the chapter's main lines.

• Throughout the book, the most important positions are highlighted in **blue**. This format not only calls your special attention to them, but makes the process of reviewing what you've learned much quicker and more effective.

• The most important ideas and guiding principles are set in large type within boxes, what art directors refer to as "call-outs," also highlighted in **blue**, with the same effect.

• Importantly, moves and the diagram they relate to are nearly always placed on the same page-spread! Although a painstaking process for the page designer, this layout principle keeps you from having to flip back and forth from moves to diagrams.

• There are many diagrams and they are in the right places, often making it possible to study without a board.

• Main lines are given in bold and clearly separated from analysis.

• It's easy to identify main-line positions. Main-line diagrams are large throughout. All other positions, whether pure analysis or side-games, are smaller and labeled "ANALYSIS."

• Every chapter offers a brief summary of its main ideas. Carefully reading the summary after studying a chapter will help you remember the key points.

• Every chapter is followed by "Memory Markers," centrally important positions that challenge you to lock in the concepts you've learned and encourage you to use these ideas in new positions, as you'll want to do in your own games.

We want this book to be your complete reference for your entire playing career. We intend to update the book whenever necessary, as we did in this Second Edition. In between editions, you can look for updates on GM Eugene Perelshteyn's website: www.ChessOpeningsExplained. See page 203.

We want to help to make your opening studies as simple and as well organized as possible!

**You can look for updates on
www.ChessOpeningsExplained.com
See page 203.**

Chapter 3
How to Study Openings

Y ou've decided to choose a serious opening repertoire. Your idea is first to find a promising game-starting scheme, to learn it, and to stick with it. So you hit the reference books.

Petrosian's complaint

After hours or even days, what's your finding? See if this sounds familiar: "When I study White, it's always equal. When I study Black, it's always worse!" Just so you understand that we all hit this wall, regardless of rating, the complaint is in this instance voiced by none other than former world champion Tigran Petrosian.

Opening romance

It's a lucky player who finds an opening system he loves to rely on, loves to protect from those who would inflict harm on it with their new, villainous ideas.

A player and his favorite

opening are really a bit of a romance. Even a tyro in such a relationship can rise on occasion to the role of super-hero to rescue his maiden in distress.

We all know club players who will take on all opponents and all kibitzers on the topic of their favorite starting moves. How do these lucky-in-love players find their beloved beginnings? Most often, it takes place as it did with Al. He happened to see an old game with the Center Counter Defense. For no completely logical reason, the moonlight struck the board. Al was smitten. The fact that the first dates—early victories—were fun clinched the relationship.

Even on a very top level of play, these same "romantic" factors can play a part. I became known for my reliance on Alekhine's Defense. Despite the prevailing opinion that after 1. e4, the move 1. ... Nf6 was not quite correct, I played "my" Alekhine consistently at the highest levels, with rewarding results.

It's worth noting that both Al and I elected to take lesser analyzed openings that offered a shortcut—sidestepping much of the normal preparation.

Switching syndrome

Many amateurs spend too much time trying to memorize various opening moves. (That said, none of us wants to reach move 12 with such a steeply uphill battle that all the strategy and tactics in our head won't get us to the top.) Getting caught up in the switching syndrome—jumping from opening to opening, memorizing and getting discouraged, and never making much use of all the time you've invested—is as impractical as it gets.

Let's take a look at the basic points to consider when choosing an opening repertoire.

Set reasonable goals

Barring blunders from our opponents, what should we expect from a satisfactory opening?

A. Regardless of its theoretical assessment, we want a position we know how to play.

B. With White, we want a position that is at least equal; we prefer to retain some advantage, although demanding a significant advantage is usually unrealistic.

C. With Black, we want an equal position, or if it is slightly worse for us, we at least want a position we know how to hold. For example, a player who emulates attacking genius Mikhail Tal may be happy with a material deficit in exchange for an attack—even if, theoretically, it doesn't fully compensate him.

Openings are schizophrenic

Don't waste your time with the fantasy of the "tailor-made" repertoire we sometimes read about that will bring out your inner, winning you with just the right openings. Certainly, an experienced chess teacher can help you to improve much faster and absorb important principles more thoroughly than you could on your own. However, in any major opening, you can't play in a way that will guide you only to tactical terrain while preventing positional games, or vice versa.

Try staying in a "solid" Caro-Kann against someone who wants to pry the game open for an attack. Even Mikhail Botvinnik couldn't do it in 1960 against Tal. Or try playing the Sicilian for a sharp, attacking game against an expert in White's c3 system, and you'll likely find yourself in a positional struggle. Some variations of the French are passive, while some are downright counterattacks. Some forms of the Ruy Lopez are positional; some are wild and hoary. Some Giuoco Pianos are hardly *pianissimo*. Your opponent can play the Queen's Gambit like the draw-prone Carl Schlechter or like the checkmate-obsessed Frank Marshall.

Openings are schizophrenic. Whatever opening you play, you risk getting a position that doesn't match your own attitudes about aggression or passivity. Still, in some extreme cases, consider the plusses and minuses of your play, indeed of your style. If you are a pawn-loving Korchnoi fan, don't play the Benko Gambit!

Petrosian's Rule

Sometimes winning is the only acceptable outcome. In such a situation, should you adopt a wild opening, swinging for the bleachers from the first move?

The great Petrosian often counseled the young and talented Russian-Armenian master Karen Gregorian. Once Gregorian returned from an important qualifying tournament and showed Petrosian a last-round game in which the young man had played some dubious opening moves as Black and lost. Petrosian cross-examined him:

Petrosian: "Why did you play such terrible moves? Even you should understand these are bad."

Gregorian: "I had to win to qualify."

Petrosian: "Make a note. It's much easier to play for a win from an equal position than from a bad position!"

Spend only 25% of your chess time studying the openings

Opening study just doesn't deserve to be so all-consuming, especially for nonprofessionals, for two basic reasons:

1. There are lots of other areas to study in chess that will make a more dramatic difference in your results—just one compelling example is the study of tactics.

2. There have been many grandmasters who became prominent, even world-class players, using an opening system roundly condemned as at least slightly inferior.

As a rule of thumb, you should spend about 25% of your chess study time on the openings.

Should you learn a second opening?

You don't really have to learn a second opening to surprise your opponents. There are enough choices *within* most openings to allow opportunities to catch your opponent off guard. Nowadays, even most top players unabashedly specialize in a few openings—normally just enough to cover the opponent's possibilities. A few, like Kasparov, seem encyclopedic in their opening choices, but after all, they have teams of researchers and theoreticians.

Actually, the best thing about knowing a second opening is not that you can use it as a surprise weapon, but that you learn the ideas and themes of different types of positions. But once again, from the point of view of real people with jobs to do and lawns to cut, a second opening covering the same ground may steal time from other important areas of your chess development.

When the world champ gets an edge against your favorite line

We can hold our favorite openings to too high a standard, or even blame them for defeats that take place long after the opening phase. Ridiculous as it sounds, we often wind up rejecting a possibility because it ends in a loss against a top GM or even a world champion. This is a corollary to the cynical outlook that an opening is evaluated by the results of a few key games, and these games were won by the

stronger player.

Long ago as a young expert, I took up a certain system in the Sicilian. I stuck with the variation as I rose through the ranks. As a master, I contributed to the system's theory, drawing and even defeating famous grandmasters. So I kept playing it. Later, my own analysis unearthed one line that I worried about—a series of moves that left White with an edge from the opening. But no one played it against me, or against anyone else.

Then in 1971, in the semifinals for the Soviet championship, I played Black against a 20-year-old grandmaster named Anatoly Karpov, then already coached by renowned opening-theoretician Semyon Furman. Karpov opened with 1. e4, and I was soon in the familiar territory of my trusty Sicilian. And then suddenly I was in the line I had hoped I would never see in a tournament game!

Karpov had played the best moves for White and gotten a small edge. I defended well, but the game was adjourned with Karpov retaining this edge. Another six-hour session saw the game adjourned a second time, in a lost position for me. I was disgusted, feeling that everyone would now play the same line against me! So I gave it up.

I know now that my abandoning the system altogether was

a very premature reaction. After all, Karpov went on to dominate top-level chess until Kasparov arrived on the scene. The line Karpov played to get a small edge would not be to everyone's taste, nor within most GMs' abilities to maintain and convert to a win. True, I went on to a new, fruitful "relationship" with Alekhine's Defense, but perhaps for the wrong reasons.

The next time you are tempted to switch your opening because the latest *Informant* game shows how the world champ beat a tournament tailgater in 40 moves—think it over. There isn't a line that wouldn't look bad in such a match-up. And when you lose in the city championship to a smartly played mating attack by the ultimate winner, don't rush to blame the opening. The reason for your loss may lie elsewhere.

Home analysis

Whatever your playing strength, nothing will improve your opening results more than home preparation—your own work in your own home over your own board. (For the serious who have the opportunity, personal chess trainers can be a tremendous advantage, of course.)

Sometimes what you find may be a tactical trick. Perhaps with best play your find peters out to equality (or for Black, a slightly worse position) faster than the main line. But an opponent seeing it for the first time will likely slip into a brutal trap, or he may panic in the face of the unknown.

It's very likely that this book will give you the best opening foundation you've ever had. You'll understand the ideas so well that you're likely to be surprised at the innovations you come up with on your own. And in the process of trying to find better and more interesting moves, you will of course constantly increase your understanding of your openings and of chess.

Let the book do the rest

Under different circumstances, I'd have much more to say about how to study openings, how to look for TNs and for shortcuts, those effective sidelines. I would explain the techniques for cutting your job down to size, how to gather and assess material, how to organize and what to memorize. But the fact is that *Complete Openings for Black, Explained* does all of this for you.

And I'm sure you're eager to get started!

PART TWO

DEFENDING AGAINST

1. e4

Chapter 4: Connecting to the Whole History of Pushing the King's Pawn

Some Important Points to Look For

In this chapter we review Black's choices against White's most popular first move, 1. e4.

◆ Symmetry, but White is on the move and attacking. See Diagram 2.

◆ Scandinavian: cutting the Gordian knot. See Diagram 32.

◆ French: preparing ... d5. See Diagram 43.

◆ Caro-Kann: preparing ... d5. See Diagram 44.

◆ Pirc: development first, center later. See Diagram 54.

◆ The assymetrical challenge in the center. See Diagram 60.

Chapter 4

Connecting to the Whole History of Pushing the King's Pawn

Black's Choices Against 1. e4

Making connections makes us smarter. In this chapter, you're about to connect with several centuries of chess opening development. It's what we used to call "background information." It's terribly underrated by too many people—those in a rush to learn only what they "need" to know. That's an irony, because what some may see as unrelated knowledge is crucial to any creative process.

The box below gives you five specific reasons for knowing something about everything in the openings. Moreover, there's a more encompassing motive for a chess player to know a lot in general. The now gratingly unimaginative phrase (it's become a cognitive oxymoron) "thinking out of the box" means to convey that creative solutions are found by seeking breakthroughs not on the slide under our immediate, microscopic concentration. A Renaissance man of both mathematics and the liberal arts wrote:

> *The creative mind is*
> *a mind that looks for*
> *unexpected likeness.*
> *–Jacob Bronowski*

Five Reasons to Know Something About Everything in the Chess Openings

1. *You need to have some information in order to make meaningful choices.*
2. *Transpositions (shifting from one opening to another) take place frequently.*
3. *Ideas from one opening can be applied to other openings.*
4. *Sometimes you reach a position in an opening with "colors reversed"—for example, when White plays the English (1. c4) and Black responds with 1. ... e5, both players can find themselves in a "Reversed Sicilian."*
5. *You can improve your overall play by practicing in different kinds of middlegame positions resulting from various openings.*

To be creative, we need to be capable of making surprising connections through a whole universe of ideas. But we've lived for some time in an age of the expert. In our jobs and even in our hobbies, we specialize. As chess players, we are "e4-players" or "d4-players." Or perhaps you're a Colle expert. Specialization makes sense, of course. Done correctly, it can make the most of our time, and it can instill us with confidence.

Is specialization just for insects?

So having a wide general knowledge makes you a better player, but specializing in chess is a survival skill. Our moves on the chessboard permit us to direct the struggle. The yin and the yang of needing to know a lot while learning to restrict the range of possibilities is not really a contradiction. Perhaps an engineer-turned-sci-fi-icon said it best:

A human being should be able to change a diaper, plan an invasion, butcher a hog, con a ship, design a building, write a sonnet, balance accounts, build a wall, set a bone, comfort the dying, take orders, give orders, cooperate, act alone, solve equations, analyze a new problem, pitch manure, program a computer, cook a tasty meal, fight efficiently, die gallantly. Specialization is for insects.
–Robert A. Heinlein,
from The Notebooks of Lazarus Long

Daunting expectations from Heinlein, who learned to play chess at four, even before he could read! But we agree with his general idea. A good chess player should be able to conduct any phase of the game competently, wherever it takes him.

We're not going to argue against specializing in certain

Three Reasons to Study Open Games First

1. *They are the most immediately dangerous.*

2. *You'll face them most often.*

3. *You'll get practice making combinations and defending against combinations, which abound in the open games.*

chess openings. In fact, this book is all about recommending certain lines that make it possible even for amateurs to become true opening experts. It offers brand-new ideas that will put your opponents at a disadvantage.

But you should occasionally play over games from openings you yourself don't use. And you should certainly know at least the basics of all of the major openings!

A time-efficient review

We are conscious of your time constraints. You have other things to do and are reading this because you expect some time-efficient return. You want to play chess better, understand it better—and win more games as Black. So we've given this chapter very serious thought, presenting you with the most potent connections to the basic ideas of the 1. e4 openings, from Black's perspective.

What time does your opening close?

This book teaches you how to deal with any White opening scheme. But we put 1. e4 first for a reason. Usually, 1. e4 leads to "open" games. Many chess trainers continue to recommend learning the "open" games before studying "closed" positions—and for most of us, it makes sense. After all, 1. e4 is the most popular opening move among amateurs, and one of the most popular moves among masters and grandmasters.

Some openings lead more often to open positions. Other openings usually bring on closed middlegames. It's helpful to define the basics as we go along, so let's draw the distinction between *open* and *closed* in chess: Open positions offer unblocked lines of contact between the opposing armies; closed don't.

Take a look at the two columns below.

Open	*Closed*
Open files	Blocked files
Open diagonals	Blocked diagonals
Fluid or absent center pawns	Blocked center
Tactical	Positional
Attacks	Strategy
Gambits	Bind
Combinations	Regrouping
Fast	Slow
1. e4	1. d4, 1. c4, 1.Nf3

In the column on the left we list words that generally apply to open games; the column on the right describes closed games.

Prior to the end of the 19th century, the advent of Steinitz' theory and positional play, opening a chess game with 1. e4 was *de rigeur*. But even now, nearly all top grandmasters at least occasionally play 1. e4. This move still dominates the lower rungs of the tournament circuit, a popularity which isn't surprising, since 1. e4 best corresponds to the three rules of thumb about the opening phase. (See the box at the bottom of this page.)

Now let's start our review in earnest to gain some perspective on the challenge of playing against 1. e4.

A Symmetry: *Meeting the best with its shadow*

1. e4 e5

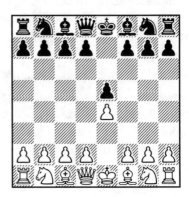

Diagram 1

After 1. ... e5

1. ... e5 is Black's most natural reply (see "Three Rules of the Opening," below). Still, being a tempo ahead in these open beginnings is an advantage. In open positions, an extra move can be important.

1. e4: best by test!
– Bobby Fischer

Three Rules of the Opening

1. *Control the center (preferably by occupying it with pawns);*

2. *Develop—bring your pieces from their starting position onto squares from which they exercise influence on the action (start with the kingside pieces because of the next rule);*

3. *Castle (usually short, since it can be accomplished most quickly and safely).*

White can try for an edge with **2. Nf3**.

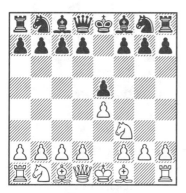

Diagram 2
After 2. Nf3

For over 100 years, this move has been viewed as the only serious try for an advantage. It not only develops and prepares castling, but it also attacks the e5-pawn. Championed by Paul Morphy, 2. Nf3 eventually triumphed over the romantic 2. f4 (the King's Gambit).

Diagram 3
King's Gambit

Don't worry about side lines now. From Black's point of view, if you find you're comfortable with 2. Nf3, you can always go back to learn the right ways to equality against less challenging

second moves, such as the King's Gambit, 2. Nc3 (Vienna), 2. Bc4, 2. d4, or 2. c3.

After 2. Nf3, theoretically best for Black is to develop with the pawn-protecting

2. ... Nc6

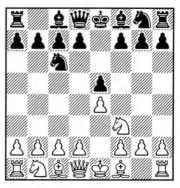

Diagram 4
After 2. ... Nc6

Why not 2. ... Bd6, protecting a pawn while developing a kingside piece, a move many beginners make?

For more than 100 years, 2. Nf3 has been viewed as the only serious follow-up to 1. e4.

Diagram 5
Bad defense: Black blocks
his development!

Diagram 6
Petroff's Defense

Because Black's pawn is stuck on d7, it doesn't influence the center, at least not for the near future. The move also blocks the most natural diagonal (c8-h3) for the c8-bishop. (Fianchettoing this bishop isn't usually a good idea in the 1. e4 e5 openings, because the bishop will be blocked by the well-protected e4-pawn. Besides, getting the piece to b7 would take an extra move.)

In the last fifteen years, as a result of the attention of world champions Anatoly Karpov and Vladimir Kramnik, and many followers, Petroff's Defense, 2. ... Nf6 has moved up in the es-

> **Petroff's Defense has moved up in the esteem of theory to nearly the equal of 2. ... Nc6.**

teem of theory from a "short cut" to nearly the equal of 2. ... Nc6. In fact, because of its new-found popularity, you'll need to study more! The more masters play an opening, the more ingenious tricks, traps and strategies they find. In other words, the more an opening is played, especially at the top, the more "theory" piles up.

Dubious, or as their proponents would say, "risky" and "enterprising" are the gambits 2. ... d5 and 2. ... f5. We show how to handle them, as well as other second moves for Black, in this volume's counterpart, *Chess Openings for White, Explained.* "Almost correct" is 2. ... d6, used by Philidor (and called the Philidor Defense).

If you'd like to study very little theory—or to have an offbeat system in reserve for a showdown with an old foe who thinks he knows your repertoire, consider 2. ... Qe7.

The top 10 reasons for having an offbeat, surprise opening alternative to defend against 1. e4.

1. You can surprise a familiar foe who thinks he knows all about your repertoire.

2. Even though he has the White pieces and is supposed to have the initiative, you can immediately put your opponent in a defensive frame of mind.

3. Many of your opponents will make mistakes under pressure to find the "right" theoretical moves.

4. Your opponent may even decide it's his job to "refute" an opening that's perfectly playable—leading to his making big mistakes in the first few moves!

5. He will likely burn up valuable clock-time calculating unfamiliar variations—imagine using your surprise in the last round of a fast-time-control tournament, with a big prize at stake!

6. If news breaks during the middle of a tournament that one of your favorite lines has been punctured by a new move from a Bulgarian grandmaster, you can fall back on your spare-tire opening.

7. You won't have to use it long anyway; such opening "refutations" generally last until the "refuter" plays someone rated even higher!

8. You get to act blasé if someone plays your own surprise against you, rattling off the best response and stifling a yawn—he's yours for life!

9. You can tell everyone it's the latest breakthrough idea from Kasparov and that the champion computer program Thresher confirms that it wins for Black against 1. e4.

10. Then you'll get to find a good surprise against 1. d4.

Diagram 7
Offbeat but sound

This system was used occasionally by Russian grandmaster Victor Kupreichik, a great attacking player. Black intends to fianchetto his dark-square bishop.

There is no way to refute this opening. Of course, with normal, good play, White should get a small edge, but remember two things: this level of advantage is not significant except among international competitors, and, secondly, White will be in unfamiliar territory. And if he presses for more, he may end up investing a lot of clock time, and being very disappointed by the result!

Let's return to **2. ... Nc6.**

Black's most vulnerable point before he has castled is the f7-square!

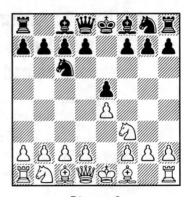

Diagram 8
After 2. ... Nc6

Now the unpretentious "knights-first" 3. Nc3

Diagram 9
After 3. Nc3

isn't without poison, but only if Black plays the natural 3. ... Bc5, allowing the archetypal (in such positions) 4. Nxe5, with an edge. (After 4. ... Nxe5, White has the pawn fork 5. d4. Black could play 4. ... Bxf2+, but after 5. Kxf2 Nxe5 6. d4 Ng6 7. Bc4, White has a strong center and will soon castle by hand.)

But instead of 3. ... Bc5, Black can go into a Four Knights Game by playing 3. ... Nf6, maintaining symmetry for one or two more moves, and this path leads to equality.

Reuben Fine

Fine moves

For 50 years, the book *The Ideas Behind the Chess Openings* by the American champion Reuben Fine held sway and determined the way we played openings. (Reuben Fine was a world-championship contender and a winner of the 1938 AVRO super-tournament.)

Here are his three tips on finding good moves in the opening.

◆ Whenever possible, make a good developing move that threatens something.

◆ Two questions must be answered prior to making a move:

    1. How it affects the center.

    2. How it fits with the development of your other men.

◆ Deviate from "book" lines only for a reason.

We're still only at move 3, and for a while, White can control the options. Let's look at 3. d4.

Diagram 10
Scotch Opening

This move was felt to be analyzed and played to death (meaning to a draw) by the early twentieth century. Theoreticians thought that White played his important central thrust too early, dissipating his latent energy. But in the 1990s, Kasparov's victories with the Scotch put it back into play. (See Fine's advice on the previous page.)

Other than the Scotch, two most promising moves for White in the main line (1. e4 e5 2. Nf3 Nc6—see Diagram 8) are 3. Bc4 and 3. Bb5. The first choice attacks the f7 square, Black's most vulnerable point before he has castled.

> **The move 3. Bc4 was Morphy's favorite and brought him many exciting victories.**

Diagram 11
After 3. Bc4

The move 3. Bc4 was Morphy's favorite and brought him many exciting victories, as it then did numerous *aficionados* of the attack.

On the Olympus of super-grandmaster play, 3. Bc4 continues to be regarded, as it has been for most of the twentieth century, as being "exhausted" and drawish. But not among the mortals, where it continues to be popular. Still, you can more or less rely on theory to provide you with the antidote to 3. Bc4. It can be 3. ... Bc5,

Diagram 12
Giuoco Piano

questionably called Giuoco Piano (Italian for the "Quiet Game"—sometimes the opening is called the Italian Game), unless White attacks with the Evans Gambit, 4. b4.

Diagram 13
Evans Gambit

Or Black can play 3. ... Nf6, appropriately called the Two Knights' Defense.

Diagram 14
Two Knights' Defense

The most popular choice for White is the positional **3. Bb5**, initiating the famous Ruy Lopez opening.

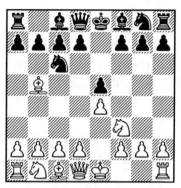

Diagram 15
Ruy Lopez

White's third move attacks the knight, which defends the e5-pawn.

The real problem is that there is a terabyte of theory in this time-honored opening. Especially over the long-term, when you are rising higher and higher in the ranks of chess players, you'd need to remember a lot to play against the Ruy. Even an historical review takes a bit of time. So settle back. It's well-worth your knowing.

After **3. ... a6**,

Diagram 16
Ruy Lopez, Morphy's Defense

the "main line" for almost a hundred years, you should be ready for Bobby Fischer's favorite, 4. Bxc6. (No, it doesn't win a pawn: after 4. ... dxc6!, 5. Nxe5 can't be recommended because of 5. ... Qd4.)

Diagram 17
After 5. ... Qd4

You need also to be ready for the more common **4. Ba4.**

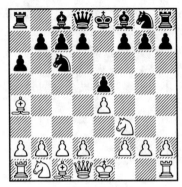

Diagram 18
After 4. Ba4

Other third moves for Black are viewed as somewhat inferior, but provide you a choice of shortcuts. Where are you, for example, on the "greed" continuum? (See the graph below.)

RESPECT FOR MATERIAL, A CONTINUUM

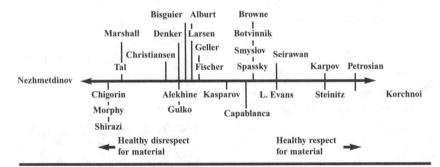

Take a look at the chart above. Since "conservatives" are most often talked about as being "on the right," we'll follow that tradition. Please keep in mind that most great players can do all things well. Petrosian detonated some drop-dead combinations. Tal ground out some ingenious endgames. The table offers only generalizations, and informed opinions may differ.

Where do you think you would fall? You'll undoubtedly profit from playing over the games of the great players near your spot on the spectrum. Pay attention to the openings and sub-variations they choose. See how you like them.

If you fall somewhere in the vicinity of Tal and Morphy, then consider playing the Schliemann, 3. ... f5.

Diagram 19

Ruy Lopez, Schliemann Variation

Even if Kasparov, Karpov and Korchnoi, from their places on our "Respect for Material Continuum," think otherwise, clearly the initiative will matter for you more than the loss of a pawn in a position similar to the one after 4. Nc3 fxe4 5. Nxe4 Nf6 6. Nxf6+ Qxf6 7. Qe2 Be7 8. Bxc6 dxc6.

Diagram 20

After 8. ... dxc6

Incidentally, only 9. Nxe5 is correct here. An attempt to both grab a pawn and exchange queens backfires: 9. Qxe5? Bg4!, and now every super-K will prefer Black! After the exchange of queens, Black enjoys better development and threatens to ruin White's kingside pawn structure.

Back to Black's third move. If, like Savielly Tartakover, you prefer to sacrifice your opponent's pawns, you still have short-cuts to choose from:

3. ... Nge7 (planning to fianchetto); the immediate fianchetto 3. ... g6; and the classic (and somewhat passive) 3. ... d6, which commits Black to giving up the center after 4. d4 exd4 5. Nxd4.

Diagram 21

Ruy Lopez, after 5. Nxd4

Siegbert Tarrasch showed that White has some slight but persistent edge here, but he was, after all, Tarrasch!

Black can even get away with moving the same piece twice with 3. ... Nd4, Bird's Defense.

Diagram 22
Ruy Lopez, Bird's Defense

Perhaps you'll put new life in the old system, as Kramnik did with the Berlin Variation, proving in his 2000 World Championship match versus Kasparov that the endgame after 1. e4 e5 2. Nf3 Nc6 3. Bb5 Nf6 4. 0-0 Nxe4 5. d4

Diagram 23
After 5. d4

5. ... Nd6 6. Bxc6 dxc6 7. dxe5 Nf5 8. Qxd8+ Kxd8 is okay for Black.

Diagram 24
Ruy Lopez, Berlin Defense

If you've decided to play "the best" 3. ... a6 (see Diagram 16) then, as we've mentioned, besides studying 4. Bxc6, you should prepare a system against the classic 4. Ba4. There are some attractive short-cuts to the main lines of theory (but even the short-cuts on a significant journey can be long!), such as the "Open Variation" (Fine called it the "Counter Attack Defense"). After normal moves, **4. Ba4 Nf6 5. 0-0,**

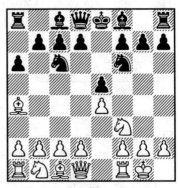

Diagram 25
After 5. 0-0

Black captures a pawn.

5. ... Nxe4 6. d4 b5 7. Bb3 d5 8. dxe5 Be6

Diagram 26
Ruy Lopez, Open Variation

Or after already learning so

much, maybe you want to study the "Champions' Defense," the Chigorin Variation, which grandmasters had in mind when they said, in the last part of the twentieth century, that nobody can become a great player without playing great Ruys. (And most world champions and challengers did play them, often from both sides.) Let's follow from Diagram 25:

5. ... Be7 6. Re1 b5 7. Bb3

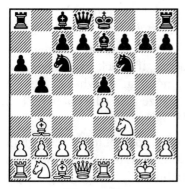

Diagram 27
After 7. Bb3

7. ... d6

Or 7. ... 0-0, if you want to lure your opponent into the Marshall Gambit after 8. c3 d5.

Diagram 28
Ruy Lopez, Marshall's Gambit

After the "classical" 7. ... d6, the play continues:

8. c3 0-0 9. h3 Na5

We're skipping some twists, such as Breyer's paradoxically good 9. ... Nb8.

10. Bc2 c5 11. d4 Qc7

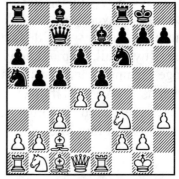

Diagram 29
Ruy Lopez, Chigorin Variation

This is the blueprint beginning of many great Ruys! (Chess players sometimes call these classic theoretical starting places "tabias.")

We've already connected to a lot of important history. Now let's move to the non-symmetrical answers to 1. e4.

Summarizing 1. ... e5

Beginners may choose 1. ... e5 because it's natural and easy to understand (therefore making it easy to find reasonable follow-up moves). The classical main line after 1. e4 e5 is the Ruy Lopez, and the stronger player you are, the more frequently you'll face the Ruy. Still, some knowledge against sharp systems, such as 1. e4 e5 2. Nf3 Nc6 3. Bc4, is required, in order to avoid panicking after 3. ... Nf6 4. Ng5.

Diagram 30
After 4. Ng5

And to avoid a waste of time like 3. ... h6?.

Diagram 31
After 3. ... h6?

B The light-square strategy:

Immediately challenging White's center

1. e4 d5

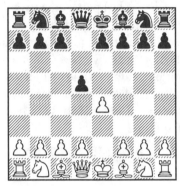

Diagram 32
The Center Counter (Scandinavian)

A basic tenet of fighting 1. e4 is that if Black can play ... d5 without a drawback, he has equalized. So why not play 1. ... d5 right away?

This attempt to cut through the Gordian knot of main lines was traditionally viewed by theory as weak. But the move was always underrated. Moreover, recently it's been given new life. After the best response, **2. exd5**, Black somewhat surprisingly has two good moves: to recapture with the queen **2. ... Qxd5**,

Diagram 33
After 2. ... Qxd5

or to play **2. ... Nf6.**

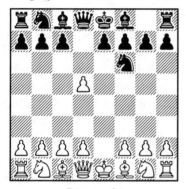

Diagram 34
After 2. ... Nf6

The legendary weakness of 2. ... Qxd5, according to traditional theory, was White's win of a tempo with 3. Nc3. The verdict was that Black exposed his queen to early harassment, allowing White to develop while Black's most powerful piece dodged bullets.

But just how important is the loss of a tempo here?

3. Nc3 Qa5 4. d4 Nf6 5. Nf3

Diagram 35
After 5. Nf3

And now Black brings out his light-square bishop before moving his e-pawn. He can choose from 5. ... Bg4, 5. ... Bf5, or even a preliminary 5. ... c6 (a useful move, securing a retreat line for the queen). For example:

5. ... c6 6. Bc4 Bg4.

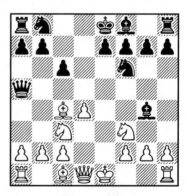

Diagram 36
After 6. ... Bg4

In all these lines, White's only hope for an edge lies in driving Black's bishop back:

7. h3 Bh5 8. g4! Bg6

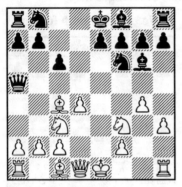

Diagram 37
After 8. ... Bg6

Here theory continues with lines that in the end are razor-sharp journeys through a tactical wonderland. Most non-specialists wouldn't dare enter, uneasy about the "weakening" g2-g4.

And where, with proper play, do even these best tries end? "Plus-over-equal"—the smallest advantage White can have, an edge truly important only on the highest levels of chess, where technique is near-perfect. But even there, such an edge is not definitive.

And if your opponents do play both h3 and g4, and keep getting an edge, consider the simple 7. ... Bxf3.

Even the best tries for White end in ±.

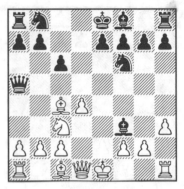

Diagram 38
After 7. ... Bxf3

Yes, on the GM level this choice winds up, again, plus-over-equal because White has the bishop pair. But among amateurs, knights are often as good, if not better, than bishops. Black's position is solid. He has no weaknesses and no bad pieces—and no long lines to remember!

Let's look at Black's other choice in the Center Counter after 2. exd5.

Diagram 39
After 2. ... Nf6

Justification for 2. ... Nf6 lies in the line 3. c4 c6 4. dxc6 (better is modest 4. d4, transferring into the Panov-Botvinnik line of the Caro-Kann) 4. ... Nxc6.

Diagram 40
After 4. ... Nxc6

And Black stands better despite a missing pawn.

Still, in Diagram 39's position, White can fight for an edge with 3. Bb5+ Bd7 4. Be2! Nxd5 5. d4.

Diagram 41
After 5. d4

Or White can play the normal 3. d4.

Diagram 42
After 3. d4.

C The light-square strategy: *Preparing ... d7-d5*

As we saw on previous pages, capturing on d5 with a piece gives White some advantage in the center, and the somewhat better game. Two major openings, the Caro-Kann and the French, solve this problem by preparing ... d7-d5 with a neighboring pawn move, in order to be able to recapture on d5 with a pawn.

1. e4 e6

Diagram 43
French

1. e4 c6

Diagram 44
Caro-Kann

Let's look what will happen after the natural **2. d4 d5** in each case.

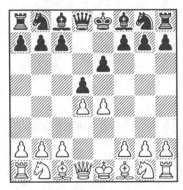

Diagram 45
French

Diagram 46
Caro-Kann

Black's ... e7-e6 opens a diagonal for his dark-square bishop and thus also facilitates early castling. The negative: the light-square bishop is restricted by the e6-pawn and often winds up a bad "French" bishop, hemmed in by its own pawns. In the Caro-Kann, the light-square bishop is free and will soon move to f5 or (after White's Nf3) to g4. On the other hand, ... c7-c6 doesn't forward Black's development (except for opening the diagonal for his queen, which is less important than developing the minor pieces), doesn't prepare for castling short, and in some cases—where ... c6-c5 will be called for—loses a tempo. Still, as practice shows, the Caro-Kann is at least as good as the French. Already we've seen its single but strong plus, keeping the light-square bishop "good." This benefit offsets the minuses.

When playing the French, you must be ready to defend against White's two main continuations, **3. Nc3** and **3. Nd2.**

In the Center Counter, after ... Bxf3, Black's position is solid. He has no weaknesses and no bad pieces— and no long lines to remember!

Diagram 47
French, White allows
3. ... Bb4

Diagram 48
French, White avoids the pin

A "busyman's" solution to learning two lines above can be found in *Pirc Alert!—a complete defense against 1. e4*, co-authored by Lev Alburt and by the Pirc's number one practitioner, GM Alex Chernin: **3. ... dxe4** (the Rubinstein French) **4. Nxe4 Bd7.**

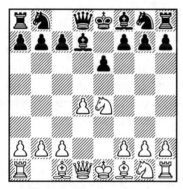

Diagram 49
After 4. ... Bd7

The game usually continues **5. Nf3 Bc6 6. Bd3 Nd7 7. 0-0 Ngf6 8. Ng3**

Diagram 50
After 8. Ng3

8. ... Bxf3!, achieving a position quite similar to Diagram 38 (from the 2. ... Qxd5 line of the Scandinavian).

For a player with more time to study and more ambition, lines of the French generally offer sharp, unbalanced positions, an explosive mixture of strategies and tactics.

The Caro-Kann main line goes:
**1. e4 c6 2. d4 d5 3. Nc3 dxe4
4. Nxe4.**

Diagram 51
After 4. Nxe4

This is a very solid, mostly positional opening, perfectly fitted to those sharing Petrosian's philosophy: with Black, seek safety first.

Both **4. ...Bf5** and **4. ... Nd7** (preparing 5. ... Ngf6) serve this goal. But be aware of neglecting tactics even in such seemingly safe positions—for instance, by playing (after 4. ... Nd7 5. Qe2)

Diagram 52
Watch Out!

Black's planned 5. ... Ngf6??, allowing 6. Nd6, "smothered" checkmate!

D Countering from the corners:
The Pirc, Modern and Alekhine
   1. e4 d6

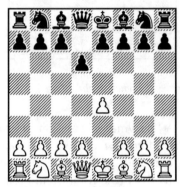

Diagram 53
Pirc Defense

Usually the game continues **2. d4 Nf6** (inviting the white knight to occupy a square in front of his pawn, as 3. Nd2, while possible, has the drawback of blocking the bishop).

   3. Nc3 g6

Diagram 54
After 3. ... g6

Black is ready to fianchetto his bishop and then to castle. He'll fight for the center later, a modernist trade off. For more on choosing the Pirc, see *Pirc Alert!*.

The Modern Defense, **1. e4 g6,**

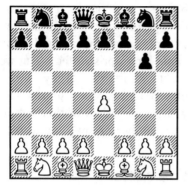

Diagram 55
The Modern Defense

is a flexible, less formal cousin (in some cases even a twin) of the Pirc.

Alekhine's Defense, **1. e4 Nf6,**

Diagram 56
After 1. ... Nf6

is a true triumph of hyper-modernism—Black provokes White to push (with tempo!) his central pawns—as in the line 2. e5 Nd5

3. c4 Nb6 4. c5.

Diagram 57
After 4. c5

Black will, however, recoup some of these tempos soon by attacking White's extended (sometimes even over-extended) pawn center. Despite a life-long effort by Lev Alburt, the theory still (correctly) favors White, but only in the modern line:

2. e5 Nd5 3. d4 d6 4. Nf3.

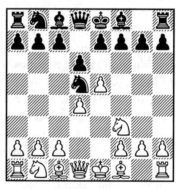

Diagram 58
After 4. Nf3

All three major replies, Lev's 4. ... Bg4 and 4. ... g6, and GM Bagirov's 4. ... c6, seem to promise White a small edge.

The good news is that White needs to know all three systems, and Black only one. And "normal," or simply "good" moves often aren't enough in sharp, unbalanced Alekhine positions to take White to safety, let alone to an advantage.

1. e4 Nc6

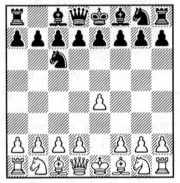

Diagram 59
After 1. ... Nc6

This Nimzovich Defense is a poor cousin of the Alekhine Defense. After 2. Nf3, Black's best move is definitely 2. ... e5. So, if you don't mind transposing into the classic 1. e4 e5 lines, or if you on occasion want to confuse an opponent who is a King's Gambit *aficionado*, 1. ... Nc6 is a good choice. But you'll have to study the line 2. d4 e5 or 2. d4 d5, where White should play first accurately, then inventively, to assure just a very small edge in some unclear, "atypical" positions.

The graphic on page 48 plots, on the unsound-to-solid continuum, Black's first-move responses to 1. e4. You can see that Black's

faux-pas openers result in a plus-over-minus (a clear advantage for White). Black's opening goal is equality.

The minor openings: 1. ... a6, 1. ... b6, 1. ... g5 are minor because they aren't good, and thus can't be recommended except in an occasional blitz game for surprise effect. (But we must admit that Tony Miles played 1. ... a6 in a tournament game against then world champion Anatoly Karpov—and won!)

E The Sicilian:
Our recommendation

Now we come to the defense we recommend against 1. e4, the Sicilian Defense, 1. ... c5.

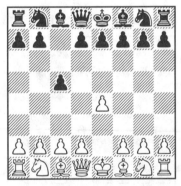

Diagram 60
After 1. ... c5

The Sicilian is currently Black's most popular defense against 1. e4. In fact, it's played more often on all levels, from the club players to super-grandmasters, than all other replies to 1. e4 combined! Not surprisingly, its popularity corresponds with very good results for Black. A search of more than 100,000 games reveals that the Sicilian yields Black the following statistics versus the classic 1. ... e5 and 1. ... e6:

	1. ... e5	1. ... e6	1. ... c5
Black won:	28.8%	25.4%	30.3%
Black drew:	31.7%	35.9%	34.9%
Black lost:	39.6%	38.6%	34.9%

So the Sicilian won the most games and lost the least! How can 1. ... c5 compete with 1. ... e6 and 1. ... e5, the logical, classical choices? After all, 1. ... c5 doesn't put a pawn in the center; doesn't develop or help to develop a piece (except for the queen, which normally isn't supposed to be brought out early in the opening); and doesn't make castling easier.

The explanation is that to try for an advantage, White has to play d2-d4. Otherwise Black will maintain at least an equal footing in the center.

2. Nf3 d6

Or 2. ... Nc6 or 2. ...e6.

3. d4 cxd4 4. Nxd4

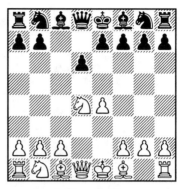

Diagram 61
After 4. Nxd4

4. ... Nf6

This induces White's next move, as other moves allow Black to equalize easily—for example, 5. Bd3 Nc6. Moves like 4. ... e6 will allow 5. c4, the Maroczy Bind, not to be overly feared, as we will show, but a different game than Black idealizes.

5. Nc3

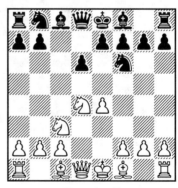

Diagram 62
After 5. Nc3

White is better developed and has more space. Black, however, has exchanged his bishop's pawn

The Unsound-to-Solid Continuum—
Black's Responses to 1. e4

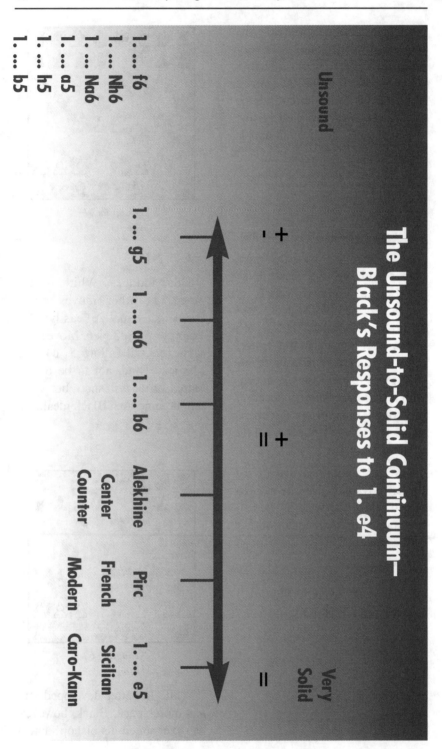

Unsound

1. ... f6
1. ... Nh6
1. ... Na6
1. ... a5
1. ... h5
1. ... b5

1. ... g5   1. ... a6   1. ... b6   Alekhine   Pirc   1. ... e5

Center   French   Sicilian
Counter

Modern   Caro-Kann

Very
Solid

±   ∓±   ∓

for the White queen's pawn, and center pawns are usually worth more. Besides, Black has potentially good play along the semi-open c-file.

Therefore White's most promising plan in the Sicilian is an attack, while "Sicilian endgames" are known to favor Black.

Black has numerous choices in the Sicilian after 5. Nc3. One popular choice is **5. ... a6**, the Najdorf.

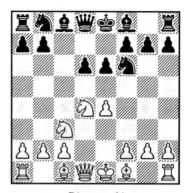

Diagram 64
Sicilian Scheveningen

Yet another choice for Black after 5. Nc3 is **5. ... Nc6**.

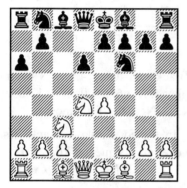

Diagram 63
Sicilian Najdorf

The idea of this move is to take control of b5—useful if Black decides to play ...e7-e5.

Another move that Black often chooses is **5. ... e6**, the Scheveningen ...

Diagram 65
After 5. ... Nc6

But these three popular lines require a defender to absorb a *lot* of detailed information, and to master a great number of tactical and strategic ideas.

Simpler to learn is the Sicilian

"SICILIAN ENDGAMES" ARE KNOWN
TO FAVOR BLACK.

Four Knights:

1. e4 c5 2. Nf3 e6 3. d4 cxd4 4. Nxd4 Nf6 5. Nc3 Nc6

Diagram 66
After 5. ... Nc6

This can lead to a small advantage for White (±) after 6. Ndb5 Bb4 7. a3 Bxc3+ 8. Nxc3 d5 9. exd5 exd5 10. Bd3 d4 11. Ne2 0-0 12. 0-0 Qd5 13. Nf4!

Diagram 67
After 13. Nf4!

13. ... Qd6 14. Nh5!

Co-author Alburt once tried to defend Black's side versus then 20-year-old Anatoly Karpov. Failing, Lev abandoned the Sicilian. That was a mistake. Very few players like to play emerging endgames, this time

slightly better for White. Those who like it would most likely lack Karpov's nearly unerring touch.

Back to Black's fourth move. After **1. e4 c5 2. Nf3 e6 3. d4 cxd4 4. Nxd4,**

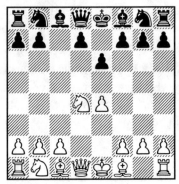

Diagram 68
After 4. Nxd4

Black can delay 4. ... Nf6 and play **4. ... a6**, the flexible Kan, or **4. ... Nc6**, the Taimanov.

In the Sveshnikov, Black first develops his queen's knight: **1. e4 c5 2. Nf3 Nc6 3. d4 cxd4 4. Nxd4.**

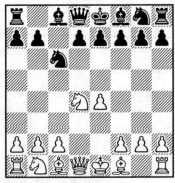

Diagram 69
After 4. Nxd4

4. ... Nf6 (although Grandmaster Sveshnikov himself nowadays prefers the immediate 4. … e5) **5. Nc3 e5!?**

Diagram 70
Sicilian Sveshnikov

Viewed as anti-positional at its creation 35 years ago, today it's very much the rage.

And of course, some players love the supersharp Dragon:

1. e4 c5 2. Nf3 d6 3. d4 cxd4 4. Nxd4 Nf6 5. Nc3 g6

Diagram 71
After 5. … g6

The variation is called the Dragon because Black's pawn formation reminded some of the mysterious beast.

Now White can choose somewhat subdued lines, in which he'll castle short. We'll have a look at those in Chapter 7.

More dangerous for Black are lines in which White castles long and then launches an attack with h2-h4-h5, sacrificing that pawn for an open path to the enemy king.

One such opening tabia arises after **6. Be3 Bg7 7. f3 0-0 8. Qd2 Nc6.**

More dangerous for Black in the Dragon are lines in which White castles long and then launches an attack with h2-h4-h5, sacrificing that pawn for an open path to the enemy king.

Diagram 72
After 8. ... Nc6

And now White follows up with either 9. 0-0-0 (where one of the main replies is 9. ... d5, now judged ±) or 9. Bc4. Black has counter play, but there is no doubt that Black's castled position is coming under fire first.

But imagine that, in the position in Diagram 72, Black's d-pawn is still on d7—and it is Black's turn to move (since he saved that tempo). In that case, Black would have an excellent game after 8. ... d5. This—an option to play … d5 in one move—is the very reason for choosing the Accelerated Dragon, our recommendation.

Summary:

Black's 1. ... e5 is the most logical response to 1. e4, and the easiest to grasp. The move 1. ... d5 can provide a time-saving "short-cut." Other assymetrical openings usually lead to complex, challenging play. Among those, our choice is Black's most successful reply: 1. ... c5, the Sicilian.

Some Practical Advice

If one of your lines has been refuted, or you're simply not too happy with it, don't despair. Search for a substitute.

And if you're quite happy with your "old" opening–say, the Pirc or Alekhine–don't abandon it. Go straight to Part III, and study the Nimzo.

Don't worry too much about matters such as a "complete, inter-connected repertoire." Yes, skipping parts of this book may create some problems later, but you will be well equipped to deal with those problems.

For instance, playing the Symmetrical English requires in this book knowledge of the Maroczy Bind, described in several Part II chapters. If you don't like the Bind, look for another line within the Symmetrical English. Or choose another first move, another system–say, 1. c4 Nf6 2. Nc3 e6 and if 3. Nf3, then 3. ... Bb4, Nimzo-style.

There are plenty of choices, and opportunities, in the opening. We hope this book will help you make choices right for you.

Connecting to the Whole History of Pushing the King's Pawn
Memory Markers!

Diagram 73
After 3. Nxe5

Diagram 74
After 4. Bc4

Diagram 75
After 5. Bxc6

Diagram 76
After 2. e5

Diagram 77
After 6. ... Bg4

Diagram 78
After 7. Qd2

Connecting to the Whole History of
Pushing the King's Pawn
Solutions to Memory Markers!

No. 1   **3. ... d6 4. Nf3 Nxe4** (not 3. ... Nxe4? 4. Qe2). See Diagram 6.

No. 2   **4. ... Nxe4**, and Black is at least equal. See note after Diagram 9.

No. 3   The right answer here and in similar positions is to take away from the center: **5. ... dxc6! 6. Ne5 Qd4!**, and Black is better. See Diagram 19.

No. 4   Black achieves a better game with **2. ... c5**. Also good is 2. ... Bf5, taking the bishop out before playing ... e6, but 2. ... c5, planning to pin the white knight with ... Bg4 (after Nf3), is even stronger. See page 38 and compare with the French.

No. 5   **7. h3.** Why not 7. Bxf7+? Because after 7. ... Kxf7 8. Ne5+ Qxe5+, Black has a piece for a pawn. See Diagram 36.

No. 6   **7. ... Ng4!.** Thus it is better for White to secure the e3-bishop with 7. f3. See page 52.

Chapter 5: The Accelerated Dragon—Intro and Main Line

Some Important Points to Look For

The Sicilian is Black's most successful defense. Our recommended move order makes White's most aggressive line against it risky after ... d5!.

◆ 8. ... a5!—one key to Black's successful play in this chapter. See Diagram 87.

◆ Black is ready to play 13. ... Nd7. He isn't afraid to exchange dark-square bishops. See Diagram 102.

◆ 9. ... d5—a typical break-through. See Diagram 120.

◆ After 15. ... Bh6, Black preserves the bishop pair. See Diagram 155.

Outline of Variations

1. e4 c5 2. Nf3 g6 3. d4 cxd4 4. Nxd4 Nc6 5. Nc3 Bg7 6. Be3 Nf6 7. Bc4 0-0 8. Bb3 a5 *(56)* **[B35]**

    A 9. a4 Ng4 10. Qxg4 Nxd4 11. Qh4 d6 12. Nd5 Re8 13. Rd1 Nxb3 *(62)*

    B 9. 0-0 d6 *(64)* [9. ... a4—p. 65; 9. ... Nxd4—p. 71]

        B1 10. Ndb5 b6 *(66)*

        B2 10. f3 Nxd4 *(66)*

        B2 10. h3 Nxd4 *(67)*

    C 9. f3 d5 *(72)*

        C1 10. exd5 Nb4 11. Nde2 a4! *(73)*

        C2 10. Bxd5 Nxd5 *(77)*

        C3 10. Nxd5 Nxd5 11. exd5 *(84)*

Chapter 5
The Accelerated Dragon
Introduction and Main Line

Every chess player must have a confident answer to White's most popular and pressing opener, 1. e4. White's aggressive first move stakes out the center and opens diagonals for both his king's bishop and queen. As we've seen in Chapter 4, Black has a number of adequate answers, but the Sicilian Defense is the fighting choice that yields Black the most victories.

A search of more than 100,000 games from international play shows that the Sicilian yields Black a 30.5% chance of

**THE SICILIAN GIVES BLACK IMPRESSIVE RESULTS—
EVEN AGAINST HIGH-LEVEL COMPETITORS WHO KNOW
HOW TO MAKE THE MOST OF THEIR INITIATIVE!**

Let's quickly review four punches packed into 1. ... c5.

1. From the very first move, Black creates an unbalanced game. Classical symmetry is out the window. The Sicilian makes mistakes both more likely and more telling!

2. To try for an advantage, most White players feel forced to play d4 to break open the d-file. Black plays ... cxd4, exchanging a flank pawn for a center pawn. The prolific chess writer Fred Reinfeld made the point that, except for some late endgames, pawns diminish in value as they approach the edges of the board. He assigned center pawns a value of one dollar and bishop pawns a value of 90 cents. So in most Sicilians, Black invests a bishop pawn for a center pawn and "keeps the change." On a larger scale of metaphor, we compare it to swapping a Mustang for a Maserati, "trading up."

3. After ... cxd4, Black gets an important semi-open file on which to place a rook and put pressure on White's position.

4. Black's superior pawn structure will favor him in the endgame. Look at it this way: White is under pressure. Every move brings him closer to an ending that favors his challenging opponent!

winning a full point and, in addition, a 34.2% of drawing. Impressive results for the second-to-move—especially against high-level competitors who know how to make the most of their opening initiative!

1. e4 c5

As we've seen, although Black doesn't occupy the center with this first move, he challenges a key square, d4, exerting control over it. So, although he temporarily keeps his center-pawns at home, he does heed Steinitz' theory.

2. Nf3

We'll look at White's alternatives, 2. Nc3 and 2. c3, in later chapters. For now, we'll follow the main line—the most often played sequence.

2. ... g6

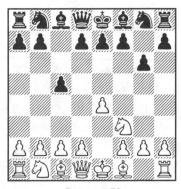

Diagram 79
After 2. ... g6

We recommend this move order (called the Hyper-Accelerated Dragon) over the usual 2. ... Nc6 to get us to the variation we want, while avoiding the Rossolimo (1. e4 c5 2. Nf3 Nc6 3. Bb5), a complex system all its own. It's true that the Rossolimo is hardly a refutation of the Sicilian, but why take time to learn a serious distraction when you can sidestep it to get a position you're prepared for? And how likely is it that you'll have to face the Rossolimo if you play the "other" second move? About 23%!

As usual, choices on the chessboard are a trade-off. We avoid the tricky Rossolimo, but must be ready for 3. c3, 3. Bc4, and even 3. d4 cxd4 4. Qxd4. They're less played than the Rossolimo, however, and we'll save these sidelines for later.

3. d4

The standard move—the center break in which White "loses money" (see page 58, left-hand column, number 2) in the pawn trade. Nearly all players of White feel forced to play d4 to seek an advantage. But the move is hardly a guarantee. Indeed, it's a testament to the Sicilian that world championship candidate GM Bent Larsen, the Great Dane of chess, termed White's ubiquitous d4 "a positional mistake."

After 3. c4 Nc6 4. d4 cxd4 5. Nxd4 Nf6 6. Nc3 d6, we transpose to the Maroczy Bind, another main branch of our system, covered in Chapters 10-15.

3. ... cxd4 4. Nxd4

We show you how to meet White's much less frequent choice, 4. Qxd4, in Chapter 8.

4. ... Nc6.

As we'll see in a later chapter on the Maroczy, this is more accurate than 4. ... Bg7.

The Accelerated Dragon—shown in Diagram 80—can be reached by 1. e4 c5 2. Nf3 Nc6 (allowing the Rossolimo, 3. Bb5) 3. d4 cxd4 4. Nxd4 g6, as well as by our move order: 1. e4 c5 2. Nf3 g6 (called the Hyper-Accelerated Dragon) 3. d4 cxd4 4. Nxd4 Nc6.

Diagram 80
After 4. ... Nc6

We've reached the basic position of the Accelerated Dragon. The main structural difference between it and the regular Dragon, where Black plays 2. ... d6 (discussed in Chapter 4), is that Black keeps his pawn on d7, giving him the option of playing ... d5! in one thrust.

This significant tempo gain sidesteps all the dangerous lines in which White castles queenside and begins a powerful "Yugoslav" attack by launching a pawn storm with h4—an approach by White that has claimed many victims over the years. (In his *My 60 Memorable Games*, Fischer sums up his own success with the system by writing, "[I] had it down to a science ... sac, sac, mate!")

In the spirit of the usual give and take, however, our recommended move order allows White to play 5. c4 (or 3. c4) and get the Maroczy Bind. (By playing c2-

c4, White blocks Black's thematic Sicilian play along the c-file and takes firm control of d5; hence the "bind.") The Maroczy is not as imminently dangerous as the Yugoslav, because the game usually develops along slow, positional routes, where both sides castle kingside.

Moreover, although in former times entering the Maroczy was off-putting for players of Black who wanted the counteraction offered by normal Sicilian lines, we'll see in Chapters 10-15 that we have the antidotes to White's plans in the Maroczy Bind—along with lots of new tactical ideas for Black. The "Bind" has lost its dreaded grip!

5. Nc3

Or 5. Be3 Nf6 6. Nc3—a simple transposition. Not dangerous to Black is 5. Nxc6 bxc6 6. Qd4 Nf6 7. e5 Nd5 8. e6 f6, as White falls behind in development.

5. ... Bg7

Black fianchettoes his dark-square bishop. This placement, and the pressure it brings to bear on the long diagonal from h8 to a1 is a key to his game plan.

6. Be3

Develop-and-defend—by far the most popular move. Chapter 7 recommends approaches for Black after the less-played, knight-retreating alternatives for

White: 6. Nde2 and 6. Nb3.

6. ... Nf6

Naturally, Black develops his knight to this time-tested square, preparing to castle, swinging his king into a safer spot and bringing his rook into play.

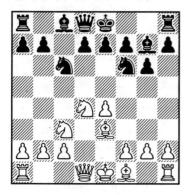

Diagram 81
After 6. ... Nf6

7. Bc4

This is the main line. White has three other, less popular and less promising seventh-move choices, examined in Chapter 6.

7. ... 0-0 8. Bb3

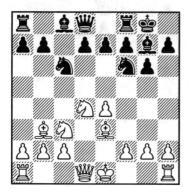

Diagram 82
After 8. Bb3

Retreating his bishop from the center is White's strongest move. The natural 8. 0-0 allows Black a "petite" equalizing combination à la Capablanca:

8. ... Nxe4! 9. Nxe4 (9. Bxf7+ Rxf7 10. Nxe4 Qa5, when, with strong central pawns and the bishop pair, Black is better)

Diagram 83
After 10. ... Qa5

9. ... d5 10. Nxc6 bxc6 11. Bd3 dxe4 12. Bxe4 Ba6!,

Diagram 84
After 12. ... Ba6!

with an equal position.

Another eighth move for White, 8. f3, allows 8. ... Qb6!.

The temporary sacrifice ... Nxe4 occurs in many openings.

Diagram 85
After 8. ... Qb6!

Now if 9. a3, then simply the developing 9. ... d6 (not 9. ... Qxb2?? 10. Na4); or 9. Bb3 Nxe4! 10. Nd5! Qa5+ 11. c3.

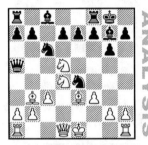

Diagram 86
After 11. c3

Here Black can choose between keeping the extra pawn (although White gets some compensation) with 11. ... Bxd4, and securing a comfortable equality

BLACK CAN CHOOSE BETWEEN KEEPING AN EXTRA PAWN AND SECURING COMFORTABLE EQUALITY.

with 11. ... Nc5 as in Fischer—Panno, 1958.

Back to 8. Bb3.

8. ... a5

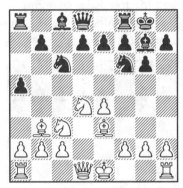

Diagram 87
After 8. ... a5

Black's idea is to play ... d5 in one move, and ... a5 helps him to achieve this by undermining the White guardians of the d5-square.

Here White has three main moves: 9. a4, 9. 0-0, and 9. f3.

A 9. a4

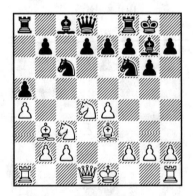

Diagram 88
After 9. a4

This move invites ... Ng4,

which gives Black a comfortable game.

9. ... Ng4 10. Qxg4

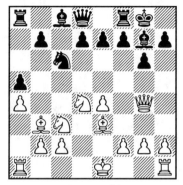

Diagram 89
After 10. Qxg4

After 10. Nxc6 Nxe3 11. Nxd8 Nxd1 12. Rxd1 Bxc3+ 13. bxc3 Rxd8, Black is better.

10. ... Nxd4

Now Black is ready to take on b3 at the most comfortable moment for him—and, thanks to 9. a4, White will have to recapture away from the center!

11. Qh4

White keeps his queen on the kingside, hoping to create an attack.

11. ... d6 12. Nd5 Re8 13. Rd1 Nxb3

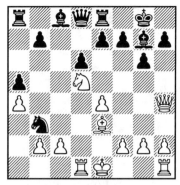

Diagram 90
After 13. ... Nxb3

Black devalues White's queenside pawns.

14. Bb6 Qd7 15. cxb3 Ra6

Black defends against the threat of Nc7.

16. Bd4 Qd8

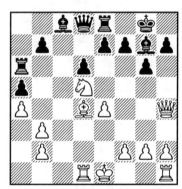

Diagram 91
After 16. ... Qd8

Black gets out of the way of his light-square bishop. He's doing fine.

17. 0-0

Or 17. Bxg7 Kxg7 18. Qg3 (White prevents ... e6) 18. ... Be6 19. 0-0 Rc6 20. Qe3 Bxd5 21. exd5 Rc5.

Diagram 92
After 21. ... Rc5

This position is about equal (Svidler–Topalov, 1999).

17. ... Be6 18. Bxg7 18. Kxg7 19. Nf4

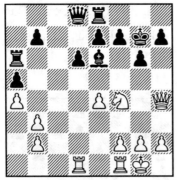

Diagram 93
After 19. Nf4

19. ... Qc8

Or 19. ... Bxb3!?–Fritz.

20. Rd3 Rc6 21. Qg3 f6

With the idea of ... Bf7. (See Almazi–Kramnik, in Part V.)

Many opening books don't even mention 9. 0-0.

B 9. 0-0

Diagram 94
After 9. 0-0

Many opening books—among them *MCO 15* (2008)—do not even mention this move, probably because after 9. ... a4 (Dzindzi's favorite) Black gets a central pawn (on e4) in exchange for his rook pawn.

Our 2005 edition recommended 9. ... d6, with the threat of 10. ... Ng4. After 10. f3 (**B2**) or 10. h3 (**B3**), we suggested 10. ... Nxd4, followed by ... B(c8)-d7-c6 and then ... Nd7, with a comfy equality. We dismissed White's 10. Ndb5 (**B1**)—avoiding the imminent exchanges—as not dangerous for Black. But this judgment has been recently challenged.

Thus, grandmaster Perelshteyn now prefers to exchange knights a move earlier (9. ... Nxd4). He believes—and you'll see why—that White's attempts to punish Black with an immediate assault won't succeed, and that other tacks will soon lead the game into the quiet and familiar **B2** and **B3** lines.

It's logical first to look at 9. ... a4 now, while examining 9. ... Nxd4 at the end of this section (after 9. ... d6).

9. ... a4 10. Nxa4 Nxe4 11. Nb5

Diagram 95
After 11. Nb5

("With the initiative," as we wrote in 2005—and then we moved on to the 9. ... d6 line.) Here the five-in-one *Encyclopedia of Chess Openings*, 2003, gives 11. ... Ra6 (to control the b6-square; riskier are 11. ... d5 and 11. ... d6) 12. c4! (12. Qe2 d5!, intending ... e6) 12. ... Na5 13. Bc2 (13. Qe2 d5! 14. cxd5 Nxb3 15. axb3 e6 ≅) 13. ... Nd6 14. Nxd6 Rxd6 15. Qe2 Nc6 ∞ (Burnoiu—Geanta, 2002). *ECO*'s comments above are by Romanian GMs Nisipeanu and Stoica.

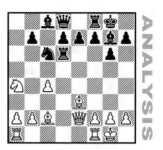

Diagram 96
After 15. ... Nc6

Rybka, however, gives the following line: 11. ... Ra6 12. f3! Nf6 13. Qe2 Na5! (Black should play ... Na5 as soon as possible in order to prevent White from extricating his light-square bishop.) 14. Rad1 d6 15. Rfe1 Bd7 16. c4.

Diagram 97
After 16. c4

And now simplifications follow: 16. ... Nxb3 17. axb3 Bxb5 18. cxb5 Ra8 19. Bb6 Qd7 20. Bd4 Rae8.

But let's go back to what is still our mainline recommendation, with some important updates:

9. ... d6

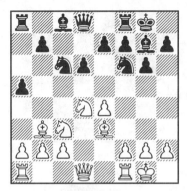

Diagram 98
After 9. ... d6

Black is threatening ... Ng4.

After 9. ... d6, White has three main choices: the reinvigorated 10. Nbd5, as well as 10. f3 and 10. h3.

B1 10. Ndb5

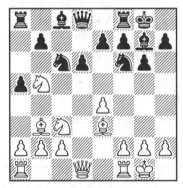

Diagram 99
After 10. Ndb5

As we've noted, this move has recently gained in popularity, but Black has ways to counter. Let's follow the 2008 game Bachmann—Iturrizaga:

10. ... b6 11. f3 Nd7 12. Bd5 Bb7 13. Qd2 Nc5 14. Rad1 Qd7 15. a4 Rac8 16. Rfe1 Nb4!

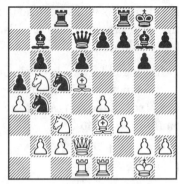

Diagram 100
After 16. ... Nb4!

17. b3 Bxd5

Now 18. exd5 Qf5 preserves equality, while 18. Nxd5, on the other hand, allows 18. ... Ne4! 19. fxe4 Rxc2 20. Nxe7+ Qxe7 21. Qxd6 Qxe4 22. Bf2 Qf5 ⩱, as in the game.

B2 10. f3

Diagram 101
After 10. f3

10. ... Nxd4 11. Bxd4 Bd7 12. a4 Bc6

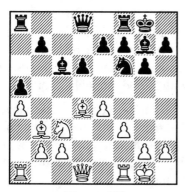

Diagram 102
After 12. ... Bc6

Black has already fulfilled the first part of his plan. Next he wants to play ... Nd7, exchange dark-square bishops, and bring his knight to c5.

The game Zulfigara—Wojtkewicz, 2002, continued: 13. Nd5 (if 13. Kh1, then simply 13. ... Nd7 14. Bxg7 Kxg7 15. Qd4+ Kg8, followed by ... Qb6 and ... Nc5, when Black is fine) 13. ... Nd7 14. c3 Nc5 15. Bc2 Bxd4+ 16. Qxd4 (or 16. cxd4 Bxd5 17. exd5 Nd7, with a good game for Black) 16. ... e5!.

Black gets a favorable pawn structure after 17. Qd2 Bxd5 18. exd5 (18. Qxd5 Qb6!) 18. ... f5, with at least equal chances.

B3 10. h3

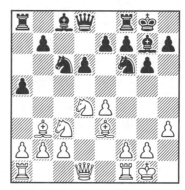

Diagram 103
After 10. h3

Black's plan here is basically the same as in the previous line, 10. f3 (**B2**).

10. ... Nxd4

The move 10. ... a4, exploiting the weakness of the e4-pawn, is also appealing. After 11. Nxa4 Nxe4 12. Nb5 Ra6, Black's d7-d6 is more useful than White's h2-h3 (cp. the 9. ... a4 line on p. 65.)

11. Bxd4 Bd7

BLACK HAS ALREADY FULFILLED THE FIRST PART OF HIS PLAN. NEXT HE WANTS TO PLAY ... ND7, EXCHANGE DARK-SQUARE BISHOPS, AND BRING HIS KNIGHT TO C5.

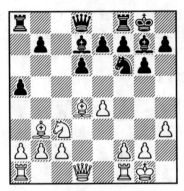

Diagram 104
After 11. ... Bd7

12. a4

After 12. Nd5, Black should not play 12. ... Nxe4?, as after 13. Bb6 Qe8 (13. ... Qb8 14. Nxe7+ and White is much better), 14. Nc7 wins the Exchange.

Instead, Black should respond to 12. Nd5 with 12. ... Nxd5 13. exd5 Bxd4 14. Qxd4 Qc7 15. Rfe1 Rfe8, when his bishop is better than White's passive counterpart.

12. ... Bc6.

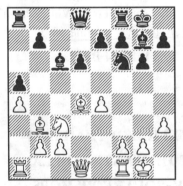

Diagram 105
After 12. ... Bc6

This is the key position of the variation. White's plan is to play in the center using the outpost on d5, and to play on the kingside with f4 and possibly f5 or e5.

Black's plan is to exchange dark-square bishops by playing ... Nd7, then to put his knight on the strong c5-outpost and to play on the dark squares.

As usual in the Sicilian, Black looks forward to the better structure in the endgame. So he welcomes the exchange of queens.

White can attack with 13. f4 or 13. Qd3.

B3a 13. f4

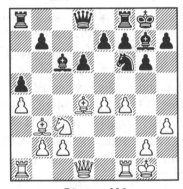

Diagram 106
After 13. f4

White gains space on the kingside and prepares e5 or f5.

13. ... Nd7

Black can't play 13. ... Nxe4? because of 14. Bxg7 Kxg7 15. Nxe4 Bxe4 16. Qd4+ and Qxe4.

14. Bxg7 Kxg7

Black has exchanged dark-square bishops and is ready to play ... Nc5.

15. Qd4+ f6 TN

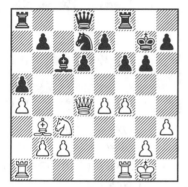

Diagram 107
After 15. ... f6

Also okay is 15. ... Kg8, as played in the game Anand–Mal-akhov, 2002. After 16. Nd5 Bxd5 17. Bxd5 Qc7 (with the idea of ... Qc5), the super-GMs got to this position.

Diagram 108
After 17. ... Qc7

Play continued 18. Kh1 Rab8 19. Bc4 Qb6 20. Rad1 Qxd4 21. Rxd4 Nc5 22. b3 Rfc8, when Black had achieved a solid posi-tion.

Our main line, 15. ... f6, is

an important novelty found by our youngest co-author in the game Friedel–Perelshteyn, 2003.

Here Black is not afraid of the weakness on e6 because White's knight can't get to it. Black wants to exchange queens with ... Qb6.

16. Nd5 Nc5 17. f5

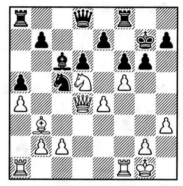

Diagram 109
After 17. f5

17. ... Nxb3 18. cxb3 Bxd5

Black prevents Nf4.

19. exd5 Rc8

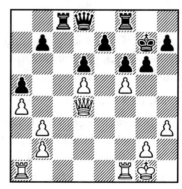

Diagram 110
After 19. ... Rc8

An interesting position! If

Black manages to exchange queens, he will be much better in the endgame (again, the Sicilian better-endgame theme), because White has too many weaknesses. (Sometimes in pressing to win before the queens come off, White leaves himself with an even worse endgame!) So White tries to create an attack.

20. Rae1 Rf7

Black defends the pawn and prepares a strong defensive setup on the kingside.

21. Re3 gxf5! 22. Rxf5 Kh8

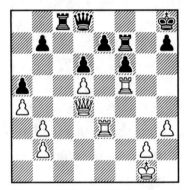

Diagram 111
After 22. ... Kh8

Now Black's king is quite safe and Black can himself take control of the g-file.

23. Rc3

White is correct to exchange a pair of rooks—Black's threat of ... Qd7, followed by doubling rooks on the g-file, is too dangerous.

23. ... Rg7 24. Kf2

The position is about even.

B3b 13. Qd3

Diagram 112
After 13. Qd3

13. ... Nd7 14. Bxg7 Kxg7 15. Rad1 Nc5

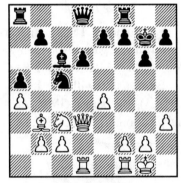

Diagram 113
After 15. ... Nc5

Black has reached the position he wanted and has a solid game. The game Movsesian—Fedorov, 2003, continued:

16. Qd4+ Kg8

Also possible is 16. ... f6!?.

17. Bd5 Qb6 18. b3 Nd7

Black, as usual, encourages the exchange of queens, looking forward to an endgame.

19. Qd2 Qc5 20. Kh1 Nf6 21. Rfe1 Rad8! 22. Bc4 e6!

Now Black controls d5.

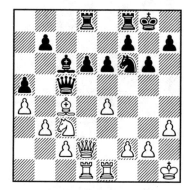

Diagram 114
After 22. ... e6!

23. Qd4 Qxd4 24. Rxd4 Rd7 25. Red1 Rfd8 26. f3 Kf8 27. Kg1

Here the players agreed to a draw. After 27. ... Ke7, Black's position is very solid.

Now that you have a knowledge of the themes and ideas in these lines, let's go back to 9. 0-0 (**B**) to take a look at GM Perelshteyn's favored response.

9. ... Nxd4 10. Bxd4 d6

Diagram 115
After 10. ... d6

The idea of this early exchange is to avoid 10. Nbd5 (**B1**), and to transfer the game into the channels similar to those in our classical lines (**B2** and **B3**).

11. Qe2

The alternative is the immediate 11. f4 Bd7 12. e5 (12. a4 Bc6 13. Kh1 Nd7 leads to familiar positions) 12. ... Ne8.

Diagram 116
After 12. ... Ne8

13. Qe2 (13. a4 fxe5 14. fxe5 Nc7) 13. ... a4 14. Bd5 Nc7!. In short, White's assault can be handled.

11. ... Bd7 12. Rad1

Diagram 117
After 12. Rad1

12. ... a4 13. Bc4 Bc6 14. f4

If 14. a3, then 14. ... Nd7, with equality (stronger than 14. ... Ra5, when 15. Nd5 led to a slight advantage in Radjabov—Tiviakov, 2007), or 14. e5 dxe5 15. Bxe5 Qb6!? (TN) 16. Nb5 Ne4=.

14. ... Nd7 15. e5

White crashes through in the center, but can he break through Black's setup? Nakamura—Wojtkewicz, 2003, continued 15. ... dxe5 16. fxe5 e6!.

Diagram 118
After 16. ... e6!

ANALYSIS

A key buffering move. Now e5 is a weakness. 17. Bc5 Qa5!? (a positional exhange sacrifice à la Petrosian) 18. Bxf8 Rxf8 19. Bb5 Nxe5 20. Bxc6 bxc6. The position is about even. However, Nakamura's over-aggressive play eventually backfired and Black won.

EUGENE'S
... 9. NxD4 SO FAR
FARES QUITE WELL!

ℭ 9. f3

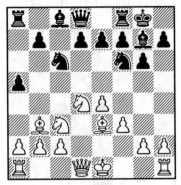

Diagram 119
After 9. f3

White intends to castle long after Qd2. His ninth move bolsters his e4-pawn, prevents ... Ng4, and leverages the pawn-charge g4. These plusses explain why it's a popular move!

9. ... d5

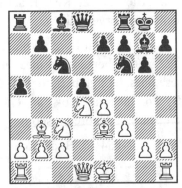

Diagram 120
After 9. ... d5

Black sacrifices his pawn to get dynamic piece play. The move is a good example of the dictum to counter an attack on the wing with a counterpunch in the center. Black's ... d5 is a common response to White's "Yugoslav Attack" intentions. Indeed, one of the great advantages of the Accelerated Dragon is that Black refrains from playing … d6 for precisely this contingency.

Now White has to play very accurately in order to avoid getting a worse position! White has three ways to capture the pawn: 10. exd5, 10. Bxd5, and 10. Nxd5?!.

C1 10. exd5 Nb4 11. Nde2 a4!

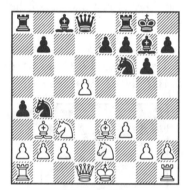

Diagram 121
After 11. … a4!

This follow-up is the whole idea behind 8. … a5. Now Black wins the d-pawn and develops a strong initiative, whether White recaptures with 12. Bxa4 or 12. Nxa4.

C1a 12. Bxa4 Nfxd5 13. Bf2

13. Bd4? loses after 13. … Bxd4 14. Nxd4 (14. Qxd4 Rxa4 15. Nxa4 Nxc2+) 14. … Ne3! 15. Qd2 Qxd4! 16. Qxd4 Nexc2+.

13. … Nxc3 14. Nxc3 Qxd1+

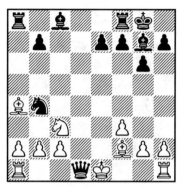

Diagram 122
After 14. … Qxd1+

15. Kxd1 Rd8+ 16. Ke2

Black can simply win his pawn back with 16. … Bxc3 17. bxc3 Rxa4 18. cxb4 Rxb4, with an equal position, or he can even play to win with 16. … Bf5!?.

Diagram 123
After 16. … Bf5!?

ANALYSIS

Black can simply win his pawn back or play for a win.

C1b 12. Nxa4 Nfxd5

Diagram 124
After 12. ... Nfxd5

13. Bf2

White's other 13th-move options are not formidable. After 13. Bd4 Bxd4 14. Qxd4 (14. Nxd4? Ne3 15. Qd2 Qxd4! 16. Qxd4 Nexc2+) 14. ... Bf5

Diagram 125
After 14. ... Bf5

White is pressed to defend c2.

15. Nac3

Here if White tries 15. Qd2?, Black plays … Bxc2!. There could follow 16. Bxc2 (relatively

better is 16. Bxd5 Rxa4∓) 16. … Ne3!.

Diagram 126
After 16. ... Ne3!

The Black horsemen mark the apocalypse. White's Judgment Day is just and harsh: he's lost.

Back to 15. Nac3: 15. ... Nxc2+ 16. Bxc2 Nxc3 17. Qxd8 Rfxd8 18. Bxf5 Nxe2 19. Kxe2 gxf5

Diagram 127
After 19. ... gxf5

The game is drawish (Petrushin–Khasin, 1976).

If 13. Bc5 Rxa4! 14. Bxa4 Qa5 15. Bxb4 Nxb4 16. c3 Rd8

THE BLACK HORSEMEN MARK WHITE'S APOCALYPSE.

Diagram 128
After 16. ... Rd8

17. cxb4!. Relatively best—even worse is 17. Qb3 Nd3+ 18. Kf1 Qa7 19. Nd4 Bxd4 20. cxd4 Qxd4 21. Qc2 Nxb2 22. Bb3

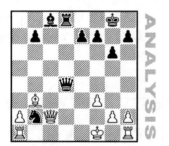

Diagram 129
After 22. Bb3

22. ... Nc4!, winning.

Finally, 13. Bd2

Diagram 130
After 13. Bd2

13. ... b5! (The classical 13. ... Bf5 is also good.) 14. Nac3 Be6.

Diagram 131
After 14. ... Be6

Black prepares to exchange White's bishop on b3.

15. Nxb5

After 15. a3 Nxc3 16. Bxc3 Bxc3+ 17. bxc3 Bxb3, Black has full compensation for a pawn.

15. ... Qb6 16. a3

Even worse is 16. Nbc3 Nxc3 17. bxc3 Bxb3.

16. ... Nxc2+ 17. Qxc2 Qxb5 ∓.

Diagram 132
After 17. ... Qxb5

Back to our main line after White's best, 13. Bf2.

13. ... Bf5

BLACK TRADES DOWN TO AN EQUAL ENDGAME.

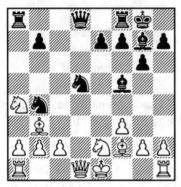

Diagram 133
After 13. ... Bf5

Now White has played 14. a3
and 14. 0-0.

C1b1 14. a3 Nxc2+

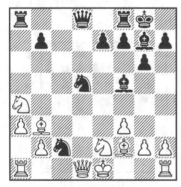

Diagram 134
After 14. ... Nxc2+

Black trades down to an
equal endgame.

15. Bxc2 Qa5+ 16. b4

16. Nac3? Nxc3 17. Nxc3
Bxc3+, winning.

Diagram 135
After 17. ... Bxc3+

**16. ... Nxb4 17. axb4 Qxb4+
18. Qd2 Qxd2+ 19. Kxd2 Bxa1
20. Rxa1**

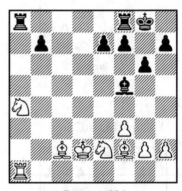

Diagram 136
After 20. Rxa1

20. ... Bxc2

Or 20. ... Rfd8+!?.

**21. Kxc2 b5 22. Nec3 bxa4
23. Rxa4 Rxa4 24. Nxa4 =.**

Diagram 137
After 24. Nxa4

C1b2 14. 0–0

White abandons his c-pawn to complete his development.

14. ... b5!

Diagram 138
After 14. ... b5!

Black attacks with his one surviving queenside foot soldier.

15. Nac3 Nxc3 16. Nxc3 Qxd1 17. Rfxd1 Bxc2 18. Bxc2 Nxc2 19. Rac1 Bxc3 20. Rxc2 Bf6

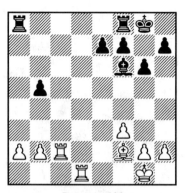

Diagram 139
After 20. ... Bf6

Black has equality (Shirov–Lautier, 1997).

C2 10. Bxd5

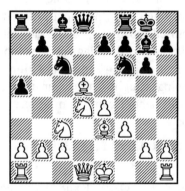

Diagram 140
After 10. Bxd5

10. ... Nxd5

Now White can choose between 11. Nxd5 and 11. exd5.

Black attacks with his one surviving foot soldier!

C2a **11. Nxd5 f5**

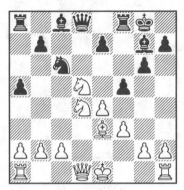

Diagram 141
After 11. ... f5

Black has a temporary advantage in development (he has castled, while White's king is still in the center), so he decides to open up the position. (In closed positions, one side can often afford a lag in development, but in open positions, being caught with your troops still in boot camp can be terminal.)

C2a1 **12. c3 fxe4 13. fxe4**

Or 13. Nxc6 bxc6 14. Nb6 Rb8 15. Qxd8 Rxd8 16. fxe4 Ba6, with the idea of ... Bd3. Black is better.

13. ... e6 14. Nf4

14. Nxc6 Qh4+ 15. g3 Qxe4

14. ... Nxd4 15. cxd4 Bxd4

16. Qxd4 Qxd4 17. Bxd4 Rxf4 18. 0–0–0 Bd7!

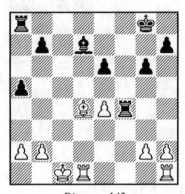

Diagram 142
After 18. ... Bd7!

White has no advantage.

C2a2 **12. Nxc6**

This move leads to the endgame. Will Black's initiative carry over to the final phase?

12. ... bxc6

Diagram 143
After 12. ... bxc6

**BLACK HAS A TEMPORARY ADVANTAGE
IN DEVELOPMENT. WHITE'S KING
IS STILL IN THE CENTER.**

13. Nb6 Rb8 14. Qxd8 Rxd8 15. Rd1 Rxd1+ 16. Kxd1

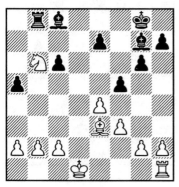

Diagram 144
After 16. Kxd1

This is the critical position. Black has tried 16. ... Bxb2 and 16. ... fxe4. We recommend capturing with the f-pawn.

16. ... fxe4 17. Nxc8

After 17. fxe4 Bxb2 18. Nxc8 Rxc8 19. Ke2 Be5,

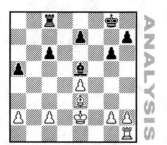

Diagram 145
After 19. ... Be5

Black threatens ... Rb8 and then ... Rb2.

20. Rb1 Bxh2 21. a4 Bc7

Black is fine (Ivanchuk–S. Polgar, 1994).

17. ... Rxc8 18. b3 exf3 19. gxf3 a4

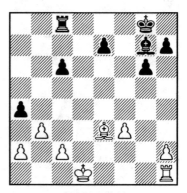

Diagram 146
After 19. ... a4

Black wants to exchange his weak pawn, and thus achieve equality.

However, even simpler and stronger is the centralization of the king.

19. ... Kf7 20. Ke2 Be5 21. a4 Ke6 22. Bb6 Ra8 23. Kd3 Bd6

Diagram 147
After 23. ... Bd6

Black prepares to play ... Rf8. He has a comfortable game. We have been following Zhan Pengxiang–Ni Hua, 2001, which ended in a draw.

C2b **11. exd5 Nb4 12. Nde2**

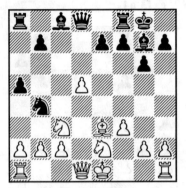

Diagram 148
After 12. Nde2

12. ... e6!

Black opens the e-file and gives his bishop on c8 a pathway into the game. Another option is 12. … Bf5 13. Rc1 b5.

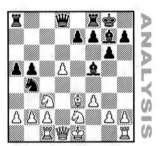

Diagram 149
After 13. ... b5

After 12. … e6!, White has three moves: 13. dxe6, 13. a3, and 13. Qd2.

C2b1 **13. dxe6**

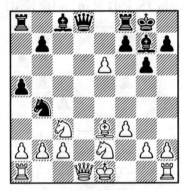

Diagram 150
After 13. dxe6

White can instead play 13. a3 or 13. Qd2 (discussed below), aiming at giving Black an isolated pawn. But 13. d6 is bad, as this pawn will be very vulnerable, for example after 13. … Ra6.

13. … Bxe6 14. a3

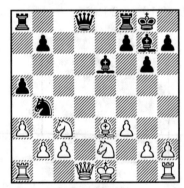

Diagram 151
After 14. a3

White is being greedy! But

BLACK OPENS THE E-FILE AND GIVES HIS BISHOP ON c8 A PATHWAY INTO THE GAME.

after 14. 0-0 Qxd1 15. Raxd1 Nxc2,

Diagram 152
After 15. ... Nxc2

Black has regained his pawn and stands better due to his active bishop pair.

14.   ... Nd5 15. Nxd5 Bxd5 16. Bd4 Re8! 17. Bxg7 Bc4!

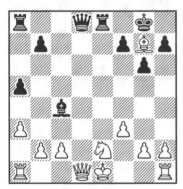

Diagram 153
After 17. ... Bc4!

Now White has to give up his queen for the rook and bishop or sacrifice an Exchange.

18. Bc3

18. 0–0? Kxg7

18.   ... Rxe2+ 19. Qxe2 Bxe2 20. Kxe2

With good winning chances for Black; White's king has no shelter.

C2b2 13. a3

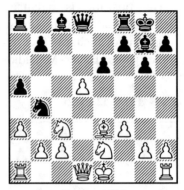

Diagram 154
After 13. a3

13. ... Nxd5 14. Nxd5 exd5 15. Bd4 Bh6!

Diagram 155
After 15. ... Bh6!

Black avoids the exchange of bishops; it would weaken his dark squares and allow White's knight to occupy d4. (Knights are the best blockaders of an isolated pawn.)

16. 0–0

(Pushing 16. h4 is too risky—for example, 16. ... Re8 17. h5 Ra6!. Black is ready to meet hxg6 with ... Rxg6.)

The position is balanced: Black's isolated d-pawn is offset by his pair of bishops. (See the sample game Bauer–Malakhov, 2003.)

C2b3 13. Qd2 exd5

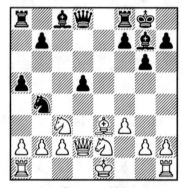

Diagram 156
After 13. ... exd5

Now if 14. a3?, Black has ... d4, with a better game. White has three reasonable moves—he can play 14. Bd4, 14. 0-0 or 14. 0-0-0.

C2b3(I) 14. Bd4 Bxd4 15. Nxd4 Qh4+

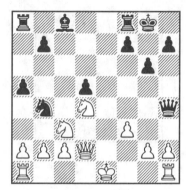

Diagram 157
After 15. ... Qh4+

15. ... Re8+ is also interesting and worthy of study.

16. Kf1 Nc6 17. Ncb5

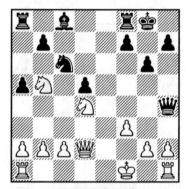

Diagram 158
After 17. Ncb5

17. ... Bd7

Black has an equal game.

BLACK IS FULLY COMPENSATED FOR THE EXCHANGE.

C2b3(II) 14. 0-0 d4!

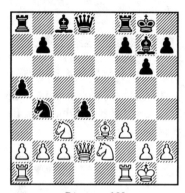

Diagram 159
After 14. ... d4!

15. Rad1 Bf5 16. Nxd4 Bxd4 17. Bxd4 Nxc2

Black is equal.

C2b3(III) 14. 0-0-0 Bf5

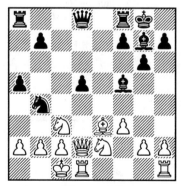

Diagram 160
After 14. ... Bf5

15. Nd4 Bxd4 16. Bxd4

Nxc2 17. Bc5 d4!

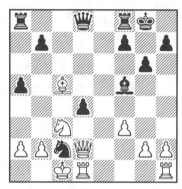

Diagram 161
After 17. ... d4!

18. Bxf8 Qxf8 19. Ne4 Bxe4 20. fxe4 Ne3

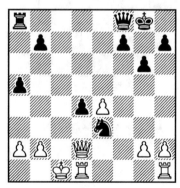

Diagram 162
After 20. ... Ne3

Black is fully compensated for the Exchange.

C3 **10. Nxd5**

The weakest recapture.

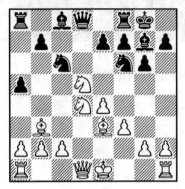

Diagram 163
After 10. Nxd5

10. ... Nxd5 11. exd5

11. Bxd5? Nxd4 12. Bxd4 Bxd4 13. Qxd4 e6, winning.

Diagram 164
After 13. ... e6

11. ... Nb4 12. c4 a4

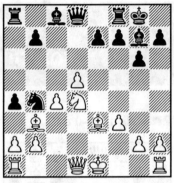

Diagram 165
After 12. ... a4

13. Bc2 (13. Bxa4? Qa5)
13. ... e5! 14. Ne2 Qh4+ 15. Bf2 Qxc4

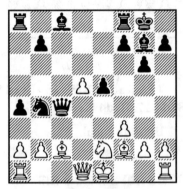

Diagram 166
After 15. ... Qxc4

Black is much better.

Summary:

In our main line, White's overaggressiveness often leaves Black with a superior endgame. But even in the middlegame, Black's sound and flexible position is resilient to attack. White has many chances to go wrong. The moves 8. ... a5 and, in case of 9. f3, 9. ... d5, are the keys to Black's counter-play.

Chapter 5: The Accelerated Dragon—Intro and Main Line
Memory Markers!

Diagram 167
After 11. Qd1

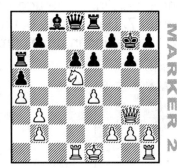

Diagram 168
After 18. ... e6

Diagram 169
After 16. Rad1

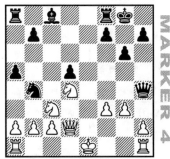

Diagram 170
After 16. g3

Solutions to Memory Markers!

No 1   **11. ... Nxb3**, forcing White to capture with the c-pawn.
         See page 63.

No. 2   **19. Qc3+** followed by **20. Nc7**, winning the Exchange.
         See page 64.

No. 3   **16. ... Qb6**, going into a favorable endgame.
         See page 69.

No. 4   **16. ... Qxd4**, winning a piece.
         See page 82.

Chapter 6: The Accelerated Dragon—Seventh-move Sidelines
Some Important Points to Look For

Of the three sidelines, the aggressive 7. Nxc6 leads to a sharp game, 7. Be2 is safe but harmless, and 7. f3 leaves White behind in development.

◆ After 8. ... Ng8, Black attacks the e5-pawn. See Diagram 174.

◆ The Black knight is well placed on f5. See Diagram 179.

◆ After 11. ... Bxd4, the endgame favors Black. See Diagram 186.

◆ Black is ready to play ... d7-d5. See Diagram 188.

Outline of Variations

1. e4 c5 2. Nf3 g6 3. d4 cxd4 4. Nxd4 Nc6 5. Nc3 Bg7 6. Be3 Nf6 *(86)*

    A 7. Nxc6 bxc6 8. e5 Ng8! *(87)* **[B34]**

        A1 9. Bd4 f6 10. f4 Qa5 11. Qe2 fxe5 12. Bxe5 Nf6 13. 0-0-0 0-0 *(88)*

        A2 9. f4 Nh6 10. Qd2 0-0 11. 0-0-0 d6! 12. exd6 exd6 13. h3 Nf5 *(89)*

    B 7. Be2 0-0 8. 0-0 d6 9. f4 Qb6 10. Qd3 Ng4! 11. Bxg4 Bxd4 (90) **[B73]**

    C 7. f3 0-0! 8. Qd2 d5 *(92)* **[B34]**

        C1 9. exd5 Nxd5 10. Nxc6 bxc6 11. Bd4 Bxd4 12. Qxd4 e5! 13. Qc5 Qb6 *(93)*

        C2 9. Nxc6 bxc6 10. e5 Nd7 11. f4 e6 12. Na4? Nxe5! 13. fxe5 Qh4+ *(93)*

Chapter 6
The Accelerated Dragon
Seventh-move Sidelines

In our main line, after Black's 6. ... Nf6, we reach this position:

Diagram 171
After 6. ... Nf6

To avoid the main continuation on move seven (7. Bc4, Chapter 5), White has three options: 7. Nxc6, 7. Be2, and 7. f3. Black can deal very effectively with all three.

Let's start with the most ambitious move.

A 7. Nxc6

Diagram 172
After 7. Nxc6

White wants to play 8. e5 to challenge Black's whole scheme.

7. ... bxc6 8. e5

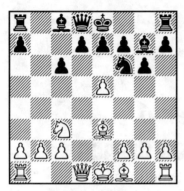

Diagram 173
After 8. e5

Diagram 174
After 8. ... Ng8!

White's idea is to give Black the apparent Hobson's choice of wasting a tempo by retreating the attacked knight to g8 or sacrificing a pawn with 8. ... Nd5!?.

We recommend playing 8. ... Ng8!, and like Brer Rabbit's enjoying the intended punishment of the "Briar Patch," Black will maneuver confidently. His important knight can head to h6 and f5. Black then follows up with ... d6, undermining White's center.

8. ... Ng8!

> We recommend playing 8. ... Ng8!. Black's important knight can head to h6 and f5. Black then follows up with ... d6, undermining White's center.

Here White has two moves:

9. Bd4 and 9. f4.

A1 9. Bd4 f6

Black provokes White into playing f4 and then further pressures e5, as exf6 cedes Black a strong center.

10. f4 Qa5 11. Qe2 fxe5

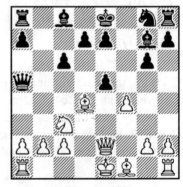

Diagram 175
After 11. ... fxe5

12. Bxe5

If White tries 12. fxe5?, Black has the star move 12. ... Rb8!, and then if 13. b3?, Black plays 13. ... c5.

12. ... Nf6 13. 0-0-0 0-0

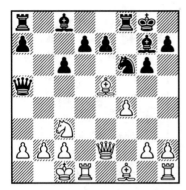

Diagram 176
After 13. ... 0-0

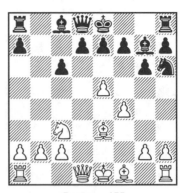

Diagram 177
After 9. ... Nh6

Black has good play—and owns the position that's more fun! White will need time to uncork his normally dominant light-square bishop. Later, Black can make threats down the semi-open b-file.

Martinez—Tiviakov, 2007, continued: 14. Bd4 e6 15. a3— and now, instead of 15. ... Nh5, Black could preserve his fun with 15. ... c5 16. Be5 (16. Qe5? d5, winning) 16. ... d5. Rybca gives this as a dynamically equal and somewhat unclear position. Homework will pay off here.

A2 9. f4 Nh6

10. Qd2 0-0 11. 0-0-0 d6!

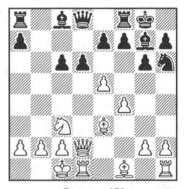

Diagram 178
After 11. ... d6!

Black undermines White's center.

12. exd6 exd6 13. h3

The pawn on d6 is untouchable: 13. Qxd6 Qxd6 14. Rxd6 Nf5 15. Rd3 Ba6, while 13. Bc5?! Bg4 gives Black dangerous counterplay.

13. ... Nf5 14. Bf2

> **Black has good play—and owns the position that's more fun!**

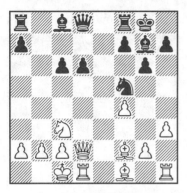

Diagram 179
After 14. Bf2

Here, Black's control over the long diagonal, together with the half-open b-file, allows him to unleash a tremendous attack!

14. ... Qa5! 15. g4 Rb8! 16. gxf5 Rxb2!

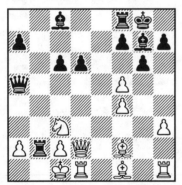

Diagram 180
After 16. ... Rxb2!

White loses, for example:

17. f6 (17. Kxb2 Qb4+ 18. Kc1 Bxc3-+). 17. ... Qa3 (with the threat of mate in one) 18. Qe3 Bxf6 19. Kd2 Bf5 20. Rc1 Qa5!.

Diagram 181
After 20. ... Qa5!

White is hopelessly pin-plagued. He has no defense against ... Rxa2 and ... Ra3.

B 7. Be2

Quietly developing with 7. Be2 transposes to the Classical Variation, a line that holds no terror for Black.

Diagram 182
After 7. Be2

7. ... 0-0 8. 0-0 d6

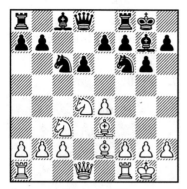

Diagram 183
After 8. ... d6

Black transposes into the normal Dragon, where White's classical setup with Be2 and 0-0 is rather harmless.

9. f4

For 9. Nb3, see 6. Nb3 in Chapter 7; if 9. h3, then 9. ... Bd7 followed by ... Nxd4 and ... Bc6.

9. ... Qb6

Black takes advantage of the fact that White's bishop is unprotected and sets up a powerful pin.

10. Qd3

10. Qd2? loses to 10. ... Nxe4 11. Nxe4 Bxd4; after 10. Na4, Black can simply play 10. ... Qa5, after which White has no better move than to retreat with 11. Nc3.

10. ... Ng4! 11. Bxg4

Or 11. Nd5 Bxd4! (Black trades his queen for three minor pieces, usually a good swap, especially when both his bishops remain on the board) 12. Nxb6 Bxe3+ 13. Kh1 Bxb6 14. Bxg4 Bxg4.

Diagram 184
After 14. ... Bxg4

Black enjoys an advantage—for example, if 15. f5 (with the threat of trapping Black's bishop with h3 and g4), then 15. ... Bh5! 16. h3 gxf5 17. exf5 f6 18. Rae1 Ne5 19. Qd2 Be8!.

Diagram 185
After 19. ... Be8!

Black will play ... Bc6, followed by ... Kh8 and ... Rg8.

11. ... Bxd4

Diagram 186
After 11. ... Bxd4

12. Bxd4 Qxd4+ 13. Qxd4 Nxd4 14. Bxc8 Rfxc8

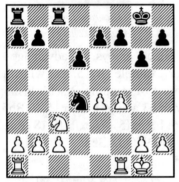

Diagram 187
After 14. ... Rfxc8

The Sicilian endgame! Black is at least equal.

C 7. f3

Taking time to bolster e4 with 7. f3 leaves White behind in development.

7. ... 0-0!

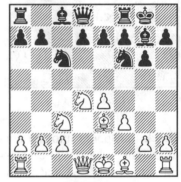

Diagram 188
After 7. ... 0-0!

White's seventh move was too passive. Now Black threatens ... Qb6 or ... d5, and White lacks an adequate response.

8. Qd2

If 8. Bc4 Qb6!, winning a pawn. (See Chapter 5, Main line: 7. Bc4, page 62.)

8. ... d5

Now White has two choices: he can capture on d5 or exchange knights and play e5.

C1 9. exd5 Nxd5

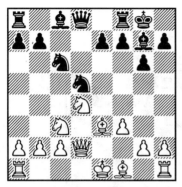

Diagram 189
After 9. ... Nxd5

10. Nxc6

Or 10. Nxd5 Qxd5 11. Nxc6 Qxc6 12. 0-0-0 Bf5, and Black's attack is overpowering.

10. ... bxc6 11. Bd4 Bxd4 12. Qxd4 e5! 13. Qc5 Qb6

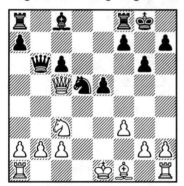

Diagram 190
After 13. ... Qb6

Black is once again better in

the upcoming endgame.

C2   9. Nxc6 bxc6 10. e5 Nd7 11. f4 e6

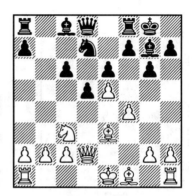

Diagram 191
After 11. ... e6

Black's idea is to play … c5. His central pawns are very strong. White's attempt to blockade them fails.

12. Na4? Nxe5! 13. fxe5 Qh4+

Black follows up with … Qxa4.

Summary:

White's three seventh-move tries to avoid our main line (7. Nxc6, 7. Be2, and 7. f3) all lead to nice games for Black. Against 7. Nxc6, Black gets positions that are promising and fun to play. The classical 7. Be2 is harmless, while the slow 7. f3 allows Black to play … d7-d5 in one move, and thus get a dangerous lead in development.

Chapter 6: The Accelerated Dragon—
Seventh-move Sidelines
Memory Markers!

Diagram 192
After 8. Qd2

Diagram 193
After 9. Bf4

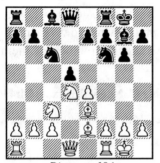

Diagram 194
After 8. ... d5

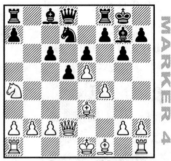

Diagram 195
After 11. Na4

Chapter 6: The Accelerated Dragon— Seventh-move Sidelines
Solutions to Memory Markers!

No. 1   **8. ... d5!.** See page 92.

No. 2   **9. ... f6** is fine here, but the preliminary **9. ... Qb6**, attacking the b2-pawn, is even stronger. See page 88.

No. 3   **9. exd5 Nxd5 10. Nxd5 Qxd5 11. Bf3**, with an advantage. Thus in Diagram 183, Black played the "modest" 8. ... d6. See page 91.

No. 4   **11. ... Nxe5!.** See page 93.

Chapter 7: The Accelerated Dragon—Sixth-move Sidelines

Some Important Points to Look For

White's sixth-move sidelines, 6. Nde2 and 6. Nb3, are easy for a prepared Black to handle. Black may even have more than one good plan at his disposal.

◆ Black expands on the queenside.
See Diagram 197.

◆ 10. ... Qc8 serves three purposes.
See Diagram 205.

◆ After 13. ... e5! Black starts central actions. See Diagram 208.

◆ Centralization.
See Diagram 227.

Outline of Variations

1. e4 c5 2. Nf3 g6 3. d4 cxd4 4. Nxd4 Nc6 5. Nc3 Bg7 *(96)* [B34]
   A 6. Nde2 Nf6 7. g3 b5 8. a3 Rb8 9. Bg2 a5 *(97)*
   B 6. Nb3 Nf6 7. Be2 0-0 8. 0-0 d6 *(98)*
     B1 9. Be3 Be6 10. f4 Qc8 *(99)*
     B2 9. Bg5 Be6 *(102)*
       B2a 10. f4 b5 *(102)*
       B2b 10. Kh1 Rc8 11. f4 Na5 12. f5 Bc4 *(103)*
     B3 9. Re1 Be6 10. Bf1 a5 11. a4 Bxb3 12. cxb3 e6 13. Bg5 h6 *(104)*
       B3a 14. Bh4 Qb6 *(105)*
       B3b 14. Be3 Nb4 *(106)*
     B4 9. f4 Be6 *(107)*

Chapter 7
The Accelerated Dragon
Sixth-move Sidelines

This chapter shows you how to play the Accelerated Dragon against less-chosen sixth moves. After **1. e4 c5 2. Nf3 g6 3. d4 cxd4 4. Nxd4 Nc6 5. Nc3**, let's look back to Chapter 5, after:

5. ... Bg7

Diagram 196
After 5 ... Bg7

Now, rather than the main-line 6. Be3, examined in Chapters 5 and 6, White can choose 6. Nde2 or 6. Nb3.

A 6. Nde2

Not surprisingly, given the passivity of this retreat, Black gets a good game:

6. ... Nf6 7. g3 b5 8. a3 Rb8 9. Bg2 a5

Diagram 197
After 9. ... a5

10. 0–0 0–0 11. h3

White makes this move in order to be able to play Be3.

11. ... b4 12. axb4 axb4 13. Nd5

Diagram 198
After 13. Nd5

13. ... Nxd5 14. exd5 Ne5

The knight has his eye on c4.

15. Nd4 Qb6

Diagram 199
After 15. ... Qb6

The game is approximately even. Note that, as Black, you should not touch your d-pawn yet because it does you yeoman service standing on its home square. It controls c6 and enables you, in some lines after dxe6, to respond with ... dxe6!—for example: 16. Re1 Nc4 17. c3 bxc3 18. bxc3 e5! 19. dxe6 (e.p.), dxe6.

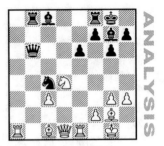

Diagram 200
After 19. ... dxe6

Also not dangerous for Black is the subtler 16. Bf4—for example: 16. ... Bb7 17. Re1 d6.

Diagram 201
After 17. ... d6

And now if 18. Bg5, then 18. ... Rfe8, preparing ... e6.

B 6. Nb3

Diagram 202
After 6. Nb3

After this move, we may transpose to the Classical Dragon, a variation Black can enter with confidence.

6. ... Nf6 7. Be2 0–0 8. 0–0 d6

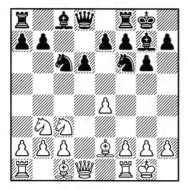

Diagram 203
After 8. ... d6

Black can also play 8. ... b6 if he wants to avoid the usual lines. GM Skembris gives: 9. Bg5 Bb7

Diagram 204
After 9. ... Bb7

10. Qd2 Rc8 11. f4 b5, when the position is unclear and worthy of home analysis. Normally, the player more familiar with a difficult position gets the point!

After 8. ... d6, White has four main moves: 9. Be3, 9. Bg5, 9. Re1, and 9. f4.

B1 9. Be3 Be6 10. f4 Qc8

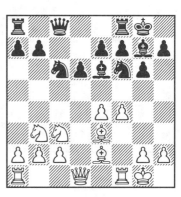

Diagram 205
After 10. ... Qc8

This move has several ideas:

1. It prevents f5;

2. It threatens ... Ng4;

3. It prepares play in the center with ... Rd8 and ... d5.

11. Kh1

White prepares a retreat square for his bishop after ... Ng4.

Or 11. h3 Rd8, with play similar to 11. Kh1.

11. ... Rd8

Black can transpose to the Classical Dragon with confidence.

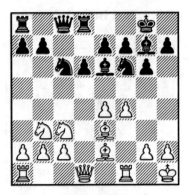

Diagram 206
After 11. ... Rd8

Black prepares ... d5.

12. Bf3.

This stops ... d5, but allows ... Bc4 and ... e5.

White can try 12. Bg1, when Black makes the advance he planned: 12. ... d5 13. e5 Ne4 14. Nxe4 dxe4 15. Qe1 f6!.

Diagram 207
After 15. ... f6!

By now a very familiar maneuver. Black opens up his bishop and at that same time rids the center of White's linchpin e5-pawn. After 16. exf6 exf6, followed by ... f5, White's pawn on f4 looks out of place, his center has collapsed, and Black stands better.

12. .... Bc4 13. Rf2 e5!

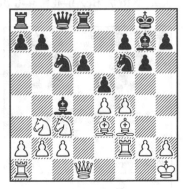

Diagram 208
After 13. ... e5!

Unexpectedly, Black starts operations in the center with a very unusual move for the Dragon setup! With ... e5, Black is threatening ... d5 and preparing ... exf4 and ... Ne5, gaining a dominant outpost for his knight on e5.

14. Rd2 exf4 15. Bxf4 Ne5

Here, after only 15 logical moves, Black completely dominates the game with his powerful knight on e5 and other active pieces. White is virtually forced to accept the pawn sacrifice. After 16. Bxe5 dxe5, Black has a pronounced advantage, thanks to his dashing bishop pair and White's bad bishop, blocked in by his own pawn.

**16. Rxd6 Rxd6 17. Qxd6 Nxf3
18. gxf3 Qh3**

Black has a strong attack.

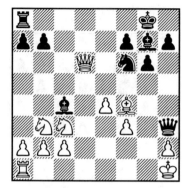

Diagram 209
After 18. ... Qh3

19. Bg3

After the more cautious 19.
Nd2 Nh5 20. Be5,

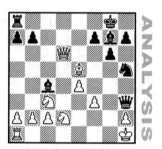

Diagram 210
After 20. Be5

there follows 20. ... Bh6 21. Rg1
(21. Nxc4? Bf4!, winning) 21. ...
Bxd2 22. Qxd2 Qxf3+ 23. Qg2
Qxg2+ 24. Rxg2

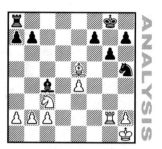

Diagram 211
After 24. Rxg2

24. ... Re8 25. Bd4 a6, and Black
is doing fine.

19. ... Nh5 20. Nd2?

Not much better is 20. Rg1
Bh6 21. Nd2 Nxg3+ 22. Rxg3
Qh4.

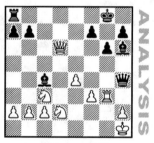

Diagram 212
After 22. ... Qh4

Black can now meet 23. Nxc4?
with ... Bf4.

20. ... Bf8!

Diagram 213
After 20. ... Bf8!

21. Qe5 f6 22. Qc7 Rc8

Final deflection. White is lost.

B2 9. Bg5

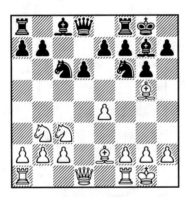

Diagram 214
After 9. Bg5

White develops his dark-square bishop on a square that establishes a once-removed pin of the key Black defensive knight. At the same time, White prepares the pawn-push f4-f5.

9. ... Be6

White has two main choices: 10. f4 and 10. Kh1.

B2a 10. f4 b5!

Diagram 215
After 10. ... b5!

11. Bf3

Or 11. Nxb5? Qb6+ 12. Kh1 Nxe4, and Black is better.

If 11. Bxb5, then 11. ... Qb6+ 12. Kh1 Nxe4 13. Bxc6 Qxc6

Diagram 216
After 13. ... Qxc6

14. Na5 (14. Nxe4 Qxe4 15. Bxe7 Rfc8) 14. ... Nxc3. The simplest. Black is at least equal.

11. ... b4 12. Nd5 Bxd5 13. exd5 Na5

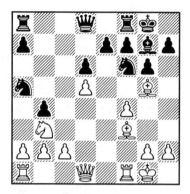

Diagram 217
After 13. ... Na5

14. Nxa5 Qxa5 15. Re1 Qc7 16. Kh1 Rfc8 17. Re2 Qb7

Diagram 218
After 17. ... Qb7

Black is in good shape. He will follow up by doubling his rooks on the c-file (Zubarev–Kacheishvili, 2000).

B2b 10. Kh1 Rc8

Black's idea is to play ... Na5, preparing counter-play on the queenside.

11. f4 Na5 12. f5 Bc4

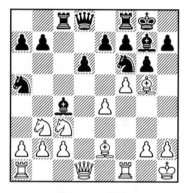

Diagram 219
After 12. ... Bc4

With equal chances—the game Khalifman–Leko, 2000, continued: 13. Bd3 b5!? 14. Qf3 (14. Nxb5 Bxb5 15. Bxb5 Nxe4 is good for Black) 14. ... b4 15. Nd5 Bxd5 16. exd5 Nc4 (with the idea of ... Ne5) 17. Bxc4 Rxc4 18. Qd3 Qc7 19. Na5!?

Black's idea is to play ... Na5, preparing counter-play on the queenside.

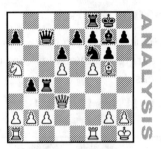

Diagram 220
After 19. Na5?!

19. ... Rxc2, and Black plans to sacrifice an Exchange for two pawns after 20. Nc6 Rc5! 21. Bxf6 Bxf6 22. Rae1 Rxc6 23. dxc6 Qxc6 24. Rc1 Qa4, with a good game for Black.

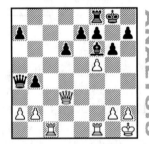

Diagram 221
After 24. ... Qa4

B3 **9. Re1**

Diagram 222
After 9. Re1

White's idea is to play Bf1 and create pressure on Black's e7-pawn after Bg5 and Nd5.

9. ... Be6 10. Bf1 a5

With the threat of ... a4, so that after the knight on b3 retreats, Black again pushes his kamikaze foot soldier to a3, creating weaknesses in White's queenside camp.

11. a4

White stops Black's pawn-push, but allows Black to capture on b3 and foul White's pawn structure.

11. ... Bxb3 12. cxb3 e6

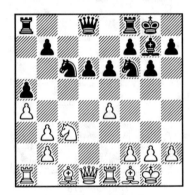

Diagram 223
After 12. ... e6

Black now has an extra pawn in the center and he plans for a timely ... d5.

13. Bg5

After 13. Nb5?! d5!, Black successfully takes over the center—for example, 14. exd5 Nxd5, when White's queenside pawn structure is ruined, and

Black's bishop and knights dominate the game.

13. ... h6

Here White has two retreats: 14. Bh4 and 14. Be3.

B3a 14. Bh4 Qb6

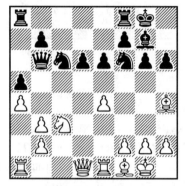

Diagram 224
After 14. ... Qb6

15. Bc4

Or 15. Qxd6 Qxb3 16. Qa3 Qxa3 17. Rxa3 Nh5,

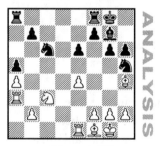

Diagram 225
After 17. ... Nh5

with the idea of playing ... g5, Black is better.

After 15. Nb5, there follows 15. ... Rfd8 16. Qf3 Ne5 17. Qe2 Rd7 (17. ... d5!) 18. Kh1 d5! 19. exd5 Nxd5.

Diagram 226
After 19. ... Nxd5

Black's knights dominate the center (Zagrebelny–Yakovich, 1997).

15. ... Rfd8 16. Rc1 Nd4

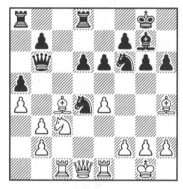

Diagram 227
After 16. ... Nd4

Black takes over key squares, leaving White no other option than to exchange the now-centralized knight.

17. Ne2 Nxe2+ 18. Qxe2

Now Black initiates a small combination to exchange his d-pawn for White's e-pawn.

18. ... g5 19. Bg3 Nxe4! 20. Qxe4 d5 21. Qf3 dxc4 22. Rxc4 Rac8

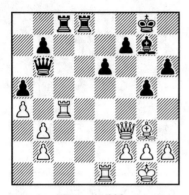

Diagram 228
After 22. ... Rac8

Black is better (Varavin–Zavgorodniy, 2002).

B3b 14. Be3 Nb4

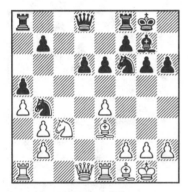

Diagram 229
After 14. ... Nb4

With the idea of ... d5.

15. Rc1 Rc8 16. Qd2 Kh7 17. Red1 d5! 18. exd5 Nfxd5

Diagram 230
After 18. ... Nfxd5

Black is fine. Arutunian–Malakhov, 2000, continued: 19. Nxd5 Qxd5 20. Rxc8 Rxc8 21. Bc4. Now after the correct 21. ... Qxd2 (21. ...Qe5?! was played in the game) 22. Rxd2 Nd5!,

Diagram 231
After 22. ... Nd5!

Black stands at least equal. White can't take on d5 because ... Rc1 delivers a back-rank mate.

B4 9. f4 Be6

Diagram 232
After 9. ... Be6

Black's pieces are active and well-coordinated, while White's attacking formation of e- and f-pawns is no longer dangerous and can become a weakness in the endgame.

Now on 10. f5, Black can play either the more complicated 10. … Bd7, or the simpler 10. … Bxb3 11. axb3 Qb6+ 12. Kh1 Qd4.

Diagram 233
After 12. ... Qd4

Summary:

White's sixth-move sidelines, 6. Nde2 and 6. Nb3, are easy for a prepared Black to handle. Against the passive 6. Nde2, Black gets a great game by castling kingside and advancing his queenside pawns. If White tries 6. Nb3, Black can confidently enter the Classical Dragon. Or he can instead play a double-fianchetto system that leads to unclear complications.

Chapter 7: The Accelerated Dragon—Sixth-move Sidelines

Memory Markers!

Diagram 234
After 18. bxc3

MARKER 1

Diagram 235
After 13. Nb5

MARKER 2

Diagram 236
After 18. Qxe2

MARKER 3

Diagram 237
After 21. Bc4

MARKER 4

Chapter 7: The Accelerated Dragon—Sixth-move Sidelines
Solutions to Memory Markers!

No. 1 **18. ... e5**; (if 19. dxe6, dxe6!). See page 98.

No. 2 **13. ... d5**, taking over the center. See page 104.

No. 3 **18. ... g5! 19. Bg3 Nxe4!,** with a better game. See page 105.

No. 4 **21 ... Qxd2 22. Rxd2 Nd5**, with a better ending. See page 106.

Chapter 8: Defending against 4. Qxd4

Some Important Points to Look For

White's 4. Qxd4—meant to punish Black for his early 2. ... g6—leads to a variety of sharp, "un-Sicilian-like" positions. This chapter shows how Black can successfully counter various White assaults.

◆ Black breaks in the center.
  See Diagram 248.

◆ White has a choice of three moves.
  See Diagram 251.

◆ Black now plays 8 ... b4. Why?
  See Diagram 258.

◆ And here comes an improvement ...
  See Diagram 276.

Outline of Variations

1. e4 c5 2. Nf3 g6 3. d4 cxd4 4. Qxd4 Nf6 *(110)* [B27]
  A 5. e5 Nc6 6. Qa4 Nd5 7. Qe4 Nb6 *(111)*
    A1 8. Nc3 d5 9. exd6 Bf5 10. Qe2 *(113)*
    A2 8. Bf4 d5! 9. exd6 Bf5 10. Qe2 Bg7 11. Nc3 *(114)*
  B 5. Bb5 a6 6. c5 axb5 7. exf6 Nc6 *(115)*
    B1 8. Qh4 Ra4 9. fxe7 Bxe7 10. Qh6 Re4+ 11. Kf1 b4 *(115)*
    B2 8. Qe3 b4 9. 0-0 e6 10. c4 Qxf6 11. Nbd2 Bg7 12. Ne4 Qe7 13. Rd1 d5 *(117)*
    B3 8. fxe7 Qxe7+ 9. Qe3 b4 10. 0-0 Qxe3 11. Bxe3 Bg7 12. Re1 0-0 *(118)*
  C 5. Nc3 Nc6 6. Qa4 d6 *(119)*

Chapter 8
Defending against 4. Qxd4

When White chooses to recapture on d4 with his queen, rather than his knight, he attempts to get an advantage in the center and to disrupt Black's normal development. Black, however, can remain completely confident.

1. e4 c5 2. Nf3 g6 3. d4 cxd4 4. Qxd4

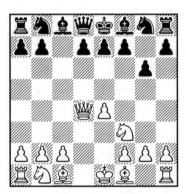

Diagram 238
After 4. Qxd4

4. ... Nf6

White has three main moves: 5. e5, 5. Bb5, and 5. Nc3.

A 5. e5 Nc6 6. Qa4 Nd5 7. Qe4

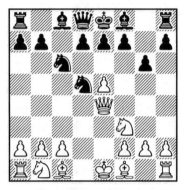

Diagram 239
After 7. Qe4

Here Black can choose between 7. ... Nc7 (our 2005 recommendation) and our current favorite, 7. ... Nb6.

The commonly played 7. ... Ndb4, with its idea of following up with ... d5 and ... Bf5, runs into problems: 8. Bb5 Qa5 9. Nc3 d5. Now, although it may seem as if Black is much better due to the threat of ... Bf5 and ... Nxc2, there follows 10. exd6! Bf5 11. Bxc6+ bxc6 (the modest 11. ... Nxc6 is better) 12. d7+ Kd8 13. Qc4!.

Diagram 240
After 13. Qc4!

Diagram 242
After 14. h5!?

And White gets a strong attack—for example: 13. ... Nxc2+ 14. Ke2 Nxa1 15. Nd4! Qe5+ 16. Be3 Qf6   17. Nxc6+ Kxd7 18. Rd1+ Ke8 19. Nb8!+−, threatening Qa4, mate.

Before examining our new main line, let's return to Diagram 239 to take a look at the still viable 7. ... Nc7, our 2005 move.

7. ... Nc7 8. Nc3 Bg7

Diagram 241
After 8. ... Bg7

9. Bc4

At the 2006 World Open, Gulamali, with White, surprised Eugene with 9. Bf4. For a while, the game remained balanced: 9. ... b5 10. h4!? b4 11. Nd5 Nxd5 12. Qxd5 Qa5 13. Qxa5 Nxa5 14. h5,

but here Black missed 14. ... h6!, maintaining   equality—e.g., 15. hxg6 fxg6 16. Bd3!? g5 17. Bg6+ Kd8!.

Returning to Diagram 241, after White's 9. Bc4, Black starts his queenside counter-play forcefully, again taking advantage of the fact that his knight on c7 reinforces ... b5.

9. ... b5! 10. Bb3

If 10. Nxb5, then 10. ... Nxb5 11. Qd5 (11. Bxb5? Qa5+) 11. ... 0-0 12. Bxb5 Bb7, when Black has compensation for the pawn.

10. ... Bb7

Diagram 243
After 10. ... Bb7

11. Qe2 a5 12. a4

After 12. Nxb5 a4 13. Bc4

Nxb5 14. Bxb5 Qc7 15. Bf4 a3!, Black gets strong play for the pawn.

12. ... b4 13. Nb5 0-0 14. Nxc7 Qxc7

Diagram 244
After 14. ... Qxc7

Black is slightly better. The game Brynell–Ward, 1998, continued: 15. Bf4 Nd8 (in order to play ... Ne6) 16. 0-0-0 Ne6 17. Bg3,

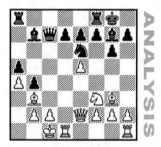

Diagram 245
After 17. Bg3

and now, both 17. ... Bxf3 and 17. ... Rac8 give Black good play, while the sharp 17. ... Nc5!? may offer even more.

So, as you can see, our 2005 recommendation, 7. ... Nc7, is alive and well. Eugene, however, now prefers the more dynamic:

7. ... Nb6

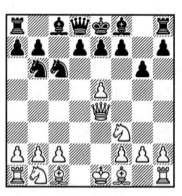

Diagram 246
After 7. ... Nb6

Black prepares the pawn sacrifice ... d7-d5!. White can now develop his queenside with either the "knights-first" 8. Nc3 or with 8. Bf4, aimed at stopping ... d7-d5.

A1 8. Nc3 d5 9. exd6 e.p. Bf5 10. Qe2

10. dxe7 Bxe7 is great for Black.

10. ... Qxd6 11. Nb5 Qb8 12. Nbd4

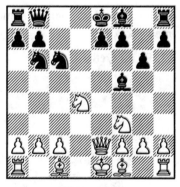

Diagram 247
After 12. Nbd4

**12. ... Bg7 13. Nxf5 gxf5
14. Qb5 e6 15. Bd3 0-0 16. 0-0
Rd8 17. Bg5 Rd5**

White's queen is in trouble
(Chen—Perleshteyn, 2006).

A2 8. Bf4 d5!

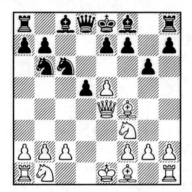

Diagram 248
After 8. ... d5

**9. exd6 Bf5 10. Qe2 Bg7
11. Nc3**

The tempting 11. dxe7 is
answered by 11. ... Nxe7∓
12. Nc3 0-0, when White's king
is stuck in a crossfire.

11. ... 0-0 12. 0-0-0 exd6

12. ... Re8!? is worth some
homework.

13. Rxd6 Qc8 14. Qb5

We've reached a
critical position
of the variation.

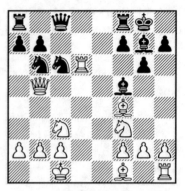

Diagram 249
After 14. Qb5

We've reached a critical position of the variation. Black is
down a pawn, but White's lack of
development and vulnerable king
give Black sufficient compensation.

14. ... Bxc3

It is always difficult to part
with such a powerful bishop. In
this case, however, it's important
to ruin White's queenside pawn
structure and create an outpost
on c4. (After 14. ... Bg4, as
played in Esserman—Perel-
shteyn, 2008, there followed
15. Bd3 Bxf3 16. gxf3 Nd4
17. Qb4, when the resulting
complex position is somewhat
more promising for White.)

15. bxc3 Re8 16. Bd3 Bxd3

Now all recaptures on d3 lead
to good play for Black, for example—17. Rxd3 (best, if 17. cxd3,
then 17. ... Re2!, with a strong
attack for Black; and if 17. Qxd3
Ne7, with a threat of ... Nf5,

when White's army is in disarray)
17. ... Qe6 18. Qb3 Qf5 19. Be3
Na5 20. Qb4 Nac4. White has to
play accurately to hold onto
equality.

B 5. Bb5

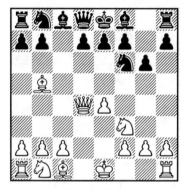

Diagram 250
After 5. Bb5

5. ... a6 6. e5

After 6. Ba4 b5 7. Bb3 Nc6,
Black develops comfortably,
winning a tempo.

6. ... axb5 7. exf6 Nc6

Diagram 251
After 7. ... Nc6

In this interesting position,
White has three moves: 8. Qh4,
8. Qe3, and 8. fxe7.

B1 8. Qh4 Ra4!

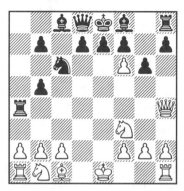

Diagram 252
After 8. ... Ra4!

Black finds a way to activate
his rook with a tempo!

9. fxe7 Bxe7 10. Qh6 Re4+

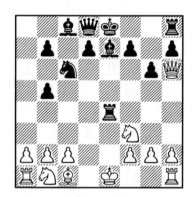

Diagram 253
After 10. ... Re4+

11. Kf1

11. Be3 Nd4 12. Nxd4 Rh4
13. 0-0 Rxh6 14. Bxh6 Qb6

> **BLACK FINDS A WAY TO
> ACTIVATE HIS ROOK
> WITH A TEMPO!**

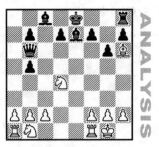

Diagram 254
After 14. ... Qb6

This leads to a sharp and unbalanced position, where Black's chances aren't worse.

11. ... b4

with complex play—for example:

12. Bg5

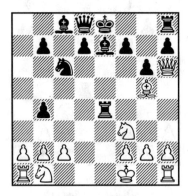

Diagram 255
After 12. Bg5

12. ...Qa5 13. Bxe7 Qb5+ 14. Kg1 Nd4!

NOW WHITE HAS TO
PLAY CAREFULLY
TO HOLD.

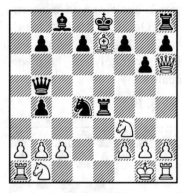

Diagram 256
After 14. ... Nd4!

15. Nc3!

If 15. Nxd4?, then 15. ... Re1 is checkmate.

15. ... bxc3 16. Nxd4 cxb2 17. Rb1

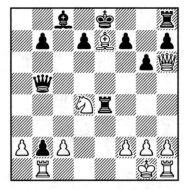

Diagram 257
After 17. Rb1

17. ... Qc4

Now White has to play carefully to hold—for example: 18. h3 (18. Qg7? 19. Qxa2) 18. ... Qxd4 19. Ba3 Re2 20. Kh2 Qe5+ 21. f4 Rxg2+, with perpetual check.

If Black wants to try for more, he can play 17. ... Qe5 18. Nf3

Qc3 (with the threat of ... Qxc2) 19. Qd2 Qxd2 20. Nxd2 Rxe7. The endgame somewhat favors Black because his bishop is stronger than White's knight.

B2 8. Qe3

Diagram 258
After 8. Qe3

8. ... b4

Black prevents Nc3.

9. 0-0 e6 10. c4

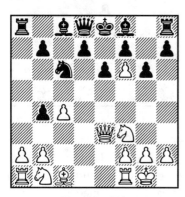

Diagram 259
After 10. c4

White sacrifices his f6-pawn to get a lead in development.

10. ... Qxf6 11. Nbd2 Bg7 12. Ne4 Qe7 13. Rd1

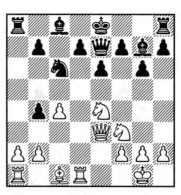

Diagram 260
After 13. Rd1

13. ... d5!

After 13. ... 0-0 14. Nd6, the knight on d6 is very unpleasant.

14. cxd5 exd5 15. Nd6+ Kf8 16. Nxc8 Qxe3 17. fxe3 Rxc8 18. Rxd5

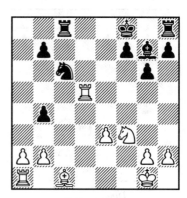

Diagram 261
After 18. Rxd5

Play is about equal.

WHITE SACRIFICES HIS F6-PAWN TO GET A LEAD IN DEVELOPMENT.

B3 8. fxe7

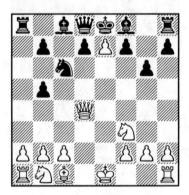

Diagram 262
After 8. fxe7

8. ... Qxe7+ 9. Qe3 b4!

Black stops Nc3 and gains more space on the queenside.

10. 0-0 Qxe3

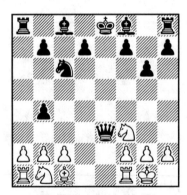

Diagram 263
After 10. ... Qxe3

11. Bxe3 Bg7 12. Re1 0-0 13. c3 d5

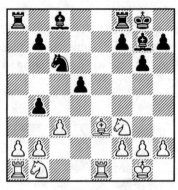

Diagram 264
After 13. ... d5

14. a3

14. Bc5! could lead to a draw by three-fold repetition after 14. ... Rd8 15. Bb6.

14. ... Bf5

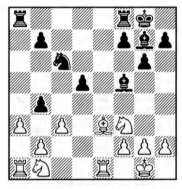

Diagram 265
After 14. ... Bf5

Black easily finishes his development, while White has trouble activating his queenside pieces. Black is slightly better.

BLACK EASILY FINISHES HIS DEVELOPMENT, WHILE WHITE HAS TROUBLE ACTIVATING HIS QUEENSIDE.

C 5. Nc3

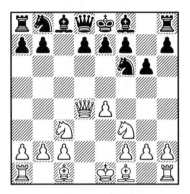

Diagram 266
After 5. Nc3

5. ... Nc6 6. Qa4

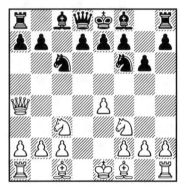

Diagram 267
After 6. Qa4

White hopes that the queen on a4 will cause Black some problems with his development.

6. ... d6 7. e5 Ng4!?

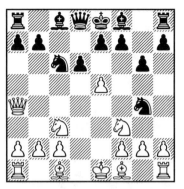

Diagram 268
After 7. ... Ng4!?

Black begins active piece play in the center and on the kingside, while White's queen no longer protects his majesty. The simpler 7. ... dxe5 8. Nxe5 Bd7 is also good.

8. exd6

Or 8. Bf4 Bg7 9. exd6 0-0 10. Bb5 e5,

Diagram 269
After 10. ... e5

> **Black begins active piece play in the center and on the kingside, while White's queen no longer protects his majesty.**

followed by ... Qxd6 with a good game for Black (Gershon–Perelshteyn, 1998).

8. ... Bg7

Black is not interested in complications after 8. ... Qb6 9. Nd5! Qxf2+ 10. Kd1.

Diagram 270
After 10. Kd1

9. h3

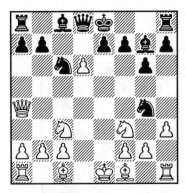

Diagram 271
After 9. h3

After 9. dxe7 Qxe7+ 10. Be2 0-0,

WHITE HAS PROBLEMS CASTLING.

Diagram 272
After 10. ... 0-0

White has problems castling.

9. ... Nge5 10. Nxe5 Bxe5

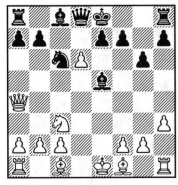

Diagram 273
After 10. ... Bxe5

11. Bh6?!

White could play better: 11. dxe7 Qxe7 12. Be3 Be6 13. Be2 0-0 14. 0-0 Rfc8.

Diagram 274
After 14. ... Rfc8

Black puts strong pressure on the c-file to compensate for his missing pawn (Skripchenko–Calzetta, 2002).

After 11. Bh6?!, Black's best plan is to take on c3, doubling White's pawns.

11. ... Bxc3+! 12. bxc3 Qxd6

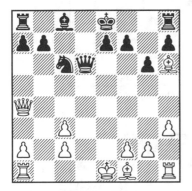

Diagram 275
After 12. ... Qxd6

Black stands better. Paschall–Perelshteyn, 2003, continued: 13. Bb5 Qe5+ 14. Kf1 Qxc3 15. Rd1

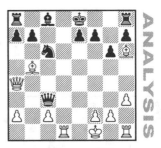

Diagram 276
After 15. Rd1

15. ... Bd7!

This is an improvement over the actual game. Black's plan is to castle long and remain up a pawn. He stands better.

Eugene instead played 15. ... Bf5?!, allowing 16. Bg7!.

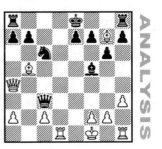

Diagram 277
After 16. Bg7!

16. ... Qxg7 17. Bxc6+ Kf8 (17. ... bxc6? 18. Qxc6+) 18. Bxb7 and White gets the pawn back.

Summary:

4. Qxd4, trying to exploit the "Hyper" in the Hyper-Accelerated Dragon (2. ... g6 rather than 2. ... Nc6), leads to sharp, non-typical Sicilian positions. However, the best White can hope for is equality.

Chapter 8: Defending against 4. Qxd4

Memory Markers!

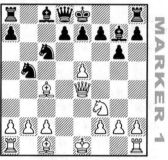

Diagram 278
After 10. ... Nxb5

MARKER 1

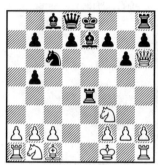

Diagram 279
After 11. Kf1

MARKER 2

Diagram 280
After 18. Qg7

MARKER 3

Diagram 281
After 11. Bh6

MARKER 4

Chapter 8: Defending against 4. Qxd4
Solutions to Memory Markers!

No. 1   **11. Qd5**. The only move, as 11. Bxb5 loses a piece. See page 112.

No. 2   **11. ... b4!**, denying White's knight the c3-square. See page 116.

No. 3   **18. ... Qxa2!**, winning. See page 116.

No. 4   **11. ... Bxc3+**, destroying White's queenside. See page 120.

Chapter 9: The Hyper-Accelerated Dragon— Third-move Sidelines

Some Important Points to Look For

This chapter deals with two of White's third-move sidelines—the center-building 3. c3, and the developing 3. Bc4. Black is in no danger if he plays accurately.

◆ Black is ready to meet 4. c3 with 4. ... e6, preparing ... d5; otherwise he'll play 4. ... Nc6, taking control of d4. See Diagram 283.

◆ Challenging White's center— exactly at the right time. See Diagram 288.

◆ Black pieces are well placed. See Diagram 292.

◆ This section (B2) is about comparisons. See Diagram 299.

Outline of Variations

1. e4 c5 2. Nf3 g6 *(124)* **[B27]**

    A 3. Bc4 Bg7 4. c3 e6 5. d4 cxd4 6. cxd4 d5 7. exd5 exd5 8. Bb5+ Bd7 9. Bxd7+ *(126)*

        9. ... Nxd7 *(126)*

        9. ... Qxd7 *(127)*

    B 3. c3 Bg7 4. d4 cxd4 5. cxd4 d5 *(127)*

        B1 6. e5 Bg4 *(127)*

            B1a 7. Nc3 Nc6 8. Be2 Bxf3 9. Bxf3 e6 10. 0-0 Nge7 11. Be3 0-0 *(128)*

            B1b 7. Nbd2 Nc6 8. h3 Bf5 9. Be2 f6 10. exf6 exf6 *(129)*

            B1c 7. Qb3 Qd7 8. Nc3 Nc6 9. Be3 Bxf3 10. gxf3 e6 11. Na4 Bf8 *(130)*

        B2 6. exd5 Nf6 7. Bb5+ Nbd7 8. d6 exd6 9. Qe2+ Qe7 10. Bf4 Qxe2+ 11. Bxe2 Ke7 *(130)*

Chapter 9
The Hyper-Accelerated Dragon
Third-move Sidelines

The previous chapters gave you the main lines of the Accelerated Dragon when White does not enter the Maroczy Bind. These chapters skipped over some less-frequently played choices for White because it was important to concentrate on the main ideas that you will see most frequently, rather than to bog down in distractions.

But of course you want to know what to do when forcibly "distracted" by White. Some of your opponents will take the chance of playing a second-rate move to catch you unprepared. So let's take a look.

We'll pick up after Black's second move:

2. ... g6

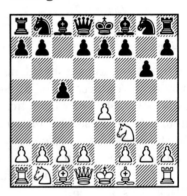

Diagram 282
After 2. ... g6

Besides 3. d4, our main line of the Accelerated Dragon, White can try: 3. Bc4 or 3. c3.

As we'll see later in **B** in this chapter, Black defends against the center-building 3. c3 with a timely ... d5, while 3. Bc4 tries to prevent this counter-play.

A 3. Bc4 Bg7

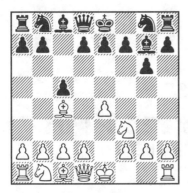

Diagram 283
After 3. ... Bg7

4. c3

On 4. 0-0, Black should not play 4. ... e6 because of 5. d4 cxd4 6. Nxd4, when he suffers from a weak d6-square. Instead, he should play 4. ... Nc6, controlling the d4-square. If White plays 5. c3 or 5. Re1, only then Black plays 5. ... e6.

4. ... e6 5. d4 cxd4 6. cxd4 d5 7. exd5

Or 7. Bb5+ Bd7, and Black is doing well. For example, 8. Bxd7+ Nxd7 (8. ... Qxd7 is playable as well) 9. e5.

> **Now both 9. ... f6 and the more "strategic" 9. ... Ne7 are both fine for Black.**

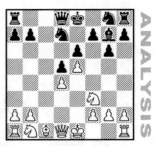

Diagram 284
After 9. e5

Now both 9. ... f6 and the more "strategic" 9. ... Ne7 (with the idea, after ... 0-0, of playing ... Nc6 and ... Qb6) are fine for Black.

7. .... exd5 8. Bb5+ Bd7 9. Bxd7+

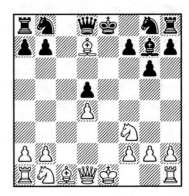

Diagram 285
After 9. Bxd7+

9. ... Nxd7

This is Black's most popular move in the position. It leads to equality. For example, 10. 0-0 Ne7 or 10. Qb3 Nb6.

Black also has a sharper and riskier option: 9. ... Qxd7 10. Ne5 Bxe5 11. dxe5 f6!?, with an unbalanced position.

Diagram 286
After 11. ... f6!?

B 3. c3

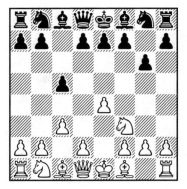

Diagram 287
After 3. c3

White plans to take over the center with d4, the same main idea we'll meet in the Alapin Variation. (See Chapter 18.)

3. ... Bg7 4. d4 cxd4 5. cxd4 d5

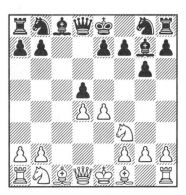

Diagram 288
After 5. ... d5

Black had to challenge White's classic center. He does it just in time.

White now has two very different plans:

1. Close off Black's bishop with 6. e5;

2. Try to open up the position after 6. exd5.

B1 6. e5 Bg4

White plans
to take over the
center with d4,
the same main
idea we'll
see in the
Alapin Variation.

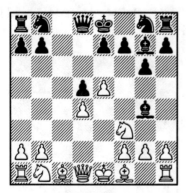

Diagram 289
After 6. ... Bg4

Here White has three ways to develop: 7. Nc3, 7. Nbd2, and the aggressive 7. Qb3.

Also possible is 7. Bb5+ Nd7! 8. 0-0 a6, and if 9. Bxd7+ Qxd7 10. Nbd2, then 10. ... Nh6, with a good game for Black.

B1a 7. Nc3 Nc6 8. Be2

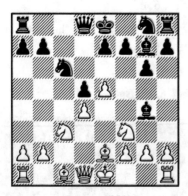

Diagram 290
After 8. Be2

8. ... Bxf3

Black has ... e6 and ... Nge7 in mind.

9. Bxf3 e6

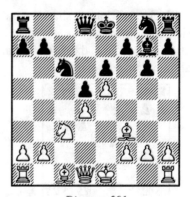

Diagram 291
After 9. ... e6

10. 0-0

Black meets 10. Nb5 with 10. ... Qa5+.

10. ... Nge7 11. Be3 0-0 12. Qd2 Nf5

Diagram 292
After 12. ... Nf5

Black has achieved a solid position. His plan is to play against White's d4-pawn and, in particular, to prepare a timely ... f6!, breaking up White's center duo and activating Black's bishop.

B1b **7. Nbd2**

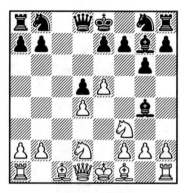

Diagram 293
After 7. Nbd2

White's idea is to play h3 and, after ... Bxf3, to recapture with the knight.

7. ... Nc6 8. h3 Bf5!

Black is not afraid to lose a tempo with this repositioning because White's knight on d2 is poorly placed.

9. Be2

After 9. Bb5 Qb6 10. Qa4 Bd7!,

Diagram 294
After 10. ... Bd7!

Black stands well. By the way, he's threatening ... Nxe5, using the "comeback" tactic that can so often be overlooked by amateurs—if Bxd7+, then ... Nxd7.

9. ... f6

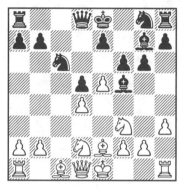

Diagram 295
After 9. ... f6

Undermining White's center is a thematic idea in this line.

10. exf6 exf6!? 11. 0–0 Nge7 12. Nb3 Qd6 13. Be3 0–0

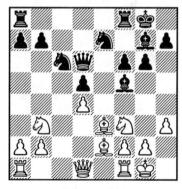

Diagram 296
After 13. ... 0-0

With equal chances (Schneider–Perelshteyn, 2000).

B1c 7. Qb3

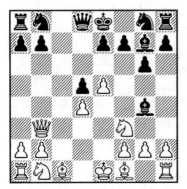

Diagram 297
After 7. Qb3

7. ... Qd7 8. Nc3 Nc6! 9. Be3 Bxf3 10. gxf3 e6 11. Na4 Bf8!

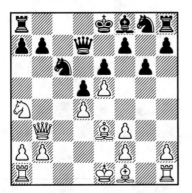

Diagram 298
After 11. ... Bf8!

Black has an equal game. His plan is to play ... Nh6-f5, ... Be7, and then bring his king to g7 via f8.

B2 6. exd5 Nf6

Diagram 299
After 6. ... Nf6

This is a position that can be reached from the Caro-Kann, Panov-Botvinnik Attack (as well as from the Alapin Variation of the Sicilian): 1. e4 c6 2. d4 d5 3. exd5 exd5 4. c4 Nf6 5. Nc3 g6 (one of three main lines) 6. cxd5.

Diagram 300
After 6. cxd5

In our case, however, White has developed his king's knight instead of his queen's knight. Because a knight on f3 doesn't support his d5-pawn, this difference favors Black.

7. Bb5+

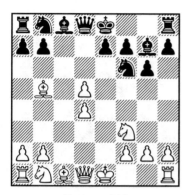

Diagram 301
After 7. Bb5+

7. Nc3 Nxd5 8. Bc4 (8.Bb5+ Bd7!) 8. ... Nb6 9. Bb3 0–0 is covered in Chapter 18, 2. c3 (Alapin).

7. ... Nbd7 8. d6

White prefers to lose his pawn on d6, changing the pawn-structure in his favor, rather than on d5. After 8. Nc3 0–0 9. 0–0 Nb6,

Diagram 302
After 9. ... Nb6

followed by ... Nfxd5, Black regains the pawn and stands better because of White's isolated d-pawn.

8. ... exd6 9. Qe2+

Diagram 303
After 9. Qe2+

Contrast this position with the line on page 223 (Chapter 18: Alapin), after 8. ... exd6 9. Qe2+ (below).

Diagram 304
After 9. Qe2+

The difference: In the Alapin, White first brings out his queen's knight, while in our text here, White has developed his king's knight. Still, Black can play 9. ... Qe7 in both cases.

9. ... Qe7 10. Bf4 Qxe2+ 11. Bxe2 Ke7

> **White prefers to lose his pawn on d6 rather than on d5.**

Diagram 305
After 11. ... Ke7

This endgame is about even. Black's control over the d5-outpost in front of White's *isolani* gives him good counter-play.

12. Nc3 Nb6 13. 0–0 h6

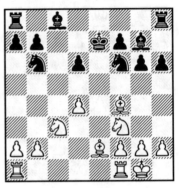

Diagram 306
After 13. ... h6

Black wants to follow up with … Be6. Sadvakasov–Bellon Lopez, 2000, continued:

14. Nd2 Nfd5 15. Nxd5+ Nxd5 16. Bg3

> This endgame is about even. Black's control over the d5-outpost in front of White's *isolani* gives him good counter-play.

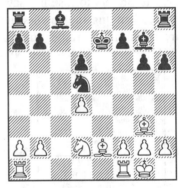

Diagram 307
After 16. Bg3

And here Black could have played

16. ... Bxd4

Bellon Lopez instead played it safe with 16. ... Be6. That move also led to a good position for Black after 17. Bf3 Rac8 18. Rfe1

Kd7 19. Ne4 Bf8 20. Rac1 Be7
21. Nc3 Nxc3 22. bxc3

Diagram 308
After 22. bxc3

22. ... Rc7=.

**17. Nc4 Bc5 18. Rad1 Be6
19. Bf3**

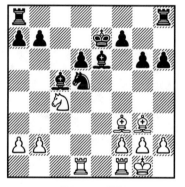

Diagram 309
After 19. Bf3

**19. ... Nc3! 20. bxc3 Bxc4
21. Rfe1+ Be6 22. Bxb7 Rab8**

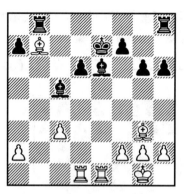

Diagram 310
After 22. ... Rab8

Black has a slightly better position.

Summary:

White's third-move sidelines are nothing to fear. Against 3. Bc4, Black can play for a safe equality with 9. ... Nxd7 or use Dzindzi's sharper 9. ... Qxd7. Against 3. c3, Black's 5. ... d5 challenges White's classical center just in time. The lines that follow give Black promising play.

Chapter 9: The Hyper-Accelerated Dragon–Third-move Sidelines

Memory Markers!

Diagram 311
After 6. Nc3

MARKER 1

Diagram 312
After 13. Bg4

MARKER 2

Diagram 313
After 7. ... Nbd7

MARKER 3

Chapter 9: The Hyper-Accelerated Dragon— Third-move Sidelines
Solutions to Memory Markers!

No. 1   **6. ... dxe4 7. Nxe4 Nh6** (with the idea ... Nf5) is the simplest. See page 127.

No. 2   **13. ... Nxe3** leads to equality. Also good is 13. ... f6. See page 128.

No. 3   **8. d6!.** See page 131.

Chapter 10: The Maroczy Bind—Introduction and 7. Be3
Some Important Points to Look For

This chapter discusses the general principles of the Maroczy Bind and then shows that 7. Be3
(with the idea of recapturing on d4 with the bishop) doesn't work because of 7. ... Ng4.

◆ The key starting position.
See Diagram 315.

◆ Black is fine.
See Diagram 316.

◆ Stunning response.
See Diagram 318.

◆ How should White play?
See Diagram 321.

Outline of Variations

1. e4 c5 2. Nf3 g6 3. d4 cxd4 4. Nxd4 Nc6 5. c4 Nf6 6. Nc3 d6 7. Be3 Ng4 8. Nxc6 Nxe3 9. Nxd8 Nxd1 10. Rxd1 Kxd8. *(136)* **[B36]**

    A 11. e5 Bg7 12. exd6 Bxc3+ 13. bxc3 exd6 *(139)*
        A1 14. c5 Re8+ 15. Be2 b6 *(139)*
        A2 14. Rxd6+ Kc7 15. Rd4 Re8+ *(139)*
    B 11. c5 Be6 12. cxd6 exd6 13. Be2 Ke7 14. Nd5+ Bxd5 15. Rxd5 Rc8 *(139)*

Chapter 10
Maroczy Bind
Introduction and 7. Be3

The Maroczy Bind setup against our Accelerated Dragon is particularly important to us. Similar or even identical positions can be reached from a number of openings in our recommended repertoire, including the symmetrical English.

White begins his "bind" with c2-c4. The pawn joins its e-pawn colleague to double-team d5, making it difficult for Black to play the typically freeing ... d7-d5 pawn push. What's more, White's pawn on c4 blocks the semi-open file, normally one of the avenues along which Black organizes his counter-play. White has time to push his c-pawn because Black hasn't played ... Nf6, which in other Sicilian lines forces White to defend his e-pawn by bringing out his knight to c3, blocking the c-pawn. So we can see that the thematic ideas are different from other lines.

Should we panic in the face of these differences? Absolutely not! This is chess, after all, and in

choosing c2-c4, White closes the door on other attractive options. But as Black, we must know how to fire back. In this section, we have some interesting, new ammunition for you!

1. e4 c5 2. Nf3 g6 3. d4 cxd4 4. Nxd4 Nc6 5. c4

Diagram 314
After 5. c4

For many years, this continuation was considered best against the Accelerated Dragon, yielding White a small but stable advantage. White's plan is straightforward: consolidate, take control of the center, and use the powerful d5-outpost for his knight—and slowly grind Black down.

However, in recent years, it has been shown that Black's position is quite promising. The powerful bishop on g7, along with the ... a6 and ... b5 pawn-storm, provides Black, who is better developed, with plenty of counter-play on the dark squares and on the queenside.

In addition, the typical end-games arising from the Be3- and Qd2-setup, or a Bg5- and Qd2-formation (discussed in the next chapters), show that Black gets a good game (as in Vallejo–Malakhov), and he may even secure good winning chances (see Rowson–Malakhov).

5. ... Nf6 6. Nc3

6. Nxc6 bxc6 7. e5? Qa5+

6. ... d6

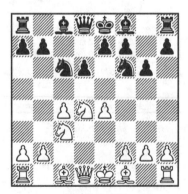

Diagram 315
After 6. ... d6

This is the key starting position, which can also arise from different move orders—for example, 1. Nf3 Nf6 2. c4 c5

3. Nc3 g6 4. d4 cxd4 5. Nd4 Nc6 6. e4 d6.

Now White has a choice between four setups:

7. Be3, 7. Be2, 7. f3, and 7. Nc2.

The first move is really a sideline that can be quickly dispensed with in this chapter. The second is the serious main line, which is divided between the next three chapters, depending on White's follow-up piece-placement. To end the section covering the Maroczy Bind, we give each of the last two moves a chapter of its own.

7. Be3 Ng4!

This move thwarts White's plan.

8. Nxc6 Nxe3

Another good choice is 8. ... bxc6.

9. Nxd8 Nxd1 10. Rxd1 Kxd8

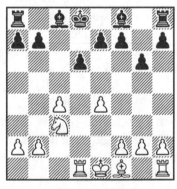

Diagram 316
After 10. ... Kxd8

Black does fine in the resulting

endgame—for example, let's look at 11. e5 and 11. c5.

A 11. e5 Bg7 12. exd6 Bxc3+ 13. bxc3 exd6

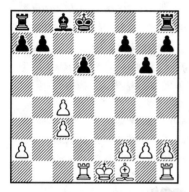

Diagram 317
After 13. ... exd6

White here tries 14. c5 and 14. Rxd6+.

A1 14. c5 Re8+ 15. Be2

Here Black has a stunning reply!

15. ... b6!

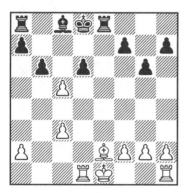

Diagram 318
After 15. ... b6!

16. Rxd6+

16. cxd6 Ba6 17. Rd2 Kd7

18. Kd1 Bxe2+ 19. Rxe2 Rxe2 20. Kxe2 Kxd6∓

16. ... Kc7 17. Rd2 bxc5

The position is equal.

A2 14. Rxd6+ Kc7 15. Rd4 Re8+

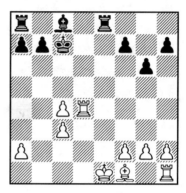

Diagram 319
After 15. ... Re8+

Equal. Black is down a meaningless pawn—White's queenside pawn structure is ruined.

B 11. c5 Be6

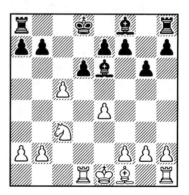

Diagram 320
After 11. ... Be6

**12. cxd6 exd6 13. Be2 Ke7
14. Nd5+ Bxd5 15. Rxd5 Rc8**

with some annoying threats.

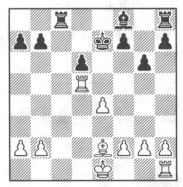

Diagram 321
After 15. ... Rc8

Summary:

   *White's Maroczy Bind setup
is particularly important
because it can crop up in our
repertoire from a number of
move-orders. Playing an early
c4, White tries to
suppress Black's natural play
in the Sicilian by blocking
the semi-open c-file and
over-protecting d5. White
has a number of piece-place-
ments, which we will examine
in the next five chapters.
His 7. Be3, discussed in
this chapter, is nullified as
an attempt to get any
advantage by 7. ... Ng4!.*

Chapter 10: Maroczy Bind—Introduction and 7. Be3
Memory Markers!

Diagram 322
After 7. e5

Diagram 323
After 17. Kd2

Chapter 10: Maroczy Bind—Introduction and 7. Be3
Solutions to Memory Markers!

No. 1   **7. ... Qa5+**. See page 138.

No. 2   **17. ... Rac8** and **18. ... Kb8**, targeting White's weak queenside pawns. See page 139.

Chapter 11: Maroczy Bind—7. Be2, with Be3 and Qd2
Some Important Points to Look For

In the main line of the Maroczy Bind, Black attacks the Bind with all his pieces, and sometimes even pawns (... a6 and ... b5)—and gets equality.

◆ Black prepares. See Diagram 327.

◆ The endgame is even.
See Diagram 333.

◆ Black has his dream position.
See Diagram 364.

◆ White has two options.
See Diagram 370.

Outline of Variations

**1. e4 c5 2. Nf3 g6 3. d4 cxd4 4. Nxd4 Nc6 5. c4 Nf6
6. Nc3 d6 7. Be2 Nxd4! 8. Qxd4 Bg7 9. Be3 0-0
10. Qd2 Be6.** *(142)* [B36]

  A 11. Rc1 Qa5 12. f3 Rfc8 13. b3 a6 *(144)*
    A1 14. a4 Nd7 15. Nd5 Qxd2+
      16. Kxd2 Bxd5 17. exd5 *(145)*
    A2 14. Nd5 Qxd2+ 15. Kxd2 Nxd5
      16. cxd5 *(146)*
    A3 14. Na4 Qxd2+ 15. Kxd2 Nd7
      16. g4 *(147)*
      A3a 16. ... f5 17. exf5 *(147)*
      A3b 16. ... Rc6 17. h3 *(148)*
  B 11. 0-0 Qa5 *(149)*
    B1 12. f3 Rfc8 13. Rfc1 *(149)*
    B2 12. Rab1 Rfc8 *(150)*

    B2a 13. Rfc1 Bxc4 *(150)*
    B2b 13. b4 Qd8 *(151)*
    B2c 13. b3 Ng4! *(151)*
      B2c1 14. Bd4 Bxd4 *(152)*
      B2c2 14. Nd5 Qxd2 *(152)*
  B3 12. Rfc1 Rfc8 13. b3 Ng4 *(153)*
  B4 12. Rac1 Rfc8 13. b3 a6 *(154)*
    B4a 14. f3 b5! *(154)*
      B4a1 15. cxb5 axb5
      16. Bxb5 *(154)*
      B4a2 15. Nd5 Qxd2
      16. Bxd2 Nxd5 *(155)*
    B4b 14. f4 b5! 15. f5! Bd7 *(156)*
      B4b1 16. b4 Qxb4 *(156)*
      B4b2 16. fxg6 hxg6 *(157)*

Chapter 11
Maroczy Bind
7. Be2, with Be3 and Qd2

In this chapter, you'll learn how to turn the tables on the most often-played line of the Maroczy Bind. After the moves **1. e4 c5 2. Nf3 g6 3. d4 cxd4 4. Nxd4 Nc6 5. c4 Nf6 6. Nc3 d6**

White usually plays

7. Be2

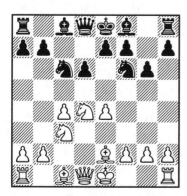

Diagram 324
After 7. Be2

White develops his bishop, takes control of the g4 square (to allow the upcoming Be3), and gets ready to castle.

7. ... Nxd4!

As a rule, trading pieces is favorable for the side with less space. This position is no exception. Additionally, Black will win a tempo after White's queen retreats from d4.

8. Qxd4 Bg7

Here White has several setups: 9. Be3 followed by Qd2 (this chapter), 9. Bg5 followed by Qd2 or Qe3 (Chapter 12), 9. 0-0 followed by Qd3 or Qe3 (Chapter 13).

9. Be3

Trading pieces
is favorable
for the side with
less space.

Diagram 325
After 9. Be3

White's plan is to meet 9. ... 0-0 with Qd2, possibly followed by Rc1, b3, and f3 to maintain a powerful, restrictive bind in the center.

9. ... 0-0

Black threatens ... Ng4.

10. Qd2 Be6

Black is first to complete his development. The bishop is best placed on e6, where it attacks the c4-pawn and leaves d7 open to give the knight a route to transfer to the queenside.

Black's plan is to play first ... Qa5 and ... Rfc8, and then to stir up queenside action with ... a6 and ... b5.

White has two main moves:

11. Rc1 and 11. 0-0. (11. f3 Qa5 12. Rc1! transposes into **A**.)

A 11. Rc1

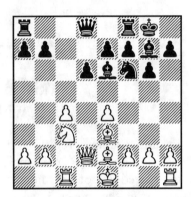

Diagram 326
After 11. Rc1

White delays castling in favor of creating a strong bind after f3 and b3. His plan is to meet ... Qa5 with Na4 or Nd5, usually transposing into an endgame after ... Qxd2.

11. ... Qa5 12. f3 Rfc8

Why this rook?

◆ First, to be able to attack the knight with ... Kf8 (in lines such as 13. b3 a6 14. 0-0 b5 15. Nd5 Qxd2 16. Nxe7+?);

◆ Second, both rooks are needed on the queenside, where decisive action will be taking place.

13. b3 a6

BLACK'S PLAN IS TO PLAY FIRST ... QA5 AND ... RFC8, AND THEN TO STIR UP QUEENSIDE ACTION WITH ... A6 AND ... B5.

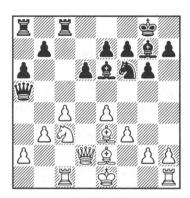

Diagram 327
After 13. ... a6

With the idea of ... b5!.

Now White has several continuations: 14. a4, 14. Nd5, and 14. Na4. All of them lead to some sort of endgame. (14. 0-0 transposes to **B4a**.)

A1 14. a4

White stops ... b5, but weakens his b3-pawn as well as c5 and b4 squares.

14. ... Nd7

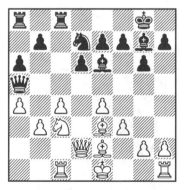

Diagram 328
After 14. ... Nd7

Black's knight has his eye on c5.

15. Nd5 Qxd2+ 16. Kxd2 Bxd5 17. exd5

After 17. cxd5 Kf8 18. Rxc8+ Rxc8 19. Rc1 Rxc1 20. Kxc1 Ke8,

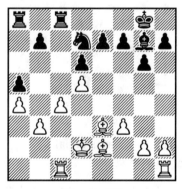

Diagram 329
After 20. ... Ke8

the endgame is about equal. The plan for Black is shown in the sample game Vallejo–Malakhov, 2003.

17. ... a5!

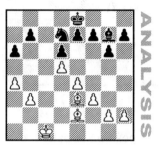

Diagram 330
After 17. ... a5!

Black's move secures the outposts on c5 and b4.

18. Bd3 Re8!

Black prepares ... e6.

19. Rce1 Nc5 20. Bc2 e6 21. dxe6 Rxe6

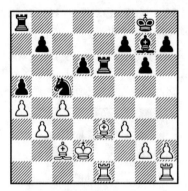

Diagram 331
After 21. ... Rxe6

The position is balanced, as in the game Korneev–Vokarev, 2000, which continued: 22. Bf2 Be5 23. g3 Rae8 24. f4 Bb2 25. Rxe6 Rxe6 26. Re1 Rxe1 27. Kxe1 f5.

Diagram 332
After 27. ... f5

The position is equal.

A2 14. Nd5

After this move, the resulting endgame is again equal.

14. ... Qxd2+ 15. Kxd2 Nxd5

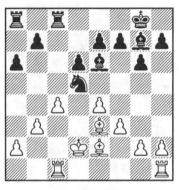

Diagram 333
After 15. ... Nxd5

16. cxd5

After 16. exd5 Bd7 17. a4 (to stop ... b5) 17. ... Bb2!

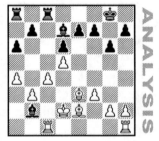

Diagram 334
After 17. ... Bb2!

(the bishop is going to c5 via a3) 18. Rc2 Ba3 19. Ra1 Bb4+ 20. Kd1 a5 21. Bd3 Bc5 22. Re2

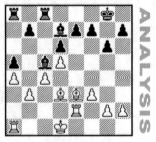

Diagram 335
After 22. Re2

22. ... e5! 23. dxe6 fxe6 24. Raa2

Kf7, when Black is at least equal (Godoy– Calfucura, 1997).

16. ... Bd7 17. Rxc8+ Rxc8 18. Rc1 Rxc1 19. Kxc1

Diagram 336
After 19. Kxc1

This is another key endgame in Maroczy Bind. Here, Black has several ways to play, but the plan with ... e6 is the easiest way to get comfortable play. The game Xie Jun–Kamsky, 1996, continued: 19. ... Kf8 20. Kd2 e6 21. Bc4 Ke7 22. Bg5+ Bf6 23. Bxf6+ Kxf6

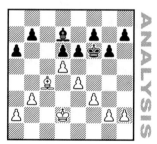

Diagram 337
After 23. ... Kxf6

24. dxe6 fxe6, with equality.

A3 14. Na4 Qxd2+ 15. Kxd2 Nd7

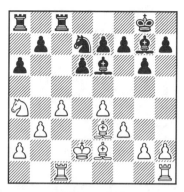

Diagram 338
After 15. ... Nd7

One of the most important endgames in the Maroczy Bind. White's plan could be to gain space on the kingside with g4, h3, and f4; or to place his knight on d5.

But Black's position is very solid and without any weaknesses.

16. g4

If 16. Nc3, then the prophylactic 16. ... Kf8, ready to meet 17. Nd5 with 17. ... Bxd5 (cp. Malakhov's Illustrative Games, #3 and #4, covering both of White's recaptures); 17. ... a5, delaying Black's capture, also deserves attention.

After 16. g4, Black has two good responses, 16. ... f5, with counter-play on the kingside, and 16. ...Rc6, followed by ... Nc5, with the idea of exchanging White's knight on a4.

A3a 16. ... f5 17. exf5

Or 17. gxf5 gxf5 18. Rhg1 Kh8 19. Bd3 f4!

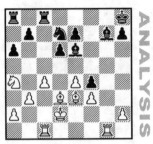

Diagram 339
After 19. ... f4!

20. Bf2 (after 20. Bxf4 Rf8 21. Ke3 Rxf4! 22. Kxf4 Bd4!, and White's king is in trouble—for example, 23. Rg5 Ne5 24. Rd1 Rf8+ 25. Rf5 Nxd3+ 26. Rxd3 Be5+ 27. Ke3 Bxf5 28. exf5 Rxf5 ∓) 20. ... Bf7 21. Nb6 Nxb6 22. Bxb6 Bb2 23. Rc2 Be5=.

17. ... gxf5 18. h3 Rf8 19. f4 Rad8 20. g5 Nc5!

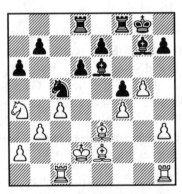

Diagram 340
After 20. ... Nc5!

The game is equal.

21. Nc3

21. Nxc5 dxc5+ 22. Ke1 Bd4 23. Kf2, and the players agreed to a draw in Motylev–Tiviakov, 2003.

21. ... Ne4+ 22. Nxe4 fxe4 23. Bg4 Bf5

Black follows up with ... e5, with an equal position (Nijboer–Tiviakov, 2003).

A3b 16. ... Rc6

Diagram 341
After 16. ... Rc6

17. h3

One of the most important endgames in the Maroczy Bind.

White prepares f4-f5.

17. ... Rac8 18. f4 Nc5!

Black forces the exchange of knights.

19. Nxc5

19. Nc3? Bxc3+ 20. Kxc3 Nxe4+.

19. ... dxc5 20. e5 f6!

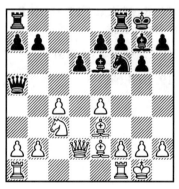

Diagram 342
After 20. ... f6!

The position is about equal.

B 11. 0-0 Qa5

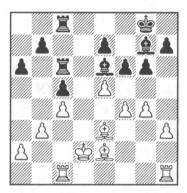

Diagram 343
After 11. ... Qa5

Here White has four moves: 12. f3, 12. Rab1, 12. Rfc1, and

12. Rac1.

B1

12. f3 Rfc8 13. Rfc1

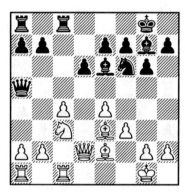

Diagram 344
After 13. Rfc1

White temporarily sacrifices a pawn.

13. ... a6

Or Black can even play 13. ... Bxc4 right away.

14. Rab1 Bxc4 15. Nd5 Qxd2 16. Nxe7+ Kf8 17. Bxd2 Kxe7 18. Bxc4

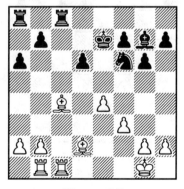

Diagram 345
After 18. Bxc4

This endgame is equal, as Black's powerful bishop and centralized king make up for his d-pawn, which is somewhat weak. White can't create any serious threats to that pawn because it is easily guarded.

18. ... b5 19. Bb3 Nd7 20. Bg5+ Bf6 21. Bxf6+ Nxf6,

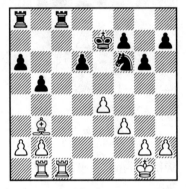

Diagram 346
After 21. ... Nxf6

with an equal game (Nik-cevic–Bakre, 2001).

B2 12. Rab1

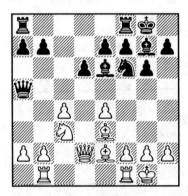

Diagram 347
After 12. Rab1

This move is currently White's favorite choice among top grand-masters. The seemingly harmless rook-move is aimed, as you will see shortly, at countering the play Black hopes to get with … b5.

12. ... Rfc8

Now White has the choice of three moves: 13. Rfc1, 13. b4, and 13. b3.

B2a 13. Rfc1

Once again, we're following the path to an equal endgame:

13. ... Bxc4 14. Nd5 Qxd2 15. Nxe7+ Kf8

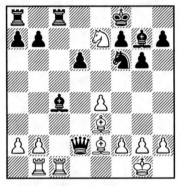

Diagram 348
After 15. ... Kf8

16. Bxd2 Kxe7 17. Rxc4 Rxc4 18. Bxc4 Rc8

18. ... Nxe4? 19. Re1

19. Bd3 Nd7

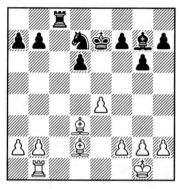

Diagram 349
After 19. ... Nd7

The game is even (Kveinys–Tiviakov, 2002).

B2b 13. b4

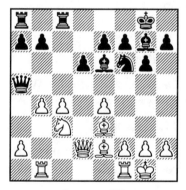

Diagram 350
After 13. b4

13. ... Qd8

And now the c4-pawn becomes a target.

B2c 13. b3

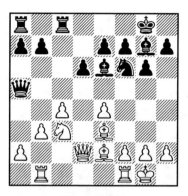

Diagram 351
After 13. b3

13. ... Ng4!

White's idea becomes clear after 13. ... b5?! 14. b4!

Diagram 352
After 14. b4!

14. ... Qc7 15. e5! dxe5 16. Nxb5,

Diagram 353
After 16. Nxb5

and Black is left with a terrible

pawn structure. But since White hasn't played f2-f3, ... Ng4 is playable.

After 13. ... Ng4, White has two moves: 14. Bd4 and 14. Nd5.

B2c1 14. Bd4

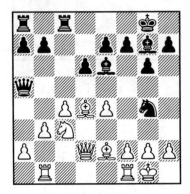

Diagram 354
After 14. Bb4

14. ... Bxd4 15. Qxd4 Qc5 16. Qd3

16. Qxc5 dxc5 17. Bxg4 Bxg4 18. Nd5 Kf8, and the game is equal.

16. ... Nf6 17. Kh1

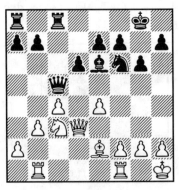

Diagram 355
After 17. Kh1

White's idea is to play f4;

Black's plan is to play ... a5, ... Bd7, and ... Bc6.

17. ... a5 18. f4 Bd7 19. a4 Bc6 20. Nd5 Re8!?

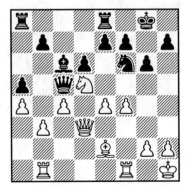

Diagram 356
After 20. ... Re8!?

Another choice is 20. ... Bxd5.

21. Rbd1

Or 21. Nxf6+ exf6, and White's e-pawn becomes a target.

21. ... Rad8

The position offers equal chances (Korneev–Tiviakov, 1998).

B2c2 14. Nd5

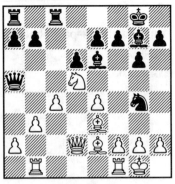

Diagram 357
After 14. Nd5

14. ... Qxd2 15. Bxd2 Kf8 16. Bg5

Or 16. Bxg4 Bxg4 17. Bg5 f6 18. Bd2 Be6 19. a4 f5 20. Bg5 Bxd5 21. exd5 Bc3 22. Be3, draw (Berkvens–Van der Weide, 2000).

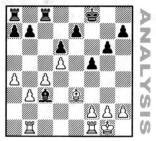

Diagram 358
After 22. Be3

16. ... Bxd5

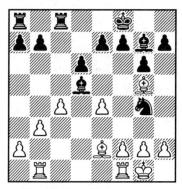

Diagram 359
After 16. ... Bxd5

17. exd5

Both 17. cxd5 Nf6 18. Bd3 Rc3, and 17. Bxg4 Be6 yield even positions.

17. ... Nf6

We've reached another critical endgame in the Maroczy. (See sample game Rowson–Malakhov, 2003.)

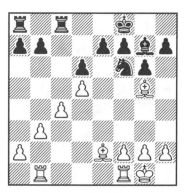

Diagram 360
After 17. ... Nf6

B3 12. Rfc1

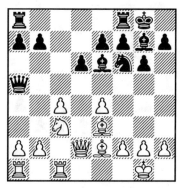

Diagram 361
After 12. Rfc1

12. ... Rfc8 13. b3 Ng4

Black executes a typical plan to simplify the position by trading pieces. Also, 13. ... a6 is interesting.

14. Bxg4 Bxg4 15. Bd4

Or 15. Rab1 Be6 16. Nd5 Qxd2 17. Bxd2 Kf8, and the players agreed to a draw in Socko—Gdanski, 2000.

15. ... Bd7 16. Bxg7 Kxg7 17. Qd4+

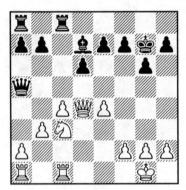

Diagram 362
After 17. Qd4+

And now the best is 17. ... f6—for example, 18. Nd5 e5!, with equality.

B4 12. Rac1

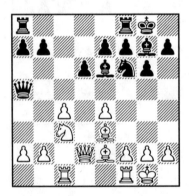

Diagram 363
After 12. Rac1

White's plan is to play on the kingside with f4-f5, so he first secures the queenside.

12. ... Rfc8 13. b3 a6

Black is getting ready to counter-attack on the queenside with ... b5!.

Let's consider 14. f3 and the more ambitious 14. f4.

B4a 14. f3 b5!

Black plays the counter-attacking move anyway.

Diagram 364
After 14. ... b5!

Black has achieved the dream position in the Maroczy Bind. White did set up the bind—but so what? His queenside, against which nearly every Black piece is directed, is now under serious pressure. White's best is to simplify into an endgame to avoid being worse in the middlegame.

B4a1 15. cxb5 axb5

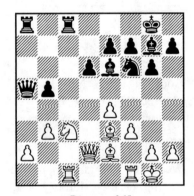

Diagram 365
After 15. ... axb5

White can't win a pawn: 16. Nxb5 is met by 16. ... Qxd2 17. Rxc8+ Bxc8 18. Bxd2 Rxa2, and Black is better in the endgame; and if 16. Bxb5 Rxc3! 17. Qxc3 Qxb5,

Diagram 366
After 17. ... Qxb5

threatening both ... Nxe4 and ... Rxa2. Black's two minor pieces are much stronger than the rook and pawn.

And here's what happened in Sells—Perelshteyn, 2007, from Diagram 365: 16. Bd4 Bd7 (threatening 17. ... b4, as the a4-square is now under the control of Black's bishop) 17. e5 dxe5 18. Bxe5 Bc6 19. Qe3

Diagram 367
After 19. Qe3

19. ... b4 20. Na4 Nd5 21. Qd4 Nc3 22. Nxc3 Bxe5 23. Qe3 Bxc3, 0-1.

B4a2 15. Nd5 Qxd2 16. Bxd2 Nxd5

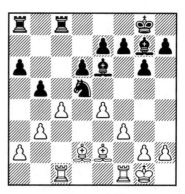

Diagram 368
After 16. ... Nxd5

17. exd5

Or 17. cxd5 Bd4+ 18. Kh1 Bd7, with equality.

17. ... Bd4+ 18. Kh1 Bd7

Now after 19. Bc3 Bxc3 20. Rxc3 b4 21. Re3 Kf8 22. Kg1 a5 23. a4

Black has achieved the dream position in the Maroczy Bind ... Nearly every Black piece is directed against White's queenside!

Diagram 369
After 23. a4

23. ... Rc5 (23. ... bxa3 24. Ra1) 24. f4 Re8 25. Rd1, the players agreed to a draw in Uribe–Perelshteyn, 1998.

B4b 14. f4 b5! 15. f5! Bd7

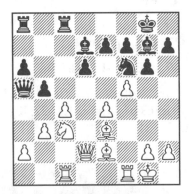

Diagram 370
After 15. ... Bd7

This is the critical position of the opening. White's attack on the kingside is met by Black's solid defenses, while Black is ready to take over the initiative on the queenside.

Now White has two options: 16. b4 and 16. fxg6.

B4b1 16. b4

White fires out another pawn, going all out to get to Black's king. Analysis shows, however, that Black is the shooter still standing after the smoke clears.

16. ... Qxb4

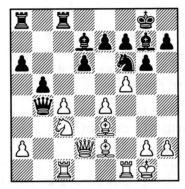

Diagram 371
After 16. ... Qxb4

17. e5 dxe5 18. fxg6 Be6 19. gxf7+ Bxf7 20. Bh6 Bxh6 21. Qxh6

Black is the shooter still standing after the smoke clears ...

White's attack was more heart than head.

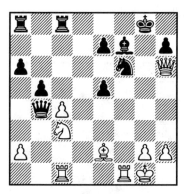

Diagram 372
After 21. Qxh6

21. ... Bxc4!

Strong and simple. White's attack was more heart than head.

22. Qg5+ Kh8 23. Rxf6

The last try at making the attack amount to something.

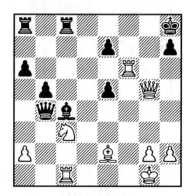

Diagram 373
After 23. Rxf6

23. ... Rg8!

Now Black is winning.

24. Qxe5 exf6 25. Qxf6+ Rg7

Ivanchuk–Anand, 1994, continued: 26. Qd4 Rc8 27. Ne4 Qe7 28. Bxc4 Qa7 29. Qxa7 Rxa7

30. Re1 Rxc4

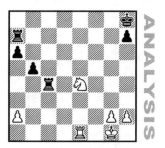

Diagram 374
After 30. ... Rxc4

31. Nd6 Rc2 32. Nf5 Ra8 33. a3 Rc3 0-1.

B4b2 16. fxg6 hxg6

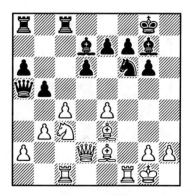

Diagram 375
After 16. ... hxg6

Here White has tried c5 and e5 to break through Black's defense. In both cases, Black obtains good play. We'll make 17. e5 our main line. But first let's take a look at how Black comes out on top if White plays 17. c5.

After 17. c5 dxc5! 18. e5 Ng4

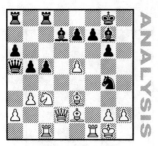

Diagram 376
After 18. ... Ng4

19. Nd5 (19. Qxd7 Nxe3 20. Nd5 Nxd5 21. Qxd5 e6 ∓) 19. ... Qxd2 20. Bxd2 Re8!

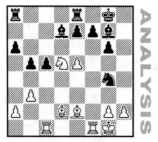

Diagram 377
After 20. ... Re8!

21. Nc7 Bxe5 22. Bxg4 Bxg4 23. Nxa8 Bd4+ 24. Kh1 Rxa8

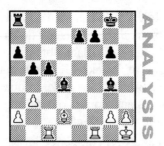

Diagram 378
After 24. ... Rxa8

Black is better because he has the bishop pair and two pawns for the Exchange. What's more,

White has the "redundant" rook.

17. e5 b4!

Diagram 379
After 17. ... b4!

A crucial resource!

18. exf6

After 18. Na4 Ne4 19. Qd4

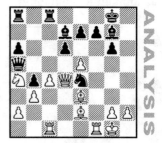

Diagram 380
After 19. Qd4

19. ... Bxa4 20. Qxe4 Bc6 21. Qf4 Qxe5 22. Qxf7+ Kh7

Diagram 381
After 22. ... Kh7

Black's king is safe, while White is faced with problems on the e-file.

18. ... bxc3 19. Rxc3 Bxf6

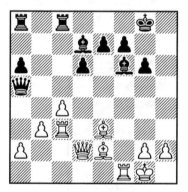

Diagram 382
After 19. ... Bxf6

20. Rxf6?!

White's idea is to create an attack on the dark squares after playing Bd4 and Qf4. But even after his best scenario, 20. Bd4 Bxd4+ 21. Qxd4 Qc5 22. Qxc5 Rxc5, Black is *at least* equal!

20. ... exf6 21. Bf3 Bc6 22. Bd4 Bxf3 23. Qf4 Qg5!

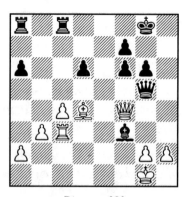

Diagram 383
After 23. ... Qg5!

24. Qxf3 Re8

Now Black gets a slightly better endgame.

25. Qxf6 Re1+ 26. Kf2 Qxf6+ 27. Bxf6 Rae8

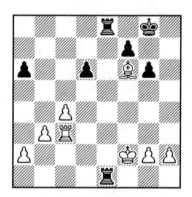

Diagram 384
After 27. ... Rae8

(Spassky–Panno, 1969).

Summary:

The usual plan for Black is: ... Qa5, ... Be6, ... Rfc8, ... a6 (with the idea of ... b5), and often ... Ng4 or ... Nd7.

Important: Endgames are okay for Black! (Sometimes, of course, accuracy will be required.)

Many transpositions are possible, but even if you don't recognize one, your understanding of the ideas should show you the right way.

Chapter 11: Maroczy Bind—7. Be2, with Be3 and Qd2

Memory Markers!

MARKER 1

Diagram 385
After 8. ... Nxd4

MARKER 2

Diagram 386
After 13. ... a6

MARKER 3

Diagram 387
After 17. Bxg4

MARKER 4

Diagram 388
After 18. fxg6

Chapter 11: Maroczy Bind—7. Be2, with Be3 and Qd2
Solutions to Memory Markers!

No. 1 **9. Bxd4!**. See page 143.

No. 2 **14. Nd5!** (if 14 ... Qxd2, 15. Nxe7+). See page 144.

No. 3 **17. ... Be6 =.** See page 153.

No. 4 **18. ... Be6!** (18. ... hxg6 19. Rxf6). See page 156.

Chapter 12: Maroczy Bind—7. Be2 with Bg5 and Qd2
Some Important Points to Look For

Many ideas in this chapter are similar to those studied in Chapter 11. While the bishop can be more active on g5 than on e3, it is also more vulnerable.

◆ The b-pawn is irrepressible.
See Diagram 390.

◆ It's a *Zwischenzug*-battle!
See Diagram 394.

◆ Black recruits a brave rook.
See Diagram 396.

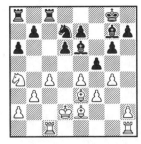

◆ Transposing to equality.
See Diagram 401.

Outline of Variations

**1. e4 c5 2. Nf3 g6 3. d4 cxd4 4. Nxd4 Nc6 5. c4 Nf6 6. Nc3 d6 7. Be2 Nxd4 8. Qxd4 Bg7
9. Bg5 0-0 10. Qd2 Be6** *(162)* [B36]

   A 11. 0-0 Qa5 12. Rac1 Rfc8 13. b3 a6 14. f4 Rc5! *(164)*

   B 11. Rc1 Qa5 12. f3 Rfc8 13. b3 a6 14. Na4 Qxd2+ 15. Kxd2 *(166)*

      B1 15. ... Nd7 16. g4 f6 17. Be3 f5 *(166)*

      B2 15. ... Rc6 16. Nc3 Kf8 17. Nd5 Bxd5 18. cxd5 Rcc8 *(167)*

Chapter 12
Maroczy Bind
7. Be2 with Bg5 and Qd2

In this variation of the Bind, White elects to develop his dark-square bishop to a more active position.

1. e4 c5 2. Nf3 g6 3. d4 cxd4 4. Nxd4 Nc6 5. c4 Nf6 6. Nc3 d6 7. Be2 Nxd4 8. Qxd4 Bg7 9. Bg5

Diagram 389
After 9. Bg5

White develops his bishop and prepares to retreat his queen to d2 or e3.

9. ... 0–0 10. Qd2

10. Qe3 is another possibility for White. Black's main idea here is similar to his plan against the 9. 0–0 and Qe3 line studied in Chapter 13: 10. ... Be6 11. 0–0 Qb6! 12. Qxb6 axb6 13. Rac1 Rfc8 14. b3 b5!.

Diagram 390
After 14. ... b5!

Again, the b-pawn is irrepressible! 15. cxb5 (15. Nxb5 Rxa2) 15. ... Rxc3!. Black sacrifices the Exchange to win White's central pawn. 16. Rxc3 Nxe4

> # White elects to develop his dark-square bishop to a more active position.

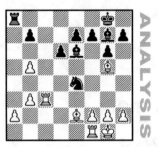

Diagram 391
After 16. ... Nxe4

17. Re3 Nxg5 18. h4 Rxa2
19. hxg5 Bd4 20. Re4 Bc5

Diagram 392
After 20. ... Bc5

White's shattered pawns give
Black sufficient compensation.

10. ... Be6

Here White has two main
moves: 11. 0–0 and 11. Rc1.

A 11. 0–0

> **White's shattered
> pawns give Black
> sufficient
> compensation.**

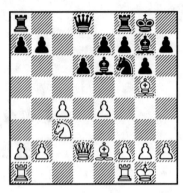

Diagram 393
After 11. 0-0

11. ... Qa5 12. Rac1

Not dangerous here is the dis-
covered attack after 12. Nd5,
because after 12. ... Qxd2,
White's e-pawn is unprotected.

12. Rad1 leads to the following
interesting endgame: 12. ... Rfc8
13. b3 a6 14. Bxf6 Bxf6 15. Nd5.
White's idea is to double up
Black's pawn after the
Zwischenzug Nxf6: 15. ... Qxd2
16. Nxf6+ Kg7!.

Diagram 394
After 16. ... Kg7!

That's the whole point! Black
chooses to take the knight on h5
with ... gxh5, which is better
than ... exf6. 17. Nh5+ gxh5 18.
Rxd2 Rc5 19. f4 f6

Diagram 395
After 19. ... f6

White can't take advantage of Black's weak h5 pawn because it's easily defended. Black, on the other hand, is ready to start his play on the queenside with ... b5!.

12. ... Rfc8 13. b3 a6 14. f4

White's idea is to play f5, creating a dangerous attack (14. f3 is met by 14. ... b5!).

14. ... Rc5!

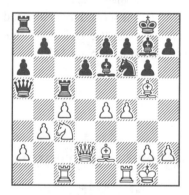

Diagram 396
After 14. ... Rc5!

Black's brave rook stops White's attack!

15. Qe3

(Or 15. Bf3 Re8 16. Qe3 Nd7,

transposing.)

Here we recommend a quiet move that guards the pawn on e7.

15. ... Re8!

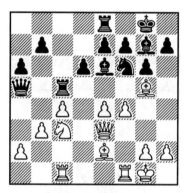

Diagram 397
After 15. ... Re8!

In the first edition, we suggested 15. ... h6 16. Bh4 Re8! (still best here). It now seems, however, that there is no need to drive White's bishop from g5 to a more promising diocese on e1, by way of h4.

After 15. ... Re8!, Black has a good game—for instance: 16. Bf3 Nd7!, and now if 17. Nd5, then 17. ... Bxd5 18. exd5 Qxa2!,

Diagram 398
After 18. ... Qxa2!

19. Bg4 (19. f5 Qb2, with the idea of ... Qd4) 19. ... Nf6 20. Be2 (Timoshenko—Moldovan, 2007). Here Rybka favors Black after 20. ... h6 21. Bh4 e6!.

B 11. Rc1

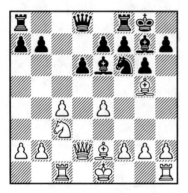

Diagram 399
After 11. Rc1

11. ... Qa5 12. f3 Rfc8 13. b3 a6 14. Na4

Diagram 400
After 14. Na4

This move leads to an endgame similar to that in the Be3, Qd2 line.

14. ... Qxd2+ 15. Kxd2

Here Black has two good ways of playing: 15. ... Nd7 with the idea of ... f5 and 15. ... Rc6.

B1 15. ... Nd7 16. g4

16. Bxe7? Bh6+ 17. Kc2 Bxc1 18. Rxc1 d5!

16. ... f6 17. Be3 f5

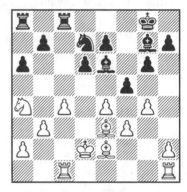

Diagram 401
After 17. ... f5

We've transposed to a balanced position as in the Be3, Qd2 line (see line **A3a** on page 147).

Black improves his king's position for the coming endgame.

B2 **15. ... Rc6 16. Nc3**

White's idea is to play Nd5, and after ... Bxd5, gain the bishop pair.

16. ... Kf8

Black improves his king's position in preparation for the coming endgame.

17. Nd5 Bxd5 18. cxd5 Rcc8

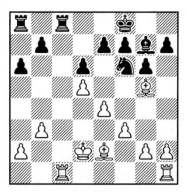

Diagram 402
After 18. ... Rcc8

This position occurred in the game Vallejo–Malakhov, 2003, where Black demonstrated the correct way to maintain equality. (See the complete game annotated in Part V.)

Summary:

Many ideas in this chapter are similar to those already explained in Chapter 11. Black successfully employs tactics to hold his own in the various emerging endgames.

Chapter 12: Maroczy Bind—7. Be2 with Bg5 and Qd2

Memory Markers!

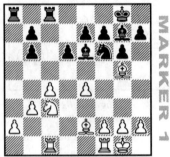

Diagram 403
After 14. b3

MARKER 1

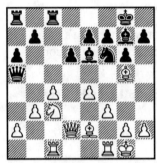

Diagram 404
After 14. f3

MARKER 2

Diagram 405
After 17. Bf2

MARKER 3

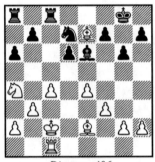

Diagram 406
After 18. Rxc1

MARKER 4

Chapter 12: Maroczy Bind—7. Be2 with Bg5 and Qd2
Solutions to Memory Markers!

No. 1   **14. ... b5!.** See page 163.

No. 2   **14. ... b5!.** See page 165.

No. 3   **17. ... Rcc8,** with equality. See page 165.

No. 4   **18. ... d5.** See page 166.

Chapter 13: Maroczy Bind—7. Be2, with 0-0 and Qd3 (or Qe3)

Some Important Points to Look For

Avoiding the main line is not promising for White. On e3, the queen blocks her bishop; on d3, she is vulnerable to the knight's attack.

◆ A surprise!
  See Diagram 410.

◆ Already familiar.
  See Diagram 413.

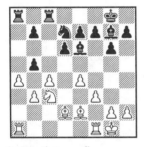

◆ Into the crossfire.
  See Diagram 418.

◆ Black dominates the dark squares.
  See Diagram 426.

Outline of Variations

1. e4 c5 2. Nf3 g6 3. d4 cxd4 4. Nxd4 Nc6 5. c4 Nf6 6. Nc3 d6 7. Be2 Nxd4 8. Qxd4 Bg7 9. 0-0 0-0 *(170)* [B36]

    A 10. Qe3 Be6 *(172)*
        A1 11. Rb1 Qb6! 12. Qd3 Nd7 *(172)*
        A2 11. Bd2 Qb6! 12. Qxb6 axb6 *(173)*
            A2a 13. a4 Nd7 14. Ra3 Nc5 *(173)*
            A2b 13. f3 Rfc8 14. b3 Nd7 *(174)*
    B 10. Qd3 Be6 11. Be3 Nd7 12. Qd2 Nc5 13. f3 a5 *(175)*

Chapter 13
Maroczy Bind
7. Be2, with 0-0 and Qd3 (or Qe3)

In this chapter, we again see White setting up the Maroczy Bind, but this time finding a different placement for his queen than d2. He thereby avoids the pin in the Qd2 vs. Qa5 positions explained in Chapters 11 and 12. But, as usual, there are trade-offs—by avoiding one problem, White creates other opportunities for Black.

1. e4 c5 2. Nf3 g6 3. d4 cxd4 4. Nxd4 Nc6 5. c4 Nf6 6. Nc3 d6 7. Be2

Diagram 407
After 7. Be2

By taking on d4 now, Black gains a tempo because White's queen won't be comfortable for long on d4.

7. ... Nxd4 8. Qxd4 Bg7 9. 0–0 0–0

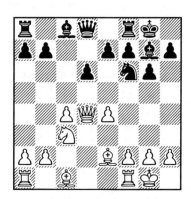

Diagram 408
After 9. ... 0-0

White's two main moves are: 10. Qe3 (but that blocks the bishop) and 10. Qd3 (but that allows Black to transfer his knight to c5 with tempo).

A 10. Qe3

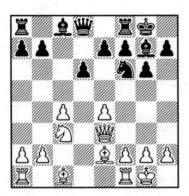

Diagram 409
After 10. Qe3

White's idea is to develop his bishop on d2; from there he can control the a5-square. His queen can help to enforce the f4 and e5 pushes. We'll see, however, that Black has enough counter-play!

10. ... Be6

White has two main moves: 11. Rb1 and 11. Bd2.

A1 11. Rb1 Qb6!

Diagram 410
After 11. ... Qb6!

12. Qd3

Or 12. Qxb6 axb6 13. Be3

Rfc8 14. b3 b5!.

12. ... Nd7 13. Nd5 Bxd5 14. exd5 Rfc8 15. Qh3 Nc5 16. Bg5

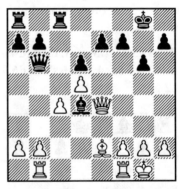

Diagram 411
After 16. Bg5

16. ... Ne4! 17. Be3 Bd4 18. Qh4 Bxe3 19. Qxe4 Bd4

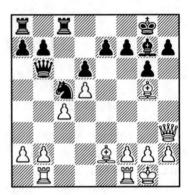

Diagram 412
After 19. ... Bd4

20. b4

If 20. Qxe7? Re8, with a winning position.

20. ... Bf6 21. Rfc1 Qd4 22. Qxd4

White enters an absolutely drawn ending.

22. ... Bxd4 23. Rc2 b6 24. Rd1 Be5 25. g3 a5 26. f4 Bf6 27. b5 Kg7, draw (Nijboer–Tiviakov, 2000).

A2 11. Bd2 Qb6!

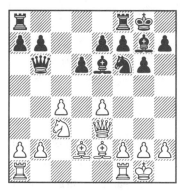

Diagram 413
After 11. ... Qb6!

Again Black offers to exchange queens, voluntarily breaking up his own pawn structure. We'll see why shortly.

12. Qxb6

After 12. b3 Qxe3 13. Bxe3 Ng4 14. Bd2 Be5 15. Bxg4 Bxg4,

Diagram 414
After 15. ... Bxg4

the position is equal.

12. ... axb6

Now White can play 13. a4 or 13. f3.

A2a 13. a4

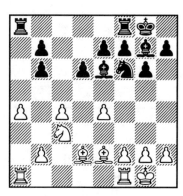

Diagram 415
After 13. a4

13. ... Nd7

As in the game Morozevich–Topalov, 2001.

14. Ra3 Nc5 15. Rfa1

White sacrifices a pawn.

15. ... Bxc3 16. Bxc3 Nxe4 17. Bd4 Rfc8 18. Re3 Bxc4!

Black offers to exchange queens, voluntarily breaking up his own pawn structure.

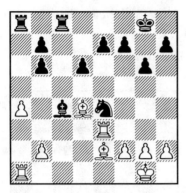

Diagram 416
After 18. ... Bxc4!

The tactics are in Black's favor: 19. Rxe4 Bxe2 20. Bc3 (20. Rxe2? Rxa4! and White loses) 20. ... Bb5 21. Rxe7 Bxa4 22. Rxb7 Bc6 23. Rba7 Rxa7 24. Rxa7 Ra8, even though Black's extra pawn is not enough to win due to the opposite-color bishops.

A2b 13. f3

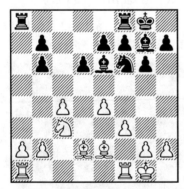

Diagram 417
After 13. f3

13. ... Rfc8 14. b3 Nd7 15. a4 b5!

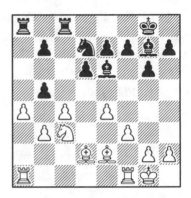

Diagram 418
After 15. ... b5!

A truly amazing move! Black throws his pawn into a three-way crossfire—and it turns out that all captures on b5 are in Black's favor!

16. axb5

16. Nxb5 Bxa1; 16. cxb5? Bxc3

16. ... Nc5! 17. Rxa8 Rxa8

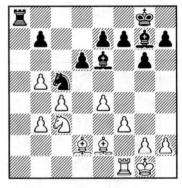

Diagram 419
After 17. ... Rxa8

18. Rb1

Or 18. b4?! Nb3 19. Be1 Nc1!.

Diagram 420
After 19. ... Nc1!

There is no defense against ... Nxe2 and ... Bxc4.

Also unsatisfactory for White is 18. Bd1 Bd4+! 19. Kh1 Ra1 with the idea ... Nxb3.

18. ... Ra3

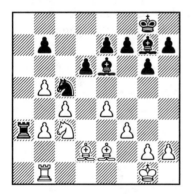

Diagram 421
After 18. ... Ra3

Now the b3-pawn falls.

If 19. Bd1, then 19. ... Bxc4 20. bxc4 Bxc3—and Black is much better.

B 10. Qd3

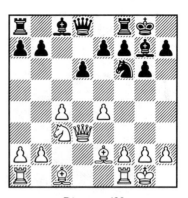

Diagram 422
After 10. Qd3

10. ... Be6 11. Be3 Nd7

The knight is heading to c5.

12. Qd2 Nc5 13. f3 a5

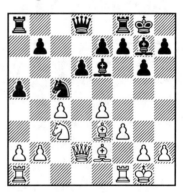

Diagram 423
After 13. ... a5

Black secures his knight. His plan is to play ... Qb6, ... Rfc8 and ... Qd8, with these ideas:

◆ The rook on c8 will put pressure on the c-pawn;

◆ The queen can move to f8 both to support ... f5 and to help guard the dark squares around the king.

14. b3 Qb6 15. Rab1 Rfc8 16. Nd5 Qd8

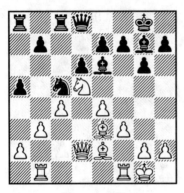

Diagram 424
After 16. ... Qd8

Black temporarily delays capture on d5. The game L'Ami–Krivoshey, 2001, continued:

17. Kh1 Rab8 18. Bg5 Bxd5 19. exd5 Bf6!

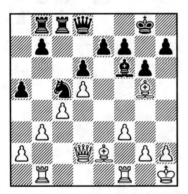

Diagram 425
After 19. ... Bf6!

The exchange of dark-square bishops is favorable for Black because his knight is better than White's bishop.

20. Be3 b6 21. a4?!

Now the knight on c5 is even more powerful. But other plans, such as preparing b3-b4, aren't promising either.

21. ... Qf8 22. Bd1 Qg7

Diagram 426
After 22. ... Qg7

Black dominates the dark squares. He may start active play in the center (with ... e7-e6) after first placing his rooks on e8 and d8, with the better game.

Summary:

Neither 10. Qe3 nor 10. Qd3 gives White any chance for an advantage. The former is challenged by ... Qb6 (the exchange on b6 is okay for Black, who gets extra influence over the a-file), the latter by a tempo-winning ... Nd7-c5.

Chapter 13: Maroczy Bind—7. Be2, with 0-0 and Qd3 (or Qe3)
Memory Markers!

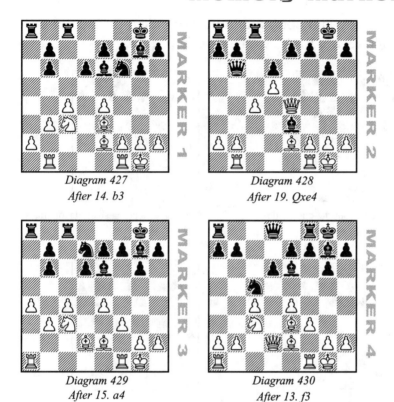

Diagram 427
After 14. b3

Diagram 428
After 19. Qxe4

Diagram 429
After 15. a4

Diagram 430
After 13. f3

Chapter 13: Maroczy Bind—7. Be2, with 0-0 and Qd3 (or Qe3)
Solutions to Memory Markers!

No. 1   **14. ... b5!**. See page 172.

No. 2   **19. ... Bd4**. If 20. Qxe7?, then 20. ... Re8, winning. See page172.

No. 3   **15. ... b5!**. See page 174.

No. 4   **13. ... a5**, securing the c5-knight. See page 175.

Chapter 14: Maroczy Bind—7. f3 System
Some Important Points to Look For

Black achieves a good game by expanding on the queens-side with ... a5, then ... a4 and even ... a3.

◆ Black stakes out the queenside.
See Diagram 432.

◆ Endgames here usually favor Black.
See Diagram 433.

◆ Black's knight on c5 will be very
strong. See Diagram 434.

◆ Favorable exchanges lead Black to a
good endgame. See Diagram 435.

Outline of Variations

1. e4 c5 2. Nf3 g6 3. d4 cxd4 4. Nxd4 Nc6 5. c4 Nf6 6. Nc3 d6 7. f3 Nxd4! 8. Qxd4 Bg7
9. Be3 0-0 10. Qd2 a5! *(178)* [B36]

Chapter 14
Maroczy Bind
7. f3 System

By playing 7. f3, White shores up his center right away, immediately tightening the bind. But as we've seen before in other variations, taking time for this move this early is a bit passive and allows Black to counter effectively right away.

1. e4 c5 2. Nf3 g6 3. d4 cxd4 4. Nxd4 Nc6 5. c4 Nf6 6. Nc3 d6 7. f3

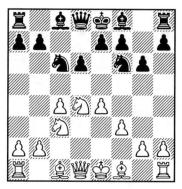

Diagram 431
After 7. f3

White defends the center immediately, even before developing his king's bishop.

7. ... Nxd4! 8. Qxd4 Bg7

9. Be3 0–0 10. Qd2 a5!

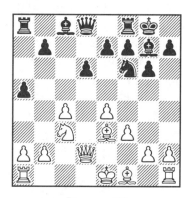

Diagram 432
After 10. ... a5!

Black has in mind to play ... a4, to stake out even more space on the queenside and secure an outpost on c5 for his knight.

11. Be2 a4 12. Rc1

Or 12. 0–0 Be6 13. Rac1 Nd7 (with the idea of ... Nc5) 14. Bd4?!.

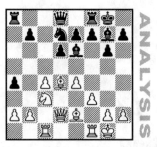

Diagram 433
After 14. Bd4

(In these types of positions, the exchange of dark-square bishops is often favorable for Black, because White's dark squares become much weaker. But what other promising plan is there for White?) 14. ... Bxd4+ 15. Qxd4 Qa5 16. Nd5 Bxd5 17. cxd5 Rfc8 18. Rfd1 Rc5 19. Rxc5 Qxc5

Diagram 434
After 19. ... Qxc5

Black achieves a comfortable endgame (Kozamernik–Mikac, 2003).

12. ... Be6 13. Nd5

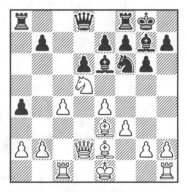

Diagram 435
After 13. Nd5

13. ... Nd7!

Paradoxically, the knight on d5 is not as dangerous as Black's, which is headed for c5.

14. 0–0 Nc5 15. Rfd1

The game J. Polgar–Tiviakov, 2002, continued:

15. ... Re8 16. Bd4

Diagram 436
After 16. Bd4

16. ... Bxd5 17. cxd5 Qa5 18. Rc3 Qb4 19. Bxg7 Kxg7 20. Qc2

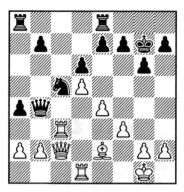

Diagram 437
After 20. Qc2

20. ... Rec8 21. Rc4 Qa5 22. Qc3+ Qxc3 23. Rxc3 a3

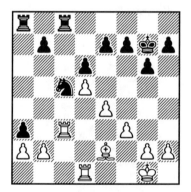

Diagram 438
After 23. ... a3

24. b3 Na6 25. Rxc8 Rxc8 26. Bxa6 bxa6

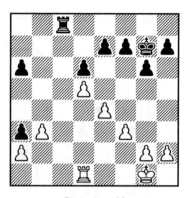

Diagram 439
After 26. ... bxa6

Black has a favorable rook endgame.

Summary:

An early f3 doesn't give White any visible benefits, while allowing Black to gain space on the queenside with ... a5 and then ... a4 (and in some cases even ... a3). The endings that emerge (almost inevitably) are even more favorable for Black than endgames achieved in the main lines (which are usually equal).

Chapter 14: Maroczy Bind—7. f3 System
Memory Markers!

Diagram 440
After 7. ... Bg7

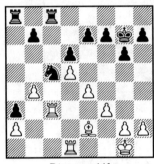

Diagram 441
After 24. b4

Chapter 14: Maroczy Bind—7. f3 System
Solutions to Memory Markers!

No. 1   **8. Be3;** if 8. ... Nxd4, 9. Bxd4.
Gains a tempo for White compared to lines where Black
timely captured on d4, forcing the White queen to recapture.
See page 179.

No. 2   **24. ... Na4 25. Rxa3 Nc3**, with advantage. See page 181.

Chapter 15: Maroczy Bind—7. Nc2
Some Important Points to Look For

White loses time avoiding the exchange of knights on d4. So his strategy, although sound, allows Black tactical solutions that lead him to the better game.

♦ Black has the better pawn structure.
  See Diagram 446.

♦ Black's ... Nd4 is a thematic thrust.
  See Diagram 449.

♦ Black gains space—and the a5-square for the queen.
  See Diagram 451.

♦ After the thematic ... f5.
  See Diagram 452.

Outline of Variations

1. e4 c5 2. Nf3 g6 3. d4 cxd4 4. Nxd4 Nc6 5. c4 Nf6 6. Nc3 d6 7. Nc2 Bg7 8. Be2 0-0
9. 0-0 Nd7 10. Bd2 a5. *(184)* [B37]
    A 11. Na3 Nc5 12. Nab5 Nd4! *(186)*
    B 11. Rb1 Nc5 12. f3 f5 *(187)*
    C 11. Be3 Nc5 12. f3 a4 *(188)*
    D 11. Kh1 Nc5 12. f3 f5! *(188)*
    E 11. Qc1 Nc5 12. Bh6 Be6 *(189)*

Chapter 15
Maroczy Bind
7. Nc2

In this final chapter on the Maroczy, White avoids the exchange of knights, following the rule that the side with more space should avoid trading pieces. However, the knight leaves the center, and does this at the cost of a tempo, allowing Black to create counter-play on the kingside with … f5.

1. e4 c5 2. Nf3 g6 3. d4 cxd4 4. Nxd4 Nc6 5. c4 Nf6 6. Nc3 d6 7. Nc2

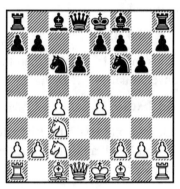

Diagram 442
After 7. Nc2

So the knight avoids the trade, but has moved three times in the first seven moves.

7. ... Bg7 8. Be2 0–0 9. 0–0 Nd7

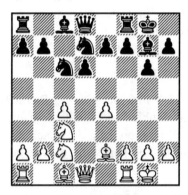

Diagram 443
After 9. ... Nd7

Black's plan is to put the knight on c5, where it will control key central squares, and then to play f5, undermining White's center.

The same position (with colors reversed and an extra tempo for the anti-Bind side) occurs after 1. c4 c5 2. Nc3 Nf6 3. Nf3 d5 4. cxd5 Nxd5 5. g3 Nc6 6. Bg2 Nc7 7. 0-0 e5 8. d3 Be7 9. Nd2.

Diagram 444
After 9. Nd2

Even though in our line Black is a tempo down, compared to the position in the "reversed" line above, his active play fully compensates him for his opponent's stronger center.

10. Bd2

If White permits ... Bg7xc3, his doubled and isolated c-pawns will be more of a drawback than his bishop-pair will be an advantage.

10. ... a5

Black stops b4 and prepares ... Nc5. Riskier is 10. ... Nc5 right away: 11. b4! Bxc3 12. Bxc3 Nxe4 13. Bb2, with an attack.

After 10. ... a5, White has five choices: 11. Na3, 11. Rb1, 11. Be3, 11. Kh1, and 11. Qc1.

A 11. Na3

Diagram 445
After 11. Na3

White seeks to take over the b5-square.

11. ... Nc5 12. Nab5 Nd4!

Black offers the trade of knights.

13. Nxd4 Bxd4

Black's knight has moved twice while White's has moved six times!

14. Bh6 Bxc3!

This move is stronger than the conventional 14. ... Bg7.

15. bxc3

Or 15. Bxf8 Bxb2 16. Rb1 Bf6 17. Bh6 Nxe4, and Black has the advantage.

IF WHITE PERMITS ... BG7XC3, HIS DOUBLED AND
ISOLATED C-PAWNS WILL BE MORE OF A DRAWBACK
THAN HIS BISHOP-PAIR WILL BE AN ADVANTAGE.

15. ... Re8

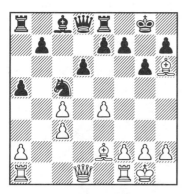

Diagram 446
After 15. ... Re8

Black is doing fine; his idea is to play ... e5 and ... f6, with a small edge.

B 11. Rb1

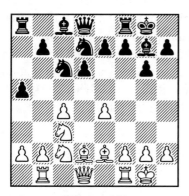

Diagram 447
After 11. Rb1

White protects his b2-pawn, freeing the c3-knight.

11. ... Nc5 12. f3 f5

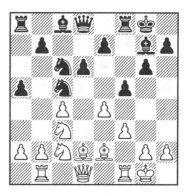

Diagram 448
After 12. ... f5

Black keeps the pressure on e4.

13. Kh1

White avoids a check along the a7-g1 diagonal—for example, from … Qb6, which could come at an inopportune moment.

13. … fxe4 14. Nxe4 Bf5!

Black is better, for example: 15. Ng3 Bxc2 16. Qxc2 Nd4!.

Diagram 449
After 16. ... Nd4!

Black completely dominates the center.

C 11. Be3

Diagram 450
After 11. Be3

White puts the bishop in a more active position. This is possible because after ... a7-a5, taking the a5-square from his queen, Black has less incentive to trade on c3.

By developing his bishop on e3, White also guards against the possibility of checks on the a7-g1 diagonal.

11. ... Nc5 12. f3 a4

Diagram 451
After 12. ... a4

Black's idea is to gain more

space on the queenside and to play ... Qa5. (12. ... f5 is also possible.)

13. Qd2 Qa5

After 14. Rab1 f5 15. exf5 Bxf5, Black stood better (Yermolisky–Donaldson, 1996).

Diagram 452
After 15. ... Bxf5

In the more recent game Charbonneau—Kudrin, 2007, play continued: 14. Na3 Be6 (here, too, 14. ... f5 was fine) 15. Rac1 Rac8! (even better than 15. ... Rfc8, as in the game) 16. Rfd1 Qb4 17. Rc2 f5!, with active play for Black.

D 11. Kh1

Once again, White invests a tempo to avoid untimely checks on the a7-g1 diagonal.

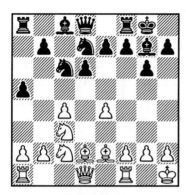

Diagram 453
After 11. Kh1

11. ... Nc5 12. f3 f5!

By now, a familiar thrust. Black has successfully executed his plan. The game Woitkiewicz–Donaldson, 2001, continued: 13. exf5 Bxf5 14. Ne3 Nd4! (Black has taken over key central squares) 15. Nxf5 Nxf5 16. g4 Nd4. Black is better. His minor pieces dominate the position.

E 11. Qc1 Nc5

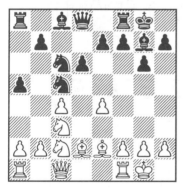

Diagram 454
After 11. ... Nc5

Black doesn't mind trading the dark-square bishops, because he occupies the dark squares himself.

12. Bh6 Be6 13. Bxg7 Kxg7 14. Qd2 f6 15. Kh1 Bf7 16. Rab1 Qb6 17. f3 a4 18. b4 axb3 19. axb3 Rfc8 20. b4

Diagram 455
After 20. b4

20. ... Na4! 21. Nd5 Qd8 22. f4 Nb6 23. Nde3 Ra2

Control of the a-file gives Black the edge. The game Predojevic—Perelshteyn, 2007, continued: 24. Ra1 Rca8 25. Rxa2 Rxa2 26. Qc3 Qa8 27. h4 Na4 28. Qb3 Nb6 29. Qc3, draw.

Black could, however, play better: 28. ... Rb2! 29. Qa3 Nxb4 30. Bd1 Qa5 31. Nxb4 Rxb4 32. Bb3 b6! 33. Nc2 Rxb3 34. Qxb3 Nc5 ∓, winning a second pawn for an Exchange.

Diagram 455a
After 34. ... Nc5

Summary:

White's 7. Nc2 is justified strategically, but costs too much time. Black uses this time to bring his knight to c5, and does it while winning tempos: ... Nd7 creates the positional threat ... Bxc3, forcing White to defend his knight with the passive Bd2; then ... Nc5 creates a threat to win the e-pawn.

Later, Black continues his attack on White's center by the bold (and thematic) ... f5, achieving promising positions, in which his pieces often dominate the center.

Chapter 15: Maroczy Bind—7. Nc2
Memory Markers!

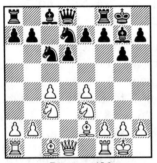

Diagram 456
After 9. Ne3

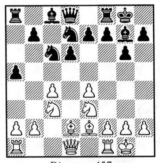

Diagram 457
After 11. Ne3

Diagram 458
After 15. ... Nxe4

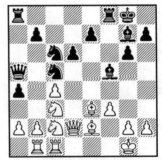

Diagram 459
After 16. Rfc1

Chapter 15: Maroczy Bind—7. Nc2
Solutions to Memory Markers!

No. 1   **9. ... Bxc3,** doubling White's pawns. See page 186.

No. 2   **11. ... Nc5 12. f3 a4!,** creating threats on the queenside. See page 186.

No. 3   **16. Qd4,** followed by Bxf8—not 16. Bxf8 Nxc3, with two pawns for the Exchange. See page 187.

No. 4   **16. ... Bxc3,** ambitious and strong. Also good is waiting with 16. ... Rf7—the knight won't run away. See page 188.

Chapter 16: The Closed Sicilian—2. Nc3 followed by g3

Some Important Points to Look For

White's play is slower than in other lines and flexible. But Black has an effective series of counterpunches for whatever plan White chooses.

◆ Black plays an instructive maneuver.
See Diagram 463.

◆ Black blocks a possible d4.
See Diagram 465.

◆ Dzindzi's favorite!
See Diagram 474.

◆ White's attack isn't dangerous.
See Diagram 478.

Outline of Variations

1. e4 c5 2. Nc3 g6 3. g3 Bg7 4. Bg2 Nc6 5. d3 d6. *(192)* [B25-26]

   A 6. Nge2 Nf6 7. 0-0 0-0 8. h3 Ne8! 9. Be3 Nd4 *(194)*

   B 6. Be3 Nf6 7. h3 0-0 8. Qd2 Nd4! 9. Nd1 e5! *(196)*

   C 6. f4 Nf6 7. Nf3 Bg4! 8. 0-0 0-0 9. h3 Bxf3 10.Qxf3 Rb8 11. Be3 *(198)*

Chapter 16
The Closed Sicilian
2. Nc3 followed by g3

This variation is marked by the absence of White's d4 thrust. White plays a King's Indian-like formation with an extra move. Play is slower and the central pawn formations tend to be locked—hence the name "Closed" Sicilian. World champion Boris Spassky's success with this line popularized it in the 1970s and 1980s.

The line appeals to players of White who prefer a slower buildup for an attack. Interestingly, White avoids playing an early d4, thereby retaining his d-pawn in the center.

1. e4 c5 2. Nc3

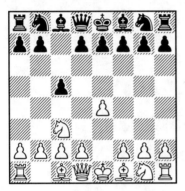

Diagram 460
After 2. Nc3

White's second move is flexible and the transpositions—the possibilities of slipping into other variations—can be tricky. Black doesn't know yet whether his opponent is heading for the Grand Prix attack with f4 and Bc4 or Bb5, or for the Closed Sicilian with g3 and Bg2. For that matter, White could still play Nf3 (or Nge2) and d4.

2. ... g6

Likewise, Black plays the flexible move that fits into his plan against all of the possibilities.

3. g3

Both 3. Nge2 Nc6 4. d4 cxd4 5. Nxd4 Bg7, and 3. Nf3 Bg7 (to avoid the Rossolimo—3. ... Nc6 4. Bb5) 4. d4 cxd4 5. Nxd4 Nc6 transpose to main lines.

Or if 3. d4 cxd4 4. Qxd4 Nf6, and then if 5. e5 (5. Bb5 a6) 5. ... Nc6 6. Qe3, 6. ... Ng4 gives

Black a good game—for example, 7. Qe2 d6!? ∓; or 7. Qg3 Ngxe5 8. f4! Nb4.

3. ... Bg7 4. Bg2 Nc6 5. d3 d6

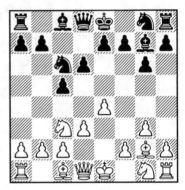

Diagram 461
After 5. ... d6

Here White has the choice of three main setups:

◆ Playing Nge2 and 0-0;
◆ Playing Be3 and Qd2, with the idea of castling long and launching an immediate attack against Black's kingside;
◆ Playing f4, Nf3 and 0-0.

A 6. Nge2 Nf6

Here 6. ... e6, with the idea of ... Nge7, is a reasonable alternative and a way to take a step off the most traveled path.

7. 0-0

Or, if 7. h3 0-0 8. Be3, Black plays 8. ... e5!, stopping d4. 9. 0-0 Nd4 10. Kh2 Nh5 11. Nd5 Be6 12. c3 Nxe2, and the game was soon drawn (Rublevsky—Gelfand, 2007).

7. ... 0–0 8. h3

Diagram 462
After 8. h3

White's plan is to throw a pawn storm at the kingside with f4 and g4, followed by f5 and g5. From e2 the knight can go to g3 or f4 to support the attack.

If instead 8. f4 immediately, then Black plays ... Bg4 with similar play to **C**, below.

8. ... Ne8!

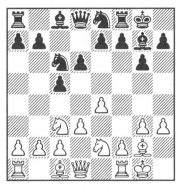

Diagram 463
After 8. ... Ne8!

9. Be3

Or White can try 9. f4 f5 10. Be3 Nd4 11. Rb1, with the idea of b4. But then Black coun-

ters with 11. ... a5!, using the strategy of containment. Now it's tough for White to come up with a reasonable plan. If 12. a4 Nc7 13. exf5 gxf5 14. Kh2 Rb8 15. Ng1 Bd7 16. Nf3 Bc6 17. Qd2 Qd7, we've reached the following position:

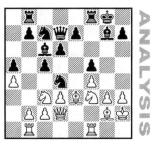

Diagram 464
After 17. ... Qd7

Black stands well, as in the game Smirin–Huzman, 2000.

9. ... Nd4

8. ... Ne8 is a multi-purpose move:

1. Black is ready to meet 9. f4 with the thematic ... f5!, which would stop White's attack;

2. Black meets 9. Be3 with ... Nd4!; he stops White from playing d4 & occupies a key central square.

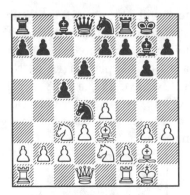

Diagram 465
After 9. ... Nd4

10. Qd2 Rb8 11. f4 f5 12. Nd1

White retreats his knight so that he can play c3, forcing Black's much better placed knight to give up his outpost on d4.

12. ... b5 13. c3 Nxe2+ 14. Qxe2 b4

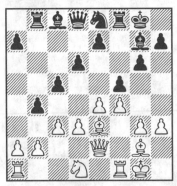

Diagram 466
After 14. ... b4

We've followed the game Sofronie–Motylev, 1999. Black has a promising position.

Black's fianchettoed bishop, aided by his queenside pawns,

puts pressure on the dark squares. At the same time, his pawn on f5 pressures e4, making it difficult for White to play d4 to take the heat off c3.

B. 6. Be3

Diagram 467
After 6. Be3

6. ... Nf6

Another plan is 6. ... e6, followed by ... Nge7.

7. h3

White prevents ... Ng4.

7. ... 0–0 8. Qd2

White prepares Bh6—to pin and trade off Black's important bishop at the right moment—and 0-0-0. The idea is a direct attack, first with a pawn storm and then with pieces.

Instead, 8. f4 Nd4 (or 8. ... e5!—e.g., 9. Nf3 Nh5, or 9. Nge2 Nd4) 9. Nge2 Ne8 10. Qd2 f5 11. 0–0 transposes to **A**, above. If 8. Nge2, then 8. ... e5! 9. 0-0 Nd4 transposes to Rublevsky—Gelfand, 2007 (see page 194, end of right-hand column).

8. ... Nd4!

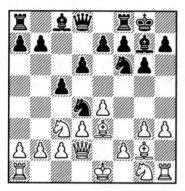

Diagram 468
After 8. ... Nd4!

A thematic move in all Closed Sicilian positions: Black takes over the center and stops White from getting in Bh6, since then … Bxh6 and Qxh6 would leave the c2-pawn unguarded.

9. Nd1

As in line **A**, White feels compelled to regroup to be able to play c3 to oust Black's central knight from his outpost.

9. ... e5!

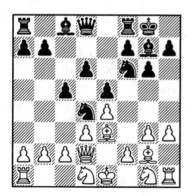

Diagram 469
After 9. ... e5!

Another move central to Black's strategy in this line. The move:

1. Stops White, after his intended c3, from playing d4;

2. Anticipates the exchange of dark-square bishops and improves Black's pawn structure, blocking White's light-square bishop on g2.

10. c3 Nc6 11. Ne2

Black gets a great position after 11. Bh6.

11. ... b6

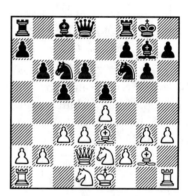

Diagram 470
After 11. ... b6

Black bolsters his pawn on c5 and intends … d5. He stands well—for example: 12. f4 d5! 13. fxe5 (13. 0–0 dxe4 14. dxe4 Qxd2 15. Bxd2 Ba6 16. Re1 Rad8

Diagram 471
After 16. ... Rad8

and Black is better) 13. ... Nxe5

Diagram 472
After 13. ... Nxe5

14. exd5 Nxd5, and now, in a worse position, White's aggressive 15. c4? loses to 15. ... Nxe3 16. Bxa8? Nxd3+.

Diagram 473
After 16. ... Nxd3+

This position, with White's king smothered by his queen and all four knights, seems as if it must come from a problemist's impractical fantasies rather than

from the hurly-burly of a real master game! White is forced to give up his queen.

By the way, notice how similar a role the knights play in the Accelerated Dragon's main line. (See Chapter 5.)

C. 6. f4 Nf6

Once again, the now-familiar ... e6 is okay here too.

7. Nf3 Bg4!

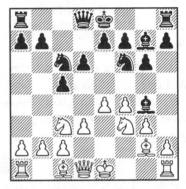

Diagram 474
After 7. ... Bg4!

This is Dzindzi's preference. Black's plan is to advance his queenside pawns and establish control over the dark squares in the center. To this end, he eliminates White's knight on f3, increasing the power of Black's bishop on g7, exchanging his only passive piece (which would be a burden after White plays f5).

8. 0–0 0–0 9. h3 Bxf3 10. Qxf3 Rb8 11. Be3

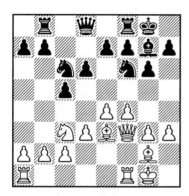

Diagram 475
After 11. Be3

11. ... Nd7

If 11. ... b5? now, White plays 12. e5, and both Black knights hang.

12. a4

White tries to prevent the move Black prepares, ... b5.

12. ... a6

13. g4 Nd4!

Without a passive bishop on c8, Black doesn't fear White's f5. Moreover, the pawn-push would further weaken White's dark squares. In the meantime, the fruit on the queenside is getting ripe!

14. Qf2

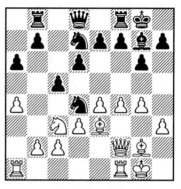

Diagram 476
After 14. Qf2

14. ... b5 15. axb5 axb5

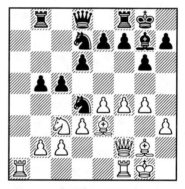

Diagram 477
After 15. ... axb5

Black's plan is to play ... b4 and put pressure on White's queenside. Meanwhile, White has difficulties making serious progress on the kingside—for example: 16. f5 b4 17. Nd5 Nf6! (not 17. ... e6 18. f6!) 18. Nxf6+ Bxf6 19. g5 Be5

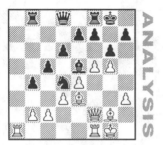

Diagram 478
After 19. ... Be5

Diagram 480
After 23. ... Re8

20. c3? Bg3!. But even the stronger 20. Kh1—preparing c3—favors Black: 20. ... Nb5 21. Rab1 Ra8.

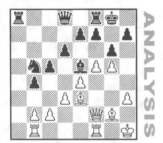

Diagram 479
After 21. ... Ra8

Black has a promising plan —queenside pressure. White's attack is illusory—22. f6 exf6 23. gxf6 Re8,

planning to play ... Re6.

Let's go back to Diagram 478 to see how Black reacts to the hasty 20. f6?!:

Diagram 481
After 20. f6?!

20. ... exf6 21. gxf6 Qxf6! 22. Qxf6 Bxf6 23. Rxf6 Nxc2!, winning material.

Summary:

Black has very effective counterpunches to all of White's plans:

If White plays f4 and Nf3, Black plays ... Bg4! and trades his bishop for the knight, enabling him to gain full control of d4. His light-square bishop then no longer plays a passive role on the queenside (after White follows up with f4-f5). If White plays an early Be3 and Qd2, Black must play a timely ... Nd4! and ... e5!, securing full control over d4. If White plays h3, preventing ... Bg4, Black continues with his queenside play. This time, however, he prepares a just-in-time ... f5! to stop White's kingside attack.

Vassily Smyslov and Boris Spassky–
Great Contributors to the Closed Sicilian

Vassily Smyslov, seventh world champion

Boris Spassky, tenth world champion

Chapter 16: The Closed Sicilian—2. Nc3 followed by g3
Memory Markers!

Diagram 482
After 9. ... Nc7

Diagram 483
After 9. Nd1

MARKER 1

MARKER 2

Chapter 16: The Closed Sicilian—2. Nc3 followed by g3
Solutions to Memory Markers!

No. 1　　**10. d4! ±**. The Black knight has taken several moves to get onto the c7-square, which in this position is less than wonderful. Thus Black should have played 9. ... Nd4!, with a good game. See page 195.

No. 2　　**9. ... e5!**. White's posture with the Qd2/Be3 battery is aimed at exchanging dark-square bishops, so Black's space-grabbing move is completely justified. See page 197.

Chapter 17: Grand Prix Attack—And a Grander Defense
Some Important Points to Look For

White's search for better chances against the Sicilian have led to yet another offshoot, the tricky Grand Prix Attack. This short chapter gives you the antidotes.

◆ White avoids Nc3–and pays a price! See Diagram 486.

◆ Black will restrict White's c4-bishop with 5. ... e6. See Diagram 488.

◆ Capturing on e6 with the d-pawn is more solid. See Diagram 496.

◆ On 5. Bb5, Black moves his knight to d4. See Diagram 499.

Outline of Variations

1. e4 c5. *(204)*

    A 2. f4 g6 3. Nf3 Bg7 *(205)* **[B21]**
        A1 4. Bc4 e6 5. d4 d5! 6. Bb5+ Bd7!
        (206)
        A2 4. c3 Nc6 5. d4 cxd4 6. cxd4 d5!
        (206)
    B 2. Nc3 g6 3. f4 Bg7 4. Nf3 Nc6 *(206)*
    [B23]
        B1 5. Bc4 e6 *(206)*
            B1a 6. 0-0 Nge7 *(207)*
                B1a1 7. e5 d5 8. exd6 Qxd6
                9. Ne4 Qc7 *(207)*
                B1a2 7. d3 d5 8. Bb3 0-0
                9. Qe1 Na5 10. Qh4 *(208)*
            B1b 6. f5 Nge7 7. fxe6 dxe6
            8. 0-0 0-0 9. d3 Na5
            10. Bb3 Nxb3 11. axb3 e5 *(209)*

    B2 5. Bb5 Nd4 *(209)*
        B2a 6. Bd3 d6 7. Nxd4 cxd4
        8. Ne2 Nf6 *(210)*
            B2a1 9. Bb5+ Bd7 10. Bxd7+
            Qxd7 11. d3 e5 12. 0 0 0-0
            13. f5 *(211)*
            B2a2 9. Nxd4 Nxe4 10. Bxe4
            Bxd4 11. c3 Bg7
            12. Qf3 Qb6 *(211)*
            B2a3 9. c3 dxc3 10. dxc3 0-0
            11. 0-0 b5!? *(212)*
        B2b 6. 0-0 e6 7. d3 Ne7 8. Nxd4
        cxd4 9. Ne2 0-0 10. Ba4 *(213)*

Chapter 17
Grand Prix Attack
And a Grander Defense

The Grand Prix is a popular choice against the Sicilian for players looking for an aggressive method that doesn't give away pawns and that may catch Black off guard. White plays f4 and uses the f-pawn to break open lines against Black's king.

1. e4 c5

White has two ways to play the Grand Prix attack on the second move: f4 and Nc3. White chooses 2. f4 to avoid the main lines of the other, more common move. But we recommend a way of playing for Black that will force White to transpose to the main 2. Nc3 lines or accept a disadvantage.

A. 2. f4

Diagram 484
After 2. f4

2. ... g6 3. Nf3 Bg7

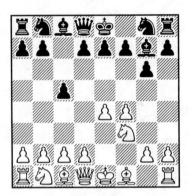

Diagram 485
After 3. ... Bg7

Now White should play 4. Nc3 and transpose into **B**, below. His attempt to avoid the main line with either 4. Bc4 or 4. c3 doesn't turn out well. For example:

A1 4. Bc4 e6 5. d4 d5!

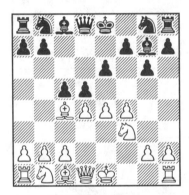

Diagram 486
After 5. ... d5!

6. Bb5+ Bd7!

After the light-squared bishops are traded off, White's plan of playing e5 is not dangerous.

A2 4. c3 Nc6 5. d4 cxd4 6. cxd4 d5!

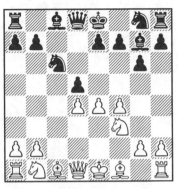

Diagram 487
After 6. ... d5!

Now if 7. e5, Black answers with 7. ... Bg4, and White has problems guarding his d-pawn in light of the coming ... Nh6-f5.

B 2. Nc3 g6 3. f4 Bg7 4. Nf3 Nc6

Here again White has two main moves: 5. Bc4 and 5. Bb5.

B1 5. Bc4

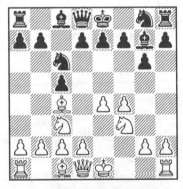

Diagram 488
After 5. Bc4

White's idea is to start an immediate attack on the kingside with f5.

5. ... e6

Here White has two main moves: 6. 0–0 and 6. f5.

B1a 6. 0–0

White finishes his development.

6. ... Nge7

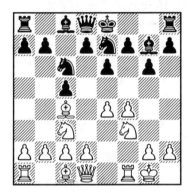

Diagram 489
After 6. ... Nge7

But now it's much harder for White to play f5. White can try 7. e5 or 7. d3.

B1a1 7. e5 d5

Now if 8. Be2, Black has 8. ... f6!, freeing his bishop.

8. exd6

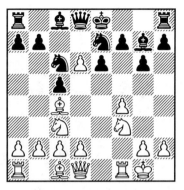

Diagram 490
After 8. exd6

8. ... Qxd6 9. Ne4 Qc7

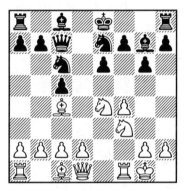

Diagram 491
After 9. ... Qc7

10. d3

If 10. Nxc5?, then 10. ... Nd4.

10. ... b6

Black will fianchetto his light-square bishop and achieve a sound and flexible position.

BLACK WILL FIANCHETTO HIS LIGHT-SQUARE BISHOP AND ACHIEVE A SOUND AND FLEXIBLE POSITION.

B1a2 7. d3

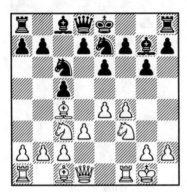

Diagram 492
After 7. d3

7. ... d5 8. Bb3 0–0 9. Qe1

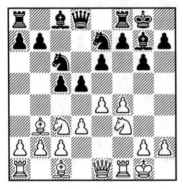

Diagram 493
After 9. Qe1

White intends to bring the queen to the kingside.

9. ... Na5 10. Qh4

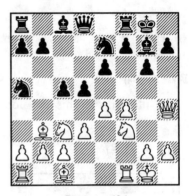

Diagram 494
After 10. Qh4

10. ... Nec6

Black welcomes the exchange of queens because his chances in the endgame are better.

11. Qf2

Or 11. Qxd8 Rxd8 12. exd5 Nxb3 13. axb3 exd5 ∓.

11. ... b6

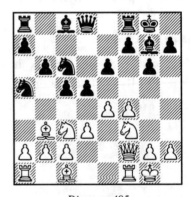

Diagram 495
After 11. ... b6

The game we're following is Carlier–Rogers, 1991. Black stands at least equal due to his control of d4.

Black welcomes the exchange of queens.

B1b 6. f5 Nge7 7. fxe6 dxe6

Diagram 496
After 7. ... dxe6

This move, rather than 7. ... fxe6, leads to solid play.

8. 0–0 0–0 9. d3 Na5 10. Bb3 Nxb3 11. axb3 e5

Diagram 497
After 11. ... e5

Black will put his light-square bishop on e6.

12. Qe1 f6 13. Qh4 Be6 14. Bh6 Nc6 15. Bxg7 Kxg7

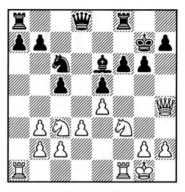

Diagram 498
After 15. ... Kxg7

Black has no problems (Gasanov–Selin, 2002.)

Now let's go back to White's other fifth-move choice:

B2 5. Bb5

Diagram 499
After 5. Bb5

White picks a more positional approach. He is ready to trade on c6 and play against Black's doubled pawns.

5. ... Nd4

Here White has two main choices: 6. Bd3 and the stronger 6. 0–0. Others turn out badly for White—for example: 6. a4 Nf6!

Diagram 500
After 6. ... Nf6!

7. e5 Nh5 8. Nxd4 cxd4 9. Ne2 a6.

Diagram 501
After 9. ... a6

Black's idea is to play ... d6, attacking e5 while preventing g4.

Also in Black's favor is 6. Nxd4 cxd4

Diagram 502
After 6. ... cxd4

7. Ne2 Qb6 8. Bd3 d5! 9. e5 f6!

Diagram 503
After 9. ... f6!

10. c4 fxe5∓ (Romanishin–Sisniega, 1985).

B2a 6. Bd3

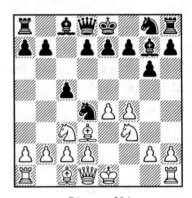

Diagram 504
After 6. Bd3

6. ... d6 7. Nxd4 cxd4 8. Ne2 Nf6

Diagram 505
After 8. ... Nf6

Now White has three main tries: 9. Bb5+, 9. Nxd4 and 9. c3.

B2a1 9. Bb5+

The bishop goes back to its first choice of squares.

9. ... Bd7 10. Bxd7+ Qxd7 11. d3 e5 12. 0–0 0–0 13. f5

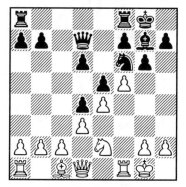

Diagram 506
After 13. f5

13. ... d5! 14. Ng3 dxe4 15. dxe4 Rac8 16. Bg5 h6

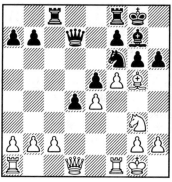

Diagram 507
After 16. ... h6

Black has good play.

B2a2 9. Nxd4

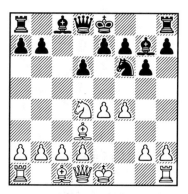

Diagram 508
After 9. Nxd4

9. ... Nxe4 10. Bxe4 Bxd4 11. c3 Bg7 12. Qf3 Qb6

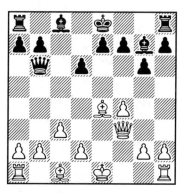

Diagram 509
After 12. ... Qb6

Black's queen move protects the b7-pawn while preventing White from castling. (The alternative, 12. ... 0–0 is interesting but unnecessarily risky.)

Black stands better—for example, 13. d4 0-0, ready to meet 14. 0-0 with 14. ... e5. If 14. f5, then Black has the thematic 14. ... gxf5 (or 14. ... Bxf5)

Diagram 510
After 14. ... gxf5

15. Bxf5 Bxf5 16. Qxf5 e6!,

Diagram 511
After 16. ... e6!

followed by ... e5. Black has better development and an edge.

B2a3 9. c3

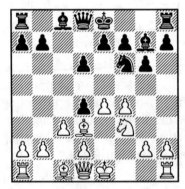

Diagram 512
After 9. c3

9. ... dxc3 10. dxc3 0-0 11. 0-0 b5!?

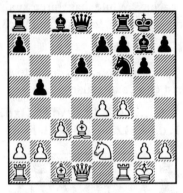

Diagram 513
After 11. ... b5!?

Or Black can choose, rather than action on the wing, more solid play in the center:

11. ... e5!

Diagram 514
After 11. ... e5!

12. h3 (or 12. Qe1 exf4 13. Rxf4 Re8 14. Ng3 d5!) 12. ... d5! 13. Ng3 Qb6+ 14. Kh1

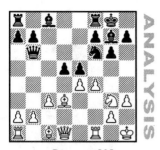

Diagram 515
After 14. Kh1

14. ... exf4 15. Rxf4 Re8, and Black is better and more harmoniously developed, as in the game Guidarelli–Bu Xiangzhi, 2004.

After 11. ... b5!?, Black's idea is to play ... Bb7 and put pressure on White's e-pawn—for example: 12. Ng3 (12. Bxb5? Qb6+) 12. ... Bb7 13. Qe2 h5, threatening ... h4—and sometimes the kamikaze-pawn will travel all the way to h3!

Diagram 516
After 13. ... h5

B2b. 6. 0-0 e6

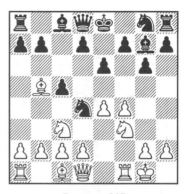

Diagram 517
After 6. ... e6

Black continues his development and keeps control of the d4-outpost.

7. d3

After 7. e5 a6 8. Bd3 Nxf3+ 9. Qxf3

Diagram 518
After 9. Qxf3

9. ... d5, Black gets a comfortable position, as in the game Plaskett–Pedersen, 1998: 10. exd6 Qxd6 11. b3 Nf6 12. Bb2 0–0 13. Na4 Nd7 = .

Diagram 519
After 13. ... Nd7=

7. ... Ne7

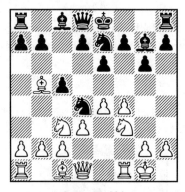

Diagram 520
After 7. ... Ne7

8. Nxd4 cxd4 9. Ne2 0–0 10. Ba4

Diagram 521
After 10. Ba4

10. ... d5 11. e5 f6 12. exf6 Bxf6 13. Bb3

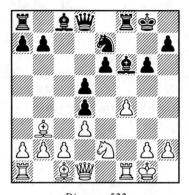

Diagram 522
After 13. Bb3

There are chances for both sides (Perelshteyn–Battsetseg, 2003).

Summary:

   The Grand Prix Attack can be a dangerous weapon in the hands of a good attacking player. But if you're well-prepared, you have little to worry about. If White puts his bishop on c4, you should restrict it with ... e6 and, if possible, attack with ... d5. Play ... Nd4 if White's bishop comes to b5. Try to keep your g7-bishop active—if necessary, by playing ... f6 to exchange White's e5-pawn.

Chapter 17: The Grand Prix Attack—And a Grander Defense
Memory Markers!

Diagram 523
After 10. Nxc5

Diagram 524
After 9. ... 0-0

Chapter 17: The Grand Prix Attack—And a Grander Defense
Solutions to Memory Markers!

No. 1   **10. ... Nd4,** and Black wins. See page 207.

No. 2   **10. g4,** winning a piece. See page 210.

Ken Smith

Smith, of Smith-Morra Gambit fame,
was also a championship poker player.

Chapter 18: Alapin Variation—2. c3 and the Smith-Morra Gambit
Some Important Points to Look For

This brief chapter gives you a rare but effective line that counters two important tries, the Alapin and the Smith-Morra. Best of all, it uses the ideas you've already learned!

◆ Just in time! See Diagram 527.

◆ Black pieces dominate the board.
   See Diagram 536.

◆ A good line for Black from the Panov–Botvinnik Caro-Kann.
   See Diagram 540.

◆ Black controls key squares.
   See Diagram 551.

Outline of Variations

1. e4 c5 2. c3 g6 3. d4 cxd4 4. cxd4 d5 *(218)* **[B22]**

    A 5. e5 Bg7 6. Nc3 Nc6 7. Bb5 f6 *(220)*

        A1 8. exf6 exf6 9. Nge2 Be6 10. Nf4 Bf7 11. 0-0 Nge7 *(220)*

        A2 8. f4 Nh6 9. Nf3 Bg4 10. Be3 0-0 11. 0-0 Nf5! *(222)*

    B 5. cxd5 Nf6 *(223)*

        B1 6. Bb5+ Nbd7 7. Nc3 Bg7 8. d6 0-0 *(223)* [8. ... exd6—p. 223]

        B2 6. Nc3 Nxd5 7. Bc4 Nb6 8. Bb3 Bg7 9. Nf3 0-0 *(224)*

            B2a 10. h3 Nc6 11. Be3 Na5 *(225)*

                B2a1 12. 0-0 Nxb3 13. axb3 Be6 *(225)*

                B2a2 12. Bc2 Nac4 13. Bc1 Be6 *(226)*

            B2b 10. 0-0 Nc6 11. d5 Na5 12. Re1 Bg4 *(226)*

Chapter 18
Alapin Variation
2. c3 and the Smith-Morra Gambit

1. e4 c5 2. c3

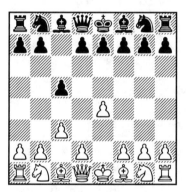

Diagram 525
After 2. c3

White's idea is to take control of the center with d4.

2. ... g6

To cut down on your study time, we concentrate on a line in which you develop your bishop to g7. Here the ideas of counterplay in the center are similar to those in the Hyper-Accelerated Dragon, which we're already prepared to play (See Chapter 9). Besides, these lines will be less well-known to your opponent than the more common 2. ... d5 and 2. ... Nf6.

The same system can be used (reaching exactly the same positions) against Alapin's pugnacious twin, the Smith-Morra Gambit. Simply meet 2. d4 with 2. ... cxd4 and 3. c3 with 3. ... g6, and after 4. cxd4 d5, you'll get Diagram 527. For 4. Bc4, see the next page. (For White, 4. Qxd4 is an inferior version of our Chapter 8, where instead of c3, Nf3 was played.)

Of course, there are other ways to fight the Smith-Morra, which is viewed as only semi-correct. After 2. d4 cxd4 3. c3 dxc3!, it's White who should struggle for equality.

3. d4 cxd4 4. cxd4

White can instead play 4. Bc4, still hoping for a true Smith-Morra. Besides accepting the gambit, Black has two other choices. He can opt for a positional approach with 4. ... d3; or he can play the sharp 4. ... Nf6, and after 5. e5, counter-attack with 5. ... d5.

Diagram 526
After 5. ... d5

4. ... d5

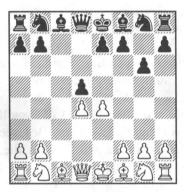

Diagram 527
After 4. ... d5

Here White has two main moves: 5. e5 and 5. exd5.

If 5. Nc3, then 5. ... dxe4 6. Bc4 Nf6 7. Qb3 e6 8. d5 exd5 9. Nxd5 Bg7

Diagram 528
After 9. ... Bg7

Zhigalko—Guseinov, 2008, continued: 10. Bg5 0-0 11. Rd1 Nbd7 12. Ne2 h6! 13. Nxf6+ Bxf6 14. Bxh6, draw.

A 5. e5 Bg7 6. Nc3

Developing the other knight with 6. Nf3 transposes to 2. Nf3 and 3. c3 lines. (See Chapter 9.)

6. ... Nc6 7. Bb5 f6

Diagram 529
After 7. ... f6

Black immediately undermines White's center. The first player has two main choices: 8. exf6 and 8. f4.

A1 8. exf6 exf6 9. Nge2 Be6 10. Nf4 Bf7 11. 0–0 Nge7

Diagram 530
After 11. ... Nge7

The game is about even—for example:

12. Bxc6+ bxc6 13. Na4 0–0 14. Nc5

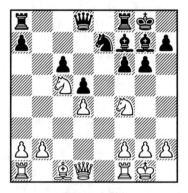

Diagram 531
After 14. Nc5

14. ... Qc8

White's outpost on c5 is matched by Black's bishop pair.

15. Re1 Re8 16. Qd3 g5!

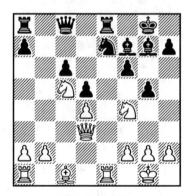

Diagram 532
After 16. ... g5!

17. Ne2

If 17. Nfe6?, then 17. ... Ng6, and White is pinned along the e-file.

17. ... Bg6 18. Qc3 Nf5

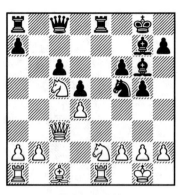

Diagram 533
After 18. ... Nf5

The game Pavasovic—Zelcic, 2002, continued: 19. Bd2 Nd6 20. Be3 Ne4 21. Nxe4 Rxe4 22. Rac1 Re6 23. Qd2 Qa6,

Diagram 534
After 23. ... Qa6

with chances for both sides.

A2 8. f4

Diagram 535
After 8. f4

Shoring up the stone wall against the g7-bishop.

8. ... Nh6 9. Nf3 Bg4 10. Be3 0–0 11. 0–0 Nf5!

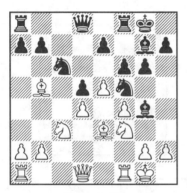

Diagram 536
After 11. ... Nf5!

Black's pieces have taken all the key squares. After the mandatory 12. Qd2, Black can play 12. ... Qb6, forcing 13. Bxc6 bxc6, with a somewhat better game. Black, however, can choose the even stronger 12. ... Rc8—for example, 13. Kh1 (to prepare a retreat for the bishop)

13. ... a6 14. Ba4?! Na5!.

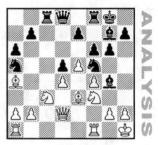

Diagram 537
After 14. ... Na5!

In the game Tzermiadinos –Ehlvest, 2002, Black continued with 12. ... fxe5?. And White quickly returned the favor. We offer the game because it's an interesting tactical fight.

13. Bxc6?

This is a bad intermezzo, or in-between, move. Better is 13. Nxe5!, when White is fine.

Diagram 538
After 13. Bxc6?

13. ... Nxe3! 14. Qxe3 exf4

On the other hand, Black plays a nice intermezzo!

15. Bxd5+ Qxd5 16. Qxf4 Qd7!

Winning a pawn.

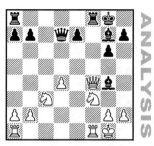

Diagram 539
After 16. ... Qd7!

B 5. exd5 Nf6

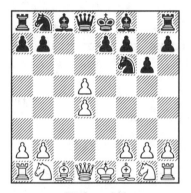

Diagram 540
After 5. ... Nf6

White has 6. Bb5+ and 6. Nc3.

B1 6. Bb5+ Nbd7 7. Nc3 Bg7 8. d6!

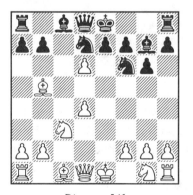

Diagram 541
After 8. d6!

In our first edition, we suggested 8. ... exd6 9. Qe2+ Kf8, followed by 10. Nf3 (or 10. Bc4 Nb6 11. Bb3 Qe7 12. Bf4 Bg4!—improving over 12. ... Qxe2 13. Ngxe2 ±; if 13. f3, Be6) 10. ... Nb6 11. 0-0 h6 12. Bf4

Diagram 542
After 12. Bf4

12. .... Be6 13. Rfe1 Kg8, preparing 14. ... Kh7. But Lev's correspondent Canadian Eric Van Dusen noted that 14. Bd3 prevents Kh7, writing that "Black appears to be in trouble."

How can Black's play be improved? First, in the line above, Black should play 12. ... Bf5. (White may still be a bit better here.)

Second, Dzindzi has rehabilitated the line 9. ... Qe7 10. Bf4 Qxe2+ 11. Be2 Ke7, which was deemed bad for Black after 12. Bf3.

Diagram 543
After 12. Bf3

The salvation is in the audacious pawn sac 12. ... Nb6 13. Nge2 Bg4!—a line worth studying.

And our current main line employs a pawn sacrifice even earlier. Let's continue from Diagram 541.

8. ... 0-0 9. dxe7 Qxe7+ 10. Nge2 a6

Diagram 544
After 10. ... a6

The position is balanced—for example: 11. Bd3 (11. Bxd7 Qxd7 12. Bf4 b5 13. Be5 Bb7 14. 0-0 Rfe8 15. Qb3 Nd5 16. Bxg7 Kxg7, when Black's powerful bishop and active pieces fully compensate for his

pawn minus) 11. ... b5 12. 0-0 Bb7 13. Re1 Rfe8 14. Bf4

Diagram 545
After 14. Bf4

14. ... Nh5! **TN**, with a comforable game for Black—e.g., 15. Be3 b4 16. Na4 Qd6 17. Ng3 (17. Rc1? Qd5-+) 17. ... Nf4 18. Bf1 Nd5= (Rotstein—Burmakin, 2008).

B2 6. Nc3 Nxd5

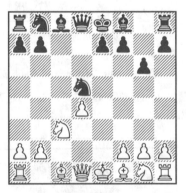

Diagram 546
After 6. ... Nxd5

We've reached a position, good for Black, from the Panov-Botvinnik Attack of the Caro-Kann: 1. e4 c6 2. d4 d5 3. exd5 cxd5 4. c4 Nf6 5. Nc3 g6, when White has played 6. cxd5 and Black has recaptured with his knight. White's 6. cxd5 isn't as dangerous as 6. Qb3 and allows Black to equalize, as we'll show.

7. Bc4

7. Bb5+ is met by 7. ... Bd7!; if 7. Qb3, then 7. ... Nb6, e.g. 8. Nf3 Bg7 9. Bb5+ Bd7 10. Ne5 0-0 11. Nxd7

Diagram 547
After 11. Nxd7

11. ... N6xd7! (the b8-knight is destined for the c6-square).

7. ... Nb6

7. ... Nxc3? 8. Qb3!

8. Bb3 Bg7 9. Nf3

Or 9. Be3 Nc6 10. d5 Ne5!, with a good game.

9. ... 0-0

Diagram 548
After 9. ... 0-0

Now White can play either 10. h3 (preventing the pin) or he can castle.

B2a 10. h3 Nc6 11. Be3 Na5

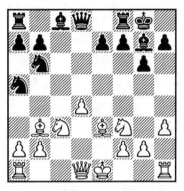

Diagram 549
After 11. ... Na5

B2a1 12. 0-0 Nxb3 13. axb3

Or 13. Qxb3 Be6.

13. ... Be6

With advantage to Black.

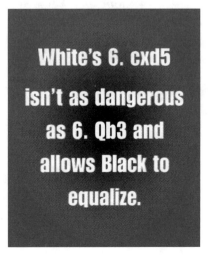

White's 6. cxd5 isn't as dangerous as 6. Qb3 and allows Black to equalize.

B2a2 12. Bc2 Nac4

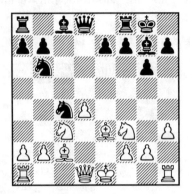

Diagram 550
After 12. ... Nac4

**13. Bc1 Be6 14. 0–0 Rc8
15. Re1 Bd5 16. Nxd5 Nxd5**

Diagram 551
After 16. ... Nxd5

Black stands better due to his control of key squares.

B2b. 10. 0-0 Nc6 11. d5 Na5
12. Re1 Bg4

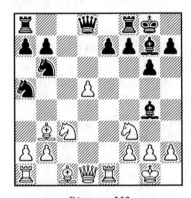

Diagram 552
After 12. ... Bg4

Black has finished his development and stands well. After 13. h3 Bxf3 14. Qxf3 Re8, the game Lein–Seirawan, 2003, continued: 15. Bg5 Nxb3 16. axb3.

Diagram 553
After 16. axb3

Here Black simplified to the rook endgame—up a pawn: 16. ... Bxc3 17. bxc3 Qxd5 18. Qxd5 Nxd5 19. c4 f6!

Diagram 554
After 19. ... f6!

20. cxd5 fxg5, when Black is a pawn ahead, but it's hard for him to win the game: 21. Rac1 b5 22. b4 Kf7 23. Rc7 Rad8 24. Re5. Here the game finished in a draw after a three-fold repitition: 24. ... Kf6 25. Re6+ Kf7 26. Re5 Kf6.

In a recent game (Mamedy-arov—Kamsky, 2008), White protected the d5-pawn with 15. Rd1, followed by ... Nxb3 16. axb3 Nc8!=.

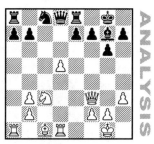

Diagram 555
After 16. ... Nc8!

Black transfers his knight to d6 and stands well: 17. h4 Nd6 18. h5 Qb6 19. h6 Bh8 20. Ne4 Nxe4 21. Qxe4 Qxb3.

Summary:
   In this chapter, we offer a rarely used method to counter both the Alapin and the Smith-Morra, capitalizing on our already acquired repertoire. Black fianchettoes his king's bishop and challenges the just-created e4/d4 center with ... d5!, achieving a good game after each of White's replies.

Simon Alapin

Chapter 18: The Alapin Variation—2. c3 and the Smith-Morra Gambit
Memory Markers!

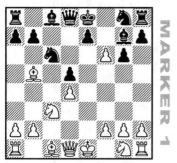

Diagram 556
After 8. exf6

Diagram 557
After 7. ... Nxc3

Chapter 18: The Alapin Variation—2. c3 and the Smith-Morra Gambit
Solutions to Memory Markers!

No. 1   **8. ... exf6,** keeping the pawns intact. See page 220.

No. 2   **8. Qb3,** a typical response to Black's ill-timed capture. See page 225.

Chapter 19: Wing Gambit and 2. b3
Some Important Points to Look For

White wants to finish Black before, as Frank Marshall puts it, he "can light his pipe." But by countering in the center, Black will enjoy himself, even in the non-smoking section.

◆ Black strikes back in the center. See Diagram 560.

◆ Tactical defense! See Diagram 567.

◆ Yet another blow in the center. See Diagram 569.

◆ White has no compensation for his lost pawn. See Diagram 577.

Outline of Variations

1. e4 c5 2. b4 cxb4 *(230)* [B20]
    A 3. a3 d5 4. exd5 Qxd5 5. Nf3 e5 6. axb4 Bxb4 7. c3 Bc5 8. Na3 Nf6 9. Bc4 *(232)*
    B 3. d4 d5! *(235)*
        B1 4. exd5 Qxd5 5. Nf3 Nc6 6. c4 bxc3 7. Nxc3 Qa5 *(235)*
        B2 4. e5 Nc6 5. Nf3 Bg4 6. Bb2 e6 *(236)*

Chapter 19
Wing Gambit and 2. b3

1. e4 c5 2. b4

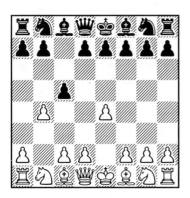

Diagram 558
After 2. b4

The Wing Gambit was the

darling of the swash-buckling American champion Frank Marshall in the early days of Sicilian theory. Although rare on the GM level, the gambit can crop up at amateur levels. (Anyone who has just read or re-read the delightful *Marshall's Best Games of Chess* finds it hard to resist trying to emulate the quick kills this idea compiled before defensive technique was perfected.)

White's idea is to deflect Black's c-pawn from the center with a "wing" (flank) pawn and then play d4. An unprepared defender can succumb to a flashy attack. With good play, however, Black finishes his development easily and ends up with an extra pawn.

Melting the Wax

With the Wing Gambit, White tries to soar above common sense. We're reminded of the Greek legend of Daedalus and his son Icarus. To escape from the labyrinth, which they had been commissioned to construct to house the monstrous Minotaur, the father and son donned feather wings held together with wax. The plan worked well until the impetuous Icarus failed to heed his father's warning. The young daredevil flew too close to the sun, melting the wax, and plummeted to his death in the ocean below.

However, a more modest "Wing Play" (2. b3) doesn't soar and isn't dangerous for Black either. He has several solid schemes to choose from, for example: 2. ... Nc6 3. Bb2 e5 4. Bb5 Nge7!,

Diagram 559
After 4. ... Nge7!

followed by ... g6 and ... Bg7.

2. ... cxb4

Here White has two main moves, 3. a3 and 3. d4.

A 3. a3 d5!

Diagram 560
After 3. ... d5!

Black strikes back in the center. The axiom is time-tested: when confronted with a demonstration on the wing, counter in the center!

4. exd5 Qxd5 5. Nf3

If 5. axb4?, Black wins material with 5. ... Qe5+. If 5. Bb2, then 5. ... e5!.

5. ... e5 6. axb4 Bxb4

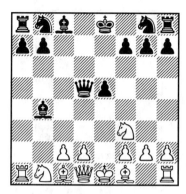

Diagram 561
After 6. ... Bxb4

7. c3

After 7. Na3, Black can play the simple 7. ... Bxa3 8. Bxa3 Nc6.

Diagram 562
After 8. ... Nc6

(Black is ready to finish his development with ... Nge7 and ... 0-0.) 9. c4!? Qd8

Diagram 563
After 9. ... Qd8

10. Qb1 Nge7 11. Bd3 f5, with an equal game. There could follow 12. Bxe7 Qxe7 13. Bxf5 Bxf5 14. Qxf5 Qf7

Diagram 564
After 14. ... Qf7

(Bronstein–Benko, 1949).

The game is even.

7. ... Bc5

THE AXIOM IS TIME TESTED: WHEN CONFRONTED WITH A DEMONSTRATION ON THE WING, COUNTER IN THE CENTER!

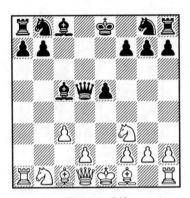

Diagram 565
After 7. ... Bc5

8. Na3 Nf6 9. Bc4

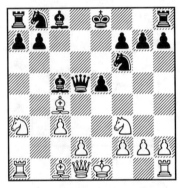

Diagram 566
After 9. Bc4

Black meets 9. Nb5 with 9. ... 0-0 10. Nc7 Bxf2+! 11. Kxf2 Qc5+.

Diagram 567
After 11. ... Qc5+

9. ... Qe4+ 10. Be2 0-0 11. Nb5 Na6

Diagram 568
After 11. ... Na6

Black easily finishes his development and keeps the extra pawn as in the game Porramaa –Kask, 1987.

BLACK EASILY FINISHES HIS DEVELOPMENT AND KEEPS THE EXTRA PAWN.

B. 3. d4 d5!

Diagram 569
After 3. ... d5!

Now White has two moves, 4. exd5 and 4. e5.

B1. 4. exd5 Qxd5

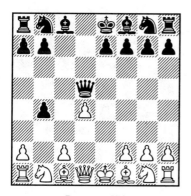

Diagram 570
After 4. ... Qxd5

5. Nf3   Nc6   6. c4   bxc3
7. Nxc3 Qa5

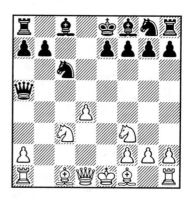

Diagram 571
After 7. ... Qa5

8. d5

Or 8. Bd2 e6 9. Nb5 (9. Be2 Bb4) 9. ... Qd8! and Black is better.

Diagram 572
After 9. ... Qd8!

8. ... e6

8. ... Qxc3+ 9. Bd2 Qf6 10. dxc6 gives White an uncomfortable advantage in development.

Diagram 573
After 10. dxc6

9. dxc6 Bb4

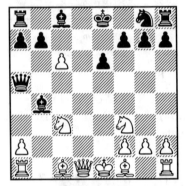

Diagram 574
After 9. ... Bb4

10. Bd2

If 10. cxb7, then 10. ... Bxb7
11. Bb5+? Qxb5.

10. ... Bxc3

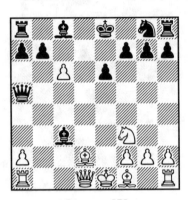

Diagram 575
After 10. ... Bxc3

White has insufficient compensation for the pawn.

B2. 4. e5 Nc6

Diagram 576
After 4. ... Nc6

5. Nf3

Or 5. a3 Qb6 6. Be3 Bf5.

5. ... Bg4 6. Bb2 e6

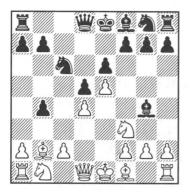

Diagram 577
After 6. ... e6

Black is up a pawn with a better position. The game Manolov–V. Georgiev, 1999, continued: 7. Nbd2 Nge7 8. Bd3

Nc8 9. 0-0 Nb6 10. Rb1 Be7 11. h3 Bh5.

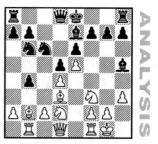

Diagram 578
After 11. ... Bh5

Black's idea is to play ... Bg6. Black is clearly better.

Summary:

White's quick-kill intentions are thwarted when Black follows the classic injunction to answer an attack on the flank with a demonstration in the center. After 3. ... d5!, Black emerges with either an easy equality (as in the Bronstein–Benko line) or a better game.

Chapter 19: Wing Gambit and 2. b3

Memory Markers!

MARKER 1

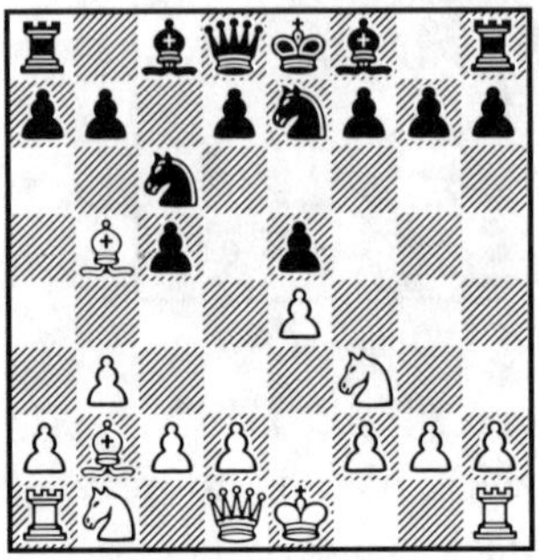

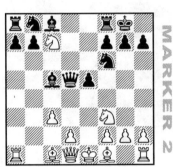

Diagram 579
After 5. Nf3

MARKER 2

Diagram 580
After 10. Nc7

MARKER 3

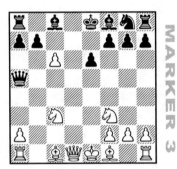

Diagram 581
After 9. dxc6

MARKER 4

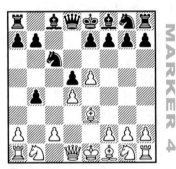

Diagram 582
After 5. Be3

Chapter 19: Wing Gambit and 2. b3

Solutions to Memory Markers!

No. 1 **5. ... d6**, followed by ... g6. See page 232.

No. 2 **10. ... Bxf2+ 11. Kxf2** (11. Ke2 Qc4+) **11. ... Qc5+**. See page 234.

No. 3 **9. ... Bb4!**. See page 236.

No. 4 **5. ... Bf5**, and only then 6. ... e6. See page 236.

PART THREE

DEFENDING AGAINST 1. d4

Chapter 20: The Development of the Closed Openings
Some Important Points to Look For

The Age of 1. d4—like the Age of Aquarius—may last thousands of years. It's as good as 1. e4, but Black has a wide choice of unrefuted defenses.

◆ The classic Queen's Gambit.
See Diagram 585.

◆ Nimzo: quick development, control over the e4-square.
See Diagram 611.

◆ The Hyper-Modern Gruenfeld.
See Diagram 613.

◆ Who'll get there first?
See Diagram 624.

◆ Lev's favorite, the Benko Gambit.
See Diagram 629.

◆ Dutch Defense–a mirror image of the Sicilian. See Diagram 631.

Chapter 20
The Development of the Closed Openings
How to play against 1. d4

The move 1. d4 acquired popularity together with the positional school of Wilhelm Steinitz and Siegbert Tarrasch. At first glance, 1. d4 doesn't adhere to the three immediate goals of the opening (see page 26) as well as 1. e4 does. While d2-d4 puts the pawn in the center and opens lines for his c1-bishop and his queen, it definitely doesn't assist in castling short. Still, both analytically and statistically, 1. e4 and 1. d4 are of equal strength.

Diagram 583
After 1. e4

Diagram 584
After 1. d4

1. e4 occupies the center, frees a bishop, and forwards castling short.

1. d4 occupies the center, frees a bishop, but does not help to prepare castling short. The two opening moves, however, are equal.

WHY CAN'T BLACK TAKE ADVANTAGE OF WHITE'S 1. D4 "MISTAKE"?

The symmetrical 1. ... d5 leaves White with an extra tempo. The "super-principled" 1. ... e5 loses a pawn—there's compensation, to be sure, but worth no more than half a pawn.

All other moves, including the various "Indian" defenses emanating from 1. ... Nf6, leave White with more pawns in the center, and thus with more space–no refutation here either.

What you should know to start preparing for 1. d4

A The Classical Symmetry:
Queen's Gambit

1. d4 d5 2. c4

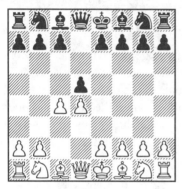

Diagram 585
After 2. c4

With his second move, White—who is, after all, a tempo up and thus should welcome opening up of the game—attacks Black's central pawn. Without this thrust, either now or a move or two later, White's chances for an edge are next to zero.

Black now has three major choices: to take on c4 (Queen's Gambit Accepted), to protect the d5-pawn with one of its neighbors (Queen's Gambit Declined), or to play the sharp Chigorin Defense, 2. ... Nc6.

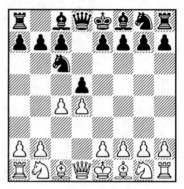

Diagram 586
After 2. ... Nc6

Black aims at quick development and often cedes White the bishop pair. The once disparaged Chigorin, named after the great Russian player, theoretician and contrarian Mikhail Chigorin, has been made border-line acceptable in modern play, mostly by the efforts of Alex Morozevich.

While Albin's Counter Gambit, 2. ... e5,

Diagram 587
2. ... e5

is generally still regarded with skepticism by leading GMs, it is often played by beginners. On the other hand, the American champion Frank Marshall's old favorite, 2. ... Nf6, gives White a strong center for free (after 3. cxd5 Nxd5 4. e4) and therefore isn't a good choice.

The idea of the Queen's Gambit Accepted **2. ... dxc4**

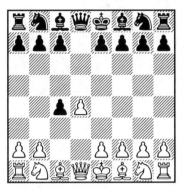

Diagram 588
After 2. ... dxc4

can be summed up in Reuben Fine's words: "A more comfortable game gets priority; equality in the center will come later."

After **3. Nf3**, Black shouldn't try to hold onto the c4-pawn, as 3. ... b5 4. a4 c6 5. e3 Bb7 (or 5. ... a6) 6. axb5 cxb5

Diagram 589
After 6. ... cxb5

7. b3! brings White back the "lost" pawn—and yields him the better game due to a superior pawn structure.

Better is **3. ... Nf6**

Diagram 590
After 3. ... Nf6

4. e3 e6 5. Bxc4 c5, attacking White's center. Often the game will lead either to a close-to-equal endgame, or to an archetypal position with a White *isolani* on d4.

A more comfortable game gets priority; equality in the center will come later.

– Reuben Fine

"Strong-point" Defenses: 2. ... e6 and 2. ... c6

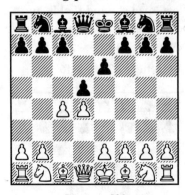

Diagram 591
Orthodox

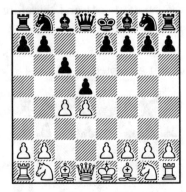

Diagram 592
Slav

Positive: **2. ... e6** helps facilitate kingside development, and early castling; it also preserves an option to play ... c7-c5 in one move. Negative: the bishop on c8 is now blocked by the e6-pawn. (Often the bishop will later be developed to b7.)

Positive: **2. ... c6** keeps the c8-h3 diagonal open. Negative: it offers Black none of the benefits of its cousin, 2. ... e6.

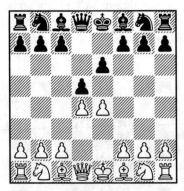

Diagram 593
French

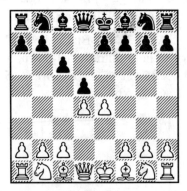

Diagram 594
Caro-Kann

The Queen's Gambit Declined, Orthodox Defense, and the Slav Defense resemble in some ways the French and Caro-Kann.

Just as they were 100 years ago, both the Queen's Gambit Declined (Orthodox) and the Slav Defense are today generally regarded as being equally playable.

In the Orthodox Defense, after the natural **3. Nc3** (the Catalan, 3. Nf3 Nf6 4. g3, is also a good try for White),

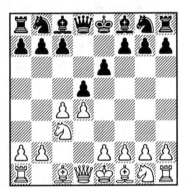

Diagram 595
After 3. Nc3

Black could play **3. ... c5,**

Diagram 596
After 3. ... c5

the Tarrasch Defense, accepting the *isolani* after **4. cxd5 exd5 5. Nf3** (5. dxc5 doesn't win a pawn,

as Black counters with 5. ... d4) **5. ... Nc6 6. g3.**

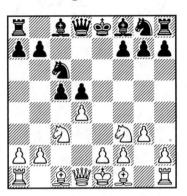

Diagram 597
After 6. g3

Akiba Rubinstein's idea—to better pressure the d5-pawn. **6. ... Nf6** (less common, but viable, is 6. ... c4) **7. Bg2 Be7 8. 0-0 0-0**

Just as they were 100 years ago, both the Queen's Gambit Declined (Orthodox) and the Slav Defense are today generally regarded as being equally playable.

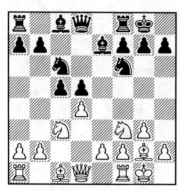

Diagram 598
After 8. ... 0-0

And now White usually prefers **9. Bg5** to Fine's recommendation, 9. dxc5 (but chess fashions often move in cycles).

The Tarrasch served Garry Kasparov well in the early '80s, and visa versa. It is less popular nowadays and awaits another champion to take up its cause.

The true Orthodox usually continues: **3. ... Nf6 4. Bg5 Nbd7**

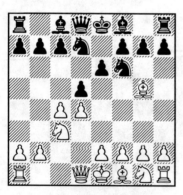

Diagram 599
After 4. ... Nbd7

(or 4. ... Be7, but the knight's move is equally good—and sets a trap)

5. Nf3 (White can't win a pawn: 5. cxd5 exd5 6. Nxd5? Nxd5!, and Black wins) **5. ... Be7 6. e3 0-0**

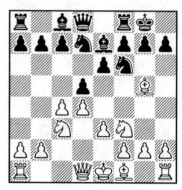

Diagram 600
After 6. ... 0-0

Here White usually delays moving his king's bishop—in order to avoid moving it again, after ... dxc4. Fortunately for him, White has useful moves: Qc2, Rc1, even a3. Often this tabia leads to White's minority attack, b4,

Diagram 601
Minority Attack

while Black will soon be attacking the White king.

But sometimes White even castles long and attacks with kingside pawns!

The history and theory of the QGD-Orthodox is rich in great names: Lasker's Variation, Capablanca's exchange maneuver, Botvinnik's central thrust. This is a solid opening, inexhaustible and irrefutable!

The same can be said about the Slav: **1. d4 d5 2. c4 c6**.

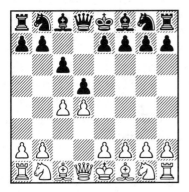

Diagram 602
After 2. ... c6

Interestingly, the symmetrical position after 3. Nf3 Nf6 4. cxd5 cxd5 5. Nc3 Nc6 6. Bf4 Bf5

Diagram 603
After 6. ... Bf5

is viewed by theory as equal. Even after 3. Nf3 Nf6 4. Nc3 a6 (paradoxical, but solid),

Diagram 604
After 4. ... a6

the exchange on d5 is worthless. Here is a popular line in the Slav:

3. Nf3 Nf6 4. Nc3

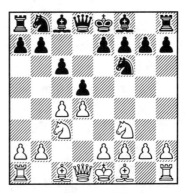

Diagram 605
After 4. Nc3

4. ... dxc4 5. a4 (to stop ... b5) **5. ... Bf5**

The QGD, Orthodox Defense, is solid, inexhaustible and irrefutable!

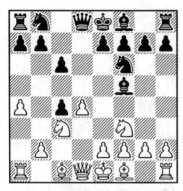

Diagram 606
After 5. ... Bf5

and nowadays **6. Ne5**, preparing to restrict Black's bishop by f3 and e4, is viewed as somewhat more promising than the straight-forward 6. e3.

Another popular line starts on move 4: instead of capturing on c4, Black plays **4. ... e6**.

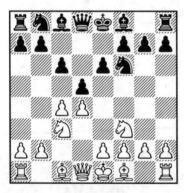

Diagram 607
After 4. ... e6

Black seems to reach back to the Orthodox, except that now 5. Bg5 runs into the super-sharp Botvinnik Variation: 5. ... dxc4 6. e4 b5 7. e5 h6,

Diagram 608
After 6. ... Bf5

which is still very much alive and well, or into the equally sharp Moscow Variation: 5. ... h6 6. Bh4 (6. Bxf6 leads to quieter, close-to-equal play) 6. ... dxc4 7. e4 g5 8. Bg3 b5, which occurred, for instance, in several key games of the 2007 World Championship in Mexico City.

Thus White often plays the more cautious **5. e3**, which is best met by **5. ... Nbd7**.

Diagram 609
After 5. ... Nbd7

Now the "normal" **6. Bd3** leads to *another* super-sharp variation, the Meran:

6. ... dxc4 7. Bxc4 b5

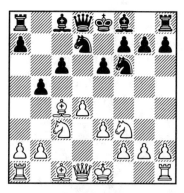

Diagram 610
After 7. ... b5

Nowadays White often tries to avoid the Meran by playing 6. Qc2—still with sharp play and mutual chances.

To conclude, the classic, symmetrical 1. ... d5 is a good, solid choice that has passed the test of time. It offers a rich blend of strategic as well as sharply charged tactical positions, and the choice is often in Black's hands.

B Asymmetrical Defenses:

If not 1. ... d5, then what?

The move 1. d4 became popular with the advent of Steinitz' theory, and for several decades the symmetrical 1. ... d5, preventing e4, was viewed as the only fully correct reply. But early in the twentieth century, players began to rely on asymmetrical approaches.

The Nimzo-Indian Defense
1. d4 Nf6 2. c4 e6 3. Nc3 Bb4

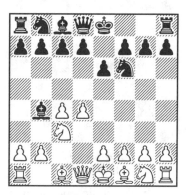

Diagram 611
After 3. ... Bb4

was the first of the "modernist" openings. It is also the most flexible and solid—and it's our choice for Black in this book. No informed player ever seriously hopes to refute the Nimzo. It's built on a super-solid strategic foundation: Black develops harmoniously and very quickly (ready to castle on move four, if he wishes), while denying White an uncontested control over the center (the e4-square).

If White avoids the pinning of his knight by playing **3. Nf3,**

> The Nimzo-Indian is flexible and solid— and it's our choice for Black.

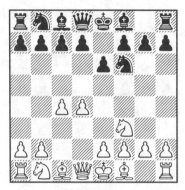

Diagram 612
After 3. Nf3

Black has a choice between the sharp 3. ... c5, the solid 3. ... b6 (Queen's Indian) and our choice—3. ... Bb4+ (the Bogo-Indian, named after GM Efim Bogolubov). As you can see, the Nimzo-Indian and Bogo-Indian closely resemble one another.

Moves 3. g3 and 3. Bg5 are rarely played and often transpose—after our trusty 3. ... Bb4+—into the Nimzo-Bogo. Thus we'll look at them at the end of Chapter 32, the last chapter on the Bogo. And if White plays 3. a3 to prevent the check on b4, Black can play 3. ... d5 and then try to steer the game into those lines of the Orthodox Variation of the Queen's Gambit Declined, in which the move a2-a3 isn't that useful. Or Black can go into the Symmetrical Tarrasch with 3. ... c5 4. e3 d5. In that line, a2-a3 is often played—but the overall evaluation, according to the *Encyclopedia of Chess Openings,* for example, is equal.

Give White a Center in Order to Attack It

The "modern" Nimzo-Indian was followed by the "hyper-modern" Gruenfeld Defense:

1. d4 Nf6 2. c4 g6 3. Nc3 (ready to play e4) **3. ... d5**

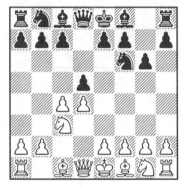

Diagram 613
After 3. ... d5

After **4. cxd5** (still the most popular move) **4. ... Nxd5 5. e4 Nxc3 6. bxc3**

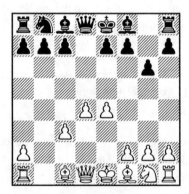

Diagram 614
After 6. bxc3

White has a strong center; Black has better development and a natural way to attack that center with ... c5, ... Nc6, and other moves that hit at d4. Until the '70s, the only acceptable line for White was to put his bishop on c4 and his knight on e2 (to avoid a pin). Nowadays, the main line goes:

6. ... Bg7 7. Nf3!? c5! 8. Rb1

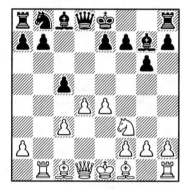

Diagram 615
After 8. Rb1

If you're ready for these lines as Black, then you can move to other White systems against the Gruenfeld, such as 4. Qb3

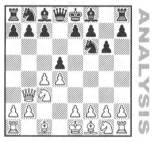

Diagram 616
After 4. Qb3

or 4. Bf4 Bg7 5. e3. Study games by Boris Gulko and Garry Kasparov, two of the Gruenfeld's top experts.

Development Above All: King's Indian Defense

1. d4 Nf6 2. c4 g6 3. Nc3 Bg7 4. e4

Diagram 617
After 4. e4

4. ... 0-0

Or 4. ... d6. This is an innocent transposition; Bobby Fischer proved that 5. e5—after 4. ... 0-0—leads to a sharp but equal game.

In the King's Indian, Black allows his opponent to play e4 and to build a strong center. Black uses this time to develop his kingside pieces to excellent squares and to castle, ready to claim his stake in the center by a later ... e5, or to attack White's center, Sicilian-like, with ... c5.

Not surprisingly, White has many systems to choose from against this "non-contact" opening. He can play the ambitious 5. f4 d6 6. Nf3. Or he can choose the solid fianchetto (with 4. Nf3 rather than 4. e4, 4. ... 0-0 5. g3 d6 6. Bg2).

Diagram 618
After 6. Bg2

Or he can try the aggressive Saemisch: 5. f3 d6,

Diagram 619
After 5. ... d6

and now either the "modern" 6. Bg5 or the classic 6. Be3. White can also choose the subtle Averbach: 5. Be2 d6 6. Bg5.

Diagram 620
After 6. Bg5

And finally, the most popular 5. Nf3 d6 6. Be2

Diagram 621
After 6. Be2

followed by the logical 6. ... e5 7. 0-0.

Diagram 622
After 7. 0-0

The main line today, and for the last 40 years or more, is the challenging 7. ... Nc6, which usually leads to sharp positions where White storms on the queenside while Black attacks the White king, e.g., 8. d5 Ne7 9. Ne1 (or the now popular 9. b4!)

Diagram 623
After 9. Ne1

9. ... Nd7 10. f3 f5 11. Be3 f4 12. Bf2 g5

Diagram 624
After 12. ... g5

You should keep track of the great players and the moves they're making to stay informed about what's going on in this system, which is often analyzed deeply—to 20 or more moves, or you can develop your own shortcut.

The move 7. ... Nbd7,

Diagram 625
Bronstein's 7. ... Nbd7

which brought David Bronstein many brilliant victories in the late '40s and '50s, may be a good shortcut—it would save you 80% or more of the time needed for preparation, as well as the need for extensive memorization. Less popular among the elite than the now fashionable 7. ... Nc6, Bronstein's 7. ... Nbd7 was never refuted; it is easy to grasp and is strategically, as well as tactically, solid. Recently, 7. ... Na6, an improved version of 7. ... Nbd7 (the knight doesn't block the bishop and controls the b4-square), became quite popular.

* * *

Less popular than the King's Indian, but still playable, are various systems where Black fianchettoes his king's bishop while keeping the knight on g8 for a while, and uses this nuance to attack the d4-pawn with ... d6 and ... e5, and sometimes with ... Nc6 and ... e5.

Also playable is the Old Indian: 1. d4 Nf6 2. c4 d6 3. Nc3 e5

Diagram 626
Old Indian

as well as various Benonis:

1. d4 c5 2. d5 e5 3. Nc3 d6 4. e4 Be7, planning ... Bg5 and the exchange (generally favorable for Black) of his "bad" bishop for White's "good" bishop, or

1. d4 Nf6 2. c4 c5 3. d5 e5.

Diagram 627
Old Benoni

Black can choose the Modern Benoni (Mikhail Tal's favorite): 1. d4 Nf6 2. c4 c5 3. d5 e6.

Diagram 628
Modern Benoni

Or Black can play Alburt's favorite, the Benko Gambit:

1. d4 Nf6 2. c4 c5 3. d5 b5,

Diagram 629
Benko Gambit

nowadays, a mainstream, even

solid choice, which is naturally often discussed in his books. (See, for instance, the last chapter of *Building Up Your Chess*.)

Less mainstream is the Budapest Gambit: 1. d4 Nf6 2. c4 e5 3. dxe5.

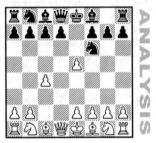

Diagram 630
Budapest Defense

Now 3. … Ne4 is tempting, but risky (at least in a sense that White, with best play, should get his plus-over-equal), while 3. … Ng4 enjoys a more acceptable reputation among the GMs.

Finally, one should consider, as an answer to 1. d4, the Dutch Defense: 1. … f5,

Diagram 631
Dutch Defense

even if only out of trust in Botvinnik's opening intuition, which was usually superb. Yes, this move doesn't develop, nor does it bring castling closer. And it somewhat exposes Black's king. But it also takes control of the e4-square. And remember how in the King's Indian, Black had to move his f6-knight to prepare the attacking ... f5; in some cases, the Dutch can save Black a tempo, or even two!

Summary:

After 1. d4, Black has a panoply of choices, from popular openings (requiring a lot of study time) to risky or somewhat passive shortcuts. Our choice, the Nimzo-Bogo complex, is both enterprising and rock-solid.

Chapter 20: The Development of the Closed Openings
Memory Markers!

Diagram 632
After 4. ... Nf6

MARKER 1

Diagram 633
After 5. ... cxb5

MARKER 2

Diagram 634
After 4. Bg5

MARKER 3

Diagram 635
After 6. ... e5

MARKER 4

Chapter 20: The Development of the Closed Openings
Solutions to Memory Markers!

No. 1   **5. f3,** preserving the center (5. Nc3 e5! equalizes). See page 243.

No. 2   **6. Qf3,** winning. See page 243.

No. 3   **4. ... Ne4,** with an equal game. See page 250.

No. 4   **7. dxe5 dxe5 8. Qxd8 Rxd8 9. Nd5,** winning a pawn. See page 252.

Chapter 21: Nimzo-Indian Defense–Introduction and 4. a3

Some Important Points to Look For

The Nimzo-Indian has been the choice of top players faced with 1. d4 since the days of the modernist revolution against classical dogma. Against 4. a3, Dzindzi's TNs will give you a great game.

◆ Here comes the creative novelty! See Diagram 641.

◆ And another: same square, same piece! See Diagram 650.

◆ Black's kingside knight can also attack c4. See Diagram 658.

◆ Black's queen will again shine on c8. See Diagram 660.

Outline of Variations

1. d4 Nf6 2. c4 e6 3. Nc3 Bb4 4. a3 Bxc3+ 5. bxc3 b6 6. f3 Ba6 7. e4 Nc6 *(258)* **[E24]**
    A 8. Bd3 Na5 9. Qe2 Qc8 10. e5 Ng8 11. f4 Ne7 12. Nf3 d5 13. cxd5 Bxd3 14. Qxd3 exd5 *(261)*
    B 8. Bg5 Qc8 9. Bd3 Na5 10. Qe2 Qb7 11. d5 Nh3 12. Rb1 Nc5 *(264)*
        B1 13. Be3 Nxd3+ 14. Qxd3 exd5 15. exd5 0-0 16. Bg5 Ne8 *(266)*
        B2 13. Nh3 d6 *(266)*
    C 8. e5 Ng8 9. Nh3 Na5 10. Qa4 Qc8 11. Bd3 c5 12. Ng5 Qc6 *(266)*

Chapter 21
Nimzo-Indian Defense
Introduction and 4. a3

After **1. d4**, we recommend the flexible **1. ... Nf6**. This move prevents e2-e4 and develops Black's knight to a square that will be good regardless of the coming play.

Here's one great advantage to a Black player looking for a solid-but-fighting repertoire: the move order we recommend throughout this section retains many of the same ideas and themes, regardless of the specific opening.

GMs generally agree that to try for any advantage, White must now play **2. c4**. Then, with **2. ... e6**, Black frees his bishop, ready to go to b4.

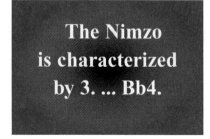

The Nimzo is characterized by 3. ... Bb4.

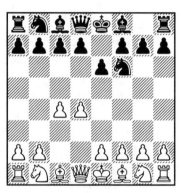

Diagram 636
After 2. ... e6

Now White must choose which knight to bring out. The most "principled" move is 3. Nc3—and against this move we'll play the Nimzo-Indian. The opening is named in honor of Aaron Nimzovich, one of the strongest players of the early twentieth century and a founder of the "modern" school, which re-examined and sometimes debunked dogma of the classical school represented by Tarrasch. The Nimzo is characterized by 3. ... Bb4.

3. Nc3 Bb4

Diagram 637
After 3. ... Bb4

The Nimzo is motivated by a different idea than the classical defenses. Rather than match White in the center, pawn for pawn (with ... d7-d5), Black develops quickly. He's ready to castle by the fourth move. He controls e4 with the joint efforts of his knight and bishop.

White's biggest plus in the Nimzo is that he normally sports the stronger center and often enjoys the bishop pair against Black's bishop and knight. For the last four decades, the Nimzo-Indian has consistently enjoyed an excellent reputation.

On his fourth move, White has tried a wide variety of moves over the years as the Nimzo thwarted the intentions of ambitious White players: 4. a3, 4. Qc2 (currently the most popular), 4. e3 (the classical setup involving Bd3 and Nf3), 4. e3 (followed by 5. Ne2), 4. f3, 4. g3, 4. Bg5 (the Leningrad System), 4. Qb3,

4. Bd2, and 4. Nf3. (This last normally transposes to the classical setup after 4. ... c5 5. e3 b6 6. Bd3 Bb7.)

We'll take a close look at each of these choices. The most immediately challenging choice is putting the question to the bishop.

4. a3

White's idea is to force Black to take on c3, and then to play f3 and e4 to gain control of the center. This is called the Saemisch Variation, named after Friedrich Saemisch, who was a strong player, but plagued by indecision. (Near the end of his career, in a tournament in Linkoeping in 1969, he lost all 13 games on time!)

4. ... Bxc3+ 5. bxc3 b6

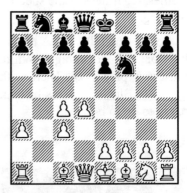

Diagram 638
After 5. ... b6

Black plans to attack White's weak pawn on c4 right away with ... Ba6 and ... Nc6-a5.

6. f3

White immediately takes control of the center. On several occasions, White instead tried 6. Bg5, preserving the f3-square for his knight. 6. ... h6 7. Bh4

Diagram 639
After 7. Bh4

7. ... Ba6 (or 7. ... Nc6 8. Nf3 Bb7 9. Nd2 Ne7 10. e3 g5 11. Bg3 Nf5, with approximate equality) 8. e3 (the aggresive 8. e4 fails to 8. ... g5—9. e5 gxh4 10. Qf3 d5!, and Black takes the initiative: 11. exf6 Bb7, Muci—Graf, 2001, when the f6 pawn is doomed) 8. ... Nc6 9. Nf3 Na5 10. Nd2 g5 11. Bg3 Bb7 12. Qc2 Qe7, followed by ... d6 and ... 0-0-0, when Black is fine.

6. ... Ba6 7. e4 Nc6

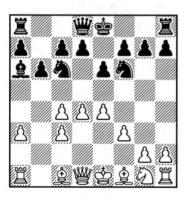

Diagram 640
After 7. ... Nc6

Here White has three main continuations: 8. Bd3, 8. Bg5, and 8. e5 (8. Nh3 Na5 merely transposes).

A 8. Bd3 Na5 9. Qe2

Diagram 641
After 9. Qe2

9. ... Qc8! TN

This theoretical novelty amounts to a very strong positional insight. The purpose of the maneuver becomes clear in a few moves.

10. e5 Ng8

White has made too many pawn moves, so Black's retreating the knight to g8 does not yield White any advantage in development.

11. f4

White's plan is to play Nf3 and 0–0, after which he is ready to attack. Black, however, has strong counter-play on the queenside.

11. ... Ne7 12. Nf3 d5!

Diagram 642
After 12. ... d5!

Black strikes the center just in time!

13. cxd5

Not 13. exd6 cxd6 14. Nd2 d5, when Black dominates the light squares.

13. ... Bxd3 14. Qxd3 exd5

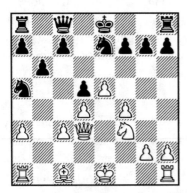

Diagram 643
After 14. ... exd5

With a vice-grip on the light squares, Black has a very comfortable position.

15. Nh4

If 15. 0–0, then ... g6!, with the idea of meeting Nh4 with

... Nf5 (not 15. ... h5, which allows 16. Nh4 and f5).

15. ... g6

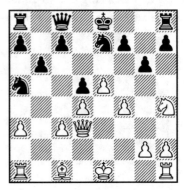

Diagram 644
After 15. ... g6

Black intends ... Nf5, with a blockade on the light squares.

16. f5!?

White temporarily sacrifices his pawn in order to create play on the kingside.

After 16. 0–0 Nf5 17. Nxf5 Qxf5 18. Qxf5 gxf5,

ANALYSIS

Diagram 645
After 18. ... gxf5

Black enjoys a clear advantage in the endgame, due to the superiority of his knight over White's bad bishop, blocked by its own pawns.

16. ... Nxf5 17. Nxf5 Qxf5 18. Qxf5 gxf5 19. 0–0

Now it may seem that White stands better, since he's ready to capture on f5 and double up on the f-file. But Black plays a thematic pawn-punch just at the right moment.

19. ... c5!

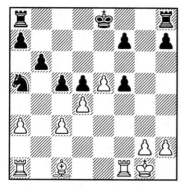

Diagram 646
After 19. ... c5!

Now White cannot comfortably regain the pawn; for example:

20. dxc5

If 20. Rxf5? cxd4 21. cxd4 Nb3,

Diagram 647
After 21. ... Nb3

and the fork costs White his d-pawn.

20. ... Nb3 21. Ra2

If 21. Rb1 Nxc5 22. Rxf5 Rc8, followed by Ne4,

Diagram 648
After 22. ... Rc8

when Black stands better.

21. ... bxc5 22. Bg5 Rg8 23. Rxf5

Black enjoys a clear advantage in the endgame. His knight is much better than White's bishop.

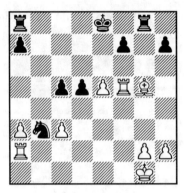

Diagram 649
After 23. Rxf5

23. ... Rb8 24. Raf2 Rb7

Black is fine.

B 8. Bg5 Qc8 TN

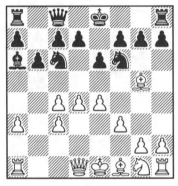

Diagram 650
After 8. ... Qc8

Dzindzi's theoretical novelty: attacking the c4-pawn with the queen after ... Na5, ... Qb7, and ... Qc6.

9. Bd3

If 9. e5 Ng8 10. Nh3 Na5 11. Qa4,

Diagram 651
After 11. Qa4

then 11. ... Qb7, followed by ... Qc6, with a pleasant endgame for Black.

Or on 9. Bxf6 gxf6, Black is not afraid of his doubled pawns—10. Qd2 Na5 11. Qh6 Qd8 12. Qg7 Rf8 13. Qxh7 Qe7,

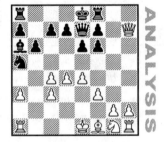

Diagram 652
After 13. ... Qe7

followed by ... Bxc4 and ... 0–0–0, and Black is better.

9. ... Na5 10. Qe2 Qb7

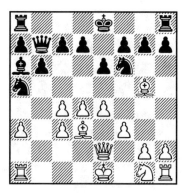

Diagram 653
After 10. .. Qb7

Black's idea is … Qc6.

11. d5

If 11. e5 Ng8 12. Be4 Qc8!,

Diagram 654
After 12. ... Qc8!

White either has to accept a repetition of the position with Bd3 or has to play 13. Bxa8. In the latter case, Black plays 13. ... Qxa8, when he has more than sufficient compensation for the Exchange, due to his full control of the light squares after ... Bxc4.

If 11. Nh3 Qc6 12. e5,

Diagram 655
After 12. e5

Black has a nice move, 12. ... Nd5!, taking advantage of his pin on the c4-pawn.

11. ... Nb3 12. Rb1 Nc5

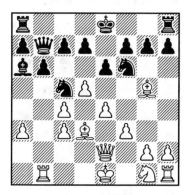

Diagram 656
After 12. ... Nc5

Black places his knight in a dominating position, pressuring White's center and the bishop on d3. White has two moves: 13. Be3, and 13. Nh3 (13. e5? is answered by 13. … Nxd5).

B1 13. Be3

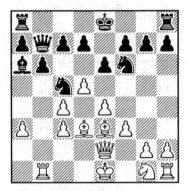

Diagram 657
After 13. Be3

13. ... Nxd3+ 14. Qxd3 exd5 15. exd5 0–0 16. Bg5 Ne8!

Diagram 658
After 16. ... Ne8!

With this "backward" move, Black completely turns the tables! After 17. Be7 Nd6 18. Bxf8 (18. Bxd6 cxd6 and Black eventually wins the c4 pawn and enjoys a clear advantage) 18. ... Bxc4 is followed by ... Rxf8 with overwhelming compensation.

B2 13. Nh3 d6

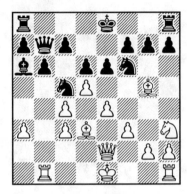

Diagram 659
After 13. ... d6

Black intends ... 0–0–0 or ... c6 and is clearly better.

C 8. e5 Ng8

Diagram 660
After 8. ... Ng8

9. Nh3 Na5 10. Qa4 Qc8

Black's counter-play hinges on ... c5.

11. Bd3 c5 12. Ng5

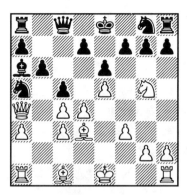

Diagram 661
After 12. Ng5

White loses his c4-pawn. He tries to create counter-play by putting his knight on e4.

12. ... Qc6 13. Qc2 Bxc4 14. Ne4 Bxd3 15. Qxd3 Nb7

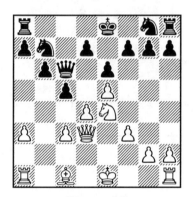

Diagram 662
After 15. ... Nb7

Black defends the weak d6-square. Jonasson–Browne, 1986 continued:

16. Bg5 h6 17. Bh4 Ne7 18. Bxe7 Kxe7 19. 0–0 d5

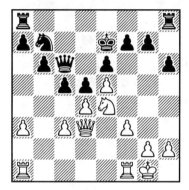

Diagram 663
After 19. ... d5

20. exd6+ Nxd6

White lacks sufficient compensation for the pawn.

Summary:

In the Saemisch, White gains a strong center, but his c4-pawn is a constant problem. Black attacks it with his bishop, knight and queen—and does quite well. Dzindzi's TNs work wonders and provide you with some uncomfortable surprises for your opponents!

Chapter 21: Nimzo-Indian—Introduction and 4. a3
Memory Markers!

Diagram 664
After 5. bxc3

MARKER 1

Diagram 665
After 15. 0-0

MARKER 2

Diagram 666
After 12. Bd3

MARKER 3

Diagram 667
After 12. d5

MARKER 4

Chapter 21: Nimzo-Indian–Introduction and 4. a3
Solutions to Memory Markers!

No. 1   **5. ... b6.** Black has many good choices. We recommend the TN-rich 5. ... b6. See page 260.

No. 2   **15. ... g6!,** controlling the f5-square.
If 16. Nh4, then ... Nf5! with an advantage. See page 262.

No. 3   **12. ... Qc6!,** winning a pawn. See page 264.

No. 4   **12. ... Qa4** (not 12. ... exd5?? 13. exd5+). See page 265.

Chapter 22: Nimzo-Indian Defense with 4. Qc2
Some Important Points to Look For

In this popular variation, White avoids the doubling of his c-pawn. With the enterprising 4. ... Nc6, Black tests White's preparation and resolve.

◆ White has four choices.
See Diagram 673.

◆ Black's knight heads to f4 while freeing the way for his f-pawn.
See Diagram 675.

◆ Black is ready to play ... e5.
See Diagram 677.

◆ Tactics save the day.
See Diagram 689.

Outline of Variations

1. d4 Nf6 2. c4 e6 3. Nc3 Bb4 4. Qc2 Nc6 5. Nf3 d6 *(270)* [E33]
  A 6. Bd2 0-0 7. a3 Bxc3 8. Bxc3 Qe7 *(272)*
    A1 9. e4 e5 10. d5 Nb8 11. Be2 Nh5 12. Nxe5 Nf6 13. Nf3 Nxe4 14. 0-0 Nxc3
      15. Qxc3 Bg4 *(273)*
    A2 9. b4 c5 10. d5 Nb8 11. c4 Nh5 12. g3 f5 *(274)*
    A3 9. e3 a5 *(274)*
      A3a 10. b3 e5 11. dxe5 dxe5 12. Be2 Bg4 *(275)*
      A3b 10. Bd3 e5 11. dxe5 dxe5 *(276)*
        A3b1 12. 0-0 Re8 13. Bf5 Bxf5 14. Qxf5 Qe6 *(276)*
        A3b2 12. Ng5 h6 13. Ne4 Nxe4 14. Bxe4 Nd4 *(277)*
    A4 9. g3 e5 10. d5 Nb8 11. Bg2 Ne8 *(278)*
  B 6. Bg5 h6 *(278)*
  C 6. e4 e5 7. d5 Bxc3+ 8. Qxc3 Ne7 9. Bd3 0-0 10. 0-0 Nh5 *(279)*
  D 6. a3 Bxc3+7. Qxc3 a5 8. b3 0-0 9. Bb2 Re8 10. g3 e5 *(280)*

Chapter 22
Nimzo-Indian Defense
with 4. Qc2

Currently White's most popular continuation against the Nimzo, this variation, along with 4. e3 and 4. Nf3, is one of the classical approaches. White avoids the doubled pawns on c3 and c4, while reinforcing e4.

1. d4 Nf6 2. c4 e6 3. Nc3 Bb4 4. Qc2

Diagram 668
After 4. Qc2

4. ... Nc6

We recommend this line; it gives Black easy play and a strategy similar to the Bogo-Indian, our recommended "partner" to the Nimzo. This system was pioneered in the 1930s by Nimzovich and by world champion Alexander Alekhine. In the 1940s, it was successfully used by top players, including Mikhail Botvinnik, Vassily Smyslov and Samuel Reshevsky. Currently, this system can be seen as part of the arsenal of American GMs Alex Yermolinsky and Joel Benjamin.

5. Nf3

Less popular is 5. e3, because it allows Black to execute his plan unhindered: 5. ... 0–0 6. Ne2 d6 7. a3 Bxc3+ 8. Nxc3

4. ... Nc6 gives Black easy play and a strategy similar to the Bogo-Indian, our recommended "partner" to the Nimzo.

Diagram 669
After 8. Nxc3

8. ... e5 9. d5 Ne7 10. Bd3 (10. e4 Ne8, with the idea of ... f5), and now Black gets strong play in the center with 10. ... c6 11. dxc6 (after 11. e4, Black can play either 11. ... Ng6 or 11. ... cxd5 12. cxd5

Diagram 670
After 12. cxd5

12. ... Nh5, and now if 13. Qe2 Nf4, or 13. 0-0 f5!) 11. ... bxc6 12. 0–0 d5.

Diagram 671
After 12. ... d5

Black takes control of the center—for example: 13. Rd1 e4 14. Be2 (14. Bxe4?! Nxe4 15. Nxe4 Bf5 16. f3

Diagram 672
After 16. f3

16. ... Qe8!, with a big advantage) 14. ... Qc7 15. cxd5 cxd5, with a comfortable position for Black.

5. ... d6

Black's plan is to exchange his dark-square bishop for the knight and play ... e5. White has four main moves: 6. Bd2, 6. Bg5, 6. e4, and 6. a3.

A 6. Bd2 0–0 7. a3 Bxc3 8. Bxc3 Qe7

Diagram 673
After 8. ... Qe7

Here White has four continuations: 9. e4 immediately takes control of the center; 9. b4 gains space on the queenside; 9. e3 is less aggressive, but White hopes to exploit his two-bishop advantage in the middlegame; and 9. g3 leads to a Bogo-Indian type of game.

A1 9. e4

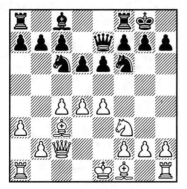

Diagram 674
After 9. e4

White plays his most aggressive move, with the threat of e5.

9. ... e5 10. d5 Nb8

Black's retreat to b8 does not give White any lead in development because he still needs to bring out his bishop and then castle.

11. Be2 Nh5

Diagram 675
After 11. ... Nh5

The knight heads for f4 and gets out of the way of the f7-pawn's advance.

12. Nxe5

If 12. 0–0, then 12. ... Nf4, followed by ... f5.

It seems as though Black loses a pawn after 12. ... dxe5 13. Bxh5, but he has a surprising "retreat."

12. ... Nf6! 13. Nf3 Nxe4 14. 0–0 Nxc3 15. Qxc3 Bg4

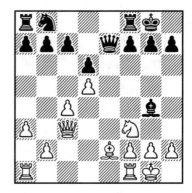

Diagram 676
After 15. ... Bg4

Black doesn't fall for 15. ...

Qxe2? 16. Rfe1, when his queen is trapped. After 15. ... Bg4, Black follows up with ... Nd7 and has an easy game.

A2 9. b4

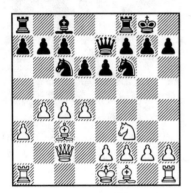

Diagram 677
After 9. b4

White grabs even more space on the queenside. Because of White's lack of development, however, Black gets strong counter-play in the center and on the kingside.

9. ... e5 10. d5

If 10. dxe5, then 10. ... Nxe5 11. e3 b6.

Diagram 678
After 11. ... b6

Black follows up with ... Bb7, with comfortable play.

10. ... Nb8 11. e4 Nh5

For 12. g3 f5, with strong kingside play, see the sample game Goldin—Yermolinsky, 2002.

12. Be2 or 12. Bd3 are met by 12. ... Nf4. In Khenkin—Yusapov, 20006, Black also got a promising game attack: 12. Nd2 f5 13. Be2 Nf4 14. Bf3 Qg5 15. 0-0-0, when the players agreed to a draw.

Diagram 679
After 15. 0-0-0

After 15. ... a5 16. Kb2 c6, the White king is the more vulnerable, and we prefer Black.

A3 9. e3

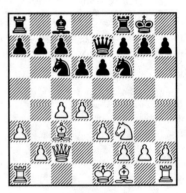

Diagram 680
After 9. e3

White wants to finish developing and use his two bishops in the middlegame. Black must play accurately to neutralize White's bishop pair.

9. ... a5

9. ... e5 is also possible. After 10. dxe5 Nxe5 (10. ... dxe5 11. b4, with pressure on e5) 11. Be2 Ng6 12. Nd2 (preventing Ne4) 12. ... Nh4!? 13. 0-0 Bf5 14. Qc1 Rfe8 =, with active piece play.

After 9. ... a5, White usually plays 10. b3 or 10. Bd3. Beliavsky (vs. Short, in 2008), tried 10. Be2. Short replied 10. ... e5 (Rybka prefers a4) 11. d5 Nb8 12. b4 axb4 13. axb4 Rxa1+ 14. Bxa1 b5

Black undermines White's queenside. 15. 0-0 bxc4 16. Qxc4 Bb7 17 Rd1 Rc8 (with the idea of c6) 18. b5 (White concedes c5) 18. ... Nbd7 19. e4, and now 19. ... Nc5! 20. Nd2 Ra8, with the idea of ... Ra4 ∓.

A3a 10. b3 e5 11. dxe5

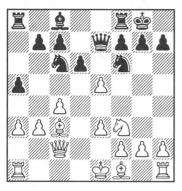

Diagram 681
After 11. dxe5

If 11. d5, then ... Nb8 12. Nd2 c6 13. dxc6 (13. e4 Nh5, with the idea of ... f5) 13. ... Nxc6 14. Bd3

Diagram 682
After 14. Bd3

14. ... Be6 15. 0-0 d5 =.

11. ... dxe5 12. Be2 Bg4

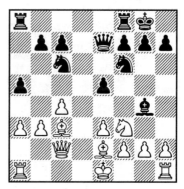

Diagram 683
After 12. ... Bg4

Black comfortably finishes his development and maintains an even game. This position occurred in the game Rago-zin–Botvinnik. After 13. 0–0 Rfe8 14. h3 Bh5 15. b4 axb4 16. axb4 Rxa1 17. Rxa1 Bxf3 18. Bxf3 e4

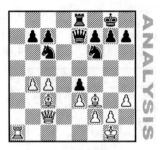

Diagram 684
After 18. ... e4

19. Be2 Nxb4 20. Qb2 c5 21. Rb1 b6 22. Bxb4 cxb4 23. Qxb4 Qxb4 24. Rxb4 Re6, they agreed to a draw.

A3b 10. Bd3

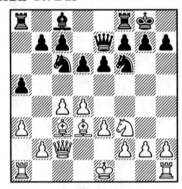

Diagram 685
After 10. Bd3

10. ... e5 11. dxe5 dxe5

Now White has 12. 0-0 and the better 12. Ng5!.

A3b1 12. 0–0 Re8

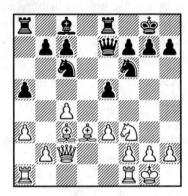

Diagram 686
After 12. ... Re8

13. Bf5

If 13. Nd2 or Ng5, Black plays 13. ... e4.

13. ... Bxf5 14. Qxf5 Qe6

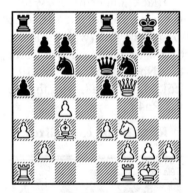

Diagram 687
After 14. ... Qe6

The position is even—for example: 15. Qxe6 Rxe6 16. b4. (White overestimates his chances; better was 16. b3.) 16. ... Ne4! 17. Bb2 f6 18. b5 Ne7, and Black is better in this endgame because of his outpost on c5 (Euwe–Reshevsky, 1948).

A3b2 12. Ng5!

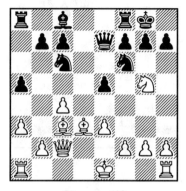

Diagram 688
After 12. Ng5!

This is an improvement over the Euwe–Reshevsky game.

12. ... h6 13. Ne4

White's idea is to exchange the knight on f6, after which he would have a small but solid advantage as a result of his bishop pair. However, Black has a beautiful reply to this idea.

13. ... Nxe4 14. Bxe4 Nd4!

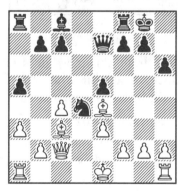

Diagram 689
After 14. ... Nd4!

This tactical shot quickly equalizes the game.

If White tries 15. Qd1, Black follows up with 15. ... Qh4!—for example: 16. 0–0 (16. Bd3 Bg4∓) 16. ... Qxe4 17. exd4 exd4 18. Re1 Qh4, with an equal position.

If White plays 15. exd4, then 15. ... exd4, and there could follow 16. Bxd4 f5 17. 0–0 fxe4.

Diagram 690
After 17. ... fxe4

Black has won his piece back, and the position is equal because of the opposite-color bishops—for example: 18. Rae1 Bf5 19. Re3 (19. f3 is met by 19. ... Qd7) 19. ... Rad8 20. Bc3 b6. Black is not afraid of 21. Rg3. After 21. ... Rf7 22. Qc1 Rd3!,

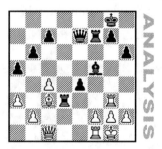

Diagram 691
After 22. ... Rd3!

Black is fine.

A4 9. g3

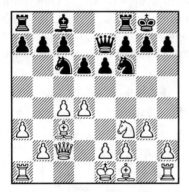

Diagram 692
After 9. g3

This position is similar to the Bogo-Indian, 6. Nc3 variation (see Chapter 31). The difference is that White has kept his bishop pair, but lost two tempi playing a3 and Qc2. Black's plan is to play ... e5, creating play in the center and on the kingside.

9. ... e5 10. d5

After 10. dxe5 dxe5 11. Bg2 Rd8 (with the idea of ... Nd4) 12. 0–0 Nd4 13. Bxd4 exd4, Black got a good position in the game Stotika–Taimanov, 1997.

10. ... Nb8 11. Bg2 Ne8

> **Black's plan is to play ... e5, creating play in the center and on the kingside.**

Diagram 693
After 11. ... Ne8

Black plans to play ... f5, with a good game.

B 6. Bg5

Diagram 694
After 6. Bg5

In truth, this move does not achieve much, since after 6. ... h6, the bishop must retreat to d2.

6. ... h6 7. Bd2

If 7. Bxf6 Qxf6 8. a3 Bxc3+ 9. Qxc3 0–0 10. Rd1 e5 11. d5 Ne7 12. g3 Qg6 13. Bg2 f5 14. 0–0 f4!,

Diagram 695
After 14. ... f4!

with the attack; while 7. Bh4? loses a pawn: 7. ... g5 8. Bg3 g4.

Now after 9. Nd2 Nxd4, White can't win a piece with 10. Qa4+ Bd7 11. Qxb4? because of 11. ... Nc2+. Even the stronger 9. d5! also favors Black after 9. ... exd5 10. exd5 Nxd5 11. Bh4 Qd7.

7. ... 0–0

Black has transposed to line **A**, with the addition of the useful move ... h6.

C 6. e4

The game Anderson–Nimzovich, 1933, demonstrates an instructive plan for Black.

6. ... e5

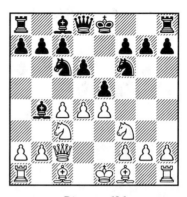

Diagram 696
After 6. ... e5

7. d5 Bxc3+ 8. Qxc3 Ne7 9. Bd3 0–0 10. 0–0

If 10. Bg5, Black plays 10. ... Ng6, followed by ... h6.

10. ... Nh5

Black plans ... Ng6 to take over the f4-square. After White's weakening g3, Black will play ... f5, with strong play on light squares. It would be dubious for White to play 11. Nxe5? here, because of 11. ... dxe5 12. Qxe5 f5, with a winning position for Black.

Black has transposed to line A, with the addition of the useful move ... h6.

◨ 6. a3 Bxc3+ 7. Qxc3

Diagram 697
After 6. a3

7. ... a5

Also interesting is 7. ... 0-0 8. b4 e5, offering a pawn.

8. b3 0-0 9. Bb2

Other options: 9. e3 Re8 10. Be2 e5 11. d5 Ne7; 9. g3, usually transposing into a main line; or 9. Bg5?! h610. Bh4 g5!.

9. ... Re8 10. g3

Or 10. Rd1 Qe7 11. e3 e5 12. Be2 Bg4, with a good game

for Black (Miton—Perelshteyn, 2007).

10. ... e5

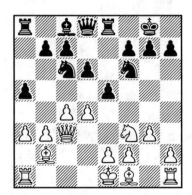

Diagram 698
After 10. ... e5

11. dxe5

Or 11. d5 Nb8! 12. Bg2 c6! 13. dxc6 bxc6 14. 0-0 Nbd7, with the idea of ... Qc7, ... Bb7, and ... c5.

11. ... dxe5 12. Bg2 Bg4! 13. 0-0 Bxf3 14. Bxf3 Nd4 15. Rfe1 c5! ∓

(Skalski-Azarov, 2005).

Summary:

Against White's most popular 4. Qc2, Black has a dynamic defense, 4. ... Nc6. One reason we like the move is that some emerging lines resemble the Bogo-Indian, which we'll study later. Of course, Black has, as is normal in the Nimzo, many other good choices: 4. ... 0-0, 4. ... c5, 4. ... d5, 4. ... b6—the usual suspects. Still, our line is as good as any—and rich in Roman's and Eugene's home analysis! Black is ready to trade his b4-bishop for the knight; meanwhile, he activates his remaining bishop with ... d6 and ... e5.

Chapter 22: Nimzo-Indian Defense with 4. Qc2
Memory Markers!

Diagram 699
After 13. 0-0

Diagram 700
After 12. Nxe5

Diagram 701
After 13. e4

Diagram 702
After 7. d5

Chapter 22: Nimzo-Indian Defense with 4. Qc2
Solutions to Memory Markers!

No. 1   **13. ... f5!,** See page 272.

No. 2   **12. ... Nf6,** and Black saves a pawn. See page 273.

No. 3   **13. ... Bg4,** undermining the d4-square. See page 276.

No. 4   **7. ... Bxc3+.** See page 279.

Chapter 23: Nimzo-Indian with 4. e3 and 5. Bd3
Some Important Points to Look For

Against White's classical set up, Black fianchettoes his queen's bishop, pressuring the center and kingside.

◆ Black fianchettoes.
See Diagram 706.

◆ An interesting pawn structure.
See Diagram 709.

◆ Black has a choice.
See Diagram 727.

◆ Black retreats to the right square.
See Diagram 744.

Outline of Variations

1. d4 Nf6 2. c4 e6 3. Nc3 Bb4 4. e3 b6 5. Bd3 Bb7 *(282)* [E43]

  A 6. Nf3 0-0 7. 0-0 c5 *(284)*
   A1 8. Na4 cxd4 *(284)*
     A1a 9. exd4 Re8 10. a3 Bf8 11. b4 d6 12. Bb2 Nbd7 13. Re1 Rc8 14. Nc3 a6
          15. Bf1 Qc7 *(284)*
     A1b 9. a3 Bd6 10. exd4 Bxf3 11. Qxf3 Nc6 12. Be3 e5 *(287)*
   A2 8. Bd2 cxd4 9. cxd4 d5 10. cxd5 Nxd5 *(289)*
     A2a 11. Qe2 Nc6 12. Rfd1 Be7 13. Rac1 Rc8 14. a3 Nxc3 15. Bxc3 Nb8 *(290)*
     A2b 11. Nxd5 Bxd2 12. Nxb6 axb6 13. Nxd2 Qxd4 *(292)*
     A2c 11. Rc1 Nf6 12. Re1 Nc6 13. Bf4 Rc8 14. Bf4 Rc8 15. Bb1 Na5
          16. Ne5 Nc4 17. Nxc4 Rxc4 18. Be5 Rc8 *(292)*
     A2d 11. Ne5 Nd7 *(293)*
  B 6. Ne2 Bxg2 7. Rg1 Bf3 8. Rxg7 Ng4 *(294)*

Chapter 23
Nimzo-Indian
with 4. e3 and 5. Bd3

In this variation, White neither immediately attacks Black's bishop on b4 nor guards against the doubling of his c-pawns. Instead, he relies on straightforward, classical development in the center, posting his light-square bishop on a traditional square and preparing for kingside castling.

1. d4 Nf6 2. c4 e6 3. Nc3 Bb4 4. e3 b6

Our reply–the fianchetto!

Diagram 703
After 4. ... b6

Here White has two popular setups, 5. Bd3 followed by Nf3 (this chapter), and 5. Ne2, which does avoid the doubling of the c-pawn (Chapter 24).

5. Bd3

5. Nf3 leads to a transposition after 5. ... Bb7 6. Bd3. After 5. f3 0–0 (5. ... c5 is also possible) 6. e4 (White must lose a tempo) 6. ... Ba6 7. Bg5 h6 8. Bh4

Diagram 704
After 8. Bh4

8. ... d6 (stopping e5, but 8. ... Be7 is another good move) 9. Bd3 c5 10. a3 Bxc3+ 11. bxc3 Nc6 12. Ne2 ∓ e5 13. 0–0 g5 14. Bf2 Nh5,

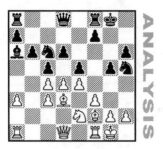

Diagram 705
After 14. ... Nh5

play could continue 15. Ng3
Nxg3 16. hxg3 Kg7 17. f4 f6,
with a very solid position for
Black (Milov–Milos, 2000).

5. ... Bb7

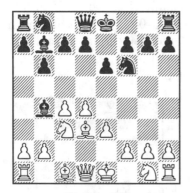

Diagram 706
After 5. ... Bb7

Now White can play 6. Nf3
or 6. Ne2.

A 6. Nf3 0–0 7. 0–0 c5

Here, White can play 8. Na4
(the most popular) or 8. Bd2.

A1 8. Na4

White's idea is to play a3
without giving Black the chance
to double the c-pawns.

8. ... cxd4

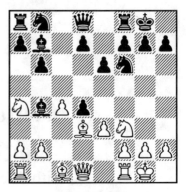

Diagram 707
After 8. ... cxd4

White can play 9. exd4 or 9.
a3.

A1a 9. exd4

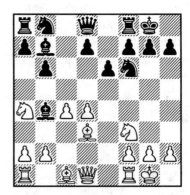

Diagram 708
After 9. exd4

9. ... Re8

Black prepares to retreat his
bishop to f8.

10. a3 Bf8

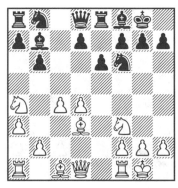

Diagram 709
After 10. ... Bf8

We have reached the topical position of the variation.

The position resembles a hedgehog structure. The main difference is that White's e4-pawn has moved to d4. This change favors Black because:

1. White does not have the usual pressure on the d-file;

2. Black can create strong counter-play in the center with ... d6, ... Nbd7 and ... e5;

3. Black's light-square bishop is very powerful and White's only way of neutralizing it is by playing d5, which is difficult to execute and allows Black to play his planned ... e5, with strong play on the kingside.

White's plan is to win even more space on the queenside with b4 and to put pressure on Black's cramped position, possibly breaking through the center with a timely d5.

Black's plan is to play ... d6 and ... Nbd7, possibly launching a central breakthrough with ... e5. Typical ideas also include ... Rc8, ... a6, and the transfer of the queen to the long diagonal either by ... Rc7, ... Qa8 or .... Qc7-b8-a8. In addition, after ... g6 and ... Bg7, Black's dark-square bishop becomes more active.

11. b4

Moves such as Nc3, Re1, and Bg5 do not create any problems for Black and often transpose to main lines. Black should simply develop with ... d6 and ... Ndb7.

11. ... d6 12. Bb2 Nbd7 13. Re1

This stops a possible ... e5.

13. ... Rc8 14. Nc3

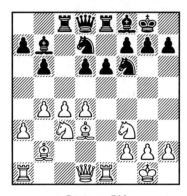

Diagram 710
After 14. Nc3

14. ... a6

Black prepares to transfer his queen to a8. Weaker is 14. ... e5 15. dxe5 dxe5 16. Ne4 Bxe4 17. Bxe4

Diagram 711
After 17. Bxe4

17. … Qc7 (if 17. … Rxc4 18. Bd3! Rc6 19. Bb5, and White has strong compensation for a pawn) 18. Bf5! g6 19. Bh3.

Diagram 712
After 19. Bh3

White's bishop pair dominates the board.

15. Bf1 Qc7

> **Black plays on the kingside. White tries to break through on the queenside.**

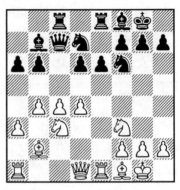

Diagram 713
After 15. … Qc7

16. Nd2

With the idea of meeting … Qa8 with f3. After 16. d5 Ne5 (16. … e5 leads to a complex position with plenty of fighting still to come; Black's plan is to play … g6, prepare … f5, and to play on the kingside while White tries to break through on the queenside with a4-a5) 17. Nxe5 dxe5 18. dxe6 Rxe6,

Diagram 714
After 18. … Rxe6

Black maintains equality—for example: 19. Nd5 Nxd5 20. cxd5 Ree8 21. Rc1 Qd6 22. Rxc8 Bxc8 23. f4 e4 24. Be5 Qd7 followed by … f6 and … Bb7.

16. … Qb8 17. Rb1 Qa8

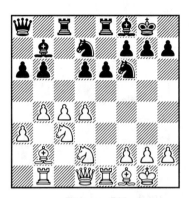

Diagram 715
After 17. ... Qa8

18. f3

The position is dynamically equal. Izoria–Tiviakov, 2002, continued:

18. ... Rc7 19. Kh1 Rec8 20. Nb3 e5

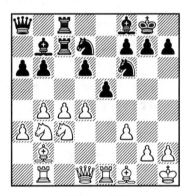

Diagram 716
After 20. ... e5

21. dxe5

21. d5 b5!, and White's d5-pawn falls.

21. ... Nxe5

Black's active piece play compensates for the weak pawn on d6.

22. Na4 Nfd7 23. Nd2 Bc6 24. Nc3 Nf6

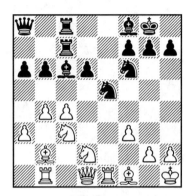

Diagram 717
After 24. ... Nf6

25. Na4 Nfd7

The game ended in a draw by three-fold repetition.

A1b **9. a3**

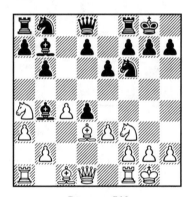

Diagram 718
After 9. a3

Of course, Black can retreat his bishop to e7, followed by ... d6 and ... Nbd7, with the same plan as in the main line. However, we recommend:

9. ... Bd6!? 10. exd4 Bxf3 11. Qxf3 Nc6 12. Be3 e5!

Diagram 719
After 12. ... e5!

This leads to interesting and sharp play. Let's look at some possible continuations:

a) 13. d5 e4! 14. Bxe4 Ne5 15. Qf5 g6 16. Qf4

Diagram 720
After 16. Qf4

16. ... Nxc4 17. Qh4 Nxe4 18. Qxe4 Nxe3 19. Qxe3

Diagram 721
After 19. Qxe3

Black stands better. His bishop is superior to White's knight.

b) 13. c5!?

Diagram 722
After 13. c5!?

White creates even bigger tactical complications!

13. ... exd4 14. Bg5 bxc5 15. Qf5

Black stands better. His bishop is superior to White's knight.

Diagram 723
After 15. Qf5

White's threat is Bxf6 and Qxh7. 15. ... g6! 16. Qxf6 Be7 17. Qf3 Bxg5 18. Nxc5 d6!

Diagram 724
After 18. ... d6!

Black keeps his extra pawn. If 19. Qxc6, then 19. ... Rc8.

c) 13. dxe5 (White's best move!) 13. ... Nxe5

Diagram 725
After 13. ... Nxe5

14. Qd1 Qc7 15. h3 Nxd3 16. Qxd3 Bh2+ 17. Kh1 Bf4

Diagram 726
After 17. ... Bf4

The position is about equal, as Black's only weakness on d7 is well-defended by his knight.

A2 8. Bd2

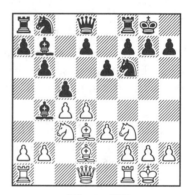

Diagram 727
After 8. Bd2

8. ... cxd4

If you don't like to play against the *isolani*, 8. ... d6 is a reasonable alternative—for example: 9. a3 Bxc3!.

9. exd4 d5 10. cxd5 Nxd5

Diagram 728
After 10. ... Nxd5

We've reached an isolated-pawn position similar to those often reached in the Caro-Kann Defense, Panov Variation. The main difference is that Black has already developed his bishop to b7 and his knight is still on b8, from where it can jump to d7 or c6.

After 10. ... Nxd5, White can play 11. Qe2, 11. Nxd5, 11. Rc1, or 11. Ne5!?.

A2a 11. Qe2

White has Qe4 in mind.

11. ... Nc6 12. Rfd1

If 12. Qe4, then ... Nf6 13. Qh4 Be7

Diagram 729
After 13. ... Be7

14. Ne4 (14. Bg5 g6!—e.g., 15. Rad1 Nb4, or 15. a3 Nh5) 14. ... Nxe4 15. Qxe4 g6 16. Bh6 Re8,

When playing against the isolated d-pawn, keep these important points in mind:

1. *The endgame is favorable for Black, so you should welcome the exchange of pieces;*

2. *Pay close attention to White's attacking chances and try to exchange White's knight when he reaches the e5 outpost;*

3. *Try to pressure the d4-pawn directly; and*

4. *Control d5.*

Diagram 730
After 16. ... Re8

with a solid position for Black, who meets 17. Bb5 with 17. ... Qd5.

12. ... Be7 13. Rac1 Rc8 14. a3 Nxc3

Diagram 731
After 14. ... Nxc3

Now if 15. bxc3, the a3-pawn becomes vulnerable.

15. Bxc3 Nb8!

Black intends to put his bishop on d5.

16. Be4 Bd5 17. Ne5 Nc6 18. Qf3 f6

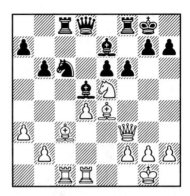

Diagram 732
After 18. ... f6

Trading pieces is good for Black.

19. Nxc6 Rxc6 20. Re1 Rf7

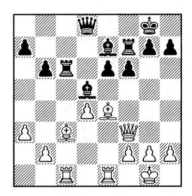

Diagram 733
After 20. ... Rf7

21. Bxd5 Qxd5 22. Qxd5 exd5 =

Gligoric–Keres, 1963.

A2b 11. Nxd5

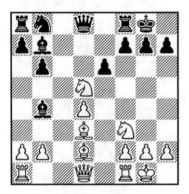

Diagram 734
After 11. Nxd5

11. ... Bxd2 12. Nxb6 axb6 13. Nxd2

13. Qxd2 Bxf3 14. gxf3 Ra5, and Black has a strong attack.

13. ... Qxd4

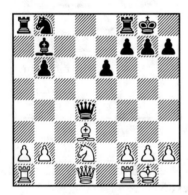

Diagram 735
After 13. ... Qxd4

Black is fine—Korelov –Keres, 1965.

A2c 11. Rc1 Nf6

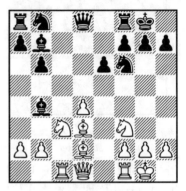

Diagram 736
After 11. ... Nf6

The knight retreats to f6 in order to defend the king and open up the bishop. We do not recommend capturing on c3 because after 12. bxc3, White improves his pawn structure.

12. a3 Be7 13. Re1 Nc6

Black threatens to win the d4-pawn.

14. Bf4

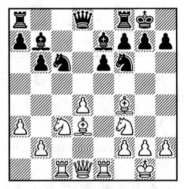

Diagram 737
After 14. Bf4

14. ... Rc8

Not 14. ... Nxd4? 15. Nxd4 Qxd4 16. Bxh7+.

15. Bb1 Na5

Black takes control of c4 and b3.

16. Ne5 Nc4!

It's important to exchange White's strong knight.

17. Nxc4

17. Re2 Nxe5 18. Bxe5 Ng4, with a structure similar to the main line.

17. ... Rxc4 18. Be5

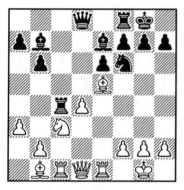

Diagram 738
After 18. Be5

With the threat of 19. Bxf6 Bxf6 20. Qd3.

18. ... Rc8 19. Qd3 g6 20. Qh3 Nd7 21. Bg3 Nf6

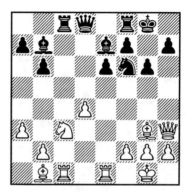

Diagram 739
After 21. ... Nf6

Here Bareev–Timman, 1995, ended in a draw by three-fold repetition.

A2d 11. Ne5!?

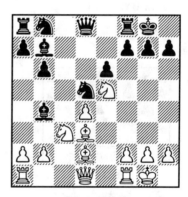

Diagram 740
After 11. Ne5!?

White would like to see 11. ... Nc6?! 12. Ba6±.

11. ... Nd7!

Black has a good game, with play similar to lines we're already familiar with.

B 6. Ne2

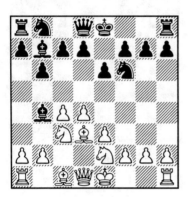

Diagram 741
After 6. Ne2

White sacrifices his g2-pawn for the initiative.

6. ... Bxg2 7. Rg1

It's very risky now to play 7. ... Be4.

Diagram 742
After 7. ... Be4

After 8. a3 (8. Rxg7? Bg6 traps the rook, or 8. Bxe4? Nxe4 9. Rxg7 Nxf2! 10. Kxf2 Qf6+, and White loses the rook) 8. ... Bxc3+ 9. Nxc3 Bxd3 10. Qxd3 0–0 (if 10. ... Nh5, then 11. e4! is even stronger than it is after 10. ... 0-0, Dzindzi–deFirmian, 1996, when White had more than enough compensation for the pawn) 11. e4!

Diagram 743
After 11. e4!

White, with his broad center and semi-open g-file, has a strong attack. Thus, instead of 7. ... Be4, we recommend ...

7. ... Bf3!

Diagram 744
After 7. ... Bf3!

8. Rxg7

8. Rg3 Bh5 (with ... Bg6 in mind); or 8. Qc2 0-0! 9. e4

Diagram 745
After 9. e4

9. ... Bxc3+ 10. bxc3 (10. Nxc3
Nc6) 10. ... e5!, and Black is better—for example: 11. dxe5 Ng4,
or 11. Bh6 Ne8 12. dxe5 f6!?.

8. ... Ng4

Black stands better because
his pieces are very active, e.g.
9. h3 f5! 10. hxg4 Qf6, trapping
the rook.

Summary:

*White's plan with 4. e3 and 5. Bd3 runs into Black's
natural defense based on fianchettoing his queen's bishop. We
then encounter a variety of middlegame positions. In all cases,
from "quasi-hedgehog" to isolani—even to pawn-grabbing
with ... Bxg2—Black holds his own.*

Chapter 23: Nimzo-Indian with 4. e3 and 5. Bd3
Memory Markers!

Diagram 746
After 5. Qf3

Diagram 747
After 21. d5

Diagram 748
After 13. d5

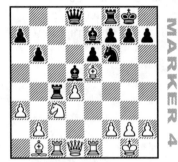

Diagram 749
After 18. ... Bd5

Chapter 23: Nimzo-Indian with 4. e3 and 5. Bd3
Solutions to Memory Markers!

No. 1   **5. ... Nc6**. Also good is 5. ... d5. See page 283.

No. 2   **21. ... b5!**. See page 287.

No. 3   **13. ... e4**. See page 288.

No. 4   **19. Qd3 g6 20. Nxd5** wins a pawn. See page 293.

The Nimzo-Indian Variations

Diagram 750, the Nimzo

Diagram 751, Chapter 21

Diagram 752, Chapter 22

Diagram 753, Chapter 23

Diagram 754, Chapter 24

Diagram 755, Chapter 25

Diagram 756, Chapter 26

Diagram 757, Chapter 27

Diagram 758, Chapter 28

Diagram 759, Chapter 29

Chapter 24: Nimzo-Indian with 4. e3 and 5. Ne2
Some Important Points to Look For

In this variation, White can prevent the doubling of his c-pawns—but then Black gets better development. If White acquiesces to doubled pawns, Black gets a good endgame.

◆ Black's active pieces guarantee him equal chances. See Diagram 764.

◆ Black does okay in this tough ending. See Diagram 769.

◆ White has two choices—neither of them promising. See Diagram 775.

◆ Portisch finally took Fischer's rook—but got a bad game. See Diagram 777.

Outline of Variations

1. d4 Nf6 2. c4 e6 3. Nc3 Bb4 4. e3 b6 5. Ne2 Ba6 *(298)* [E45]

A 6. a3 Bxc3+ 7. Nxc3 d5 8. b3 0-0 9. Be2 dxc4 10. bxc4 Nc6 *(299)*

B 6. Ng3 Bxc3+ 7. bxc3 d5 *(300)*

    B1 8. Ba3 Bxc4 9. Bxc4 dxc4 *(301)*

        B1a 10. e4 Qd7 11. 0-0 Qb5 12. Rb1 Qa6 13. Qc1 Nbd7
            14. Rd1 0-0-0 *(301)*

        B1b 10. Qa4+ Qd7 11. Qxc4 Qc6 12. Qxc6+ Nxc6
            13. c4 0-0-0 *(301)*

    B2 8. cxd5 Bxf1 9. Kxf1 Qxd5 10. Qd3 0-0 11. e4 Qa5 12. e5 Nd5
        013. Ne4 f5 *(302)*

    B3 8. Qf3 0-0 *(303)*

        B3a 9. e4 dxe4 10. Nxe4 Nxe4 11. Qxe4 Qd7 *(303)*

        B3b 9. cxd5 Qxd5 10. e4 Qa5 *(304)*

Chapter 24
Nimzo-Indian
with 4. e3 and 5. Ne2

In this variation, named after the great Akiba Rubinstein, White develops his king's knight to e2 so that he can recapture on c3 with a piece, keeping his pawn structure intact. Rubinstein played it in the early twentieth century; in modern times, Victor Korchnoi and Svetozar Gligoric were prominent practitioners.

1. d4 Nf6 2. c4 e6 3. Nc3 Bb4 4. e3 b6 5. Ne2

Diagram 760
After 5. Ne2

5. ... Ba6

Black uses White's somewhat awkward development to create immediate counter-play against the c4-pawn. Here White's main moves are 6. a3 and 6. Ng3.

A 6. a3 Bxc3+

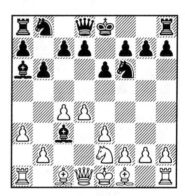

Diagram 761
After 6. ... Bxc3+

7. Nxc3 d5

Black's idea is to exchange light-square bishops, leaving White with a bishop that is restricted by the central formation he has chosen.

8. b3

Now 8. cxd5 Bxf1 9. Kxf1 Nxd5 is fine for Black. If 8. Qf3 c6 9. b3 0-0 10. g4!?. White's aggressive pawn thrust is not dangerous for Black: 10. ... Nbd7 11. g5 Ne8 12. cxd5

Diagram 762
After 12. cxd5

12. ... Bxf1 13. dxc6 Ba6, and Black stands well.

8. ... 0–0 9. Be2 dxc4 10. bxc4 Nc6

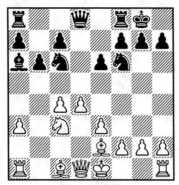

Diagram 763
After 10. ... Nc6

Black has ... Na5 in mind.

11. a4

White intends to meet ... Na5 with Nb5.

After 11. Qa4 Na5 12. 0–0 Qd7, White's weaknesses become even more apparent.

11. ... Na5 12. Nb5 c6 13. Na3 c5

Diagram 764
After 13. ... c5

With about equal play (M. Gurevich–Vladimirov, 2001).

B 6. Ng3

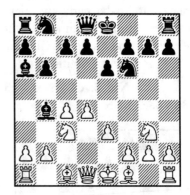

Diagram 765
After 6. Ng3

White's idea is to play e4 and create a strong center; Black in turn prepares immediate counterplay in the center and tries to exchange light-square bishops.

6. ... Bxc3+ 7. bxc3 d5

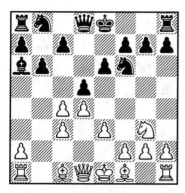

Diagram 766
After 7. ... d5

White's strongest move now is 8. Ba3. Two other tries, 8. cxd5 and 8. Qf3, lead to good play for Black.

B1 8. Ba3 Bxc4 9. Bxc4 dxc4

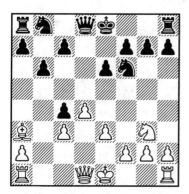

Diagram 767
After 9. ... dxc4

Now White can play for the initiative with 10. e4 or win the pawn back with 10. Qa4+.

B1a 10. e4 Qd7 11. 0–0 Qb5 12. Rb1 Qa6 13. Qc1 Nbd7 14. Rd1 0–0–0

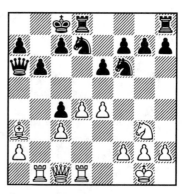

Diagram 768
After 14. ... 0-0-0

With complex play. See the illustrative game Epishin–Berg, 2002.

B1b 10. Qa4+ Qd7 11. Qxc4 Qc6 12. Qxc6+ Nxc6 13. c4 0–0–0

Diagram 769
After 13. ... 0-0-0

This endgame is one of the key positions in the 6. Ng3 variation. White has a strong center and his plan is to gain even more space with f3 and e4. Black needs to keep the pressure on d4 in order to prevent e4, and to counter with ... Na5 and ... c5.

After 14. Ke2 Rd7 15. f3

Rhd8 16. h4 Kb7 17. Rhd1 Na5
18. Rac1 c5!,

Diagram 770
After 18. ... c5!

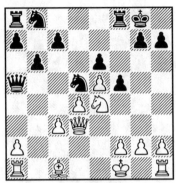

Diagram 772
After 13. ... f5!

the position, from Gulko–Rech-
lis, 2000, is equal. If 19. dxc5?,
then 19. ... Rxd1 20. Rxd1 Rxd1
21. Kxd1 Nxc4.

B2 8. cxd5 Bxf1 9. Kxf1

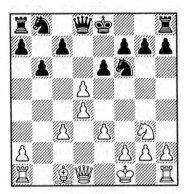

Diagram 771
After 9. Kxf1

9. ... Qxd5 10. Qd3 0–0

Black's position is very solid,
while White's king is misplaced
and his queenside pawns are
weak.

**11. e4 Qa5 12. e5 Nd5 13.
Ne4 f5!**

14. Ng5

Or 14. exf6 Nxf6, with a better position for Black. White's
king is in danger.

**14. ... Re8 15. Bd2 h6 16.
Nf3 c5**

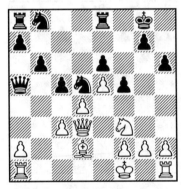

Diagram 773
After 16. ... c5

17. g3

A better move for White is
17. c4, but after 17. ... Qa6
18. Qe2 Ne7, Black has an easy
game.

17. ... cxd4 18. cxd4 Qa6!

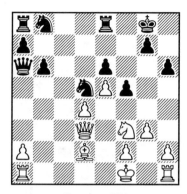

Diagram 774
After 18. ... Qa6!

Black has a better endgame, as in Santos–Leitao, 2001.

B3 **8. Qf3 0–0**

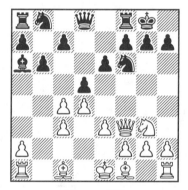

Diagram 775
After 8. ... 0-0

White has 9. e4 or 9. cxd5.

B3a **9. e4 dxe4 10. Nxe4 Nxe4 11. Qxe4 Qd7!**

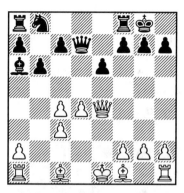

Diagram 776
After 11. ... Qd7!

Black stands better. He plans to play … Nc6-a5, attacking the weak c4-pawn.

12. Ba3

12. Qxa8 Nc6 13. Qxf8+ Kxf8 ∓. White's pawns eventually fall.

12. ... Re8 13. Bd3 f5!

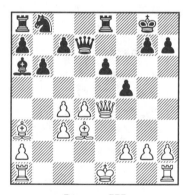

Diagram 777
After 13. ... f5!

14. Qxa8 Nc6 15. Qxe8+ Qxe8 ∓

Even after all of White's improvements, his restricted rooks here are inferior to Black's queen, which has plenty of easy targets (Portisch–Fischer, 1966).

B3b 9. cxd5 Qxd5

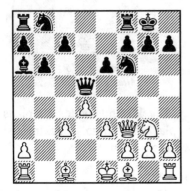

Diagram 778
After 9. ... Qxd5

10. e4 Qa5

The game Sadler–Brunner, 1999, continued: 11. Be2 Bxe2 12. Nxe2 Nbd7 13. 0–0 c5 14. Ng3 cxd4 15. cxd4 Rac8,

Diagram 779
After 15. ... Rac8

with a comfortable position for Black, who controls the only open file.

Summary:

If, after 5. Ne2 Ba6, White goes for the bishop pair, Black's better development provides him with sufficient counter-play. If White allows the doubling of his c-pawn with 6. Ng3 after all, it leads to a dynamic game.

Chapter 24: Nimzo-Indian with 4. e3 and 5. Ne2
Memory Markers!

Diagram 780
After 17. Bb2

Diagram 781
After 6. ... d5

Diagram 782
After 17. c4

Diagram 783
After 10. Bxa6

Chapter 24: Nimzo-Indian with 4. e3 and 5. Ne2
Solutions to Memory Markers!

No. 1   **17. ... Qd7.** By attacking the a-pawn, Black forces the transition to a safe ending: 18. dxc5 Qxd1 19. Bxd1 bxc5. See page 300.

No. 2   **7. Qa4+,** winning a piece. See page 300.

No. 3   **17. ... Qa6.** See page 302.

No. 4   **10. ... Qxf3,** with a good endgame. See page 304.

Chapter 25: Nimzo-Indian with 4. f3
Some Important Points to Look For

White's 4. f3 has a lot in common with the Saemisch (Chapter 21). But here Black can counter in the center before White can play e4.

♦ The pawn is untouchable. See Diagram 785.

♦ With strong play on the dark squares. See Diagram 789.

♦ Black has important outposts on d4 and c5. See Diagram 792.

♦ An important improvement: 17. ... a4!. See Diagram 793.

Outline of Variations

1. d4 Nf6 2. c4 e6 3. Nc3 Bb4 4. f3 d5 5. a3 Be7! 6. e4 dxe4 7. fxe4 e5! 8. d5 Bc5 *(306)* [E20]

Chapter 25
Nimzo-Indian
with 4. f3

Popular in the early 1990s, when teenage Alexei Shirov used it to score some well-publicized victories, 4. f3 has a lot in common with the Saemisch. White attempts to take control of the center right away without wasting time on 4. a3.

Black found the answers, and the variation lost fashion, but it's still seen on the club level. Black should counterattack in the center before White can comfortably execute his planned e4.

1. d4 Nf6 2. c4 e6 3. Nc3 Bb4 4. f3

Diagram 784
After 4. f3

4. ... d5 5. a3

Now that Black has played ... d5, White is not afraid of 5. ... Bxc3+, because after he recaptures and plays e3, he would have a strong center and an opportunity to exchange one of his doubled pawns. But Black has a better move, preserving his bishop.

5. ... Be7! 6. e4 dxe4 7. fxe4 e5!

Black should counterattack in the center before White can comfortably execute his planned e4.

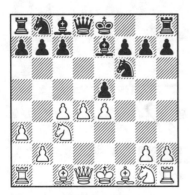

Diagram 785
After 7. ... e5!

This important move weakens the dark squares in White's camp.

8. d5

After 8. dxe5 Qxd1+ 9. Kxd1 Ng4, threatening ... Nf2+ and ... Nxe5, White's position is ruined.

8. ... Bc5

Diagram 786
After 8. ... Bc5

Now on 9. Be2, we play 9. ... Ng4!.

After 10. Bxg4 Qh4+ 11. g3 Qxg4, Black stands better because he owns the bishop pair

and because White has weaknesses in his position. After 9. Bg5 Bd4!

Diagram 787
After 9. ... Bd4!

10. Bd3 (10. Nf3 Bxc3+ 11. bxc3 Qd6 12. Bd3 Na6 13. 0–0 Nc5 14. Qc2 h6 as in the game Formanek–McCambridge, 1995, Black stands well) 10. ... h6 11. Bh4 c6 12. Nge2 Bg4

Diagram 788
After 12. ... Bg4

Black wants to exchange his light-square bishop to create more breathing room for his remaining pieces.

13. Qc2 Bxe2 14. Nxe2 Be3 15. Ng3 g6 16. Nf1 Bd4 17. 0–0–0 Nbd7

Diagram 789
After 17. ... Nbd7

With strong play on the dark squares, as in the game Georghiu–Keres, 1964.

Now back to the main line (Diagram 786).

9. Nf3 Bg4

Black should not be tempted by 9. ... Ng4?, because after 10. b4! Bf2+ 11. Ke2 and now, 11. ... c5 12. Nb5! a6 13. Qa4!, followed by h3, yields White a strong initiative.

10. h3

This is White's main move. After 10. b4 Bd4, Black's dark-square bishop becomes extremely powerful. And after 10. Be2 Bxf3 11. Bxf3 Nbd7,

Diagram 790
After 11. ... Nbd7

Black will play ... c6, with a possible ... Qb6 and ... Bd4 to follow, giving him a very active position and good play on the dark squares.

White must solve the problem of where to castle. Castling kingside is impossible, and Black is ready to attack White's king on the queenside with ... c6 and ... b5.

10. ... Bxf3 11. Qxf3

Diagram 791
After 11. Qxf3

11. ... Nbd7 12. Bd3 a5

Or 12. ... c6 13. Bd2 a5, and starting a pawn storm is not good for White: 14. g4 0-0 15. g5 Ne8 16. h4 Bd4.

Diagram 792
After 16. ... Bd4

In Boor—Perelshteyn, 2006, White sacrificed with 17. Ne2, and soon Eugene was winning.

After our main-line 12. ... a5, Black secures an outpost on c5. He plans to put his bishop on d4 and his knight on c5.

13. Bd2 0–0 14. 0–0–0

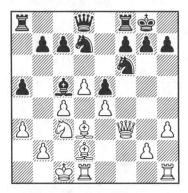

Diagram 793
After 14. 0-0-0

The position is from Volkov–Shaposhnikov, 2001. Black will use the outposts on d4 and c5 and, with a timely ... c6 and ... b5, mount an attack on White's

Summary:

The goal of 4. f3 is clear—to play e2-e4 and to dominate the center. To counter this plan, Black preserves his dark-square bishop and, playing along the dark squares, gets an excellent, dynamic game.

king. The game continued:

14. ... Ne8

Black transfers his knight to a better square, d6, where it helps with the attack on White's king.

15. Kb1 Nd6 16. Rc1 Qe7 17. Rhe1

It's hard for White to get any attacking chances as Black's king is quite safe.

17. ... a4!

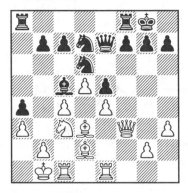

Diagram 794
After 17. ... a4!

An improvement to the game, in which Black played 17. ... Rfb8, allowing Na4. With the new move, Black stops Na4 and secures the b3-square.

18. Ka2 c6!

Black dominates on the queenside, with the possibilities of ... Bd4 and ... Nc5 controlling all the key outposts.

Chapter 25: Nimzo-Indian with 4. f3
Memory Markers!

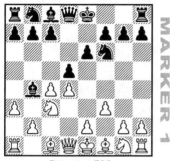

Diagram 795
After 5. a3

MARKER 1

Diagram 796
After 7. fxe4

MARKER 2

Diagram 797
After 12. Bd3

MARKER 3

Diagram 798
After 17. ... Rfb8

MARKER 4

Chapter 25: Nimzo-Indian with 4. f3
Solutions to Memory Markers!

No. 1   **5. ... Be7!,** preserving the bishop. See page 307.

No. 2   **7. ... e5!,** taking control of dark squares. (The pawn is untouchable.) See page 307.

No. 3   **12. ... a5.** Black secures an outpost on c5 for his bishop, and potentially, for his knight. See page 309.

No. 4   **18. Na4!,** stopping Black's assault. See page 310.

Chapter 26: Nimzo-Indian with 4. g3
Some Important Points to Look For

White temporarily ignores the pin on his knight, playing 4. g3 to prevent Black's fianchetto. But the plan is slow, allowing a prepared defender to seize the initiative.

◆ Black attacks the c3-knight.
  See Diagram 800.

◆ White's queen is unprotected on c2.
  See Diagram 802.

◆ ... d5 is the important liberating thrust. See Diagram 806.

◆ Black has played a surprising but logical retreat! See Diagram 812.

Outline of Variations
1. d4 Nf6 2. c4 e6 3. Nc3 Bb4 4. g3 c5 5. Nf3 Ne4 6. Qd3 cxd4 7. Nxd4 Qa5 *(312)* [E20]

Chapter 26
Nimzo-Indian
with 4. g3

White's immediate preparation to fianchetto his light-square bishop is called the Romanishin Variation, after the Ukrainian grandmaster Oleg Romanishin.

1. d4 Nf6 2. c4 e6 3. Nc3 Bb4 4. g3

Nowadays the line is sometimes referred to as the Romanishin–Kasparov System because of Garry Kasparov's contributions to its theory.

White ignores the pin, striving for fast development. He intends Bg2, Nf3, and 0–0, putting pressure on the long diagonal.

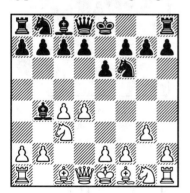

Diagram 799
After 4. g3

4. ... c5

Black answers the wing demonstration with an attack in the center.

5. Nf3 Ne4

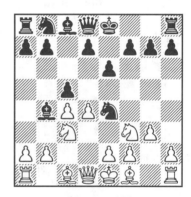

Diagram 800
After 5. ... Ne4

Black doubles the pressure on the pinned knight, temporarily putting White on the defensive.

6. Qd3

White could also play the weaker 6. Qc2 cxd4 7. Nxd4 (7. Qxe4 dxc3) 7. ... Qa5.

Diagram 801
After 7. ... Qa5

If 8. Nb3?, Black should not play 8. ... Nxc3? 9. Nxa5 Ne4+ 10. Bd2 (10. Kd1? Nxf2, checkmate) 10. ... Bxd2+ 11. Kd1, when White keeps the queen with a winning position.

However, the answer to White's second-choice line is 8. ... Qf5!.

Diagram 802
After 8. ... Qf5!

Black takes advantage of the fact that White's queen is unprotected. Now White cannot defend against numerous threats: ... Qxf2, ... Nxc3 or ... Nxg3—for example, 9. f3 loses a piece: 9. ... Nxc3 10. Qxf5 Na4+, followed by ... exf5.

6. ... cxd4 7. Nxd4

If 7. Qxd4, then 7. ... Qf6 or 7. ... Bxc3+ 8. bxc3 Nf6 are both good for Black.

7. ... Qa5

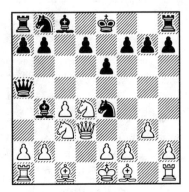

Diagram 803
After 7. ... Qa5

8. Nb3

8. Qxe4? Bxc3+

8. ... Nxc3 9. Bd2

9. Nxa5 Ne4+ 10. Bd2 (10. Kd1? loses after 10. ... Nxf2+ and ... Nxd3) 10. ... Bxd2+ 11. Qxd2 Nxd2 12. Kxd2 Nc6 =.

Diagram 804
After 12. ... Nc6 =

If 13. Nxc6, then 13. ... dxc6, followed by ... e5.

9. ... Ne4 10. Qxe4

10. Nxa5 transposes to

9. Nxa5.

10. ... Bxd2+ 11. Nxd2

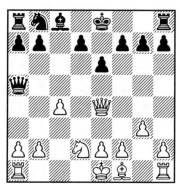

Diagram 805
After 11. Nxd2

After some forced play, the position has been clarified. White still needs to make three moves to finish his development: Bg2, Qe3, and 0–0. In the meantime, Black castles and takes over the center.

11. ... 0–0 12. Bg2 Nc6 13. Qe3 d5

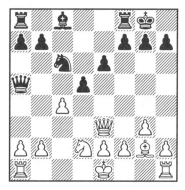

Diagram 806
After 13. ... d5

14. 0–0

14. cxd5 exd5 15. 0–0 d4

16. Qd3

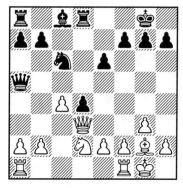

Diagram 807
After 16. Qd3

(16. Qf4? g5) 16. ... Bf5, with active piece play for Black.

14. ... d4 15. Qd3 Rd8

Diagram 808
After 15. ... Rd8

16. a3

After 16. Rfd1 e5 17. a3 Qc7 18. b4 Ne7 (with the idea ... Bf5), the game Christiansen–de-Firmian, 2000, continued: 19. c5

Diagram 809
After 19. c5

19. ... Bf5 20. Qf3 Rab8 21. Ne4 Bxe4 22. Qxe4 Nd5 (the knight is heading to c3) 23. Rd2 a5 24. Qd3 axb4 25. Qc4 Nb6 26. Qb5 Nd5 27. axb4 Nc3 28. Qc4 Ra8 29. Rxa8 Rxa8, draw.

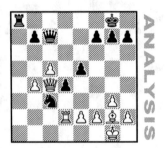

Diagram 810
After 29. ... Rxa8

16. ... Qc7

Cheparinov—Bacrot, 2008, reached an equal ending after 16. ... Ne5 17. b4 Nxd3 18. bxa5 Nc5 19. Rab1 Rb8 20. Ne4 Na4! 21. Rb4 Bd7.

After our main-line 16. ... Qc7, Black's idea becomes clear in a few moves.

17. b4 Ne5! 18. Qe4

Diagram 811
After 18. Qe4

18. ... Ng6 19. c5 f5 20. Qd3 e5 21. Nc4 e4 22. Qd2 Nh8!

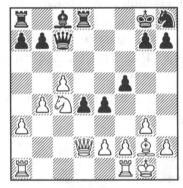

Diagram 812
After 22. ... Nh8!

Black plans to play ... Nf7, completely controlling the center.

23. Nd6 Nf7 24. Qxd4 Nxd6 25. cxd6 Qxd6 26. Qxd6 Rxd6

Black plans to play ... Nf7, completely controlling the center.

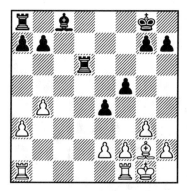

Diagram 813
After 26. ... Rxd6

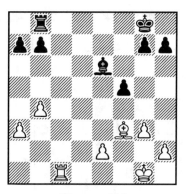

Diagram 814
After 31. Rc1

The endgame is equal—for example:

27. Rfd1 Rxd1+ 28. Rxd1 Be6 29. f3 exf3 30. Bxf3 Rb8 31. Rc1

31. ... Rc8! =

Summary:

The purpose of 4. g3 is to prevent Black's queenside fianchetto. White's play here is slow. Black can wrest the initiative with 4. ... c5 and 5. ... Ne4, increasing the pressure on White's pinned knight. Then White has to be very careful. The best he can hope for after accurate play is an even endgame.

Chapter 26: Nimzo-Indian with 4. g3

Memory Markers!

Diagram 815
After 5. d5

MARKER 1

Diagram 816
After 8. Nc2

MARKER 2

Diagram 817
After 14. f4

MARKER 3

Diagram 818
After 13. Qf4

MARKER 4

Chapter 26: Nimzo-Indian with 4. g3
Solutions to Memory
Markers!

No. 1   **5. ... b5! 6. dxe6 fxe6 7. cxb5 d5**. Black has more than adequate compensation for his sacrificed pawn. Also good is the solid 5. ... Ne4 6. Bd2 ∓ (6. Qc2? Qf6, winning a pawn—Vaganian–Karpov. 1969). See page 313.

No. 2   **8. ... Bxc3+ 9. bxc3 Nc5** ∓. See page 314.

No. 3   **14. ... e5!**. (Also good is the modest 14. ... f6, preparing ... e5.) Black's bishop has been freed and, if 15. fxe5, White's e5-pawn will be very weak. See page 314.

No. 4   **13. ... e5! 14. Qe3 Nd4**, with equality. See page 315.

Chapter 27: Nimzo-Indian with 4. Bg5—the Leningrad System
Some Important Points to Look For

With 4. ... h6, Black puts the question to White's Leningrad bishop. After its retreat, Black follows up with ... c5, playing for a closed position in which he can pressure White's doubled pawns.

◆ The key move.
  See Diagram 825.

◆ In this closed position,
  Black's king is quite comfortable.
  See Diagram 828.

◆ White's attack goes nowhere.
  See Diagram 830.

◆ Black isn't concerned about
  the opening of the h-file.
  See Diagram 839.

Outline of Varaitions

1. d4 Nf6 2. c4 e6 3. Nc3 Bb4 4. Bg5 h6 5. Bh4 c5 6. d5 Bxc3+ 7. bxc3 d6 8.e3 e5 *(320)* [E31]

    A 9. f3 Bf5! *(322)*

        A1 10. e4 Bc8! 11. Bd3 Nbd7 12. Ne2 Qe7 13. Bf2 *(323)*

        A2 10. Bd3 Bxd3 11. Qxd3 Nbd7 12. Ne2 0-0 13. 0-0 Qa5 *(325)*

        A3 10. Qb3 b6 11. h3 Nbd7 12. g4 Bh7 13. Ne2 g5 14. Bf2 h5!? *(326)*

    B 9. Bd3 e4! 10. Bc2 g5 11. Bg3 Qe7 12. h4 *(326)*

    C 9. Qc2 Qe7! 10. Nf3 Nbd7 11. Nd2 *(327)*

Chapter 27
Nimzo-Indian
with 4. Bg5, the Leningrad System

In the Leningrad System, White answers a pin with a pin, developing his bishop. He hopes to entice Black to play ... h6 and ... g5, when he can exploit the resulting weaknesses.

1. d4 Nf6 2. c4 e6 3. Nc3 Bb4 4. Bg5

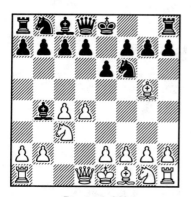

Diagram 819
After 4. Bg5

4. ... h6 5. Bh4 c5 6. d5

On 6. e3, Black seizes the initiative with 6. ... cxd4 7. exd4 Qa5 8. Qc2 Ne4

Diagram 820
After 8. ... Ne4

Now after 9. Rc1 d5 10. Bd3 Qxa2 11. Bxe4 dxe4 12. Nge2 Qxc4

Diagram 821
After 12. ... Qxc4

13. Qxe4 0–0, White does not have sufficient compensation for the pawn (Klossner–A. Sokolov, 1994).

6. ... Bxc3+ 7. bxc3 d6

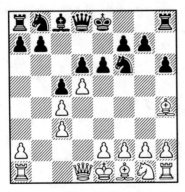

Diagram 822
After 7. ... d6

Black's idea is to set up his pawns on dark squares—e5, d6, and c5—and to keep the center closed. Then White's ownership of the two bishops becomes insignificant; he will be left with the chronic weakness of doubled c-pawns.

8. e3

After 8. dxe6 Bxe6 9. e3 g5 10. Bg3

Diagram 823
After 10. Bg3

10. ... Ne4 11. Qc2 Nxg3 12. hxg3 Nc6 13. Nf3 Qe7 14. Bd3 0–0–0

Diagram 824
After 14. ... 0-0-0

Black is much better, due to White's weak c-pawns. Additionally, it's hard for White to castle because 0–0 invites the threatening ... h5-h4 push.

8. ... e5

Play starts to branch off here. White can choose 9. f3, 9. Bd3, or 9. Qc2.

A 9. f3 Bf5!

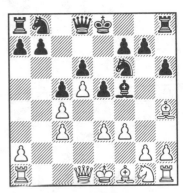

Diagram 825
After 9. ... Bf5!

Black's idea is to exchange light-square bishops if White plays 10. Bd3, or otherwise provoke 10. e4, which, as we will see shortly, only plays into

Black's hands.

Now White can choose from 10. e4, 10. Bd3, and 10. Qb3.

A1 10. e4 Bc8!

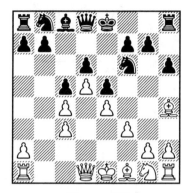

Diagram 826
After 10. ... Bc8!

Black initiates a very strong maneuver intended to lock up White's light-square bishop while leaving his own active. (Of course he shouldn't play 10. ... Bg6 or 10. ... Bh7, when his bishop is caged in by White's pawns.) Black's plan is ... Nbd7, ... Nf8, ... g5, and ... Ng6.

11. Bd3 Nbd7 12. Ne2 Qe7

Black's last is a useful move that prepares an escape for his king to c7 via d8.

13. Bf2

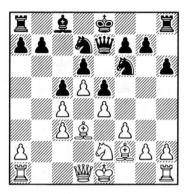

Diagram 827
After 13. Bf2

After 13. 0–0 g5 14. Bf2 Nf8, followed by ... Ng6, Black gets strong play on the kingside.

13. ... Nh5 14. Be3 Qf6

With the idea of ... Nf4.

15. Qd2 g5 16. Nc1 Nf8 17. Rb1 Kd8

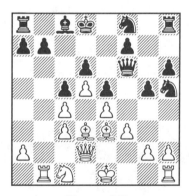

Diagram 828
After 17. ... Kd8

18. a4 a5

Black stops a5 and sets up a fortress with ... Ra6 and ... b6.

19. g3 Kc7 20. Rf1 Ng6

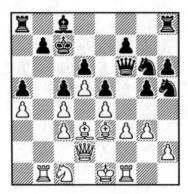

Diagram 829
After 20. ... Ng6

Black successfully executed his plan in the game Yermolinsky–Chow, 1993, which continued:

21. Qd1

For the next few moves, both sides are redeploying their forces. Their slow maneuvers are characteristic of these closed positions.

21. ... Qe7 22. Qb3 Ra6

Black's idea is to play ... b6.

23. Rf2 Ng7 24. Rfb2

Slow maneuvers
are characteristic
of these
closed positions.

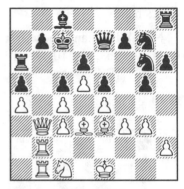

Diagram 830
After 24. Rfb2

24. ... b6

This puts an end once and for all to White's attack.

25. Qc2 Bd7 26. Be2 Qe8 27. Bd1 f5!

White's attack on the queenside has been stymied. Black starts timely counter-play on the kingside.

28. Nd3

Diagram 831
After 28. Nd3

28. ... f4

Gaining even more space!

29. Bf2 Qe7 30. Qd2 h5 31. gxf4 gxf4 32. Ke2 h4

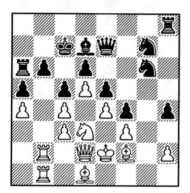

Diagram 832
After 32. ... h4

Although the players agreed to a draw, Black's position is slightly better because of his kingside space advantage.

A2 10. Bd3 Bxd3 11. Qxd3 Nbd7 12. Ne2

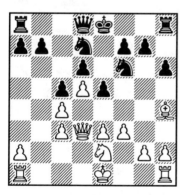

Diagram 833
After 12. Ne2

Black has a solid position with several good plans, for example:

12. ... 0–0 13. 0–0 Qa5

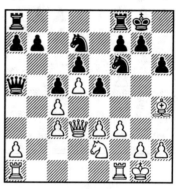

Diagram 834
After 13. ... Qa5

with the idea of playing ... Rae8 and ... e4, or if White answers with e4, playing ... Nh7, and preparing ... Qa4 and ... Nb6, attacking the c4 pawn.

After 14. Bxf6 (14. Ng3 right away loses to 14. ... g5) 14. ... Nxf6 15. Ng3 g6 16. f4 e4! 17. Nxe4 Nxe4 18. Qxe4,

Diagram 835
After 18. Qxe4

18. ... Qxc3 leads to an equal game.

A3 10. Qb3   **B** 9. Bd3

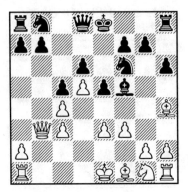

Diagram 836
After 10. Qb3

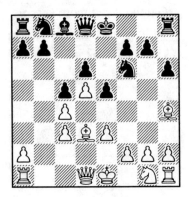

Diagram 838
After 9. Bd3

10. ... b6 11. h3 Nbd7 12. g4 Bh7 13. Ne2 g5 14. Bf2 h5!?

9. ... e4! 10. Bc2

10. Bxe4? loses a piece after 10. ... g5; and 10. Bxf6 Qxf6 11. Bxe4 Qxc3+ is also good for Black.

10. ... g5 11. Bg3 Qe7 12. h4

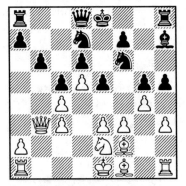

Diagram 837
After 14. ... h5

Black prepares an interesting counterattack.

15. h4 e4!

With active play where the tactics are in Black's favor. See sample game Timman–Dzindzi, 1977.

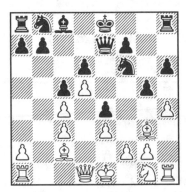

Diagram 839
After 12. h4

12. ... Rg8

Black is not afraid of the opening of the h-file because his king safely goes to c7.

13. hxg5 hxg5 14. Ne2 Kd8

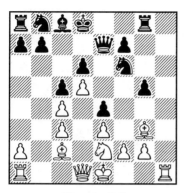

Diagram 840
After 14. ... Kd8

Black follows up with ... Kc7 and ... Nbd7, with a solid position.

ⓒ 9. Qc2

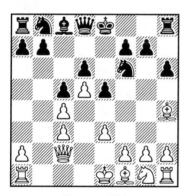

Diagram 841
After 9. Qc2

With the idea of playing Bd3 next, thus preventing ... e4.

9. ... Qe7! 10. Nf3

10. Bd3 is now met by 10. ... g5 11. Bg3 e4.

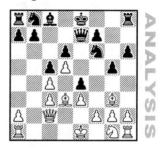

Diagram 842
After 11. ... e4

10. ... Nbd7 11. Nd2

Now one possible good continuation is 11. ... g5 12. Bg3 e4! (anyway!) 13. h4 Rg8.

Diagram 843
After 13. ... Rg8

Black's plan is to put his king on c7 and, when possible, play ... Ne5 with a very solid position.

White plays 9. Qc2 with the idea of Bd3, preventing ... e4.

Gokhale—Kacheishvili, 2001, continued: 14. Be2 Kd8 15. Rb1 Kc7 16. Rb5 b6 17. Rb2 (White has no active plan), and here Black missed a chance to play 17. ... Ne5!,

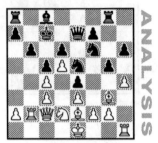

Diagram 844
After 17. ... Ne5

with a better game. Black's e-pawn is practically untouchable.

After 18. hxg5 hxg5 19. Nxe4? Bf5 ∓ 20. f3 g4, White's position collapses.

Summary:

Against 4. Bg5, we recommend first playing 4. ... h6, forcing White's bishop to commit to h4. Then we continue with 5. ... c5, aiming for a locked position in which White suffers doubled c-pawns. In all lines, Black does well— even coming out on top.

Chapter 27: Nimzo-Indian with 4. Bg5—the Leningrad System
Memory Markers!

Diagram 845
After 18. ... Kc7

MARKER 1

Diagram 846
After 27. Bd1

MARKER 2

Diagram 847
After 16. f4

MARKER 3

Diagram 848
After 14. Ne2

MARKER 4

Chapter 27: Nimzo-Indian with 4. Bg5—the Leningrad System
Solutions to Memory Markers!

No. 1   **19. a5!,** preventing Black from building a queen-side fortress. See page 323.

No. 2   **27. ... f5,** starting a kingside attack. See page 324.

No. 3   **16. ... e4!.** See page 325.

No. 4   **14. ... Kd8!.** Black's king will be safe on c7. See page 327.

Chapter 28: Nimzo-Indian with 4. Qb3

Some Important Points to Look For

White's 4. Qb3 attacks Black's bishop and defends against doubled pawns. But Black attacks and defends with 4. ... c5 and gets an easy game.

◆ The defining move of the line. See Diagram 849.

◆ A familiar knight-jump comes next. See Diagram 850.

◆ Black has a comfortable game. See Diagram 851.

◆ White lacks compensation for the pawn. See Diagram 852.

Outline of Variations

1. d4 Nf6 2. c4 e6 3. Nc3 Bb4 4. Qb3 c5 5. dxc5 Nc6 6. Nf3 *(330)* [E22]

Chapter 28
Nimzo-Indian
with 4. Qb3

This system is sometimes called the Spielmann Variation, after the Viennese GM R udolf Spielmann, a master of aggression, who played the line three times during the Carlsbad tournament in 1929. Although it both attacks Black's unprotected bishop and defends against doubled pawns, it's less popular than other lines—White's queen is often misplaced on b3 and Black gets comfortable play.

1. d4 Nf6 2. c4 e6 3. Nc3 Bb4 4. Qb3

Diagram 849
After 4. Qb3

4. ... c5

We recommend this move, although 4. ... Nc6 also leads to equality.

5. dxc5 Nc6

5. ... Na6 is fine too.

6. Nf3

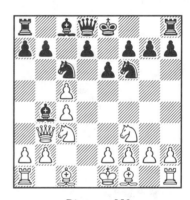

Diagram 850
After 6. Nf3

6. ... Ne4 7. Bd2 Nxd2 8. Nxd2 0-0 9. e3 Bxc5 10. Nde4 b6 11. Be2 Be7

Diagram 851
After 11. ... Be7

Diagram 852
After 17. ... Kh8!

Black has comfortable play—for example: 12. 0–0–0!? a6 13. g4 Qc7 14. g5? (reckless) 14. ... Na5 15. Qc2 Nxc4 16. Bxc4 Qxc4 17. Rhg1 Kh8! (prophylaxis).

White lacks sufficient compensation for the pawn (Blanco–Lautier, 1999).

Summary:

At first glance, 4. Qb3 is stronger than 4. Qc2 and played with the same idea—to be able to retake on c3 with his queen, preserving White's pawn formation. After all, 4. Qb3 also attacks Black's bishop.

However, Black can protect his bishop with a natural developing move, and at the same time use the e4-square, which White's queen has abandoned. Black gets a comfortable, easy game.

Chapter 28: Nimzo-Indian with 4. Qb3
Memory Markers!

Diagram 853
After 5. a3

MARKER 1

Diagram 854
After 9. Nde4

MARKER 2

Diagram 855
After 10. a3

MARKER 3

Diagram 856
After 17. Rhg1

MARKER 4

Chapter 28: Nimzo-Indian with 4. Qb3
Solutions to Memory Markers!

No. 1   **5. ... Nxd4,** winning a pawn (6. Qxb4?? Nc2+). See page 331.

No. 2   **9. ... f5,** winning back a pawn. See page 331.

No. 3   **10. ... Qa5,** and the c5-pawn falls anyway. The White queen on b3 blocks White's b-pawn. See page 331.

No. 4   **17. ... Kh8!.** See page 332.

Chapter 29: Nimzo-Indian with 4. Bd2

Some Important Points to Look For

White's fourth move is natural, immediately unpinning his knight. But his unchallenging choice allows Black to develop easily.

◆ Unchallenged, Black simply castles. See Diagram 857.

◆ The smoke has cleared. See Diagram 860.

◆ White's kingside is still in the barracks. See Diagram 861.

◆ Black intends ... Be4. See Diagram 862.

Outline of Variations

1. d4 Nf6 2. c4 e6 3. Nc3 Bb4 4. Bd2 0-0 5. a3 Bxc3 6. Bxc3 Ne4 7. Qc2 Nxc3 8. Qxc3 *(334)* [E20]

Chapter 29
Nimzo-Indian
with 4. Bd2

White unpins his knight immediately—a natural reaction that could come from any "park" player. The move, however, does not create any opening problems for Black, who has several good continuations.

1. d4 Nf6 2. c4 e6 3. Nc3 Bb4 4. Bd2

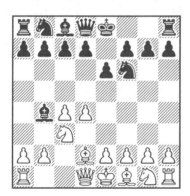

Diagram 857
After 4. Bd2

4. ... 0–0

We recommend this move. In *The Encyclopedia of Chess Openings*, GM Vadim Zvyagintsev suggests 4. ... b6 5. e4 (5. f3 Bxc3 6. bxc3 d5 7. e3 Ba6, and Black has the better game—in this line, White's dark-square bishop doesn't belong on d2!).

Diagram 858
After 7. ... Ba6

After 5. e4, Black plays 5. ... Bxc3 6. Bxc3

Diagram 859
After 6. Bxc3

6. ... Nxe4 7. Qg4 Bb7! 8. Qxg7 Rf8, with a good game.

Diagram 860
After 8. ... Rf8

5. a3

White's alternatives: 5. Nf3 b6 6. e3 Bb7 7. Bd3 c5 8. 0–0 cxd4 9. exd4 d5; or 5. e3 c5 6. Nf3 b6 7. Bd3 Bb7 8. 0–0 cxd4 9. exd4 d5, transposing to the Classical line, 8. Bd2.

5. ... Bxc3 6. Bxc3 Ne4 7. Qc2 Nxc3 8. Qxc3

Diagram 861
After 8. Qxc3

8. ... d6 9. Nf3 Qe7 10. g3 b6 11. Bg2 Bb7 12. 0–0 Nd7 13. Qc2 Nf6

Diagram 862
After 13. ... Nf6

Black intends ... Be4, with a comfortable position similar to some Bogo-Indian positions we'll study in the following chapters.

Summary:

Natural-looking and thus popular among beginners, the pin-breaker 4. Bd2 in fact misplaces White's bishop. Black has several good lines to choose from—we provide you with two of these.

Chapter 29: Nimzo-Indian with 4. Bd2
Memory Markers!

Diagram 863
After 5. e4

MARKER 1

Diagram 864
After 7. Qg4

MARKER 2

Diagram 865
After 10. g3

MARKER 3

Chapter 29: Nimzo-Indian with 4. Bd2
Solutions to Memory Markers!

No. 1 **5. ... Bxc3.** See page 335.

No. 2 **7. ... Bb7! 8. Qxg7 Rf8,** with a good game. See page 335.

No. 3 **10. ... b6 11. Bg2 Bb7.** Black contests the long diagonal.
See page 336.

Chapter 30: Bogo-Indian—Introduction and 4. Bd2 with 6. Bg2
Some Important Points to Look For

When White avoids the Nimzo-Indian by playing 3. Nf3, Black continues with 3. ... Bb4+, the Bogo-Indian. If White then plays 4. Bd2 and fianchettoes his other bishop, Black replies 4. ... Qe7 and 5. ... Nc6, pressuring White's center.

◆ The action begins.
    See Diagram 869.

◆ The key position.
    See Diagram 875.

◆ After the e-pawn recaptures.
    See Diagram 883.

◆ After the c-pawn recaptures.
    See Diagram 894.

Outline of Variations

1. d4 Nf6 2. c4 e6 3. Nf3 Bb4+ 4. Bd2 Qe7 5. g3 Nc6 6. Bg2 Bxd2+ 7. Nbxd2 0-0 8. 0-0 d6 9. e4 e5 10. d5 Nb8 *(338)* [E11]
    A 11. b4 a5 12. a3 Na6 13. Qb3 c6 *(343)*
    B 11. Ne1 a5 12. Nd3 Na6 *(345)*
        B1 13. a3 Bg4 14. f3 Bd7 15. b4 c6 *(346)*
        B2 13. f4 c6 *(347)*
            B2a 14. h3 cxd5 15. cxd5 Bd7 *(347)*
            B2b 14. f5 cxd5 15. exd5 e4 16. Qe2 b5! *(349)*
            B2c 14. fxe5 dxe5 *(350)*

Chapter 30
Bogo-Indian
Introduction and 4. Bd2 with 6. Bg2

When White plays 3. Nf3, he is announcing de facto that he wants to avoid the solid Nimzo, covered in the last section. He would probably prefer to play against the Queen's Indian (3. ... b6). But Black has another great choice, the Bogo-Indian.

The Bogo-Indian became popular in the 1980s and has taken hold as a solid and enterprising way of defending against 3. Nf3— and of avoiding reams of Queen's Indian analysis.

Think of the Bogo-Indian as the tag-team partner of the Nimzo-Indian. (Let's be less formal; we're all going to be close friends with these openings, so let's call them the Bogo and the Nimzo, as most of their fans do.)

When White plays d4 and c4 and then opts for Nc3, the Nimzo jumps in the ring. On the other hand, when White chooses Nf3 first, the Bogo jumps the ropes, ready to grapple. And there are times— when White first plays Nf3 and then switches direction with a quick Nc3 —that the Bogo will then tag up, letting the Nimzo take over again.

The Bogo, named after Efim Bogolubov, is these days seen at all levels. Bogolubov, during the 1930s, the heyday of world champion Alexander Alekhine, played two title matches with the champ, with whom he had in common a love for imbibing.

(One story claims that the jovial and rotund Bogo knew only one word of English, "beer.")

"When I play White," Bogo once said, "I win because I have the first move. When I play Black, I win because I am Bogolubov." So let's take a look at the opening that bears his name. (For a sister opening, 3. g3, see page 368.)

1. d4 Nf6 2. c4 e6 3. Nf3 Bb4+

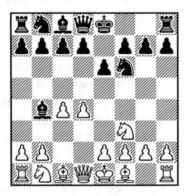

Diagram 866
After 3. ... Bb4+

After this natural developing move, White has three choices: 4. Bd2, 4. Nbd2, and 4. Nc3, switching into the Nimzo. In this chapter and the next, we'll learn what to do against 4. Bd2.

4. Bd2 Qe7

Our recommendation. Here the main move is 5. g3. After the unambitious 5. e3 Bxd2+ 6. Qxd2 0–0 7. Nc3 d6 8. Be2 e5 9. 0–0 e4,

Diagram 867
After 9. ... e4

Black has a comfortable position.

5. g3 Nc6

Preferred by Dzindzi from among Black's many options.

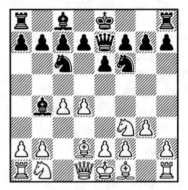

Diagram 868
After 5. ... Nc6

Now White has two continuations: 6. Bg2 and 6. Nc3 (next chapter).

6. Bg2 Bxd2+

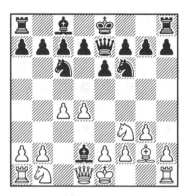

Diagram 869
After 6. ... Bxd2+

7. Nbxd2

Weaker is 7. Qxd2. After 7. ... Ne4 8. Qc2 Qb4+,

Diagram 870
After 8. ... Qb4+

White has to make an unpleasant choice.

1) 9. Kf1 d5;

2) 9. Nc3 Nxc3 10. Qxc3 Qxc3+ 11. bxc3 b6

Diagram 871
After 11. ... b6

and White's weak pawn structure will be a liability in the endgame.

3) 9. Nbd2 Nxd2 10. Qxd2

Diagram 872
After 10. Qxd2

(Or 10. Nxd2 Nxd4 ∓) 10. ... Qxc4 does not give White sufficient compensation for the pawn. Back to Diagram 869 and 7. Nbxd2.

7. ... 0–0

White's weak pawn structure will be a liability in the endgame.

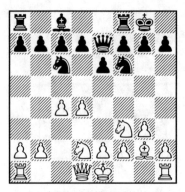

Diagram 873
After 7. ... 0-0

Castling is more accurate than 7. ... d6 8. Nf1 0–0 9. Ne3 e5 10. 0–0,

ANALYSIS

Diagram 874
After 10. 0-0

followed by dxe5 and Nd5, with a slight edge for White.

8. 0–0

Now after 8. Nf1, Black has 8. ... Qb4+.

8. ... d6 9. e4 e5 10. d5 Nb8

Diagram 875
After 10. ... Nb8

This is the key position of the opening. Notice that the pawn structure in the center closely resembles the King's Indian Defense. Yet, there are three major differences:

1) Black has exchanged the dark-square bishops;

2) White's knight on d2 is misplaced;

3) White has a tepid (it's not truly "bad," but it is hardly the apple of White's eye) bishop on g2.

These differences make Black's position strategically sound.

The fact that the center is closed makes Black's lack of development on the queenside less important.

Plans for both sides:

Black's plan is to play on the queenside and in some cases even play on the kingside, with … f5. White usually transfers his knight to d3 via e1 and opts for a timely f4 or b4, c5 expansion.

After 10. … Nb8 (see Diagram 875), White has two main moves: 11. b4 and 11. Ne1. Let's look at them in order.

A 11. b4

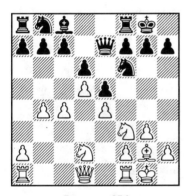

Diagram 876
After 11. b4

The battle for c5 begins. White gains space on the queenside and prepares the thematic c5 advance.

11. … a5 12. a3 Na6

Black, in turn, is fighting for the c5-square for his knight.

13. Qb3

13. bxa5 is bad because it allows an immediate 13. … Nc5, giving Black the important outpost, while 13. Ne1 transposes to 11. Ne1 (**B**) after 13. … Bg4 14. f3 Bd7.

13. … c6

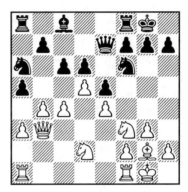

Diagram 877
After 13. … c6

Black creates his own play on the queenside.

14. Ne1

After 14. Rfc1 Bd7 15. h3, Black has an instructive positional idea: 15. … axb4 16. axb4 c5 17. b5 Nb4.

Black creates his own play on the queenside.

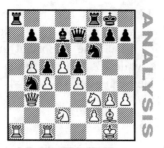

Diagram 878
After 17. ... Nb4

The knight on b4 controls key squares on the queenside, while White's pieces are tied up in defense of c2 to prevent a ... Nc2-d4 maneuver. Black will continue ... Rfb8 and ... Qd8 (in order to fight for the a-file), with a solid position.

14. ... Bd7

Pointless is 14. ... axb4 15. axb4 Nc5 16. Qb1 Rxa1 17. Qxa1 Na6 18. Nd3.

Diagram 879
After 18. Nd3

15. Nd3 cxd5

It is important to take on d5 without playing axb4 first, since after ... exd5, the opening of the a-file favors White—for example:

15. ... axb4? 16. axb4 cxd5 17. exd5 b5 18. c5 dxc5? 19. bxc5 Nxc5 20. Qb4,

Diagram 880
After 20. Qb4

and White wins.

16. exd5

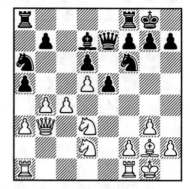

Diagram 881
After 16. exd5

Capturing with the c-pawn favors Black: 16. cxd5 a4 (or 16. ... axb4 17. axb4 Bb5 18. Nc4 Rac8 19. Rfc1 Rc7, with a promising position for Black) 17. Qb1

Diagram 882
After 17. Qb1

(17. Qb2 Bb5) 17. ... Nc7!?, and Black enjoys the prospect of a great outpost on b5. Black is better.

16. ... Bf5!

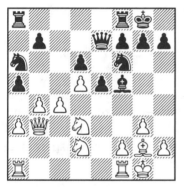

Diagram 883
After 16. ... Bf5!

Now White faces a serious problem defending b4.

17. Nb2 h5

Diagram 884
After 17. ... h5

Our recommendation—Black begins play on the kingside. His idea is to play ... h4, exchange on g3, and play ... Ng4. If White tries h4, Black continues ... e4, with the intention of ... Rfe8, ... Qe5, occupying the outpost on g4 with either bishop or knight.

It is very hard for White to make progress with his pawn majority on the queenside: b5 is always met by ... Nc5 and c5 is very difficult to accomplish.

Note that the absence of a-pawns in Diagram 884 would have favored White.

B 11. Ne1

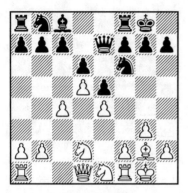

Diagram 885
After 11. Ne1

White's knight is headed for d3, where the horseman would control key squares and support either an f4 or b4-c5 advance.

11. ... a5 12. Nd3 Na6

White can now choose 13. a3 or 13. f4.

B1 13. a3 Bg4

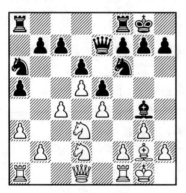

Diagram 886
After 13. ... Bg4

Although it's also possible to play 13. … Bd7 immediately, with our plan Black first forces f3. Then he plays … Bd7. In this way he contests the effect of

White's light-square bishop and weakens the g1–a7 diagonal.

14. f3

If 14. Qc2? Be2 15. Rfe1 Bxd3 16. Qxd3 Nc5 17. Qc2 a4!

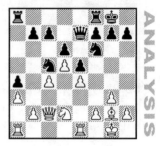

Diagram 887
After 17. ... a4!

Black has a permanent outpost on c5.

14. ... Bd7 15. b4

Or 15. b3 c6 16. dxc6 bxc6 17. Qc2 Nc5, as in the game Vucic–Dzindzi, 1999 and now after 18. b4 Ne6 19. Nb3 a4 20. Nbc1 Nd4, Black had won the strategic battle.

Diagram 888
After 20. ... Nd4

15. ... c6

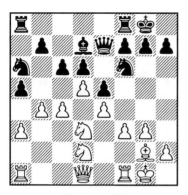

Diagram 889
After 15. ... c6

Black begins his counter-play on the queenside.

16. bxa5

If 16. dxc6 bxc6 17. Qc2 Rfb8,

Diagram 890
After 17. ... Rfb8

Black gets strong pressure on White's queenside pawns—if 18. c5, then ... d5!. For 16. Qb3, see the sample game Skembris–Beliavsky, 1994.

16. ... Qd8 17. Nb3 cxd5 18. cxd5 Bb5 19. Rf2 Nd7 20. Nb2 Nac5

With active play for Black. (See the sample game Khomyakov–Korotylev, 1999.)

B2 13. f4 c6

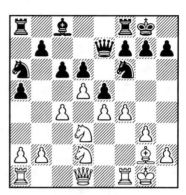

Diagram 891
After 13. ... c6

Black begins his counter-play.

B2a 14. h3

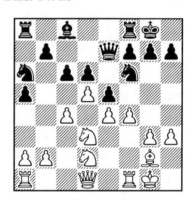

Diagram 892
After 14. h3

14. ... cxd5 15. cxd5

If 15. exd5, then 15. ... exf4 16. Nxf4 Qe5,

Diagram 893
After 16. ... Qe5

followed by ... Nc5. White's position has been weakened and Black starts to occupy the key squares.

15. ... Bd7

Diagram 894
After 15. ... Bd7

This move is played with the idea of ... Bb5. Now against either 16. Qb3 or 16. a4, Black plays 16. ... b5!. White can try to win a pawn with 16. fxe5 dxe5 17. Nc4 Bb5 18. Ncxe5, but Black again gets strong counterplay with 18. ... Nc5!

Diagram 895
After 18. ... Nc5!

19. Re1 Rfe8 20. Kh2 Bxd3 21. Nxd3 Ncxe4.

Diagram 896
After 21. ... Ncxe4

Black has regained his pawn with good chances—for example: 22. Nf2 Nxf2 23. Rxe7 Nxd1 24. Rxe8+ Nxe8 25. Rxd1 Nd6.

Diagram 897
After 25. ... Nd6

Black has the better endgame.

B2b 14. f5

White tries to use his space advantage to attack on the king-side with g4 and g5.

14. ... cxd5

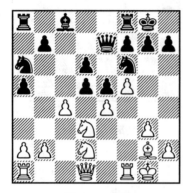

Diagram 898
After 14. ... cxd5

15. exd5

If White recaptures the other way, with 15. cxd5, then Black plays 15. ... Bd7,

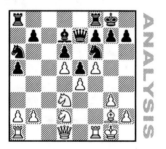

Diagram 899
After 15. ... Bd7

with a good game because his initiative on the queenside is more dangerous than White's on the kingside—for example: 16. a4 b5!.

15. ... e4 16. Qe2 b5!

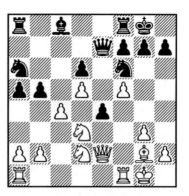

Diagram 900
After 16. ... b5!

Here we see Black's counter-play in full swing. His pieces jump to life! Now 17. c5! is White's best: 17. ... Re8 18. Rae1 Qa7 19. Nxe4 Nxe4 20. Bxe4 Nxc5 21. Nxc5 Qxc5+,

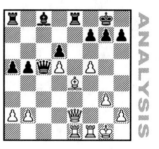

Diagram 901
After 21. ... Qxc5+

with approximate equality.

But many Whites will try to take the pawn and reap the whirl-wind: 17. cxb5 Qa7+ 18. Nf2 e3 19. bxa6 Bxa6 20. Nc4

Diagram 902
After 20. Nc4

20. ... exf2+ 21. Rxf2 Rfe8 22. Qc2 Rac8 23. b3 Ng4

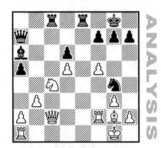

Diagram 903
After 23. ... Ng4

White is helpless in a cross-fire of pins.

B2c 14. fxe5 dxe5

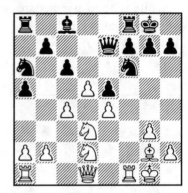

Diagram 904
After 14. ... dxe5

Followed by ... Nc5 or ... Nb4, when Black has a grip on the dark squares.

Summary:

The system with 6. Bg2 does not give White any advantage. Black gets sufficient counter-play against White's attack on either the queen- or kingside. Note the maneuver ... c6 and ... cxd5, forcing White to commit himself. When White captures with the e-pawn, he frees Black's e5-pawn, while cxd5 allows ... Bd7, threatening ... Bb5. Then if the bishop is not allowed to take the square, ... b5 follows.

Efim Bogolubov

Chapter 30: Bogo-Indian—Introduction and 4. Bd2 with 6. Bg2

Memory Markers!

Diagram 905
After 18. Re1

MARKER 1

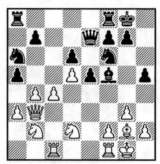

Diagram 906
After 18. Rac1

MARKER 2

Diagram 907
After 15. Rfe1

MARKER 3

Diagram 908
After 15. cxd5

MARKER 4

Chapter 30: Bogo-Indian—Introduction and 4. Bd2 with 6. Bg2
Solutions to Memory Markers!

No. 1 **18. ... Nb5.** Also good is 18. ... Bb5, with the idea of ... Ba6, and only then ... Nb5. See page 345.

No. 2 **18. ... h4,** softening the White king's defense. See page 345.

No. 3 **15. ... Bxd3 16. Qxd3 Nc5** and 17. ... a4, taking permanent control of the c5-square by preventing b4 from ever materializing. See page 346.

No. 4 **15. ... Bd7!:** very familiar by now. See page 349.

Chapter 31: Bogo-Indian with 4. Bd2 and 6. Nc3
Some Important Points to Look For

After 4. Bd2, White can follow up with 6. Nc3. Black plays
6. ... Bxc3 and does well whether White chooses a sharp
middlegame or a complex endgame.

♦ The endgame is equal.
   See Diagram 911.

♦ White has two plans.
   See Diagram 915.

♦ The right move!
   See Diagram 920.

♦ Black enjoys the ideal King's
   Indian. See Diagram 924.

Outline of Variations

1. d4 Nf6 2. c4 e6 3. Nf3 Bb4+ 4. Bd2 Qe7 5. g3 Nc6 6. Nc3 Bxc3 7. Bxc3 Ne4 *(354)* [E11]

A 8. Qc2 Nxc3 9. Qxc3 Qb4 10. Rc1 Qxc3+ 11. Rxc3 d6 12. Bg2 Bd7 *(355)*

B 8. Rc1 0-0 9. Bg2 d6 *(356)*

  B1 10. d5 Nxc3 11. Rxc3 Nb8 12. dxe6 fxe6 13. Nd4 c6 14. 0-0 Nd7 *(356)*

    B1a 15. e4 Nf6 *(357)*

      B1a1 16. e5 dxe5 17. Nf3 e4 18. Ng5 e5 19. Nxc4 Bf5 *(357)*

      B1a2 16. Rd3 e5 17. Nc2 Be6 18. Ne3 Rad8 *(358)*

    B1b 15. b4 Nf6 16. b5 e5 17. Nc2 cxb5 18. cxb5 Be6 *(359)*

  B2 10. 0-0 Nxc3 11. Rxc3 e5 12. d5 Nb8 *(360)*

    B2a 13. c5 dxc5 14. Qc2 Na6! 15. Re3 f6 *(360)*

    B2b 13. Nd2 Nd7 14. b4 f5 15. c5 e4 16. cxd6 cxd6 17. Rc7 *(360)*

    B2c 13. b4 Bg4 14. Nd2 Nd7 *(361)*

Chapter 31
Bogo-Indian
with 4. Bd2 and 6. Nc3

In the previous chapter, we noted that after 5. ... Nc6, White, instead of playing 6. Bg2, can develop his queen's knight. Here we show you how to deal with this possibility.

1. d4 Nf6 2. c4 e6 3. Nf3 Bb4+ 4. Bd2 Qe7 5. g3 Nc6 6. Nc3

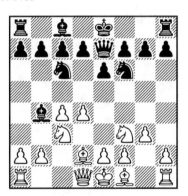

Diagram 909
After 6. Nc3

6. ... Bxc3 7. Bxc3 Ne4

Now White has two moves: 8. Qc2 and 8. Rc1.

A 8. Qc2 Nxc3 9. Qxc3 Qb4

Black's move is straightforward and good.

10. Rc1

10. Qxb4 Nxb4 11. Kd2 d6 12. Bg2 Bd7

Diagram 910
After 12. ... Bd7

13. Kc3 (13. a3 Nc6 14. b4 Rb8!=, with the idea of 15. ... Ke7, 16. ... Rac8, 17. ... Nd8, and then ... b7-b6 and ... c7-c5. The close character of the position permits such long-term planning!) 13. ... Nc6, with equal chances in the endgame— for example, 14. d5 Ne7.

10. ... Qxc3+ 11. Rxc3 d6 12. Bg2 Bd7

Black's 9. ... Qb4 is straightforward and good.

Diagram 911
After 12. ... Bd7

Black has an approximately equal ending. In the game Kaidanov–Dzindzichashvili, 1997, White played 13. d5 (13. 0-0 Rb8 =), and after 13. ... Ne7 14. dxe6 (14. Nd4 e5 15. Nb5 Kd8, with the idea of ... a6 =) 14. ... fxe6 15. Nd4 Nc6 16. Bxc6?! bxc6 17. c5 e5!

Diagram 912
After 17. ... e5!

18. Nc2 Rb8 19. b3 Ke7 ∓, ended up in a worse position.

B 8. Rc1 0–0 9. Bg2 d6

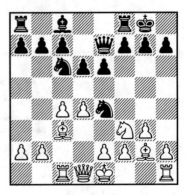

Diagram 913
After 9. ... d6

Here White can choose between 10. d5 and 10. 0-0.

B1 10. d5 Nxc3

Black prevents 11. Bb4 after the knight's retreat.

11. Rxc3

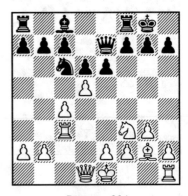

Diagram 914
After 11. Rxc3

Black's knight is heading toward f6 via d7.

11. ... Nb8

After 11. ... exd5 12. cxd5, White has a favorable pawn

structure due to the weak pawn on c7.

12. dxe6

12. 0–0 e5 transposes to 10. 0–0.

12. ... fxe6 13. Nd4

White puts a knight on a strong square and sets a small but poisonous trap.

13. ... c6

13. ... Nd7? 14. Nxe6 Qxe6 15. Bd5

14. 0–0 Nd7

Diagram 915
After 14. ... Nd7

In this position, White has two plans: to create a central bind with 15. e4, or to use his strong bishop on g2 to create play on the queenside with 15. b4 and then b5.

Black's plan is to play ... Nf6 and ... e5, followed by developing his bishop to e6 and a timely ... d6-d5-push.

B1a 15. e4

White dashes all of Black's hopes of a ... d5-push and prepares an assault along the d-file on the weak d6-pawn.

15. ... Nf6

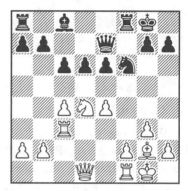

Diagram 916
After 15. ... Nf6

Now White has two moves: 16. e5 and 16. Rd3.

B1a1 16. e5 dxe5 17. Nf3 e4 18. Ng5 e5 19. Nxe4 Bf5

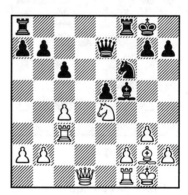

Diagram 917
After 19. ... Bf5

Now if 20. Nxf6+, 20. ... Qxf6.

20. Qd6 Qf7!

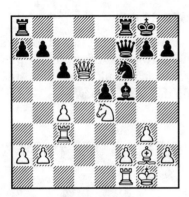

Diagram 918
After 20. ... Qf7!

21. Nxf6+

White has to take on f6. If 21. Nc5, then 21. ... Rfe8, with the idea of trapping the queen after ... Rad8. And after 21. Ng5 Qg6 22. Ne6 Ng4, Black wins a piece.

21. ... Qxf6 22. Qxf6 gxf6

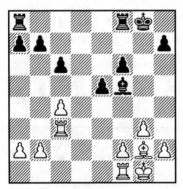

Diagram 919
After 22. ... gxf6

Black has an equal ending.

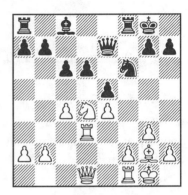

Diagram 920
After 16. ... e5

17. Nc2 Be6

Just in time!

18. Ne3

If 18. Rxd6, then 18. ... Bxc4.

18. ... Rad8

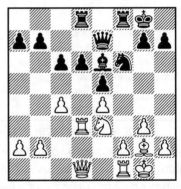

Diagram 921
After 18. ... Rad8

In this position, Black is compensated for his somewhat weakened pawn on d6 by his better placed light-square bishop and the half-open f-file. It is not easy for White to attack the d6-pawn. For example, 19. Qd2 is met by 19. ... Ng4 20. Nxg4 Bxg4, with an equal game.

B1b 15. b4

With the idea of b5.

15. ... Nf6

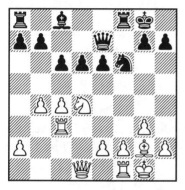

Diagram 922
After 15. ... Nf6

16. b5 e5

Black counters the attack on the flank with action in the center.

17. Nc2 cxb5 18. cxb5 Be6

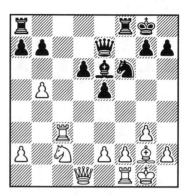

Diagram 923
After 18. ... Be6

White's queenside push did not achieve the desired results. Instead, Black has firm control of the center. In the game Karpov–Rogers, 1996, White played 19. Ne3, and after 19. ... Rac8 (19. ... a6!?), Black got a comfortable position: 20. Qd2 (20. Rd3 Rfd8 21. Nd5 Bxd5! 22. Bxd5+ Kh8, with the idea of ... Rc5 and ... Qc7; Black has a better game—he controls the c-file and influences the central squares with his knight, while White's bishop looks out over an empty diagonal) 20. ... Rxc3 21. Qxc3 Qd7 22. a4 Rc8, capturing the file.

White's queenside push did not achieve the desired results. Instead, Black has firm control of the center.

B2 **10. 0-0 Nxc3 11. Rxc3 e5 12. d5 Nb8**

Diagram 924
After 12. ... Nb8

Black owns the ideal King's Indian structure:

1) White doesn't have a knight on c3 to help him pressure Black's queenside;

2) White's light-square bishop is poorly placed;

3) Black doesn't have a passive bishop on g7.

White's temporary advantage in development is not very relevant because of the closed character of the position.

White's plan is to play on the queenside by breaking through with c5. Black's plan is to generate play on the kingside with the possibility of counter-play on the queenside and the center.

White's main options now are: 13. c5, 13. Nd2, and 13. b4. (If White plays 13. e4, Black answers with 13. ... f5.)

B2a **13. c5**

This attempt to open the c-file fails immediately.

13. ... dxc5 14. Qc2

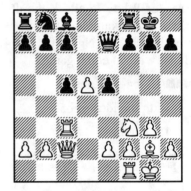

Diagram 925
After 14. Qc2

14. ... Na6!

14. ... b6? 15. Re3 f6 16. d6! Qxd6 (16. ... cxd6 17. Nxe5 Bb7 18. Qc4+ and White wins) 17. Ng5, winning.

15. Re3 f6

White is simply a pawn down.

B2b **13. Nd2**

Diagram 926
After 13. Nd2

13. ... Nd7

Not 13. ... f5?, as White can now play 14. c5! dxc5 15. Qc1 Nd7 16. Nb3, and the c5-pawn falls.

14. b4 f5 15. c5 e4

Black intends ... Ne5.

16. cxd6 cxd6

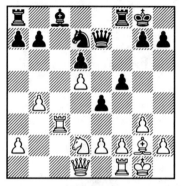

Diagram 927
After 16. ... cxd6

Now 17. Rc7 Qd8 18. Qc2 a5! 19. a3 axb4 20. axb4 Ra2!, favors Black. In a 2008 game, Postny (ELO 2661) agreed to a draw with Balinas (ELO 2571) after 17. Qb3 Nf6. Or 17. f3 a5 18. b5 (18. a3 axb4 19. axb4 exf3 20. exf3 Qf6∓, keeping the e5-square for his knight) 18. ... exf3 19. exf3 Qe5 20. Rc7 Qd4+∓.

B2c 13. b4 Bg4

With the idea of ... Nd7 and ... f5.

14. Nd2

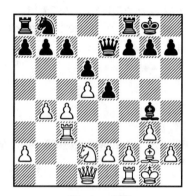

Diagram 928
After 14. Nd2

Or 14. c5 a5 15. a3 axb4 16. axb4 Na6 17. cxd6 cxd6 18. Qb3 Rfc8,

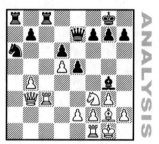

Diagram 929
After 18. ... Rfc8

when Black once again has comfortable play.

14. ... Nd7

With complex play. See the sample game Avrukh–Ibrahimov, 2001.

Summary:

White's 6. Nc3 allows him to choose between equal, although complex, endings and sharp, strategically complex middlegames. Black can do well in all of these circumstances, and sometimes even end up on top—as Australian GM Ian Rogers did playing the great Karpov himself!

Chapter 31: Bogo-Indian with 4. Bd2 and 6. Nc3
Memory Markers!

Diagram 930
After 13. ... Nd7

MARKER 1

Diagram 931
After 21. Ng5

MARKER 2

Diagram 932
After 21. Nd5

MARKER 3

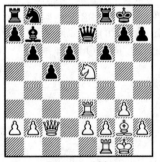

Diagram 933
After 17. ... Bb7

MARKER 4

Chapter 31: Bogo-Indian with 4. Bd2 and 6. Nc3
Solutions to Memory Markers!

No. 1   **14. Nxe6!,** if 14. ... Qe6?, 15. Bd5 +−. See page 357.

No. 2   **21. ... Qg6!,** ready to meet 22. Ne6? with 22. ... Ng4, winning. See page 358.

No. 3   **21. ... Bxd5;** the ensuing position favors Black. See page 359.

No. 4   **18. Qc4+,** winning. See page 360.

Chapter 32: Bogo-Indian with 4. Nbd2

Some Important Points to Look For

White blocks the check on move three with 4. Nd2, retaining his own bishop. Black fianchettoes on b7 and gets a comfortable game.

◆ Black controls the long diagonal.
   See Diagram 937.

◆ Ready for ... Nd4.
   See Diagram 940.

◆ This Hedgehog favors Black.
   See Diagram 941.

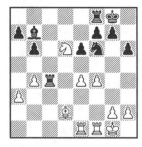

◆ Pawns can't move back!
   See Diagram 942.

Outline of Variations

1. d4 Nf6 2. c4 e6 3. Nf3 Bb4+ 4. Nbd2 b6 5. a3 Bxd2+ 6. Bxd2 h6 7. e3 Bb7 8. Bd3 d6 *(364)* [E11]

Chapter 32
Bogo-Indian
with 4. Nbd2

In this line, White meets the check on move three with 4. Nbd2 to preserve his dark-square bishop. He hopes for the advantage of the bishop pair.

1. d4 Nf6 2. c4 e6 3. Nf3

In the end of this chapter, we'll briefly review White's attempts to avoid the Nimzo-Bogo mainstream by playing 3. Bg5 and 3. g3.

3. ... Bb4+ 4. Nbd2

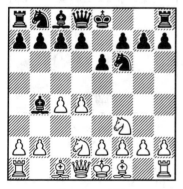

Diagram 934
After 4. Nbd2

Black has several possible moves, but we recommend the immediate fianchetto.

4. ... b6 5. a3 Bxd2+ 6. Bxd2

Or 6. Qxd2 Bb7 7. e3 0–0 8. Be2 d6 9. 0–0 Nbd7 10. b4 Ne4 11. Qc2 f5 12. Bb2 Qe7,

Diagram 935
After 12. ... Qe7

with easy play for Black—e.g.: 13. Rad1 a5 14. d5 (or 14. Ne1 axb4 15. axb4 Ra2 16. Qb3 Rfa8=) 14. ... e5 15. Bd3 c6!?, with complex play (Khenkin—Kuzubov, 2006).

6. ... h6

Black has several possible moves, but we recommend the immediate fianchetto.

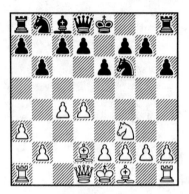

Diagram 936
After 6. ... h6

Black prevents the unpleasant pin Bg5.

7. e3

Other options aren't promising either:

1) 7. g3 Bb7 8. Bg2 0–0 9. 0–0 d6 10. b4 Nbd7 11. Bc3 Be4

Diagram 937
After 11. ... Be4

Black comfortably finishes his development and controls the e4-square.

He plans to put his queen on b7 to exert additional pressure on the long diagonal, and possibly to play ... a6 and ... b5. See the sample game Cebalo–Jakovljevic, 1999.

2) 7. Bf4 Bb7 8. e3 Nh5 (eliminating White's dark-square bishop) 9. Bg3 Nxg3 10. hxg3 d6 11. Be2 Nd7

Diagram 938
After 11. ... Nd7

Black has an easy game. His plan is to play ... Qe7 and wait to see where White castles—then castle on the same side. Back to 7. e3.

7. ... Bb7 8. Bd3 d6

Diagram 939
After 8. ... d6

We prefer this move (with the idea of ... Nbd7, followed by ... c5 or possibly ... e5) over the conventional 8. ... Ne4, when 9. Qc2 may bring White a small edge.

9. Qc2

Or 9. 0–0 Nbd7 10. Qc2, transposing.

9. ... c5

Black prevents White from getting a strong center with e4 and d5.

10. e4

10. dxc5 bxc5 11. e4 (if 11. b4, then we transpose with 11. ... e5 12. e4 Nc6; or if 11. Bc3, 11 ... 0-0, and now if 12. 0-0, Black can play 12. ... Bxf3 13. gxf3 Nbd7, with a sharp, unclear position—or if 12. Rd1, then 12. ... Nbd7 13. e4 d5!, with a good game for Black, for example: 14. Bxf6 Qxf6!.) 11. ... e5 (with the idea of ... Nc6-d4) 12. b4 Nc6,

Diagram 940
After 12. ... Nc6

followed by ... 0–0 and ... Nd4, with a balanced game.

Back to the mainline, 10. e4.

10. ... cxd4 11. Nxd4 Nbd7 12. 0–0

12. b4 is met by 12. ... Ne5; and 12. Nb5 is met by 12. ... Nc5

12. ... 0–0 13. f4 Nc5 14. Rae1 Rc8

Diagram 941
After 14. ... Rc8

This hedgehog-like position is dynamically equal. Play could continue: 15. b4 (or 15. Bc3 a6, with the idea of ... Qc7, and a good game for Black) 15. ... Nxd3 16. Qxd3 Qc7 17. Nb5 Qxc4 18. Qxc4 Rxc4 19. Nxd6

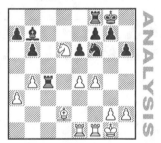

Diagram 942
After 19. Nxd6

19. ... Rd4!, which doesn't look good for White either.

Rare Third Moves

White's 3. Bg5, 3. Bf4 (which will normally transpose to other lines), and the "mini-Bogo" 3. g3 also allow Black a solid path to equality.

After 3. Bg5 Bb4+ 4. Nd2 (4. Nc3 transposes to the Nimzo) 4. ... h6 5. Bh4 c5 6. a3 Bxd2+ 7. Qxd2 g5 and 8. ... Ne4, Black quickly equalized in Seirawan—Andersson, 1983; 5. Bxf6 (as in Seirawan—Portisch, 1982) also led to equality.

The purpose of 3. g3 is to take immediate control of the long diagonal, thus limiting Black's options (for example, discouraging Black from fianchettoing his own light-square bishop), compared to the Bogo-Indian. But closing some doors to Black opens others—as is often the case.

3. ... Bb4+ 4. Bd2

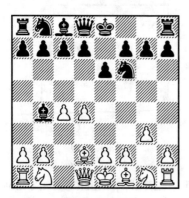

Diagram 943
After 4. Bd2

Or 4. Nd2 c5 with equality, e.g. 5. a3 Bxd2+ 6. Qxd2 cxd4 7. Nf3 b6! (Ivanchuk—Macieja, 2005).

4. ... Qe7

As in the Bogo.

5. Bg2 Nc6 6. e3

6. Nf3 transposes into the Bogo.

6. ... e5

Pushing 6. ... d5!? also deserves attention.

7. d5 Bxd2 8. Qxd2 Nb8 9. Nc3 d6 10. Nge2

The game is balanced. Flear—Adams, 1996, continued: 10. ... a5! 11. h3 Na6

Diagram 944
After 11. ... Na6

12. g4 Nd7 13. Ng3 Nb6 14. b3 g6 15. 0-0-0 Nc5 16. f4 a4!, with a good game.

Summary:
The goal of 4. Nbd2 is to get the bishop pair. White achieves this goal, but at a cost. Black fianchettoes his remaining bishop and achieves comfortable positions in all lines.

Chapter 32: Bogo-Indian with 4. Nbd2
Memory Markers!

Diagram 945
After 6. ... 0-0

Diagram 946
After 8. e3

Diagram 947
After 13. 0-0-0

Diagram 948
After 9. Qc2

Chapter 32: Bogo-Indian with 4. Nbd2
Solutions to Memory Markers!

No. 1 **7. Bg5,** and White stands better. See page 365.

No. 2 **8. ... Nh5,** ready to exchange the bishop. See page 366.

No. 3 **13. ... 0-0-0.** See page 366.

No. 4 **9. ... c5,** anticipating White's e4. See page 367.

Chapter 33: Torre Attack—1. d4 Nf6 2. Nf3 e6 3. Bg5

Some Important Points to Look For

After 3. ... h6, if White retreats his bishop, Black develops easily. If instead White captures on f6, he gives up the bishop pair without doubling Black's pawns.

◆ White has two options.
  See Diagram 951.

◆ One fianchetto ...
  See Diagram 960.

◆ ... then another.
  See Diagram 964.

◆ Can White regain his pawn?
  See Diagram 966.

Table of Mainlines—Chapter 33

1. d4 Nf6 2. Nf3 e6 3. Bg5 h6 *(370)* [A46]

  A 4. Bh4 c5 5. e3 cxd4 6. exd4 Be7 7. Bd3 0-0 *(371)*

    A1 8. c4 b6 9. Nc3 Bb7 10. 0-0 d6 11. Re1 Nbd7 *(372)*

    A2 8. c3 b6 9. Qe2 Bb7 10. Nbd2 Nc6 11. Bxf6!? *(373)*

  B 4. Bf6 Qxf6 5. e4 d6 6. Nc3 g6 7. Qd2 Bg7 8. 0-0-0 a6 *(374)*

    B1 9. Bd3 Qe7 10. Rhe1 b5 11. Kb1 Bb7 *(375)*

    B2 9. e5 Qe7 10. d5?! dxe5 11. Re1 Nd7 12. Bc4 exd5 13. Nxd5 Qd6 *(375)*

    B3 9. Qe3 Nd7 10. h4 b5 11. Re1 Bb7 *(376)*

Chapter 33
Torre Attack
1. d4 Nf6 2. Nf3 e6 3. Bg5

The Torre attack is a popular choice for White players looking for a "shortcut" to avoid lots of theory.

1. d4 Nf6 2. Nf3

By playing 2. Nf3, White discourages his opponent's bishop from coming to b4 (as in the Nimzo-Bogo).

2. ... e6 3. Bg5

For other White lines, see Chapters 34-36.

Diagram 949
After 3. Bg5

Although this opening idea was widely known at least as early as Kostic–Capablanca,

1919, when it was played in their fourth match game, the sequence was made popular by the Mexican grandmaster Carlos Torre in the 1920s.

3. ... h6

Black immediately puts the question to the bishop on g5—trade or retreat.

White has two choices: 4. Bh4 and 4. Bxf6.

A 4. Bh4

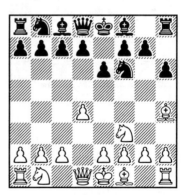

Diagram 950
After 4. Bh4

The retreat allows Black easy development.

4. ... c5 5. e3 cxd4 6. exd4 Be7 7. Bd3 0-0

Diagram 951
After 7. ... 0-0

Here White has a choice between 8. c4 and 8. c3.

A1 8. c4

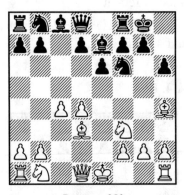

Diagram 952
After 8. c4

This move leads to hedgehog-like positions similar to those we've already encountered in the Nimzo-Indian Defense.

8. ... b6 9. Nc3 Bb7 10. 0-0 d6

In the rapid game Carl-sen—Leko, 2008, Black immediately acted in the center with 10. ... Nc6 11. Bc2 d5 12. Bxf6 Bxf6 13. cxd5 Nb4!?,

Diagram 953
After 13. ... Nb4!?

with a good game.

11. Re1 Nbd7

Black finishes his development and maintains the balance. Play could continue: 12. Rc1 Rc8 13. Qe2 Re8 14. Bg3 Nh5.

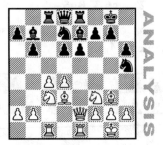

Diagram 954
After 14. ... Nh5

The game Gausel–Pigusov, 2001, continued: 15. b4 a6 16. a3 Ndf6 17. Nd2 Bf8 18. Nce4 Nxg3 19. hxg3 Nxe4 20. Bxe4 Bxe4 21. Qxe4

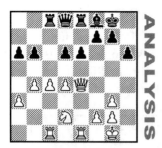

Diagram 955
After 21. Qxe4

21. ... Re7 22. Qd3 Rec7 with equal play.

A2 8. c3

Diagram 956
After 8. c3

8. ... b6 9. Qe2 Bb7 10. Nbd2 Nc6

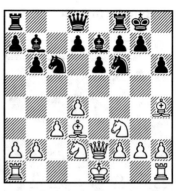

Diagram 957
After 10. ... Nc6

Black finishes his development and stands at least equal. Now if 11. 0-0, then ... Nd5! 12. Bg3 f5 and Black takes over the initiative.

11. Bxf6!?

White's idea is to attack on the kingside.

11. ... Bxf6 12. 0-0-0

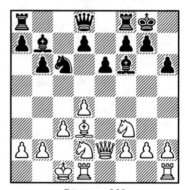

Diagram 958
After 12. 0-0-0

See the sample game Sokolov–Karpov, 1995.

B 4. Bxf6 Qxf6 5. e4

Diagram 959
After 5. e4

In return for the bishop pair, White has a powerful center. His plan is to quickly mobilize his forces after Nc3, Qd2 and 0-0-0. Black, for his part, must find the right setup to neutralize White's center and maximize the strength of his own bishops.

5. ... d6 6. Nc3 g6

Diagram 960
After 6. ... g6

Here Black's bishops are best placed on g7 and b7.

7. Qd2

7. Bd3 does not pose any serious problems to Black after 7. ... Bg7 8. 0-0 0-0 9. e5 Qe7 10. Re1 a6 11. Qd2 b5.

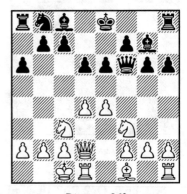

Diagram 961
After 11. ... b5

Black is fine.

7. ... Bg7 8. 0-0-0 a6

Diagram 962
After 8. ... a6

Black plans to gain space on the queenside with   ... b5 and keeps White guessing about where he will castle.

Here White has three options: 9. Bd3, 9. e5, and 9. Qe3.

B1 9. Bd3

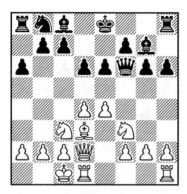

Diagram 963
After 9. Bd3

9. ... Qe7

Black anticipates e5.

10. Rhe1 b5 11. Kb1 Bb7

Diagram 964
After 11. ... Bb7

Black is ready to meet White's advances in the center. The position is balanced.

B2 9. e5

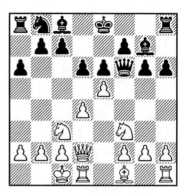

Diagram 965
After 9. e5

White immediately tries to break through in the center.

9. ... Qe7 10. d5?!

White goes all out to pry open the central files before Black can castle, but this is too optimistic.

10. ... dxe5 11. Re1 Nd7 12. Bc4 exd5 13. Nxd5 Qd6

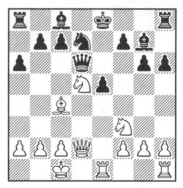

Diagram 966
After 13. ... Qd6

Black is up a pawn and it's not clear how White should continue—for example: 14. Nxe5

Nxe5 15. f4 Be6! 16. fxe5 Bxe5
17. Qe3 0-0-0 18. Qxe5 Bxd5.

Diagram 967
After 18. ... Bxd5

White is simply a pawn
down.

B3 9. Qe3

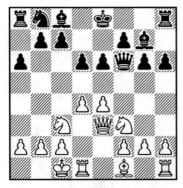

Diagram 968
After 9. Qe3

Played primarily with e4-e5
in mind.

**9. ... Nd7 10. h4 b5 11. Re1
Bb7**

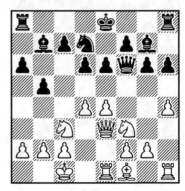

Diagram 969
After 11. ... Bb7

This position occured in
Mikhalevski–Sandipan, 2002.
White is all set to play e5, but
Black is ready to meet it.

12. e5 Qe7! 13. h5 g5!

Black easily neutralizes all
of White's offensives.

14. exd6 cxd6 15. d5

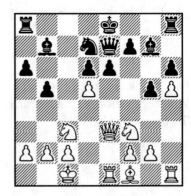

Diagram 970
After 15. d5

15. ... Ne5!

Black takes over the important outpost.

16. Nd4 0-0 17. dxe6 fxe6

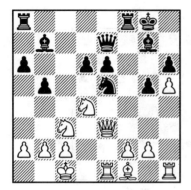

Diagram 971
After 17. ... fxe6

White's strong center has disappeared, allowing Black's bishops to rake the board. Moreover, Black's knight controls the key squares.

After 18. f3 Rac8 19. Be2, Black missed 19. ... b4! (19. ... Rc7 was played in the game), which poses immediate problems for White: 20. Na4 Qc7!.

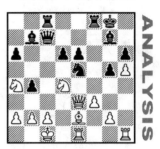

Diagram 972
After 20. ... Qc7!

With the strong threat of ... Qa5.

Summary:

After 3. ... h6, the retreat 4. Bh4 allows Black easy development. More ambitious is 4. Bxf6, giving up a bishop but gaining space. Still, with accurate play, Black will achieve an equal game.

Chapter 33: Torre Attack—1. d4 Nf6 2. Nf3 e6 3. Bg5

Memory Markers!

MARKER 1

Diagram 973
After 12. Bg3

MARKER 2

Diagram 974
After 6. Nc3

MARKER 3

Diagram 975
After 10. Rhe1

MARKER 4

Diagram 976
After 15. h5

Chapter 33: Torre Attack—1. d4 Nf6 2. Nf3 e6 3. Bg5
Solutions to Memory Markers!

No. 1   **12. ... f5,** threatening to win the bishop.
        See page 373.

No. 2   **6. ... g6.** See page 374.

No. 3   **10. ... b5.** One good fianchetto deserves another! See page 375.

No. 4   **15. ... g5,** closing the kingside. See page 376.

Chapter 34: London System—1. d4 Nf6 2. Nf3 e6 3. Bf4
Some Important Points to Look For

If you're ready for it, the London System poses no particular threat. The system recommended in this chapter guarantees Black a promising game.

◆ Black clarifies the center.
  See Diagram 978.

◆ Black is comfortable here.
  See Diagram 980.

◆ A strong knight!
  See Diagram 983.

◆ Isn't Black better?
  See Diagram 985.

Outline of Variations

1. d4 Nf6 2. Nf3 e6 3. Bf4 c5 4. e3 b6 5. Bd3 Bb7 6. Nbd2 Be7 7. c3 cxd4 8. exd4 0-0
9. 0-0 d6 10. Qe2 Nbd7 11. h3 Re8 *(380)* [A46]

Chapter 34
London System
1. d4 Nf6 2. Nf3 e6 3. Bf4

The London System is another opening employed at the club level by those who wish to keep the game in a narrow range of possibilities.

1. d4 Nf6 2. Nf3 e6 3. Bf4

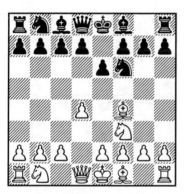

Diagram 977
After 3. Bf4

In the London System, White puts his pawns on e3 and c3, as in the Colle, but only after developing his dark-square bishop, to avoid blocking it in.

3. ... c5

Black immediately challenges White's central pawn, planning to fianchetto his queen's bishop or to play 4. ... Qb6—in both cases with easy equality.

4. e3 b6 5. Bd3 Bb7 6. Nbd2 Be7 7. c3

Diagram 978
After 7. c3

7. ... cxd4

Black wants to clarify the situation in the center and, depending on how White recaptures on d4, form his plan.

If 8. cxd4, Black can exchange his knight for White's bishop with 8. ... Nh5 9. Bg3 d6 10. 0-0 Nxg3 11. hxg3 0-0 12. e4 Nd7.

Diagram 979
After 12. ... Nd7

Black plans to play ... g6 and
... Bf6-g7, with a better game.
Thus White's best move is 8.
exd4.

8. exd4 0-0 9. 0-0 d6

Diagram 980
After 9. ... d6

Black has already reached a
comfortable position. The game
could continue:

10. Qe2 Nbd7 11. h3 Re8

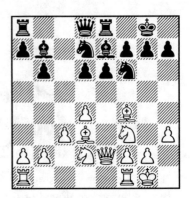

Diagram 981
After 11. ... Re8

Black plans ... Bf8 and ...
e5.

12. Ne4

Or 12. a4 a6 13. Rfe1 Bf8
(with the idea ... e5) 14. Ne4
Nxe4 15. Bxe Bxe4 16. Qxe4
Nf6

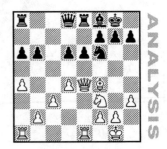

Diagram 982
After 16. ... Nf6

17. Qd3 Nd5 18. Bg3 Qd7 19. c4
Nb4 20. Qb3 a5.

Diagram 983
After 20. ... a5

Black stands well due to his strong knight on b4.

12. ... Nxe4 13. Bxe4 Bxe4 14. Qxe4 Nf6 15. Qd3

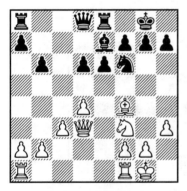

Diagram 984
After 15. Qd3

Here the game Virag–Meszaros, 2002 continued: 15. ... a6 16. Nd2 Qd7 17. a4 b5 18. axb5 axb5 19. Ne4 Nxe4 20. Qxe4 d5 21. Qd3 Qc6,

Diagram 985
After 21. ... Qc6

with at least an even game.

Summary:

Against a knowledgable opponent—like you—the London system gives White equality at best. Black's natural development—3. ... c5, 4. ... b6 (fianchettoing), and 7. ... cxd4 (forcing White to clarify the center)— guarantees the second player a first-class game.

Chapter 34: London Sytem—1. d4 Nf6 2. Nf3 e6 3. Bf4
Memory Markers!

Diagram 986
After 7. ... cxd4

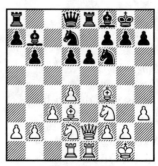

Diagram 987
After 13. Rad1

Diagram 988
After 19. c4

Diagram 989
After 23. Qd2

Chapter 34: London Sytem—1. d4 Nf6 2. Nf3 e6 3. Bf4
Solutions to Memory Markers!

No. 1   **8. exd4,** because after 8. cxd4 Nh5, Black gets the bishop pair and a somewhat better game. See page 381.

No. 2   **13. ... e5.** The pawn is secure. Also good is 13. ... a6. See page 382.

No. 3   **19. ... Nb4.** See page 382.

No. 4   **23. ... b4.** See page 383.

Chapter 35: The Fianchetto—2. Nf3 e6 3. g3
Some Important Points to Look For

With his move order, White wants to avoid the Nimzo- and Bogo-Indians. By playing Dzindzi's 3. ... b5, Black prevents White from ever getting in an effective c4. Black does well.

◆ Black has good play in the center. See Diagram 991.

◆ Black will now play ... b4. See Diagram 993.

◆ Black's ... Rb8 is a star move. See Diagram 1005.

◆ Black's 17. ... Nxe3 strikes a decisive blow. See Diagram 1010.

Outline of Variations

1. d4 Nf6 2. Nf3 e6 3. g3 b5 4. Bg2 Bb7 5. 0-0 c5 6. Bg5 Be7 7. c3 Na6 8. Nbd2 0-0 9. Qb3 Rb8! *(386)*
[A46]

Chapter 35
The Fianchetto

2. Nf3 e6 3. g3

When White puts off the decision to play c2-c4 in favor of 2. Nf3 and 3. g3, you can prevent White from ever getting in c2-c4. Black's line here is a specialty of grandmaster Dzindzichashvili. It will save you a great deal of theoretical bookwork!

1. d4 Nf6 2. Nf3 e6 3. g3 b5

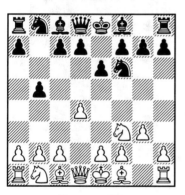

Diagram 990
After 3. ... b5

This move is as good or better than other playable alternatives: 3. ... d5 (leading to the Catalan); 3. ... b6 (leading to the Queen's Indian with ... Bb7) and 3. ... c5. It certainly requires much less study!

With 3. ... b5, Black stops White from playing c4 and prepares to develop his own bishop to b7.

Why, then, after 1. d4 Nf6 2. Nf3, shouldn't Black play ... b7-b5, or—for that matter—why shouldn't he push the b-pawn-even on move one? The answer is that after 1. d4 Nf6 2. Nf3 b5 3. e3, White attacks the b-pawn while preparing to develop his bishop. Only after White commits his bishop to the long diagonal with 3. g3 is ... b5 a good reply.

After 3. ... b5, White can, of course, attack the b5-pawn with his queen. But 4. Qd3 is not a natural developing move. So

Black equalizes: 4. Qd3 a6 5. e4 Bb7 6. e5 Nd5 7. Bg2 c5.

Diagram 991
After 7. ... c5

Black has sufficient play in the center: 8. dxc5 Bxc5 9. 0–0 Qc7 10. Nc3 Nxc3 11. Qxc3 b4 12. Qd3 d5 13. exd6 Qxd6.

Diagram 992
After 13. ... Qxd6

The position is equal (Mateuta–Bets, 2003).

Another attack on the b-pawn is likewise harmless: 4. a4

Diagram 993
After 4. a4

4. ... b4. (The idea is ... c5.) 5. Bg2 Bb7 6. 0–0 c5 7. c3 Na6 8. Nbd2 Be7 9. Re1

Diagram 994
After 9. Re1

(White wants to play e4.) 9. ... 0–0 (Not all threats should be prevented.) 10. e4 bxc3! (to gain control of the b4-square) 11. bxc3 cxd4 12. cxd4 d5 13. e5 Ne4,

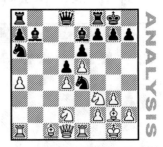

Diagram 995
After 13. ... Ne4

and Black is doing fine.

4. Bg2

The most popular move, and so it's our main line.

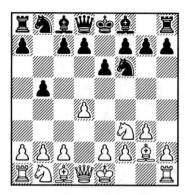

Diagram 996
After 4. Bg2

4. ... Bb7 5. 0–0

5. Bg5 transposes into the main line after 6. 0-0; 5. a4 b4 transposes to 4. a4, discussed on page 388.

5. ... c5 6. Bg5

If 6. Na3 (6. c3 Na6 7. Bg5 Be7 transposes to the main line) 6. ... a6 7. c4 cxd4 8. cxb5,

Diagram 997
After 8. cxb5

then after 8. ... Bxa3 9. bxa3 axb5 10. Bb2 0–0 11. Bxd4 Bd5 12. Bxf6 Qxf6,

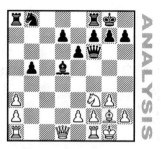

Diagram 998
After 12. ... Qxf6

Black is better (Adorjan–Timman, 1998).

6. ... Be7 7. c3

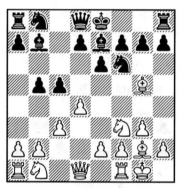

Diagram 999
After 7. c3

If 7. dxc5 Bxc5 8. Nc3 a6,

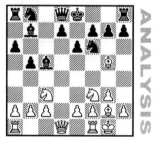

Diagram 1000
After 8. ... a6

Black is at least equal. His plan is to castle and then to play ... d5 and ... Nbd7.

7. ... Na6

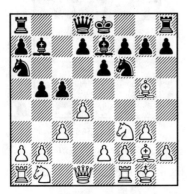

Diagram 1001
After 7. ... Na6

This is an interesting way of developing Black's knight and neutralizing the threat of Bxf6 and dxc5.

8. Nbd2 0–0 9. Qb3

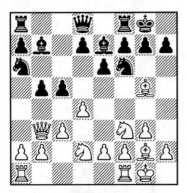

Diagram 1002
After 9. Qb3

White plans 10. e4 in response to 9. ... Qb6.

Other White choices:

9. e3 d5!

Diagram 1003
After 9. ... d5!

Black's plan is to play on the queenside. (Also good is 9. ... h6, as in Ivanchuk–Timman, 1995.)

Another alternative to 9. Qb3 is 9. Bxf6 Bxf6 10. e4 cxd4 11. cxd4 d5 12. e5 Be7.

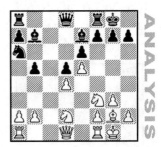

Diagram 1004
After 12. ... Be7

White has no attacking prospects on the kingside and his g2-bishop is passive, while Black has good queenside play and thus a small advantage.

9. ... Rb8!

Diagram 1005
After 9. ... Rb8!

10. Qxb5

This is the only way to try for an advantage.

10. ... Bxf3 11. Qxa6 Bxg2 12. Kxg2 Rxb2

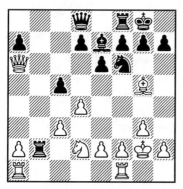

Diagram 1006
After 12. ... Rxb2

13. Nb3

If 13. Qxa7, then 13. ... cxd4 14. cxd4 h6 15. Bxf6 Bxf6.

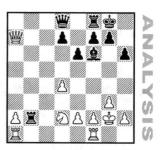

Diagram 1007
After 15. ... Bxf6

Now White can try 16. Ne4 or 16. Rfd1.

If 16. Ne4 (16. Rfd1 Qa8+ 17. Qxa8 Rxa8 =), 16. ... Rxe2 17. Nxf6+ Qxf6 18. Qxd7 Rb8.

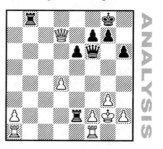

Diagram 1008
After 18. ... Rb8

With the idea of playing ... R8b2, creating strong threats on the "seventh" rank—for example: 19. Qc6 Rbb2 20. Qa8+, and the players agreed to a draw in the game Pre–Degraeve, 1997. After 20. ... Kh7 21. Qf3 Qxf3+ 22. Kxf3 Rxa2, the position is a dead draw.

**13. ... Qa8+ 14. Kg1 cxd4
15. cxd4 Qe4**

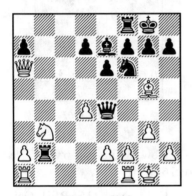

Diagram 1009
After 15. ... Qe4

Black has equalized and now goes for the advantage.

16. Bxf6

With this move, White preserved equality in Cifuentes-Parada –Marin.

Note that after 16. e3 Nd5! 17. Bxe7 Nxe3!,

Diagram 1010
After 17. ... Nxe3!

there's no defense against mate!

What if White plays 2. g3, fianchettoing a move earlier? Black then plays 2. ... d5! 3. Bg2 Bf5, with total equality,

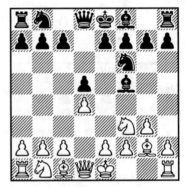

Diagram 1011
After 3. ... Bf5

ready to meet 4. c4 with 4. ... c6 5. Qb3 Qb6!.

Summary:

Playing 1. d4 Nf6 2. Nf3 e6, and now 3. g3, White wants to avoid our friends Nimzo and Bogo. But then Dzindzi's 3. ... b5 takes away White's option of playing c2-c4 later.

White can't demonstrate b5 to be a weakness. In fact, Black has experienced no problems in this opening.

Chapter 35: The Fianchetto—2. Nf3 e6 3. g3
Memory Markers!

Diagram 1012
After 2. ... b5

Diagram 1013
After 10. cxb4

Diagram 1014
After 9. ... Qb6

Diagram 1015
After 16. Rfe1

Chapter 35: The Fianchetto—2. Nf3 e6 3. g3
Solutions to Memory Markers!

No. 1   **3. e3 ±.** See page 387.
No. 2   **10. ... Nxb4,** with a better pawn structure for Black. See page 388.
No. 3   **10. e4!,** with a better game for White. See page 390.
No. 4   **16. ... Bb4.** See page 392.

Chapter 36: Colle System—1. d4 Nf6 2. Nf3 e6 3. e3
Some Important Points to Look For

The Colle is ever-popular on the amateur level. Against both its popular forms, Black plays ... d5 and ... c5, then fianchettoes his queen's bishop for a good game.

◆ Black's 9. ... Ne4 is a typical response. See Diagram 1021.

◆ Black is okay and playing for more. See Diagram 1027.

◆ A balanced position ... See Diagram 1030.

◆ ... and an unbalanced position. See Diagram 1032.

Outline of Variations

1. d4 Nf6 2. Nf3 e6 3. e3 c5 4. Bd3 d5 *(394)* [A46]

   A 5. c3 Be7 6. Nbd2 0-0 7. 0-0 b6 *(396)*

     A1 8. Ne5 Bb7 9. f4 Ne4! 10. Nxe4 dxe4 11. Bc2 f6 12. Ng4 Bd5 *(396)*

     A2 8. Qe2 Bb7 9. dxc5 bxc5 10. e4 Nc6 11. e5 Nfd7 12. Re1 Re8 *(397)*

   B 5. b3 Nbd7 6. 0-0 b6 7. Bb2 Bb7 8. Ne5 Be7 9. Nd2 0-0 10. f4 Ne4! *(399)*

Chapter 36
Colle System
The Businessman's Opening

The Colle System is named after Belgian master Edgar Colle, who played it in the 1920s. But it was his compatriot George Koltanowski, after his emigration to the U.S., who brought it, with a vengeance, to the New World.

Koltanowski, who earned the title of the United States Chess Federation's official Dean of American Chess as well as induction into the World Chess Hall of Fame in Miami, played the opening against all comers. He wrote about it in a popular monograph that went through many editions, and he taught it to his students. Sometimes he called it the "businessman's opening"— in other words, a self-contained system for White that eliminated the need to spend many hours studying theory. Perfect for the player who has a crowded schedule!

The Colle continues to be popular among the amateur ranks, and, although it appears to begin passively, in its most impressive games it can explode into a compelling kingside attack, especially after White engineers an effective e3-e4 pawn push.

But Black has found how to neutralize the Colle.

1. d4 Nf6 2. Nf3 e6 3. e3

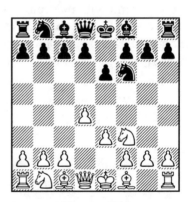

Diagram 1016
After 3. e3

White's idea is to finish his development first with Bd3 and 0-0.

3. ... c5

Black's plan is to play in the center.

If you prefer to avoid 4. c4 (see the next comment), 3. ... b6 provides an answer. Now 4. c4 leads to Nimzo/Bogo positions either discussed in this book or totally harmless to Black. In fact, the Queen's Indian without the fianchetto of White's kingside bishop is also harmless, so after, say, 3. ... b6 4. c4 Bb7 5. Bd3, there are several good ways to equality besides Bogo's 5. ... Bb4+. And, if 3. ... b6 is followed by 4. Bd3 Bb7 5. Nbd2, or 5. c3, we can switch by 5. ... c5 into the Colle lines below.

4. Bd3

If 4. c4, Black can play 4. ... d5, morphing into a safe line of the Tarrasch Defense. (The dangerous variation incorporates Rubinstein's fianchetto.) For an alternative route, see our comment after 3. ... c5.

4. ... d5

Here White has two main moves: 5. c3 and 5. b3.

A 5. c3

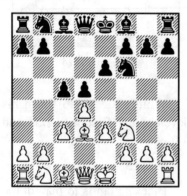

Diagram 1017
After 5. c3

This is the most popular plan, establishing the "Colle Triangle." White plans to castle and follow up with kingside play with Ne5 and f4, or play in the center with Qe2 and e4.

5. ... Be7 6. Nbd2 0-0 7. 0-0 b6

Diagram 1018
After 7. ... b6

Black develops his bishop to b7 on the long diagonal in order to contest e4, a key square.

Here White has two main moves: 8. Ne5 and 8. Qe2.

A1 8. Ne5 Bb7

Diagram 1019
After 8. ... Bb7

9. f4

White opts for a "Stonewall" formation, a sort of reversed Dutch Defense formation.

After 9. Qf3 (to prevent ... Ne4) Nbd7 10. Qh3 Nxe5 11. dxe5 Ne4 12. f3 Ng5 13. Qg3 f5!,

Diagram 1020
After 13. ... f5!

Black's plan is to play ... Nf7 and, in response to f4, play ... Kh8, ... Rg8 and ... g5, with a strong attack.

9. ... Ne4!

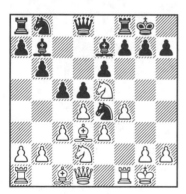

Diagram 1021
After 9. ... Ne4!

A typical move in these positions that puts the brakes on White's attack. We can now see the value of Black's choice of b7

for his bishop.

10. Nxe4 dxe4 11. Bc2 f6 12. Ng4 Bd5

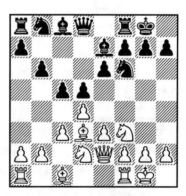

Diagram 1022
After 12. ... Bd5

Black follows up with ... Nd7. Black has ended White's attack. The position is about even.

A2 8. Qe2

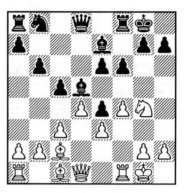

Diagram 1023
After 8. Qe2

8. ... Bb7 9. dxc5 bxc5 10. e4 Nc6

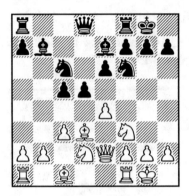

Diagram 1024
After 10. ... Nc6

11. e5

Or 11. Re1 Qc7 12. e5 Nd7
13. Nf1 Rfd8 14. Ng3 Nf8.

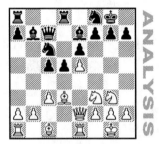

Diagram 1025
After 14. ... Nf8

11. ... Nd7

Black puts pressure on the e5
-pawn.

**Black's plan
includes transferring
his knight to f8
and then,
possibly, to g6.**

12. Re1 Re8

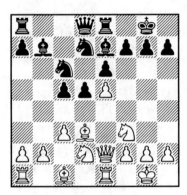

Diagram 1026
After 12. ... Re8

Black's plan includes transferring his knight to f8 and then,
possibly, to g6.

13. Nf1 Nf8 14. Bf4 a5

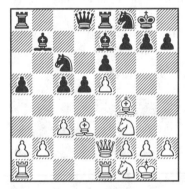

Diagram 1027
After 14. ... a5

Black is doing fine. The
game Burmakin–Aseev, 1995,
continued: 15. Rad1 a4 (gaining
space on the queenside) 16. c4
Nd4! 17. Nxd4 cxd4 18. Ng3
dxc4 19. Bxc4 Ng6.

Diagram 1028
After 19. ... Ng6

With his 18th move, Black opened up his b7-bishop. He has an important passed pawn on d4. Play continued: 20. Bc1 Qb6 21. Bd3 Red8 22. Rf1 (White anticipates Black's ... Bd5 maneuver—see White's 24th move. If 22. Qg4 Rac8 ∓.) 22. ... Bd5 23. a3 Bb3 24. Rde1 Rac8.

Diagram 1029
After 24. ... Rac8

Black is slightly better.

B 5. b3

White prepares to fianchetto his dark-square bishop. This plan was favored by the witty Savielly Tartakover, and his name is often applied to the variation. (But let's keep in mind, he was the one who said *"Erro ergo sum"*: I err, therefore I am.).

5. ... Nbd7

Black's plan of development is, in fact, somewhat similar to White's. Also good, and equalizing, is the commoner line, in which Black plays 5. ... Nc6 and 6. ... Bd6.

6. 0-0 b6 7. Bb2 Bb7

Diagram 1030
After 7. ... Bb7

The position is balanced.

8. Ne5 Be7 9. Nd2 0-0 10. f4 Ne4!

> **Also good is the commoner line, in which Black plays 5. ... Nc6 and 6. ... Bd6.**

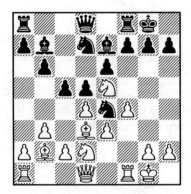

Diagram 1031
After 10. ... Ne4!

**11. Nxe4 dxe4 12. Bc4 Nxe5
13. fxe5 Bg5**

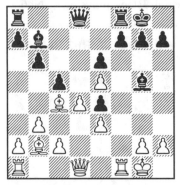

Diagram 1032
After 13. ... Bg5

The game is even. If White
protects his pawn with 14. Qe2
(to keep a rook on the f-file),
Black will play aggressively: 14.
... a6 (threatening ... b5) 15. a4
Bd5!,

Diagram 1033
After 15. ... Bd5

and if 16. Bxd5 exd5! 17. dxc5
bxc5 18. Rad1 Rb8

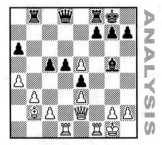

Diagram 1034
After 18. ... Rb8

19. c4 Qb6. And Black comes out
on top in a complex struggle;
while 16. Bxa6 Rxa6! 17. Qxa6
Bxe3+ 18. Kh1 Bxd4

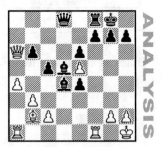

Diagram 1035
After 18. ... Bxd4

is also good for Black.

Summary:

Against both the c3- and b3-Colle, Black puts his pawns in the center—on d5 and c5. Importantly, he fianchettoes his light-square bishop. If White plays Ne5 and f4, Black counters with ... Ne4. Black also has sufficient counter-play when White plays e4-e5. Although White is alive and well in the popular Colle and has a number of options to choose from— the same can be said for Black!

Chapter 36: Colle System—1. d4 Nf6 2. Nf3 e6 3. e3
Memory Markers!

Diagram 1036
After 9. ... Nbd7

Diagram 1037
After 16. Bxa6

Chapter 36: Colle System—1. d4 Nf6 2. Nf3 e6 3. e3
Solutions to Memory Markers!

No. 1   **10. Qf3,** preventing ... Ne4. White stands better. He's ready to attack! See page 396.

No. 2   **16. ... Rxa6,** with compensation. See page 400.

Chapter 37: Veresov Opening—1. d4 Nf6 2. Nc3 d5 3. Bg5

Some Important Points to Look For

White again avoids the theoretically favored 2. c4 in favor of 2. Nc3, intending a quick e4. Black should be happy to see this choice, having two promising lines to choose from.

◆ The main line.

   See Diagram 1040.

◆ Time to triple.

   See Diagram 1042.

◆ Black's star move is 11. ... Qe5!.

   See Diagram 1044.

◆ More of the same.

   See Diagram 1055.

Outline of Variations

1. d4 Nf6 2. Nc3 d5 3. Bg5 c5!? 4. Bxf6 gxf6 5. e4 dxe4 6. dxc5 f5! *(402)* [D01]

   A 7. g4 Qc7 8. gxf5 Bg7 9. Qd5 *(404)*

   B 7. Qh5!? Nc6 8. Nh3 Bg7 9. Ng5 Bxc3+ 10. bxc3 Qd5! 11. c4 Qe5! *(405)*

   C 7. Qxd8+ Kxd8 *(406)*

      C1 8. Rd1+ Bd7 9. Bc4 e6 *(406)*

      C2 8. Nh3 Bg7 9. 0-0-0+ Bd7 10. Ne2 *(406)*

      C3 8. f3 Bg7 9. Rd1+ Bd7 10. Bc4 *(407)*

Chapter 37
Veresov Opening
A Shortcut to Theory

The Veresov Opening, or the Richter-Veresov Attack, chooses Nc3 over c4. To justify blocking his c2-pawn, White must fight for an e2-e4 thrust. Lev Alburt, still one of the world's leading authorities on the Veresov, helped popularize the opening in the 1970s, choosing it as a way to save the time he spent studying the maze of opening theory.

Nowadays, the opening is usually employed by players who like to avoid main lines or try to surprise their opponents. If Black is well prepared, he should have no problem getting a good game.

1. d4 Nf6 2. Nc3 d5 3. Bg5

> **This sharp system leads to dynamic play. Black often gets a significant edge.**

Diagram 1038
After 3. Bg5

White continues to fight for control of e4, while threatening to double Black's pawns.

3. ... c5!?

This sharp system leads to dynamic play. Black often gets a significant edge.

Also good is the solid 3. ... Nbd7 (to prevent the doubling of his pawns with Bxf6), often followed by ... g6, with a comfortable game for Black.

4. Bxf6

After the timid 4. e3 Nc6 5. Bxf6 gxf6 6. Nf3 e6,

Diagram 1039
After 6. ... e6

Black is fine. And if 4. dxc5, then 4. ... d4!, with advantage.

4. ... gxf6

4. ... exf6 leads to a calmer game. (See the Trompowsky, Chapter 38.)

5. e4

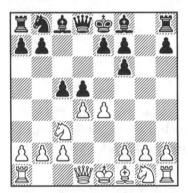

Diagram 1040
After 5. e4

The main line. White immediately opens up the center. The unambitious 5. e3 leads, at most, to equality (as in Diagram 1039).

5. ... dxe4 6. dxc5 f5!

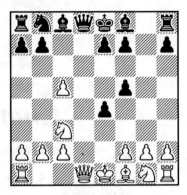

Diagram 1041
After 6. ... f5!

Black solidifies his central pawn structure and doesn't mind going into an endgame.

Here White can try three moves: 7. g4, 7. Qh5!?, and 7. Qxd8+.

A 7. g4 Qc7

7. ... Bg7 is another good choice.

8. gxf5 Bg7 9. Qd5

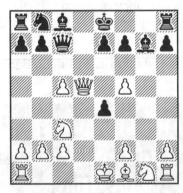

Diagram 1042
After 9. Qd5

9. ... Bxc3+ 10. bxc3 Nd7 ∓

B 7. Qh5!?

This leads to sharp play in which Black emerges on top.

7. ... Nc6

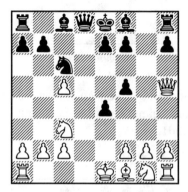

Diagram 1043
After 7. ... Nc6

8. Nh3

8. Rd1 is met by 8. ... Qa5. If 8. Bc4, then 8. ... e6.

8. ... Bg7 9. Ng5 Bxc3+ 10. bxc3 Qd5! 11. c4 Qe5!

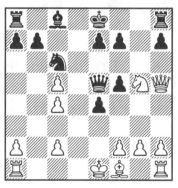

Diagram 1044
After 11. ... Qe5!

It turns out that Black's king will be quite safe on c7.

12. Qxf7+ Kd8 13. Qd5+

Or 13. Rd1+ Kc7, threatening 14. ... h6 15. Nh3 Be6.

13. ... Kc7

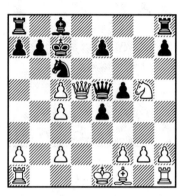

Diagram 1045
After 13. ... Kc7

Now White has to go into an endgame. After 14. Qxe5+ (14. Rd1? Qf6! 15. h4 Rd8 16. Qf7

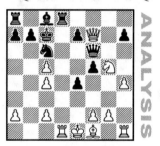

Diagram 1046
After 16. Qf7

16. ... Qc3+ wins for Black) 14. ... Nxe5, Black is clearly on top—White's tripled c-pawns are extremely weak.

C 7. Qxd8+ Kxd8

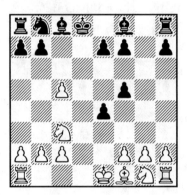

Diagram 1047
After 7. ... Kxd8

Here White has three options: 8. Rd1+, 8. Nh3, and 8. f3.

C1 8. Rd1+ Bd7 9. Bc4 e6

Diagram 1048
After 9. ... e6

Black is doing fine. If now 10. g4?! (White tries to break up Black's pawn structure, but more importantly, weakens the long diagonal.) 10. ... fxg4 11. Nxe4 Ke7 12. Ne2 Bc6 13. N2g3 f5!,

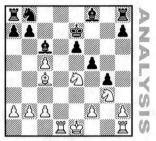

Diagram 1049
After 13. ... f5!

and Black won an Exchange in the game Vasilev–Krasenkov, 2001.

C2 8. Nh3

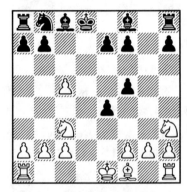

Diagram 1050
After 8. Nh3

8. ... Bg7 9. 0-0-0+ Bd7 10. Ne2

Or 10. Bc4 Bxc3! 11. bxc3 e6.

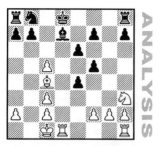

Diagram 1051
After 11. ... e6

Black follows up with ...
Ke7, and White's c-pawns are
low-hanging fruit, just waiting to
be plucked.

**10. ... Kc7 11. Nef4 e6
12. Be2 Nc6**

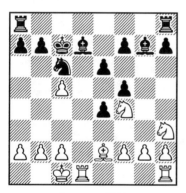

Diagram 1052
After 12. ... Nc6

With the idea of ... Ne5.
Black stands well.

C3 8. f3

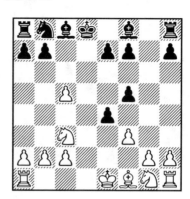

Diagram 1053
After 8. f3

8. ... Bg7 9. Rd1+

Or 9. 0-0-0+ Bd7 10. fxe4
Bxc3 11. bxc3 fxe4 ∓.

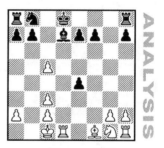

Diagram 1054
After 11. ... fxe4

9. ... Bd7 10. Bc4

White follows up with ... Ke7, and
White's pawns are low-hanging fruit,
just waiting to be plucked.

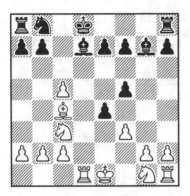

Diagram 1055
After 10. Bc4

And now: 10. ... Bxc3+! 11. bxc3 e6 12. fxe4 fxe4 13. Nh3 Ke7

Diagram 1056
After 13. ... Ke7

Black is better because of White's weak, tripled pawns. Play could continue: 14. Ng5 Rg8 15. h4 h6 16. Nxe4 Bc6 17. Nd6 Nd7 18. Rd2 Nxc5

Diagram 1057
After 18. ... Nxc5

and Black is clearly on top (∓).

Summary:

Black should be happy to see the Veresov. He can choose between a safe, perhaps somewhat better game after 3. ... Nbd7, and Dzindzi's choice—3. ... c5. This sharp reply often leads to complex endings in which Black's chances are quite good. Note that Black is normally prepared to take on c3 with his bishop, saddling White with very weak, tripled and isolated c-pawns.

Chapter 37: Veresov Opening—1. d4 Nf6 2. Nc3 d5 3. Bg5

Memory Markers!

Diagram 1058
After 4. Nf3

MARKER 1

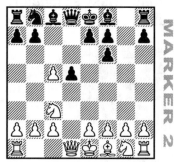

Diagram 1059
After 5. dxc5

MARKER 2

Diagram 1060
After 8. gxf5

MARKER 3

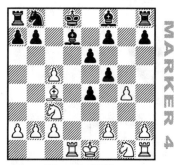

Diagram 1061
After 10. g4

MARKER 4

Chapter 37: Veresov Opening—1. d4 Nf6 2. Nc3 d5 3. Bg5

Solutions to Memory Markers!

No. 1 **4. ... g6.** Black's plan is natural and strong. See page 403.
No. 2 **5. ... d4.** See page 404.
No. 3 **8. ... Bg7,** preparing to triple White's c-pawns. See page 404.
No. 4 **10. ... fxg4!.** See page 406.

Chapter 38: The Trompowsky—1. d4 Nf6 2. Bg5
Some Important Points to Look For

This is another line whose reason for being is to avoid theory. The Trompowsky's signatory move is 2. Bg5. We play one of ours, ... c5, and Black not only survives but prevails.

◆ Our choice: 2. ... c5.
　 See Diagram 1063.

◆ Black attacks.
　 See Diagram 1067.

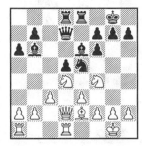

◆ Black has full compensation for his missing pawn. See Diagram 1072.

◆ White's best—he's okay, but so is Black. See Diagram 1084.

Outline of Variations

1. d4 Nf6 2. Bg5 c5 *(410)* [A45]

　A 3. Nc3 cxd4 4. Qxd4 Nc6 5. Qh4 Qa5! 6. 0-0-0 d6 7. e4 Be6 8. Bxf6 gxf6 9. Kb1 f5 10. exf5 *(412)*

　B 3. d5 Ne4 4. Bf4 Qb6 *(412)*
　　B1 5. Qc1 c4 6. e3 Qa5+ 7. Nd2 c3! 8. bxc3 Qxd5 *(412)*
　　B2 5. Bc1 e6 6. f3 Nf6 7. c4 exd5 8. cxd5 c4 *(113)*
　　B3 5. Nd2 Qxb2! 6. Nxe4 Qb4+ 7. Qd2 Qxe4 8. e3 g5 *(414)*

　C 3. Bxf6 exf6 *(415)*
　　C1 4. e3 Qb6! 5. b3 d5 6. Nf3 Nc6 7. Be2 *(415)*
　　C2 4. c3 d5 5. e3 Nc6 6. Nd2 Be7 7. dxc5 Bxc5 8. Nb3 Bb6 9. Ne2 0-0 10. Nf4 *(416)*
　　C3 4. d5 f5 5. Nc3 d6 6. e3 a6 7. a4 g6 8. Nf3 Bg7 9. Be2 Qa5
　　　　 10. Qd2 0-0 11. 0-0 Nd7 *(417)*
　　C4 4. Nc3 d5 5. e3 Be6 6. Nf3 c4 7. Be2 Bb4 8. Qd2 0-0 9. a3 Bd6 10. 0-0 a6 *(418)*

Chapter 38
The Trompowsky
1. d4 Nf6 2. Bg5

Developed by British chessplayers, the Trompowsky is used chiefly by those trying to avoid modern opening theory.

1. d4 Nf6 2. Bg5

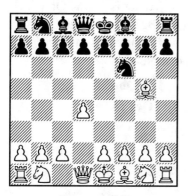

Diagram 1062
After 2. Bg5

Black has several options: 2. ... e6—for example, 3. e4 h6, forcing 4. Bxf6; 2. ... d5 or 2. ... g6, allowing 3. Bxf6; or the most popular 2. ... Ne4. But in this chapter we give Dzindzi's favorite,

2. ... c5

This move allows White fewer choices and saves Black study time.

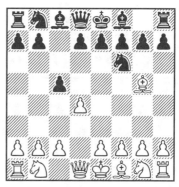

Diagram 1063
After 2. ... c5

White has three choices: 3. Nc3, 3. d5, and 3. Bxf6.

Dzindzi's favorite, ... c5, allows White fewer choices and saves Black study time.

A 3. Nc3 cxd4 4. Qxd4 Nc6 5. Qh4 Qa5! 6. 0-0-0 d6 7. e4 Be6

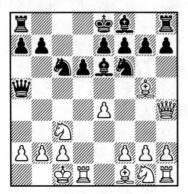

Diagram 1064
After 7. ... Be6

8. Bxf6

If 8. Kb1, ... Nxe4 should be considered now or later.

8. ... gxf6 9. Kb1 f5 10. exf5

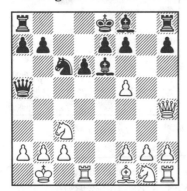

Diagram 1065
After 10. exf5

10. ... Qxf5

10. ... Bxf5? 11. Rd5 ±

Black wants to continue 11. ... Qg4, with the better endgame.

B 3. d5

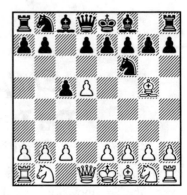

Diagram 1066
After 3. d5

3. ... Ne4 4. Bf4

Weaker is 4. Bh4 Qb6 5. Qc1 g5 6. Bg3 d6 followed by ... Bg7, when Black has a very active position.

4. ... Qb6

B1 5. Qc1 c4

Diagram 1067
After 5. ... c4

6. e3 Qa5+ 7. Nd2

Better 7. Nc3 Nxc3 8. Qd2 Qxd5 9. Qxc3 Nc6 10. Qxc4, with equality.

7. ... c3! 8. bxc3 Qxd5

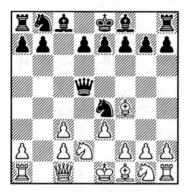

Diagram 1068
After 8. ... Qxd5

Black is better.

B2 5. Bc1 e6

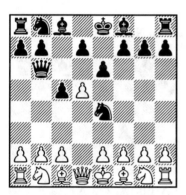

Diagram 1069
After 5. ... e6

6. f3 Nf6 7. c4 exd5 8. cxd5 c4

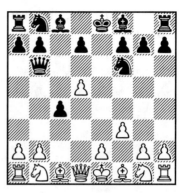

Diagram 1070
After 8. ... c4

9. e3

Or 9. e4 Bc5 10. Nh3 d6 11. Bxc4 Bxh3 12. gxh3

Diagram 1071
After 12. gxh3

12. … Nbd7, with sufficient compensation for the pawn, due to White's weak kingside pawn structure.

Black has sufficient compensation for the pawn due to White's weak kingside pawn structure.

**9. ... Bc5 10. Kf2 0–0
11. Bxc4**

Diagram 1072
After 11. Bxc4

**11. ... Re8 12. Qb3 Qd6
13. Ne2 Na6 14. Nbc3 Nc7
15. Rd1**

Diagram 1073
After 15. Rd1

15. ... b5

Also possible is 15. . . Qxh2
16. d6 Ne6, and Black is better.

**16. Nxb5 Nxb5 17. Bxb5
Rb8 18. Qd3 Qxh2**

Diagram 1074
After 18. ... Qxh2

White is in danger, as in
Milov–Landenbergue, 2002.

B3 5. Nd2 Qxb2!

Diagram 1075
After 5. ... Qxb2!

**6. Nxe4 Qb4+ 7. Qd2 Qxe4
8. e3 g5**

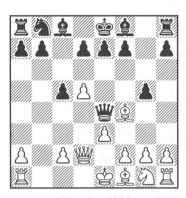

Diagram 1076
After 8. ... g5

9. Bg3

9. Bxg5? Qe5; 9. f3 Qf5 10. Bg3 Qf6 11. Rb1 Bg7 with a clear advantage for Black.

9. ... Bg7

White doesn't have sufficient compensation for the missing pawn.

C 3. Bxf6

White's best.

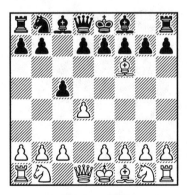

Diagram 1077
After 3. Bxf6

3. ... exf6

Taking toward the center (3. ... gxf6) also gives Black an equal game. But our recommendation is not as well-known and contains some never-before-published analysis by Dzindzi.

After 3. ... exf6, White has four moves: 4. e3, 4. c3, 4. d5, and 4. Nc3.

C1 4. e3 Qb6! 5. b3 d5 6. Nf3 Nc6 7. Be2

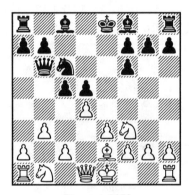

Diagram 1078
After 7. Be2

7. ... Be6

Black has an easy game—for example:

8. 0–0 Rd8

And now if White tries to put pressure on Black's central pawn by playing 9. Nc3, then after 9. ... Qa5 10. Na4 c4, Black has a superior position following the logical 11. Qe1 Bb4 12. c3 Ba3.

Diagram 1079
After 12. ... Ba3

White's knight on a4 is in jeopardy. The game Thorfinnsson–Chandler, 2001, continued: 13. Bd1 b5 14. Nc5 Bb2 15. Nb7 Qxc3 16. Nxd8 Kxd8

Diagram 1080
After 16. ... Kxd8

17. Qxc3 (17. Rb1 Bf5) 17. ... Bxc3 18. Rc1 Bb2 19. Rb1 c3 20. Ne1 Nb4.

Diagram 1081
After 20. ... Nb4

Black has an overwhelming position, e.g., 21. Nc2—and here

instead of 21. ... Bf5 (which was played in the game), 21. ... Nxa2 gives a decisive advantage to Black.

C2 4. c3

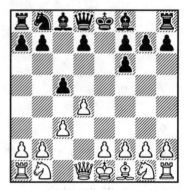

Diagram 1082
After 4. c3

This is the most strategically sound of White's fourth-move choices.

4. ... d5 5. e3 Nc6 6. Nd2 Be7 7. dxc5 Bxc5 8. Nb3 Bb6 9. Ne2 0–0 10. Nf4!

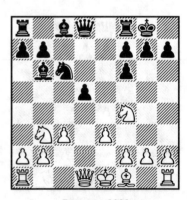

Diagram 1083
After 10. Nf4!

10. ... Be6 11. Be2 Qd7 12. 0–0 Rad8 13. Qd2 Ne5

14. Rfd1 a6 15. Nd4 Rfe8

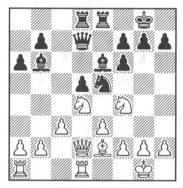

Diagram 1084
After 15. ... Rfe8

Black has a weak d5-pawn, but White does not have any reasonable way to exploit it, or to improve his position. Chances are equal. The game could continue: 16. Qc2 Qc8 17. h3 g6 18. Rd2 Bc7 19. Rad1 Bb8 20. Nf3 Qc6

Diagram 1085
After 20. ... Qc6

21. Nxe6 fxe6 22. e4 Qc7 23. g3 Ba7 24. Nxe5 fxe5 25. Kg2 d4.

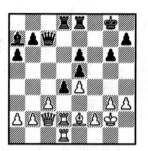

Diagram 1086
After 25. ... d4

The position is equal. If 26. f4, then ... Qc5.

C3 4. d5 f5

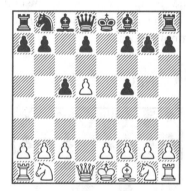

Diagram 1087
After 4. ... f5

This prevents e4.

5. Nc3 d6 6. e3 a6

Black prepares ... b5 and stops ... Bb5+.

7. a4 g6 8. Nf3 Bg7 9. Be2 Qa5 10. Qd2 0–0 11. 0–0 Nd7

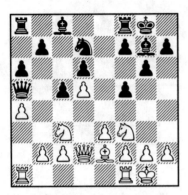

Diagram 1088
After 11. ... Nd7

With the idea of ... Ne5 or ... Nf6. Black has an advantage due to his powerful g7-bishop and the constriction of White's minor pieces.

C4 4. Nc3

Diagram 1089
After 4. Nc3

4. ... d5 5. e3

After 5. dxc5 d4 6. Ne4 Bf5, Black regains the pawn with a better position.

5. ... Be6 6. Nf3 c4

Also playable is 6. ... Nc6 7. Be2 cxd4 8. Nxd4 Bb4 9. 0–0 Bxc3 10. bxc3 0–0.

Diagram 1090
After 10. ... 0-0

Black is at least equal.

7. Be2 Bb4

Diagram 1091
After 7. ... Bb4

8. Qd2 0–0 9. a3 Bd6 10. 0–0 a6

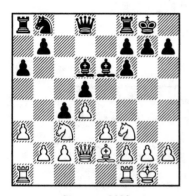

Diagram 1092
After 10. ... a6

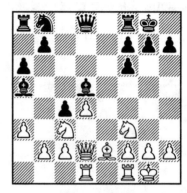

Diagram 1093
After 14. ... Ba5!

Black is doing fine, for example:

Black has a tight grip on the center.

11. e4 dxe4 12. Nxe4 Bc7!

You'll see why on move 14.

13. Rad1

Or 13. Nc5 Bd5

13. ... Bd5 14. Nc3 Ba5!

Summary:

The Trompowsky offers Black several good choices. After 2. ... c5, 3. Nc3 allows Black to win tempi by attacking the White queen; not surprisingly, Black stands better. Black does well in sharp lines after 3. d5 Ne4, followed by 4. ... Qb6 (targeting the b2-pawn left unprotected after the White bishop's signatory move, 2. Bg5). Finally, after 3. Bxf6 (doubling Black's pawn), Dzindzi's favorite 3. ... exf6 gives Black equality in positions where at times he organizes play around his isolated d-pawn.

Chapter 38: The Trompowsky—1. d4 Nf6 2. Bg5

Memory Markers!

Diagram 1094
After 10. ... Bxf5

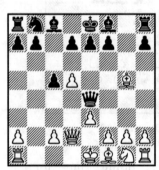

Diagram 1095
After 9. Bxg5

Diagram 1096
After 22. e4

Diagram 1097
After 6. ... g6

Chapter 38: The Trompowsky—1. d4 Nf6 2. Bg5
Solutions to Memory Markers!

No. 1   **11. Rd5 ±.** Why only ±? Because of 11. ... Bxc2+ 12. Kc1! (best). Indeed, it's ±—but not +−. See page 412.

No. 2   **9. ... Qe5 −+.** See page 415.

No. 3   **22. ... Qc7!.** See page 417.

No. 4   **7. Bb5+.** Thus we suggest 6. ... a6, stopping this check while preparing ... b5. See page 417.

Chapter 39: Blackmar-Diemer Gambit—1. d4 Nf6 2. Nc3 d5 3. e4

Some Important Points to Look For

Against a swashbuckling Blackmar-Diemer gambiteer, we force him into a less promising gambit—just a half-step before he can get into his game.

◆ The BDG with a pair of knights
gone. See Diagram 1099.

◆ Black protects his pawn.
See Diagram 1102.

◆ Black siezes the initiative.
See Diagram 1105.

◆ A brave pawn!
See Diagram 1111.

Outline of Variations

1. d4 Nf6 2. Nc3 d5 3. e4 Nxe4 4. Nxe4 dxe4 *(423)* [D00]

A 5. Be3 Bf5 6. Ne2 e6 7. Ng3 Bg6 8. h4 h5 *(424)*

B 5. f3 Bf5 6. c3 e6 7. Be3 *(424)*

C 5. Bc4 g6 6. f3 Bg7 7. c3 c5 8. Qb3 0-0 9. dxc5 Nd7 *(425)*

Chapter 39
Blackmar-Diemer Gambit
The Danish of 1. d4

There are librarians who return books late; there are Republicans who drive hybrid cars—and there are 1. d4-players who like a real gambit. More often then not, their opening of choice is the Blackmar-Diemer.

1. d4 Nf6 2. Nc3 d5 3. e4

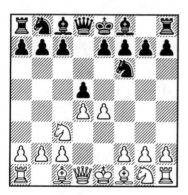

Diagram 1098
After 3. e4

Armand Edward Blackmar (1826-1888) was an American professor of music and a chess expert who played 1. d4 d5 2. e4 dxe4 3. f3 in many games. Emil Josef Diemer (1908-1990) was a German chess master who saw Blackmar's games and found the

Zwischenzug 3. Nc3. He played the gambit against all comers, leaving behind some marvelous combinations.

Nowadays the Blackmar-Diemer Gambit is rarely seen in master practice, since White gives up a pawn for less than clear compensation. But the gambit has its devotees on the amateur level, so you should be prepared.

Technically, it's not a Blackmar-Diemer until White offers f3, as a Blackmar-Diemer gambiteer will after 3. ... dxe4. But to avoid BDG mainlines—familiar to the BDG fanatic—we recommend making White live with a different gambit, a line called the Hübsch Gambit, even stronger for Black than playing 3. ... dxe4. It's available to us because we started with 1. ... Nf6 instead of 1. ... d5.

3. ... Nxe4 4. Nxe4 dxe4

Diagram 1099
After 4. ... dxe4

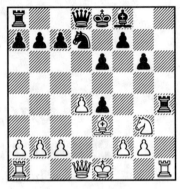

Diagram 1101
After 12. ... Rxh4

Here White can try three options: 5. Be3, 5. f3, and 5. Bc4.

Black is, again, up a pawn.

A 5. Be3 Bf5 6. Ne2 e6 7. Ng3 Bg6 8. h4

B 5. f3 Bf5

Diagram 1100
After 8. h4

Diagram 1102
After 5. ... Bf5

White tries to create play on the kingside. Black, however, easily defends against all threats.

6. c3 e6 7. Be3

8. ... h5 9. Be2 Nd7 10. Bxh5 Bxh5 11. Nxh5 g6! 12. Ng3 Rxh4

In the game Van den Berg-De Waal, 2002, after 7. ... Be7 8. fxe4 Bxe4 9. Qg4

Diagram 1103
After 9. Qg4

9. ... Bg6 10. Nf3 Nd7 11. Nd2 Nf6 12. Qd1 0-0,

Diagram 1104
After 12. ... 0-0

Black is simply up a pawn in a better position.

C 5. Bc4 g6 6. f3 Bg7 7. c3 c5

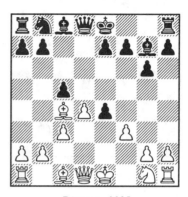

Diagram 1105
After 7. ... c5

Black immediately undermines White's central pawn.

8. Qb3

After 8. d5 exf3 9. Nxf3 0-0

Diagram 1106
After 9. ... 0-0

White has no compensation for the pawn.

8. ... 0-0 9. dxc5 Nd7

Black immediately undermines White's central pawn.

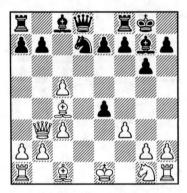

Diagram 1107
After 9. ... Nd7

This position occurred in the game Josslen–Vanderstricht, 2003. White tried to hold the c5-pawn and was quickly punished: 10. Be3 Qc7 11. Qb4

(Relatively better is 11. fxe4 Nxc5 12.Qc2 Be6 13. Bxe6 Nxe6 14. Nf3 Qc4,

Diagram 1108
After 14. ... Qc4

with a good game for Black.)

11. ... a5! 12. Qb5 Ne5.

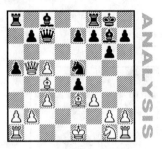

Diagram 1109
After 12. ... Ne5!

Black seizes the initiative. 13. Be2 Bf5 14. fxe4 Bxe4 15. Nf3 Bc6 16. Qb3

Diagram 1110
After 16. Qb3

Black stands better. White is behind in development and lacks adequate play. The game continued: 16. ... Nxf3+ 17. Bxf3 a4! 18. Qc4 Bxf3 19. gxf3 a3.

Diagram 1111
After 19. ... a3

Black creates even more

weaknesses in White's camp. Now White played 20. 0-0-0 and lost by force, yet it's hard to recommend anything different at this point. The game continued: 20. ... axb2+ 21. Kxb2 b5! 22. Qb4 Ra4 23. Qb3 Rfa8 24. Rd3 Qa5, White resigned.

Diagram 1112
After 24. ... Qa5

ANALYSIS

Summary:

We avoid the Blackmar-Diemer Gambit by forcing White into the Hübsch Gambit, which gives White some initiative—but not full compensation for the sacrificed pawn, and not nearly enough for the Morphy-wannabe who plays the BDG. Black plays actively to maintain his edge.

Chapter 39: Blackmar-Diemer Gambit—The Danish of 1. d4

Memory Markers!

Diagram 1113
After 7. h4

Diagram 1114
After 10. h4

Diagram 1115
After 11. Be3

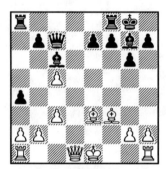

Diagram 1116
After 18. Qd1

Chapter 39: Blackmar-Diemer Gambit—The Danish of 1. d4

Solutions to Memory Markers!

No. 1   **7. ... h5.** See page 424.

No. 2   **10. ... h5.** See page 425.

No. 3   **11. ... Nb6.** See page 425.

No. 4   **18. ... a3,** with a decisive advantage. See page 426.

PART FOUR

DEFENDING AGAINST 1. c4 AND OTHER FIRST MOVES

Chapter 40: English, Part I—Overall Review and Intro to 1. ... c5

Some Important Points to Look For

The English is a subtle and deservedly popular opening that's been employed by many of the world's greatest. Black has a number of good replies. We recommend 1. ... c5.

◆ The most precise order.
   See Diagram 1122.

◆ We don't want this!
   See Diagram 1124.

◆ A timely check.
   See Diagram 1126.

◆ Two good choices.
   See Diagram 1130.

Outline of Variations

1. c4 c5 2. Nf3 g6 *(432)* [A30]
   A 3. d4 cxd4 4. Nxd4 Nc6 *(433)*
      A1 5. e4 Nf6 *(433)*
      A2 5. g3 Bg7 6. Nc2 Qa5+ 7. Bd2 Qc5 8. Bc3 Nf6 *(433)*
      A3 5. Nc3 Bg7 6. Nc2 Bxc3+ 7. bxc3 Qa5 8. Bd2 0-0 9. f3 d6 *(434)*
   B 3. e3 Nf6 4. d4 *(434)*
   C 3. Nc3 Bg7 4 g3 Nc6 5. Bg2 c5 *(435)*

Chapter 40
English, Part I
Overall Review and Intro to 1. ... c5

The English (1. c4) is one of White's most effective and subtle openings and has been a part of the repertoire of many of the world's greatest players. White does not immediately commit to any one plan of development, and transpositions abound.

1. c4

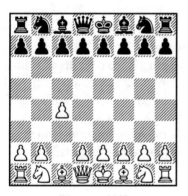

Diagram 1117
After 1. c4

White's first move takes control of d5.

Black has a number of good responses: the principled 1. ... e5, the flexible 1. ... Nf6, the symmetrical 1. ... c5, the fianchetto 1. ... g6, and 1. ... c6,

leading either to the Slav or to the Caro-Kann.

Isn't 1. ... e5 a more useful move than White's 1. c4 debut? Not according to statistics. Of course, 1. c4 e5 is a reversed Sicilian. (We've discussed the Sicilian in Chapter 4.)

After **1. ... e5 2. Nc3,**

White's most common move,

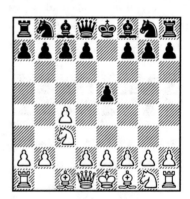

Diagram 1118
After 2. Nc3

Black can play 2. ... Nf6 and, if 3. g3, then, à la Rossolimo, 3. ... Bb4. Also popular is 2. ... Nc6, preparing to play the Grand-Prix-style 3. ... f5.

Another choice is the flexible

1. ... Nf6

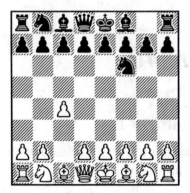

Diagram 1119
After 1. ... Nf6

Now the game often trans-forms into other openings—for example, the familiar Nimzo- (or Bogo-) Indian after 2. d4 e6. White can, however, continue 2. Nc3, and on 2. ... e6, play 3. e4, avoiding those classical open-ings.

Our move choice is **1. ... c5.**

Diagram 1120
After 1. ... c5

We recommend this symmet-rical continuation because White's popular (and best) **2. Nf3**, followed by 3. d4, leads to the Maroczy Bind positions you learn in Part II.

In the next chapter, we'll study the Panov-Botvinnik line of the Caro-Kann, reached after 2. Nf3 g6 3. e3 (or 3. Nc3) Nf6 4. d4 cxd4 5. exd4 d5 6. Nc3.

Diagram 1121
After 6. Nc3

We've seen this before—for instance, in our chapter on the Alapin (2. c3) Sicilian. And in Chapter 42, we'll study 2. Nc3, followed by the fianchetto of White's light-square bishop—closed positions in which d4 soon becomes impossible.

2. ... g6

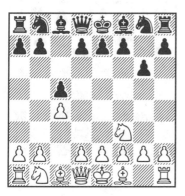

Diagram 1122
After 2. ... g6

The most precise move order, which limits White's options—and our studies.

(Also playable is the "softer" 2. ... Nf6.)

Now, what can White do?

A 3. d4 cxd4 4. Nxd4

Diagram 1123
After 4. Nxd4

4. ... Nc6

Not 4. ... Bg7 5. e4, ready to meet 5. ... Nc6 with 6. Be3.

Diagram 1124
After 6. Be3

White's choices here are: 5. e4, 5. g3, and 5. Nc3.

A1 5. e4

This move leads to familiar Maroczy Bind lines after 5. ... Nf6.

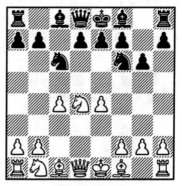

Diagram 1125
After 5. ... Nf6

A2 5. g3 Bg7 6. Nc2

The unambitious 6. e3 can be countered by 6. ... d6 7. Bg2 Bd7; if White makes another retreat—6. Nb3, then Black can play 6. ... d6 and 7. ... Be6, with a good game.

6. ... Qa5+

Diagram 1126
After 6. ... Qa5+

7. Bd2 Qc5 8. Bc3

Now the simple 8. ... Nf6 (accepting the sac is risky) gives Black a good game, as White's pieces aren't well placed after 9. Nd2 0-0.

Diagram 1127
After 9. ... 0-0

If in the position shown in Diagram 1123, after 4. ... Nc6, White plays 5. Nc3, the game could continue:

A3 5. Nc3 Bg7 6. Nc2

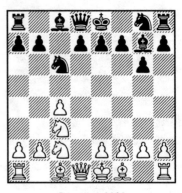

Diagram 1128
After 6. Nc2

Black has 6. ... Bxc3+ 7. bxc3 Qa5 (also good is 7. ... d6) 8. Bd2 Nf6 9. f3 d6 10. e4

Diagram 1129
After 10. e4

10. ... Qa4!, and Black is better. White's queenside pawns are weak. All endings clearly favor Black.

If, in the position shown in Diagram 1122, White continues:

B 3. e3

we recommend flexible 3. ... Nf6 to keep our options open after 4. d4.

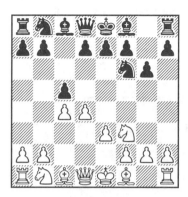

Diagram 1130
After 4. d4

Indeed, both 4. ... cxd4 5. exd4 d5 (a familiar Panov–Botvinnik line, good for Black), or the more ambitious 4. ... Bg7, delaying the exchange as well as ... d5, are good for us. And if White neither plays d4, nor prepares it with e3 early enough, Black can prevent it forever,

steering the game into the closed lines of Chapter 42. For example:

C 3. Nc3 Bg7 4. g3 Nc6 5. Bg2 e5

Diagram 1131
After 5. ... e5

Or 5. ... d6 and 6. ... e5.

In the next two chapters, we'll look at the English in more detail.

Summary:

Of all the good responses to 1. c4, we recommend the Symmetrical Variation, using our knowledge of various Sicilians. White's attempt to combine d4, Nxd4 and the g2-fianchetto doesn't turn out to his advantage in our chosen move order—2. Nf3 g6.

Chapter 40: English—Overall Review and Intro to 1. ... c5

Memory Markers!

Diagram 1132
After 5. e4

MARKER 1

Diagram 1133
After 8. Bc3

MARKER 2

Diagram 1134
After 5. d5

MARKER 3

Diagram 1135
After 6. e3

MARKER 4

Chapter 40: English—Overall Review and Intro to 1. ... c5

Solutions to Memory Markers!

No. 1   **5. ... Nf6,** entering the Maroczy Bind. See page 433.

No. 2   **8. ... Nf6,** with a good game. Taking the pawn gives White adequate compensation in the form of initiative. See page 434.

No. 3   **5. ... e6!.** We're in a sharp Benoni with an extra tempo (White will eventually have to play e4 anyway). Great! See page 435.

No. 4   **6. ... e5,** preventing d4. See page 435.

Chapter 41: English, Part II—White plays e3 and d4
Some Important Points to Look For

White wants to play in the center. Black can capture on d4 and transpose into a favorable form of the Caro-Kann. Or he can take a theoretical "shortcut," playing 5. ... 0-0.

◆ Black enters the Caro-Kann.
See Diagram 1139.

◆ A typical Black riposte.
See Diagram 1143.

◆ Bold and effective!
See Diagram 1150.

◆ A knight tango.
See Diagram 1155.

Outline of Variations

1. c4 c5 2. Nf3 g6 3. Nc3 Bg7 4. e3 Nf6 5. d4 cxd4 6. exd4 d5 *(438)* [A30➡B13]

    A 7. Be2 0-0 8. 0-0 dxc4 9. Bxc4 Bg4 *(440)*

    B 7. Bg5 Ne4 8. cxd5 Nxg5 9. Nxg5 0-0 *(441)*

      B1 10. Nf3 Nd7 11. Bc4 Nb6 12. Bb3 Bg4 13. 0-0 Bxf3 14. Qxf3 Bxd4 *(442)*

      B2 10. Qd2 Nd7 11. Bc4 Qb6 12. Rd1 Qb4 13. Bb3 a5 *(442)*

    C 7. cxd5 Nxd5 8. Bc4 Nb6 9. Bb3 Nc6 10. Be3 0-0 11. d5 Na5 *(444)*

    D 7. Qb3 dxc4 8. Bxc4 0-0 9. Ne5 e6 10. Be3 Nc6 11. Nxc6 bxc6 12. 0-0 Nd5 *(445)*

Chapter 41
English, Part II
White Plays e3 and d4

In this line, White's objective is to play in the center with d4, prepared by e3—in order to recapture with this pawn.

1. c4 c5 2. Nf3 g6

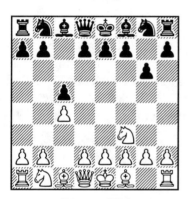

Diagram 1136
After 2. ... g6

We rely on a familiar sequence of moves to use what we've already studied. The moves leave Black options. In this line, he will have the option of transposing into a very safe form of the Panov-Botvinnik Caro-Kann. Or—if you want to eliminate the need for going over much of this chapter—you can instead play a different way—to

limit your study.

3. Nc3 Bg7 4. e3

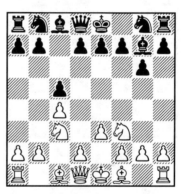

Diagram 1137
After 4. e3

4. ... Nf6 5. d4

Diagram 1138
After 5. d4

5. ... cxd4

Black can delay this exchange with 5. ... 0-0, as neither 6. dxc5 nor 6. d5 (White will have to waste a tempo by playing e4 in two moves) is promising for White. After 6. Be2 cxd4 7. exd4 d5, we'll reach **A** below.

6. exd4 d5

Diagram 1139
After 6. ... d5

We've transposed to the Panov Variation of the Caro-Kann Defense where White has played Nf3. This line does not create any problems for Black, who easily gets comfortable play. White has several continuations: 7. Be2, 7. Bg5, 7. Qb3, and 7. cxd5.

A 7. Be2 0–0 8. 0–0 dxc4

Also good is developing 8. ... Nc6—QGD Tarrasch with reversed colors. Lev Alburt played this line and preferred Black.

9. Bxc4 Bg4

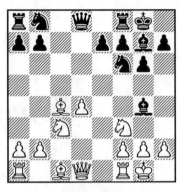

Diagram 1140
After 9. ... Bg4

Black's plan is to pressure White's isolated d-pawn, and this pin immobilizes one of the pawn's guardians.

10. Be3

White develops his bishop as another bodyguard for his d4-pawn. Or he can play 10. h3 Bxf3 11. Qxf3 Nc6 12. d5 Ne5, with play similar to the main line.

Diagram 1141
After 12. ... Ne5

10. ... Nc6

Black's play is straightforward and effective. He develops with another threat to d4.

11. d5

This is a concession.

**11. ... Bxf3 12. Qxf3 Ne5
13. Qe2 Nxc4 14. Qxc4 Qd7**

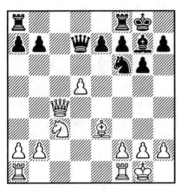

*Diagram 1142
After 14. ... Qd7*

Black has a solid position with no weaknesses. His plan is to transfer his knight to d6. As Nimzovich told us, a knight is an ideal blockader of the isolated passed pawn. Here it will also control the key squares in the center. The position is about equal.

B 7. Bg5 Ne4!

*Diagram 1143
After 7. ... Ne4!*

Black sacrifices his pawn for active play.

8. cxd5

If White plays 8. Nxd5?, he loses a piece after 8. ... Nxg5 9. Nxg5 e6!.

*Diagram 1144
After 9. ... e6!*

After 8. Bh4 Nxc3 9. bxc3 0–0 10. Qb3 dxc4 11. Bxc4 Nc6,

*Diagram 1145
After 11. ... Nc6*

Black comfortably finishes his development.

8. ... Nxg5 9. Nxg5 0–0

Black has a solid position with no weaknesses.

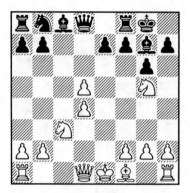

Diagram 1146
After 9. ... 0-0

White's doubled d-pawns and backward development give Black sufficient compensation for the pawn. Let's look at two tries: 10. Nf3 and 10. Qd2.

B1 10. Nf3 Nd7 11. Bc4 Nb6 12. Bb3 Bg4 13. 0–0 Bxf3 14. Qxf3

14. gxf3? weakens the king and leaves White with a broken pawn structure—14. ... Qd6, with the idea of ... Qf4.

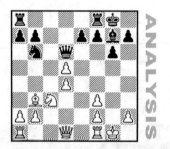

Diagram 1147
After 14. ... Qd6

Black is better.

14. ... Bxd4

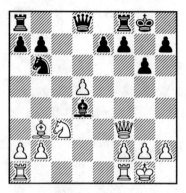

Diagram 1148
After 14. ... Bxd4

Winning the pawn back with a good position.

B2 10. Qd2

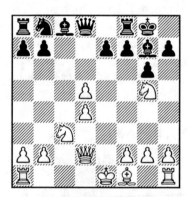

Diagram 1149
After 10. Qd2

White defends against the threat of ... Qb6 and protects the g5-knight.

10. ... Nd7 11. Bc4 Qb6 12. Rd1 Qb4 13. Bb3 a5!

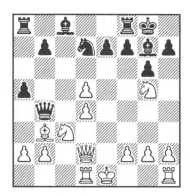

Diagram 1150
After 13. ... a5!

Black threatens ... a4.

14. Ba4 Nb6 15. a3 Qc4 16. Qe2

Black answers 16. Bb5 with 16. ... Qb3.

16. ... Bf5

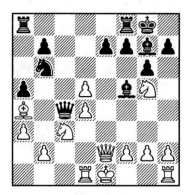

Diagram 1151
After 16. ... Bf5

Now if 17. Qxc4 Nxc4, and a pawn falls.

17. Bb5

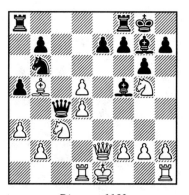

Diagram 1152
After 17. Bb5

17. ... Qxe2+ 18. Kxe2 Rad8 19. Bd3 Bxd3+ 20. Rxd3 Nxd5 21. Nxd5 Rxd5 22. Nf3

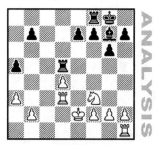

Diagram 1153
After 22. Nf3

We're following Ljubojevic-Kamsky, 1996. Black regained the pawn and stands better. (He eventually won.)

C 7. cxd5

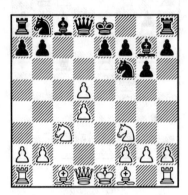

Diagram 1154
After 7. cxd5

7. ... Nxd5 8. Bc4 Nb6 9. Bb3 Nc6

For another good option, 9. ... 0-0, see page 225 (Alapin).

10. Be3 0–0 11. d5 Na5!

Diagram 1155
After 11. ... Na5!

12. Bd4

Or 12. Bc2 Nac4, with good play for Black.

12. ... Nxb3 13. Bxg7 Nxa1

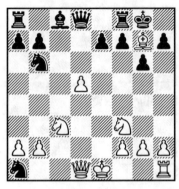

Diagram 1156
After 13. ... Nxa1

14. Bxf8 Qxf8 15. Qxa1 Bf5

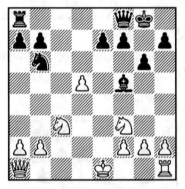

Diagram 1157
After 15. ... Bf5

Black is on top. White is left with a weak, isolated d-pawn (Sveshnikov–Dvoirys, 1996).

D 7. Qb3

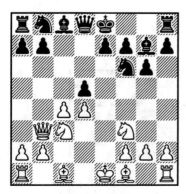

Diagram 1158
After 7. Qb3

This move is not dangerous because Black can safely take the pawn on c4 and castle.

7. ... dxc4 8. Bxc4 0–0 9. Ne5 e6 10. Be3 Nc6

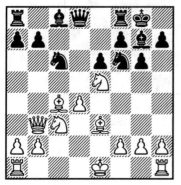

Diagram 1159
After 10. ... Nc6

Black is not afraid of his queenside pawn structure being weakened after Nxc6—in return he gets an important outpost on d5 for his remaining knight.

11. Nxc6 bxc6 12. 0–0 Nd5

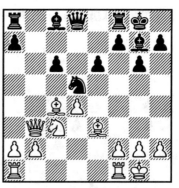

Diagram 1160
After 12. ... Nd5

With the idea of ... a5 and ... Ba6. The game is balanced.

Summary:

*The Panov-Botvinnik lines in this chapter (with Nf3 played early), lead to an equal game. Black also has a choice of delaying an exchange on d4, castling first. Then, in line **A**, both 8. ... dxc4 and 8. ... Nc6 give him an easy equality— and perhaps a bit more. Note that if you adopt the system with 5. ... 0-0, then lines **B**, **C**, and **D** cannot occur. (See our comments to 5. ... cxd4 and Memory Marker 4.)*

Chapter 41: English, Part II—White Plays e3 and d4

Memory Markers!

Diagram 1161
After 8. cxd5

Diagram 1162
After 8. Nxd5

Diagram 1163
After 14. Na4

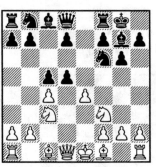

Diagram 1164
After 7. ... exd5

Chapter 41: English, Part II—White plays e3 and d4

Solutions to Memory Markers!

No. 1 **8. ... Nxg5,** a temporary pawn sacrifice, gives Black a good game—as shown in this chapter. Winning the pawn back instantly leaves White with a small edge after 8. ... Nxc3?! 9. bxc3 Qxd5, and now, for instance, 10. Qb3. See page 441.

No. 2 **8. ... Nxg5 9. Nxg5 e6** wins a piece. See page 441.

No. 3 **14. ... Qxd2+** (also interesting is 14. ... Qb5, but not 14. ... b5 15. Qxb4!) **15. Rxd2 b5.** See page 443.

No. 4 **8. exd5!,** because going into a super-sharp Modern Benoni a tempo down (after 8. cxd5) isn't a good idea. After the "symmetrical" exchange exd5, we reach a known position in which White would have an edge, if not for a lost tempo (e2-e3-e4). Now the game is even. See pages 440 and 445 (Summary).

Chapter 42: English, Part III—White Refrains from d4
Some Important Points to Look For

White can play the English without an early d4. We keep to our trusty move order, often creating a "Stonewall" formation with a later ... e5, preventing d4 forever.

◆ A space-conscious approach.
See Diagram 1168.

◆ Striking at the center!
See Diagram 1179.

◆ A universal approach.
See Diagram 1190.

◆ Here, symmetry equals equality.
See Diagram 1204.

Outline of Variations

1. c4 c5 2. Nc3 g6 3. g3 Bg7 4. Bg2 Nc6 *(448)* [A36-37]
> **A** 5. Nf3 d6 6. 0-0 e5 7. d3 Nge7 8. a3 0-0 9. Rb1 a5 10. Ne1 Be6 *(450)*
>> **A1** 11. Nd5 Rb8 12. Nxe7+ Nxe7 13. b4 axb4 14. axb4 cxb4 15. Rxb4 d5 *(452)*
>> **A2** 11. Nc2 d5 12. cxd5 Nxd5 *(453)*
> **B** 5. a3 d6 6. Rb1 a5 7. e3 e5 8. Nge2 Nge7 9. 0-0 0-0 *(454)*
> **C** 5. e3 e5 6. Nge2 Nge7 7. 0-0 0-0 8. d3 d6 9. Rb1 Rb8 10. a3 a5 11. Bd2 Be6 *(456)*
>> **C1** 12. Nd5 b5 13. Nec3 b4 *(457)*
>> **C2** 12. Qb3 f5 13. Nd5 Nxd5 14. cxd5 Bf7 15. Qc2 Ne7 *(458)*
> **D** 5. e4 d6 6. Nge2 e5 7. 0-0 Nge7 8. d3 0-0 9. a3 a5 10. Rb1 Rb8 *(458)*
>> **D1** 11. Nd5 b5 12. cxb5 Rxb5 13. Qa4 Ba6 *(459)*
>> **D2** 11. Be3 f5 12. exf5 gxf5 *(460)*
>> **D3** 11. Bd2 Be6 12. f4 Qd7 13. Nd5 Bg4 *(460)*

Chapter 42
English, Part III
White Refrains from d4

White can also play the English without pushing d4 in the early stages, keeping the center closed and allowing more time to jockey behind the lines.

1. c4 c5 2. Nc3 g6

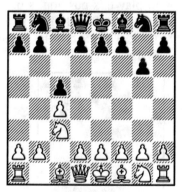

Diagram 1165
After 2. ... g6

We recommend this move order and not 2. ... Nc6. After 2. ... Nc6 3. Nf3 g6 4. e3 Bg7 (4. ...

Nf6 also isn't sufficient for equality) 5. d4, we reach an important position—and one you should avoid!

Diagram 1166
After 5. d4

White stands better, ready to push d5.

We also delay playing ... Nf6 because, unless White goes for an early d4, we're going to play ... e5 and put our king's knight on e7.

3. g3

Nix ... Nc6 if you don't see g3!
In our system, it's safe to play ... Nc6 early only if White has already played g3!

If 3. e3, then 3. ... Nf6 4. d4 Bg7, allowing 5. d5 (discussed briefly in two previous chapters). Also good is 4. ... cxd4 5. exd4 Bg7. Now if 6. Nf3, then ... d5 (English, Part II), or 6. d5 0-0 7. Nf3 e6 8. Be2 exd5 9. exd5 d6, with equality.

3. ... Bg7

Now d4 is no longer an available option. (See **C**.)

4. Bg2 Nc6

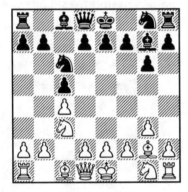

Diagram 1167
After 4. ... Nc6

We've reached a popular position in the symmetrical English. White has several choices: 5. Nf3, 5. a3, 5. e3 (with the idea of Nge2) and 5. e4 followed by Nge2 and d3.

A 5. Nf3 d6 6. 0-0 e5

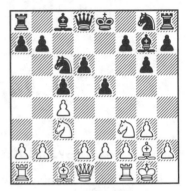

Diagram 1168
After 6. ... e5

Although we prefer this space-conscious approach—a second, symmetrical (and good) way to play this position is 6. ... Nf6 7. d3 0-0 8. Bd2 Bd7 9. a3 a6 10. Rb1 Rb8 11. b4 cxb4 12. axb4 b5!.

Diagram 1169
After 12. ... b5!

Black has stymied White's queenside play, and the position is balanced.

Black has stymied White's queenside play, and the position is balanced.

7. d3

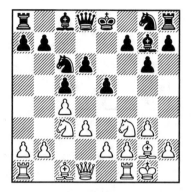

Diagram 1170
After 7. d3

7. ... Nge7 8. a3 0–0 9. Rb1 a5

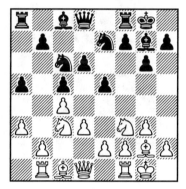

Diagram 1171
After 9. ... a5

This is the main position in the Nf3/d3 variation. White's typical plan is to occupy the d5-square after Ne1-c2-e3-d5. In the meantime, Black prepares his counter-play.

10. Ne1

After 10. Bd2 Rb8 11. Qa4 Bd7 12. Nb5 Nf5 (defending the d6-pawn and preparing Nd4)

13. Qd1 Ncd4 14. Nc3 (or 14. Nfxd4 exd4 15. b4 axb4 16. axb4 Re8!—an improvement over 16. ... b6, as played in Delchev–Brkic, 2006; Black is ready to meet 17. bxc5 dxc5 18. Bf4 with 18. ... Be5) 14. ... Nxf3+ 15. Bxf3 Nd4 16. Bg2 b5!

Diagram 1172
After 16. ... b5!

Black easily equalizes as in the game Markowski–Kasimzhanov, 2003: 17. e3 b4 18. axb4 cxb4 19. exd4 bxc3 20. Bxc3 exd4 21. Bd2

Diagram 1173
After 21. Bd2

21. ... a4 22. b4 axb3 23. Rxb3 Qc7 24. Rxb8, draw.

White's typical plan is to occupy d5 after Ne1-c2-e3-d5.

10. ... Be6

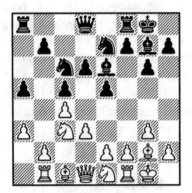

Diagram 1174
After 10. ... Be6

A1 11. Nd5 Rb8 12. Nxe7+

Or 12. Nc2 b5! 13. Nce3 bxc4 14. dxc4 f5 15. Nc3 e4 16. Bd2 Nd4

Diagram 1175
After 16. ... Nd4

Black seizes the initiative. The game Langeweg–Kavalek, 1968, continued: 17. Ncd5 Nxd5 18. Nxd5 Bxd5 19. cxd5 Nb3 20. f3 Nxd2 21. Qxd2 e3

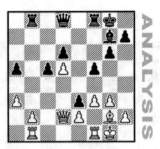

Diagram 1176
After 21. ... e3

22. Qc2 a4 23. Qxa4 Bxb2 24. f4 Qf6 25. Kh1 Rfc8 26. Rfd1 c4 27. Qc2 Qc3, and White lost.

Black also achieved dominance on all fronts and won in Pantsulaia–Karjakin, 2005, after 12. Nc2 b5 (by transposition)

Diagram 1177
After 12. ... b5

13. Bd2 a4 14. Nxe7+ Nxe7 15. e3 f5 16. f4 Qd7

12. ... Nxe7 =

Bareev–Almasi, 2002, continued:

13. b4

Diagram 1178
After 13. b4

**13. ... axb4 14. axb4 cxb4
15. Rxb4 d5!**

Diagram 1179
After 15. ... d5!

With this typical counter-blow in the center, the position quickly reduces itself to an even endgame.

16. Nc2 dxc4 17. dxc4 Nc6

**18. Ra4 Qxd1 19. Rxd1 Ra8
20. Rxa8 Rxa8 21. Bd5 Nd4
22. Nxd4 exd4 =**

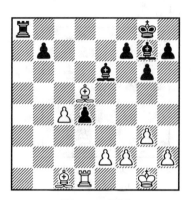

Diagram 1180
After 22. ... exd4

A2 11. Nc2 d5 12. cxd5 Nxd5

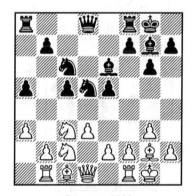

Diagram 1181
After 12. ... Nxd5

Suddenly it's Black who plays the bind.

After the typical counter-blow in the center, 15. ... d5!, the position quickly reduces itself to an even endgame.

13. Ne3

If 13. Ne4 b6 14. Ng5 Bc8 15. Ne3 Nce7 16. Nxd5 Nxd5 17. Ne4 Bb7,

Diagram 1182
After 17. ... Bb7

Black reaches a comfortable position (Lesiege–Degraeve, 2002).

13. ... Nde7

Black is fine, for example— 14. Nc4

Diagram 1183
After 14. Nc4

14. ... Rb8 15. Bg5 f6 16. Be3 b6 17. Qa4 Qc7 18. Rfc1 Kh8 19. Qd1 Qd8 = (Ruck-Huzman, 2000).

Diagram 1184
After 19. ... Qd8

B 5. a3

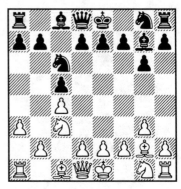

Diagram 1185
After 5. a3

White's idea is to get his queenside play rolling immediately with b4. With his tricky move, he hopes to create complications after 5. ... e5 with the pawn sacrifice 6. b4!. But Black has a better fifth move that avoids White's intentions.

5. ... d6 6. Rb1

Now after 6. b4?! cxb4 7. axb4 Nxb4 8. Qa4+ Nc6 9. Bxc6+ bxc6 10. Qxc6+ Bd7, Black is much better since White's powerful bishop is gone.

Diagram 1186
After 10. ... Bd7

6. ... a5!

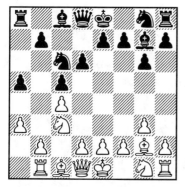

Diagram 1187
After 6. ... a5!

Black puts the permanent kibosh on White's b4. Now the game usually transposes to main lines:

7. e3

Or 7. d3 e5!

Diagram 1188
After 7. ... e5!

Black prepares ... Nge7 and stops any future attempts by White to play d4.

7. ... e5 8. Ngc2 Nge7 9. 0–0 0–0

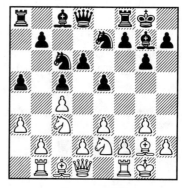

Diagram 1189
After 9. ... 0-0

Now White has to play 10. d3 because d4 is well guarded by Black's pieces. The type of positions will be similar to those in the next line.

Whenever possible, it is best for Black to create this Stonewall-like setup against the Symmetrical English.

C 5. e3 e5

Diagram 1190
After 5. ... e5

This almost universal approach is the simplest way to stop White's plan with d4. Black's idea is simple: continue development with ... Nge7 and ... 0–0, and, if White plays a3 to prepare b4, meet it with ... a5.

6. Nge2 Nge7 7. 0–0 0–0 8. d3

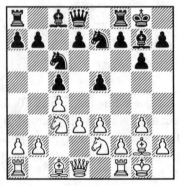

Diagram 1191
After 8. d3

Or 8. a3 d6 9. Rb1 a5 10. d3 transposes.

8. ... d6 9. Rb1

White plans to play a3 and b4.

After 9. Nd5 Nxd5 10. cxd5 Ne7,

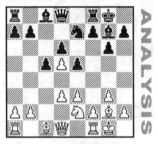

Diagram 1192
After 10. ... Ne7

Black has a very solid position and an easy game. His plan includes playing ... f5 and ... b5, fighting for a space advantage on both flanks.

9. ... Rb8

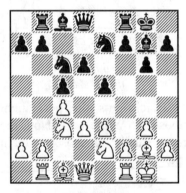

Diagram 1193
After 9. ... Rb8

A useful prophylactic move, protecting b7 and getting the rook out from under the x-ray on the long diagonal.

10. a3 a5

Also possible is 10. ... a6, with the idea of 11. b4 cxb4 12. axb4 b5!,

Diagram 1194
After 12. ... b5!

neutralizing White's play on the queenside. Now after 13. cxb5 axb5 14. Ne4 h6 (preparing ... f5) 15. Bd2, Black can play 15. ... Be6 to further prepare ... f5 by eliminating the potential check on b3, or he can even play 15. ... f5 immediately, with at least an equal game.

11. Bd2 Be6

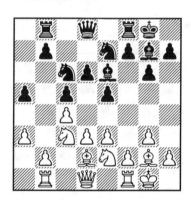

Diagram 1195
After 11. ... Be6

White has 12. Nd5 and 12. Qb3 to choose from.

C1 12. Nd5 b5!

This undermining flank move gives Black an easy game.

13. Nec3

13. Nxe7+ Nxe7 14. cxb5 Rxb5 15. b4 axb4 16. axb4 Qd7, 17. bxc5 dxc5 =,

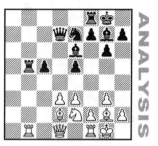

Diagram 1196
After 17. ... dxc5

as in Taimanov–Maksimenko, 2000, which continued 18. Rxb5 Qxb5 19. Qb1 Rb8 20. Qxb5 Rxb5 21. Nc3 Rb2, at which point the players called it a draw.

13. ... b4

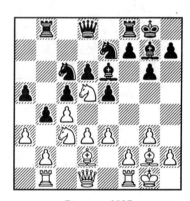

Diagram 1197
After 13. ... b4

14. axb4 axb4 15. Nxe7+ Nxe7 16. Nd5 Nxd5 17. Bxd5 Bxd5 18. cxd5

We're following David–Navara, 2001. Black can follow up with 18. ... Qd7 and then 19. ... f5, with slightly better chances.

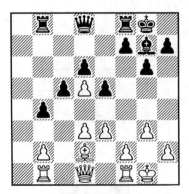

Diagram 1198
After 18. cxd5

C2 12. Qb3

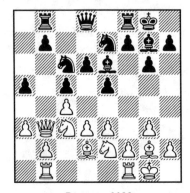

Diagram 1199
After 12. Qb3

White wants to stop ... b5 and play Nd5.

12. ... f5 13. Nd5 Nxd5!

> **Black takes advantage of the awkward position of White's queen.**

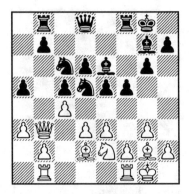

Diagram 1200
After 13. ... Nxd5!

Black takes advantage of the awkward position of White's queen.

14. cxd5 Bf7 15. Qc2 Ne7

Black has a solid position (Gurevich–Lautier, 2002).

D 5. e4 d6

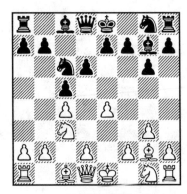

Diagram 1201
After 5. ... d6

We recommend the same setup as we used against White's 5. e3. Of course, Black has a few other good ways of developing his pieces—for instance, 5. ... e6 followed by ... Nge7. And Dzindzi's favorite, 5. ... Nf6 (with the idea, seen in several lines, of playing a later ... Ne8, ... Nc7, and ... Ne6) is also fine. Making the choice here is a matter of taste.

6. Nge2 e5 7. 0–0 Nge7 8. d3 0–0

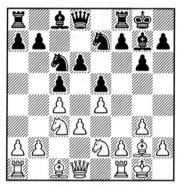

Diagram 1202
After 8. ... 0-0

This symmetrical position is balanced. White's two main plans are playing for either f4 or b4. Black's strategy is simple:

1. Play ... Be6 and ... Qd7, meeting f4 with Bg4;

2. Meet White's a3 and Rb1 with ... a5 and ... Rb8 in order to stop b4;

3. On Nd5, play ... b5!;

4. Take over the d4-outpost with a timely ... Nd4.

An extra tempo here doesn't promise White an edge.

9. a3

9. f4 exf4 10. gxf4 and here—to eliminate any worry

about the sacrificial f5—Black plays 10. ... f5!.

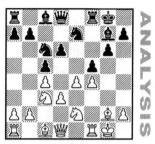

Diagram 1203
After 10. ... f5!

9. ... a5

Another possibility is 9. ... a6, with the already familiar idea of 10. Rb1 Rb8 11. b4 cxb4 12. axb4 b5!, stopping White's queenside play.

10. Rb1 Rb8

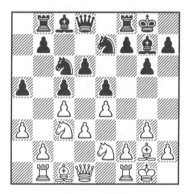

Diagram 1204
After 10. ... Rb8

White can choose between 11. Nd5, 11. Be3, and 11. Bd2.

D1 11. Nd5 b5 12. cxb5 Rxb5 13. Qa4 Ba6!

Black is fine, for example: 14. Nxe7+ Nxe7 15. b4

Diagram 1205
After 15. b4

15. ... cxb4 (15. ... Qb6? 16. Nc3) 16. axb4 Qa8, followed by ... Nc6 or ... Rfb8.

D2 11. Be3 f5

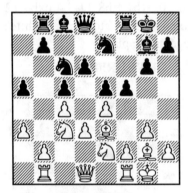

Diagram 1206
After 11. ... f5

12. exf5 gxf5

The position is approximately equal. (Compare the comments after 9. f4, page 459.)

D3 11. Bd2 Be6

Diagram 1207
After 11. ... Be6

12. f4 Qd7

Preparing ... Bg4.

13. Nd5 Bg4

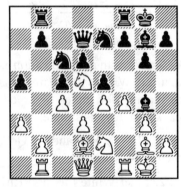

Diagram 1208
After 13. ... Bg4

14. Nb6?

White should be thinking of how to secure equality. His aggression is unwarranted by his position and simply loses time.

14. ... Qd8 15. Na4 Nd4! 16. Nac3 Nec6

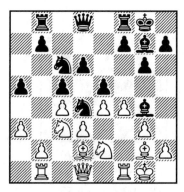

Diagram 1209
After 16. ... Nec6

Black has the better game.
Taimanov–Zhu Chen, 2000, con-
tinued: 17. h3 Bxe2 18. Nxe2
Nxe2+ 19. Qxe2 exf4 20. gxf4 b5

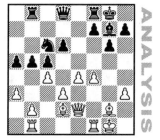

Diagram 1210
After 20. ... b5

21. cxb5 Rxb5 22. Bc3 Qb6
23. a4 Nd4 24. Qf2 Rb3 25. e5
dxe5

Diagram 1211
After 25. ... dxe5

26. fxe5 (26. Bd5 exf4) 26. ...
Qe6 27. Bxd4 cxd4 28. Qxd4
Bxe5 29. Qc4 Qb6+ 30. Kh1
Rxb2 31. Rxb2 Qxb2.

Diagram 1212
After 31. ... Qxb2

Black has a decisive advantage. White is a pawn down, and
his king is quite vulnerable.

32. Qd5 Qc3 33. Qc4 Qd2
34. Qd5 Qe3 35. Qf3 Qg5 (Black
masterfully avoids exchanges.)
36. Rb1 Bb8

Black has a decisive advantage.
White is a pawn down, and his king
is quite vulnerable.

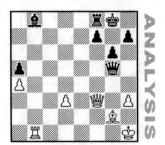

Diagram 1213
After 36. ... Bb8

37. d4 Qd8 38. Qf2 Qd6 39. Bf3 Ba7 40. Rb5 Bxd4

Diagram 1214
After 40. ... Bxd4

41. Qe1 Bb6 42. Bd5 Bc5 43. Qe4 Qf6 44. Bc4 Qf2 45. Qg2 Qd4 46. Qf1 Qe4+

Diagram 1215
After 46. ... Qe4+

47. Kh2 Bd6+ 48. Kg1 Qc2 49. Qd3 Qh2+ 50. Kf1 Bg3

Diagram 1216
After 50. ... Bg3

51. Qf3 Qxh3+ 52. Ke2 Qh4 53. Kd3 Bc7 54. Rb7 Qg3 0–1.

We've given this long game to illustrate how Black can win in a "boring" symmetrical English!

Summary:

Against White's development with 2. Nc3 and king's bishop fianchetto, Black fianchettoes his own king's bishop and, by playing ... Nc6 and then ... e5, forever prevents d4. Black's setup is good and solid after e3 or the symmetrical e4— whether White develops his knight to f3 or on e2. (In these types of positions, an extra tempo doesn't translate into an edge!) Against White's play on the queenside with a3 and b4, Black can either stop his opponent's advance temporarily with ... a5 (while being ready to play ... b5 at the right moment), or maintain symmetry with ... a6 and ... b5.

Chapter 42: English, Part III—White Refrains from d4

Memory Markers!

Diagram 1217
After 4. e3

MARKER 1

Diagram 1218
After 4. g3

MARKER 2

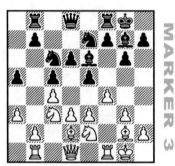

Diagram 1219
After 12. f4

MARKER 3

Diagram 1220
After 15. ... Qb6

MARKER 4

Chapter 42: English, Part III—White Refrains from d4
Solutions to Memory Markers!

No. 1   **4. ... Nf6!,** not 4. ... Nc6 5. d4 ±. See page 449.

No. 2   **4. ... Nc6!.** Now White will never be able to play d4. And, while
4. ... Nf6 is a good move, it could lead us into territory not covered in
this book after 5. d4 cxd4 6. Nxd4. See page 450.

No. 3   **12. ... d5!?.** Of course, Black has a number of good (and
non-committal) moves, but can't he grab the center? We think so, as
after 13. f5 gxf5 14. cxd5 Nxd5 15. Nxd5 Bxd5, the d3-pawn is
hanging. See page 457.

No. 4   **16. Nc3,** winning material. See page 460.

Chapter 43: Bird's Opening—1. f4

Some Important Points to Look For

With this unusual opening, White tries for a reversed Dutch with an extra move in-hand, but our recommendation avoids such lines. Black gets at least equality.

◆ Reversed Dutch.
  See Diagram 1222.

◆ A balanced position.
  See Diagram 1224.

◆ The light-square strategy.
  See Diagram 1228.

◆ Black gets a key square and an edge.
  See Diagram 1233.

Outline of Variations

1. f4 g6 2. Nf3 d5 *(467)* [A02]
  A 3. g3 Bg7 4. Bg2 Nf6 5. 0-0 0-0 6. d3 b6 7. Nc3 Bb7 *(468)*
  B 3. e3 Bg7 4. d4 Nh6 5. Be2 0-0 6. 0-0 Nf5 7. c3 Nd6 8. b3 Nd7 9. Ne5 Nf6 *(469)*

Chapter 43
Bird's Opening
1. f4

This offbeat beginning was popularized by English master Henry E. Bird at the end of the nineteenth century. It does not contribute to White's development at all, and weakens the king's position. Its only merit is taking control of a very important square, e5. The Bird can, however, lead to some dangerous attacks unless Black has a good antidote in his black bag.

1. f4

Diagram 1221
After 1. f4

White wants to create an immediate kingside initiative, and takes control of the e5-square. This is often played in order to create a colors-reversed Dutch with an extra tempo.

1. ... g6

Black plays this move order rather than 1. ... d5 to avoid 2. b3. Another good system for Black is 1. ... Nf6, 2. ... g6, 3. ... Bg7 and 4. ... 0-0—preserving the option of playing ... d6 (rather than ... d5) and ... e5.

2. Nf3

2. e4 c5 would transpose to the familiar Sicilian Defense. If you prefer to avoid it, play 1. ... d5 or 1. ... Nf6. Openings are about give and take!

2. ... d5

White wants to create an immediate kingside initiative, and takes control of the e5-square.

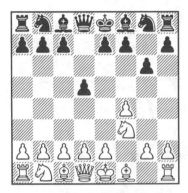

Diagram 1222
After 2. ... d5

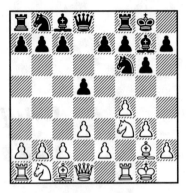

Diagram 1223
After 6. d3

We've reached a Dutch Defense with colors reversed, and, of course, with an extra tempo for the Dutch side (in this case, White). As the Dutch is a closed opening, however, the extra tempo should, at best, give White equality.

White has two main continuations: 3. g3 and 3. e3.

A 3. g3 Bg7 4. Bg2 Nf6 5. 0-0 0-0 6. d3

White's idea is to play a Dutch Defense, Leningrad Variation, up a tempo, which would occur if Black plays 6. ... c5.

6. ... b6

This is the easiest way of obtaining a good game.

7. Nc3 Bb7

Diagram 1224
After 7. ... Bb7

> **Because the Dutch is a closed opening, White's extra tempo should, at best, give him equality.**

The position is balanced. It's hard for White to play e4, and Black is ready to finish his development with ... Nbd7.

The game could continue: 8. Ne5 Nbd7 9. Nxd7 Qxd7 10. e4 dxe4 (or 10. ... c5) 11. dxe4 Rfd8,

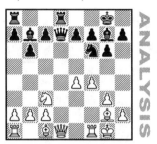

Diagram 1225
After 11. ... Rfd8

with approximately equal chances.

B 3. e3 Bg7 4. d4

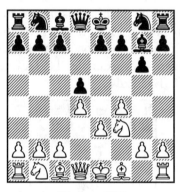

Diagram 1226
After 4. d4

This is the reversed Stonewall Dutch setup. White's plan is to play Bd3, c3, and 0-0—and try to keep the position closed while exploiting his e5 outpost.

4. Be2 doesn't change much: after 4. ... Nh6 5. 0-0 0-0, the only alternative to 6. d4 is 6. d3 b6 7. e4 dxe4 8. dxe4 Qxd1

9. Rxd1 Bb7 10. e5 Na6.

Diagram 1227
After 10. ... Na6

Black will activate his pieces after … f6, … Nf7 and … Nc5, with a game that's about even.

4. ... Nh6!?

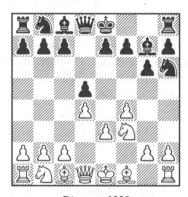

Diagram 1228
After 4. ... Nh6!?

Black's strategy is built around exploiting White's chronic weakness on e4. Black also prepares the exchange of bishops after 5. Bd3 Bf5 6. 0-0 0-0 7. c3 Bxd3 8. Qxd3 c6 9. Nbd2 Nd7.

Diagram 1229
After 9. ... Nd7

Note how Black turned his relative disadvantage, being a tempo down versus the Dutch, to his favor by developing his knight (which otherwise would be on f6) to a better square—in this line, h6.

The light-square weaknesses in White's camp are even more apparent here. Black's plan is to play ... Nf5-d6 and ... Nf6-e4, taking over the outpost on e4. Thus, White usually plays ...

5. Be2

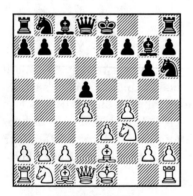

Diagram 1230
After 5. Be2

5. ... 0-0 6. 0-0 Nf5

This knight is heading

toward d6, the other toward f6.

7. c3 Nd6 8. b3 Nd7 9. Ne5 Nf6!

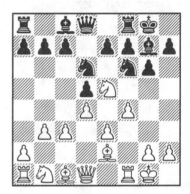

Diagram 1231
After 9. ... Nf6!

Black has successfully executed his plan and is now ready to play ... Nfe4!. After 10. h3 Nfe4, the position is in Black's favor—for example: 11. Qe1 c5 12. Ba3 cxd4

Diagram 1232
After 12. ... cxd4

13. cxd4 (13. Bxd6? exd6 14. Nf3 dxc3 15. Nd4 Qb6 leaves White in despair) 13. ... f6 14. Nd3 Bf5.

Diagram 1233
After 14. ... Bf5

The control of the e4-square—while e5 is controlled by the f6-pawn—provides Black with a small edge.

Summary:
Our recommended system, 1. ... g6, allows Black to avoid lines in which White will have the moral satisfaction of playing a familiar Dutch line with an extra tempo.

While 1. f4 can't be "refuted," Black enjoys at least full equality—and can try for more.

Chapter 43: Bird's Opening—1. f4
Memory Markers!

Diagram 1234
After 3. c4

MARKER 1

Diagram 1235
After 5. Bd3

MARKER 2

Diagram 1236
After 9. 0-0

MARKER 3

Diagram 1237
After 11. Qc2

MARKER 4

Chapter 43: Bird's Opening—1. f4
Solutions to Memory Markers!

No. 1   **3. ... Nf6.** This developing move is, in our judgment, the first among several equally good responses—such as 3. ... d4 and 3. ... dxc4.
See page 468.

No. 2   **5. ... d6** and then ... Nbd7, or ... Nc6, preparing ... e5.
See page 467.

No. 3   **9. ... Ng4.** See page 470.

No. 4   **11. ... f6.** Also strong is 11. ... c5. See page 470.

Creative Director
Jami Anson

Jami Anson has lent her creative hand to assist in the design and production of Lev Alburt's books. She is the winner of many Chess Journalist of America awards and the Cramer Award for best chess photography. Her photographs have appeared in magazines such as *Time Magazine* and *TV Guide*, as well as in many newspapers and books.

Jami has designed art for many firms—Sterling Publishing, McGraw Hill, Excalibur Electronics, Chess n' Bridge, Chess4Less, ChessCafe, Classical Games, House of Staunton, Internet Chess Club, Minuteman Press of Hyde Park, OutExcel Corp., Active Learning Corp., Lev Alburt, Susan Polgar, Lindberg Associates, World Chess Hall of Fame, Seiko and World Peace Sanctuary (affiliated with the United Nations).

After 18 years of designing and producing *Chess Life* and *Schoolmates* for the U.S. Chess Federation, Jami started her own design firm—Jadesign.

During her tenure at *Chess Life*, she maintained and built up the research libary and photos that span chess history from the early 1800s to the present day. She is currently creating a cultural center in her home town from an abandoned church. This project, called Little Apple Restoration, will include classes in art, music, theatre and, of course, chess.

Contact Jami Anson at:
jadesignfirm@aol.com

Winner of many awards for design, photography and layout

• Design • Production • Results

Jadesign is an award-winning design firm that produces cost-effective solutions for web and print.

Jadesign has over 24 years of experience in design and production.

FREE estimates
Creative Director/Owner
Jami L. Anson

Jadesign
203 Bedell Avenue,
Highland, NY 12528
845.401.9469
jadesignfirm@aol.com

Chapter 44: Sokolsky—1. b4
Some Important Points to Look For

Against 1. b4, we recommend that you go for quick development. In our line, Black wrests the initiative from White and takes over the center.

◆ How our line starts.
See Diagram 1239.

◆ This is what we want to achieve.
See Diagram 1240.

◆ Black still has enough pawns in the center. See Diagram 1243.

◆ Black dominates.
See Diagram 1245.

Outline of Variations

1. b4 e5 2. Bb2 Bxb4 3. Bxe5 Nf6 4. e3 0-0 5. Nf3 Re8 6. Be2 d5 7. 0-0 c5 8. c4 Nc6
9. Bb2 d4 10. Qb3 Ne4 11. d3 Nd6 12. e4 f5 *(474)* [A00]

Chapter 44
Sokolsky
1. b4

This offbeat flank opening goes by a number of names—the Polish, the Orangutan, and the Sokolsky, after Alexey Pavlovich Sokolsky, the Russian opening theoretician.

The story goes that Savielly Tartakover got the idea somehow from watching the climbing of apes at the zoo. But both Berthold Englisch and Carl Schlechter played it before Tartakover did.

It's an opening without a significant following, but once in a while you'll run into a lover of the eccentric who hopes to put you off your game with a bizarre surprise.

1. b4

You may run into a lover of the eccentric who hopes to put you off your game with a bizarre surprise.

Diagram 1238
After 1. b4

White's idea is to gain space on the queenside and develop his bishop on the long diagonal, pressuring the center and even the enemy kingside. The drawback? White's first move doesn't exercise control of the center, and the b-pawn will require time to defend.

Black has several good responses, one of them going into the Dutch: 1. ... f5, gaining space on the kingside.

1. ... e5

We recommend this classic move, staking out the center and

attacking White's loose pawn.

2. Bb2 Bxb4!? 3. Bxe5

Diagram 1239
After 3. Bxe5

Although it seems contradictory to trade his center pawn for White's wing pawn, Black's line allows him almost immediately to take the lead in development and reach a good position.

3. ... Nf6 4. e3

If 4. c4 0-0 5. e3 d5 is also okay for Black.

4. ... 0-0 5. Nf3 Re8 6. Be2 d5

Diagram 1240
After 6. ... d5

7. 0-0

After 7. c4 dxc4 8. Bxc4 Nc6 9. Bb2 Be6

Diagram 1241
After 9. ... Be6

10. Bxe6 (or 10. Be2 Qe7 11. 0-0 Rad8, and Black is clearly ahead in development) 10. ... Rxe6,

Diagram 1242
After 10. ... Rxe6

Black has finished his development first and stands better.

7. ... c5

Diagram 1243
After 7. ... c5

8. c4

Or 8. d3 Nc6 9. Bb2 Bf5.

Diagram 1244
After 9. ... Bf5

And Black is better.

8. ... Nc6 9. Bb2 d4!

Diagram 1245
After 9. ... d4!

Black is wresting the initiative from White and gaining more space in the center. The game can continue:

10. Qb3 Ne4 11. d3 Nd6 12. e4 f5!

Diagram 1246
After 12. ... f5!

Black has a clearly superior position.

Summary:

Our recommended system versus 1. b4 gives Black quick development with good and easy play. Yes, Black exchanges his king pawn for a knight pawn, but he'll make good use of the resulting semi-open e-file.

Chapter 44: Sokolsky—1. b4

Memory Markers!

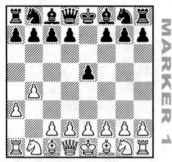

Diagram 1247
After 2. a3

Diagram 1248
After 2. ... f6

Diagram 1249
After 12. e4

Chapter 44: Sokolsky—1. b4

Solutions to Memory Markers!

No. 1   **2. ... d5 3. Bb2 f6,** and Black already stands better. See page 476.

No. 2   **3. b5!,** with an unclear position. See page 476.

No. 3   **12. ... f5.** See page 477.

These openings may not be fashionable at the top, but they have their staunch adherents!

Diagram 1250, Torre Attack, Chapter 33

Diagram 1251, London System, Chapter 34

Diagram 1252, Fianchetto, Chapter 35

Diagram 1253, Colle, Chapter 36

Diagram 1254, Veresov, Chapter 37

Diagram 1255, Trompowsky, Chapter 38

Diagram 1256, BDG, Chapter 39

Diagram 1257, Bird's Opening, Chapter 43

Diagram 1258, Sokolsky, Chapter 44

Diagram 1259, Larsen's, Chapter 45

Chapter 45: The Rest—Knights-First and the Fianchettoes

Some Important Points to Look For

We can briefly cover the last of White's reasonable opening moves using what we've already learned. Moreover, there's a reason uncommon moves are uncommon!

◆ Black transposes to Part 2. See Diagram 1263.

◆ Black transposes to Part 4. See Diagram 1264.

◆ Black's ... h6 gives his bishop a retreat. See Diagram 1268.

◆ Black blocks White's dark-square bishop. See Diagram 1271.

Outline of Variations

A 1. Nf3 c5 *(480)*
  A1 2. e4 g6 *(482)*
  A2 2. c4 g6 (482)
  A3 2. b3 d6 3. Bb2 e5 *(484)*
B 1. g3 c5 *(482)*
C 1. b3 d5 2. Bb2 Bg4 *(483)* [A01]
Rare Moves *(484)* [A00]

Chapter 45
The Rest
Knights-First and the Fianchettoes

In this chapter, we cover the rest of White's reasonable opening tries. You can relax a bit now after working so hard on the rest of the book. We don't have to go very deep in any lines, since most of these tries transpose into ideas we've already seen.

The move **A 1. Nf3**

Diagram 1260
After 1. Nf3

is one of White's "equally best" moves, a peer of 1. e4, 1. d4 and 1. c4. White develops his king's knight to a perfect square while keeping his options open. For instance, after 1. ... d5, White can switch to classicism with

2. d4, reaching the Queen's Gambit on the next move. Or he can play 2. g3, ready to go, after 2. ... c5 3. Bg2 Nc6,

Diagram 1261
After 3. ... Nc6

into a reversed Gruenfeld with 4. d4—a tempo up, of course.

Still, our previous work should spare us a lot of preparation time here. By playing **1. ... c5,**

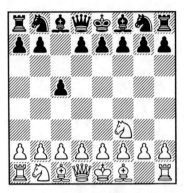

Diagram 1262
After 1. ... c5

we invite White to make up his mind. If:

A1 **2. e4**, then **2. ... g6**.

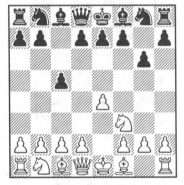

Diagram 1263
After 2. ... g6

This is our Part II, while

> On 2. g3, we can stick with 2. ... g6, eventually reaching a familiar position.

A2 **2. c4 g6**

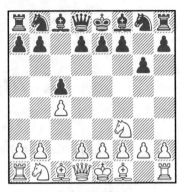

Diagram 1264
After 2. ... g6

is our Part IV, the Symmetrical English.

And on 2. g3, we can stick with 2. ... g6, eventually reaching an already familiar position, either the English or the Closed Sicilian. Or we can play 2. ... Nc6 3. Bg2 e5!

Diagram 1265
After 3. ... e5!

4. 0-0 d5.

Yes, White can now play the reversed King's Indian a tempo up, but this should suffice only to give him equality.

And we can give

B **1. g3** the same treatment:
1. ... c5!,

Diagram 1266
After 1. ... c5!

transferring the game into openings now familiar to you, as we did against 1. Nf3. Of course, there are other good, easy-to-learn systems versus 1. g3 (which, unlike Nf3, doesn't take control of any central square).

For example, there is the method Lasker used against Reti.

1. ... d5 2. Nf3 Nf6 3. Bg2 c6

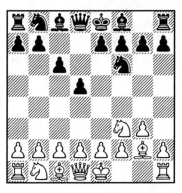

Diagram 1267
After 3. ... c6

Black blocks the diagonal.

4. 0-0 Bf5.

The game may continue **5. d3 e6 6. Nbd2 h6** (to secure a possible retreat for the bishop).

Diagram 1268
After 6. ... h6

White will prepare e4 and play in the center and on the kingside. Black will counter and try to open the game on the queenside.

What is modern theory's verdict?—Equal chances.

Larsen's Opening starts:

C **1. b3.**

Diagram 1269
After 1. b3

White can't get an edge against

several of Black's defenses. Even symmetry:

1. ... b6

is good enough for equality, and so is 1. ... f5. And, of course, 1. ... Nf6, followed by the dark-square-bishop fianchetto. Here is another interesting line:

1. ... d5 2. Bb2 Bg4

Diagram 1270
After 2. ... Bg4

3. h3 Bh5 4. Nf3 Bxf3 5. exf3 Nf6 6. f4 e6 7. g3 g6 = (Sprag-gett–Dorfman, 1991).

And if White tries to lure you into the Larsen via **1. Nf3 c5 2. b3**, we recommend:

> **When facing an unorthodox opening, don't rush. Try to understand its purpose.**

A3 2. ... d6 3. Bb2 e5.

Diagram 1271
After 3. ... e5

Black blocks the White bishop and gets a good game. Indeed, 1. ... c5 is playable against 1. b3 as well, but after 2. Bb2 d6 (or 2. ... Nc6) White can, besides 3. Nf3, play 3. f4—not a big deal, however. In fact, if you begin to worry about such minor openings, your overall opening preparedness must already be very good!

Rare Moves

White, a tempo up, can afford to make second-best moves and still preserve equality. When facing an unorthodox opening, don't rush, but try to understand its purpose. Consider where the opening may lead, and whether you have some knowledge of positions likely to emerge.

Take, for instance, 1. e3. If 1. ... e5, White will play 2. d4, in order to get an exchange French, a tempo up: 2. ... exd4 3. exd4 d5. And, if 1. ... d5, then 2. Nf3, hoping, after 2. ... c5, to play the Nimzo/Bogo-Indian—a tempo up.

Your reaction? You can play your "normal" 1. ... Nf6. Or you can consider in which opening White's e3 would be unnecessary, and perhaps reply with 1. ... f5.

Diagram 1272
After 1. ... f5

Another reverse opening, 1. a3, may invite the same answer—or perhaps Black will play 1. ... Nf6, 2. ... g6, 3. ... Bg7 and 4. ... 0-0. After all, a3 isn't particularly useful against the King's Indian!

On 1. Nc3, you can play 1. ... c5, and White's best now will be 2. e4, the familiar Sicilian. Or you can "punish" him with 1. ... d5 =, as neither the Veresov (2. d4) nor 2. e4 dxe4! 3. Nxe4

Diagram 1273
After 3. Nxe4

offer White even the slightest edge.

Summary:

Against White's serious first moves, 1. Nf3 and 1. g3, we reply 1. ... c5, transferring into systems we've studied earlier in this book. Any unusual opening moves by White that are not covered by a lot of opening theory are simply not that dangerous for Black—there is a reason for the lack of theory!

As long as you think about what your opponent's moves are intended to accomplish and come up with a favorite system, or a system in which the unusual moves are not very useful, there is nothing to fear from any of these unorthodox tries.

Chapter 45: The Rest—Knights-First and the Fianchettoes

Memory Markers!

Diagram 1274
After 2. e4

MARKER 1

Diagram 1275
After 2. c4

MARKER 2

Diagram 1276
After 4. Nf3

MARKER 3

Diagram 1277
After 3. Bb2

MARKER 4

Chapter 45: The Rest—Knights-First and the Fianchettoes

Solutions to Memory Markers!

No. 1   **2. ... g6,** transposing into our familiar Part 2. See page 482.

No. 2   **2. ... g6,** transposing into our Part 4. See page 482.

No. 3   **4. ... Bxf3 5. exf3 Nf6 6. f4 e6 7. g3 g6 =.** See page 484.

No. 4   **3. ... e5,** blocking White's bishop. See page 484.

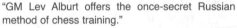
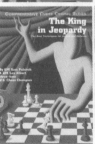

PART FIVE

ILLUSTRATIVE GAMES

Ideas into Action

List of Games

Outline of Opening Moves

Almasi—Kramnik
1. e4 c5 2. Nf3 Nc6 3. Nc3 g6 4. d4 cxd4 5. Nxd4 Bg7 6. Be3 Nf6 7. Bc4 0-0 8. Bb3 a5 9. a4 *(491)* Accelerated Dragon [B35]

Bauer—Malakhov
1. e4 c5 2. Nf3 Nc6 3. d4 cxd4 4. Nxd4 g6 5. Nc3 Bg7 6. Be3 Nf6 7. Bc4 0-0 8. Bb3 a5 9. f3 *(496)* Accelerated Dragon [B35]

Rowson—Malakhov
1. e4 c5 2. Nf3 Nc6 3. d4 cxd4 4. Nxd4 g6 5. c4 Nf6 6. Nc3 d6 7. Be2 Nxd4 8. Qxd4 Bg7 9. Be3 *(500)* Maroczy Bind [B36]

Vallejo—Malakhov
1. e4 c5 2. Nf3 Nc6 3. d4 cxd4 4. Nxd4 g6 5. c4 Nf6 6. Nc3 d6 7. Be2 Nxd4 8. Qxd4 Bg7 9. Bg5 *(502)* Maroczy Bind [B36]

Rudelis—Donaldson
1. d4 Nf6 2. c4 e6 3. Nc3 Bb4 4. a3 Bxc3+ 5. bxc3 b6 *(506)* Nimzo-Indian [E24]

Epishin—Berg
1. d4 e6 2. c4 Nf6 3. Nc3 Bb4 4. e3 b6 5. Ne2 Ba6 *(508)* Nimzo-Indian [E45]

Goldin—Yermolinsky
1. d4 Nf6 2. c4 e6 3. Nc3 Bb4 4. Qc2 *(510)* Nimzo-Indian [E33]

Timman—Dzindzichashvili
1. d4 Nf6 2. c4 e6 3. Nc3 Bb4 4. Bg5 *(514)* Nimzo-Indian [E31]

Skembris—Beliavsky
1. d4 Nf6 2. c4 e6 3. Nf3 Bb4+ 4. Bd2 Qe7 5. g3 Nc6 6. Bg2 Bxd2+ 7. Nbxd2 d6 8. 0-0 e5 9. d5 Nb8 10. e4 a5 11. Ne1 0-0 12. Nd3 Na6 13. a3 Bg4 14. f3 Bd7 15. b4 c6 16. Qb3 *(518)* Bogo-Indian [E11]

Khomyakov—Korotylev
1. d4 Nf6 2. c4 e6 3. Nf3 Bb4+ 4. Bd2 Qe7 5. g3 Nc6 6. Bg2 Bxd2+ 7. Nbxd2 d6 8. 0-0-0-0 9. e4 e5 10. d5 Nb8 11. b4 a5 12. a3 Na6 13. Ne1 Bg4 14. f3 Bd7 15. Nd3 c6 16. bxa5 *(522)* Bogo-Indian [E11]

Avrukh—Ibrahimov
1. d4 Nf6 2. c4 e6 3. Nf3 Bb4+ 4. Bd2 Qe7 5. g3 Nc6 6. Nc3 Bxc3 7. Bxc3 Ne4 *(526)* Bogo-Indian [E11]

Cebalo—Jakovjevic
1. d4 Nf6 2. c4 e6 3. Nf3 Bb4+ 4. Nbd2 b6 *(530)* Bogo-Indian [E11]

Sokolov—Karpov
1. d4 Nf6 2. Nf3 e6 3. Bg5 h6 4. Bh4 c5 *(534)* Torre Attack [A46]

Chapter 46
Illustrative Games
Ideas into Action

Game One
Accelerated Dragon

ZOLTAN ALMASI—VLADIMIR
KRAMNIK, 2003

1. e4 c5 2. Nf3 Nc6

Black does not use our recommended order, 2. ... g6, and so could have had to face the Rossolimo Variation, 3. Bb5. But White does not take this opportunity, and the game transposes to our main line.

3. Nc3 g6 4. d4 cxd4 5. Nxd4 Bg7 6. Be3 Nf6 7. Bc4

So after some differences in the move order, we've reached the main line of our Sicilian Accelerated Dragon, Diagram 81, page 61, in Chapter 5, where we've given the notes to this game through move 21.

7. ... 0–0 8. Bb3 a5

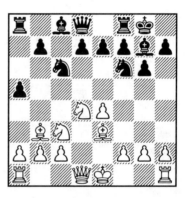

Diagram 1278
After 8. ... a5

9. a4

This is variation **A**, Chapter 5.

9. ... Ng4 10. Qxg4 Nxd4 11. Qh4 d6 12. Nd5 Re8

Black does not play 2. ... g6, and so could have had to face the Rossolimo Variation.

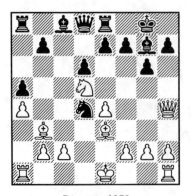

Diagram 1279
After 12. ... Re8

**13. Rd1 Nxb3 14. Bb6 Qd7
15. cxb3 Ra6 16. Bd4 Qd8**

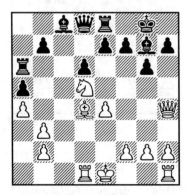

Diagram 1280
After 16. ... Qd8

**17. 0–0 Be6 18. Bxg7 Kxg7
19. Nf4 Qc8 20. Rd3 Rc6 21.
Qg3 f6**

This is where we left the game
in Chapter 5.

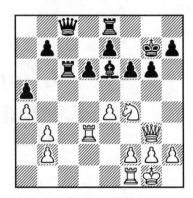

Diagram 1281
After 21. ... f6

Black prepares ... Bf7.

**22. Ne2 Bf7 23. Nd4 Rc1 24.
Qe3 Rxf1+ 25. Kxf1**

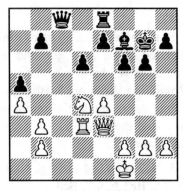

Diagram 1282

After 25. Kxf1

This position is in Black's
favor because he has an extra
pawn in the center. Pay attention
to Kramnik's technique as he
first leads the game into an
endgame, then converts his
advantage into a win.

25. ... Qd7

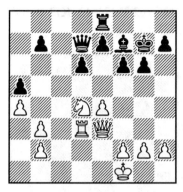

Diagram 1283
After 25. ... Qd7

With the idea of ... Rc8, taking the file.

26. Rc3 Rc8 27. f3 Rxc3 28. Qxc3

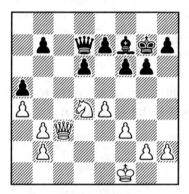

Diagram 1284
After 28. Qxc3

28. ... e5! 29. Ne2 d5

Black takes over the center.

30. exd5 Qxd5 31. b4 axb4 32. Qxb4

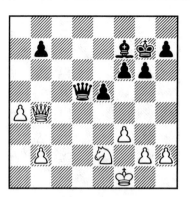

Diagram 1285
After 32. Qxb4

32. ... Qb3! 33. Qxb3 Bxb3 34. Nc3

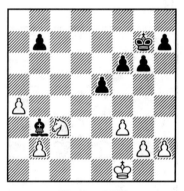

Diagram 1286
After 34. Nc3

Black has achieved what he wanted: the endgame is won because of his extra pawn on the kingside and his powerful bishop that can sweep across the board in one move. Kramnik's flawless technique will reward close study.

34. ... b6 35. Kf2 f5 36. g3 Kf6 37. f4

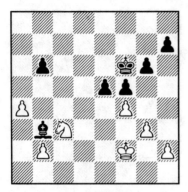

Diagram 1287
After 37. f4

37. ... g5! 38. fxe5+ Kxe5 39. Ke3 h5 40. Kf3 f4 41. gxf4+ gxf4

Diagram 1288
After 41. ... gxf4

Although the number of pawns is equal, Black has created a passed pawn. White has to guard against the possibility of its queening, so Black can use it as a diversion—an important advantage. Additionally, Kramnik has collected another advantage: he has the long-range bishop against the short-range knight in an endgame with pawns on both sides of the board.

42. Ne2 Bd5+ 43. Kf2 Bc6 44. b3 f3 45. Ng1

Diagram 1289
After 45. Ng1

45. ... Kd4! 46. b4

After 46. Nxf3+ Bxf3 47. Kxf3 Kc3, the pawn endgame is won— Black queens first. We see the value of the passed pawn as a diversion!

46. ... Bxa4 47. Kxf3 Kc4 48. Kf4 Kxb4 49. Ke3 Bd1

Diagram 1290
After 49. ... Bd1

50. Nh 3 Kc3 51. Nf4 b5 52. Nd5+ Kc4 53. Nb6+

Diagram 1291
After 53. Nb6+

Black now transfers his king to the kingside, deciding the game.

53. ... Kc5 54. Nd7+ Kd6 55. Nf6 Ke5 56. Nd7+ Kf5 57. Nc5

Diagram 1292
After 57. Nc5

We see the value of the passed pawn as a diversion!

57. ... Bc2 58. Na6 Kg4 59. Nb4 Bf5 60. Kf2 Kf4 61. Ke2 Bg4+

Diagram 1293
After 61. ... Bg4+

62. Kd2

Or 62. Kf2 Ke4, heading to support the passed b-pawn.

62. ... Kf3 63. Nd5 Kg2 64. Kc3 Kxh2 65. Kb4

Diagram 1294
After 65. Kb4

65. ... h4 66. Kxb5 Kg3 67. Ne3 h3 68. Kc5 Be2

Diagram 1295
After 68. ... Be2

White resigns.

Game Two

Accelerated Dragon

CHRISTIAN BAUER—
VLADIMIR MALAKHOV, 2003

**1. e4 c5 2. Nf3 Nc6 3. d4 cxd4
4. Nxd4 g6 5. Nc3 Bg7 6. Be3
Nf6 7. Bc4 0–0 8. Bb3 a5 9. f3**

This is Variation **C**, page 72.

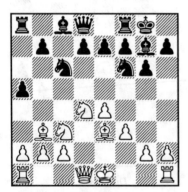

Diagram 1296
After 9. f3

**9. ... d5 10. Bxd5 Nxd5 11.
exd5 Nb4 12. Nde2 e6 13. a3
Nxd5 14. Nxd5 exd5 15. Bd4**

Bh6! 16. 0–0

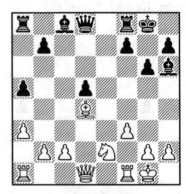

Diagram 1297
After 16. 0-0

This is where we left off in
Chapter 5, page 80. We have
reached one of the most uncon-
ventional positions in modern
theory. At first it seems that
White is simply better due to
Black's isolated d-pawn and
White's strong grip on the d4 outpost. However, a deeper analysis
shows that Black's powerful bishops crisscross White's position,
not allowing White to consolidate.

16. ... Bf5

Or 16. ... Re8, and now if 17.
Bf2 (with the idea of Nd4), 17. ...
Bf5 18. Nd4 Qf6 19. c3 a4!,

One of the most unconventional positions in modern theory!

Diagram 1298
After 19. ... a4!

with play similar to the game.

17. Ng3 Qd7 18. c3 Rfe8 19. Rf2 a4!

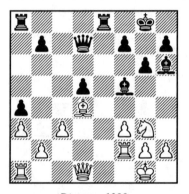

Diagram 1299
After 19. ... a4!

Black fixes White's pawn structure on the queenside, underlining White's light-square weaknesses.

20. Qf1 Bf4 21. Rd1 Be6!?

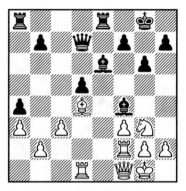

Diagram 1300
After 21. ... Be6!?

Malakhov decides to save his bishop, clearly indicating that he is playing to win.

22. Re2 Qb5 23. Rde1 Bd7 24. Qf2 Rxe2 25. Rxe2 Re8 26. Rxe8+ Bxe8

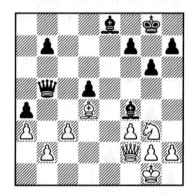

Diagram 1301
After 26. ... Bxe8

The position has simplified; Black's strong pressure on b2 and his bishop pair give him some winning chances.

27. Be3 Bc7 28. Qd2 f6 29. Bd4 Bd8 30. Nf1 Qc6 31. Qf4 Bc7!

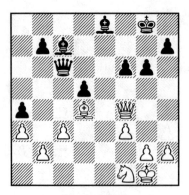

Diagram 1302
After 31. ... Bc7!

32. Qh4

If 32. Qxf6 Qxf6 33. Bxf6, then 33. ... Bf4, followed by ... Bc1.

32. ... g5 33. Qh6?!

White enters unfavorable complications. Better is 33. Qf2, holding on.

33. ... Bb6!

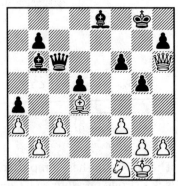

Diagram 1303
After 33. ... Bb6!

Black takes over the initiative.

34. h4 Bxd4+ 35. cxd4 Qb6 36. hxg5 Qxd4+ 37. Kh1 Bg6 38. gxf6 Qxf6

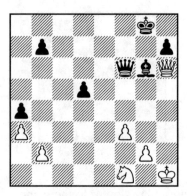

Diagram 1304
After 38. ... Qxf6

Once again, Black has a passed pawn and a clear edge.

39. Qd2 d4 40. Kg1 Qb6 41. Kf2 Kf7 42. Ke1

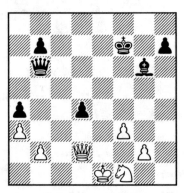

Diagram 1305
After 42. Ke1

42. ... Ke6?

Black chooses the wrong plan. The correct move is 42. ... Qd6, centralizing his queen. Then after 43. Kf2, Black plays ... h5, with the idea of ... h4, controlling the g3 square.

43. Ng3 Kd5 44. Ne2 Kc4

This gallant king-march to the

center is full of bravado, but doesn't accomplish much for Black.

45. g4 Qd6 46. f4!

Diagram 1306
After 46. f4!

Now White takes over the initiative, threatening f4-f5, advancing his own passed pawn.

46. ... Be4?

Better is 46. ... Bd3.

47. f5?

Better is 47. Qc1+! Kb3 48. Qd1+ Kxb2 49. Qxa4 ±,

Diagram 1307
After 49. Qxa4

when the Black king is at risk in enemy territory.

47. ... h5?

Diagram 1308
After 47. ... h5?

This mistake costs Black the game; his final opportunity was 47. ... b5, with chances for a draw.

48. Qf4! Qd5 49. Ng3 Bd3 50. gxh5

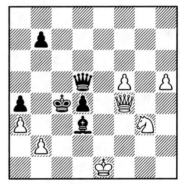

Diagram 1309
After 50. gxh5

White is winning.

50. ... Qa5+ 51. Kf2 Qb6 52. Qc1+ Kd5 53. h6 Bc4 54. h7 d3+ 55. Kg2 Qd4

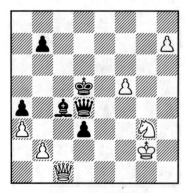

Diagram 1310
After 55. ... Qd4

**56. Qc3 Qe3 57. Qa5+ Kc6
58. Qxa4+ Kb6 59. Qb4+ Ka6
60. Qa4+ Kb6 61. Qb4+ Ka6
62. Qxc4+**

Diagram 1311
After 62. Qxc4+

Black resigns.

Game Three
Maroczy Bind

JONATHAN ROWSON—
VLADIMIR MALAKHOV, 2003

**1. e4 c5 2. Nf3 Nc6 3. d4 cxd4
4. Nxd4 g6 5. c4 Nf6**

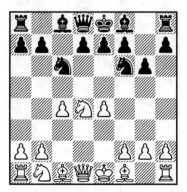

Diagram 1312
After 5. ... Nf6

**6. Nc3 d6 7. Be2 Nxd4 8.
Qxd4 Bg7 9. Be3 0–0 10. Qd2**

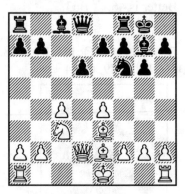

Diagram 1313
After 10. Qd2

**10. ... Be6 11. 0–0 Qa5 12.
Rab1 Rfc8 13. b3 Ng4!**

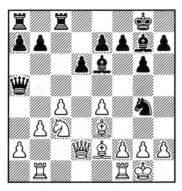

Diagram 1314
After 13. ... Ng4!

14. Nd5

This is Variation **B2c2**, Chapter 11, page 153.

14. ... Qxd2 15. Bxd2 Kf8 16. Bg5 Bxd5 17. exd5 Nf6

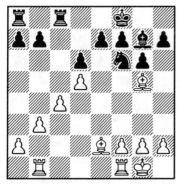

Diagram 1315
After 17. ... Nf6

We left the game here on page 153. This is the key endgame of this variation. White has a bishop pair, yet Black's position is solid, without any weaknesses. His plan is to play on the queenside.

18. Bd3 h6 19. Bd2 Nd7

This is the best square for the knight, where he controls the c5-

and e5-outposts.

20. Rfe1 a5 21. Rbc1 Rc7

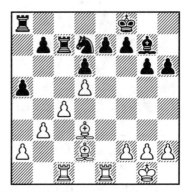

Diagram 1316
After 21. ... Rc7

With this quiet move, Mala-khov prepares a powerful attack on the queenside.

22. f4 Bd4+ 23. Kf1 a4!

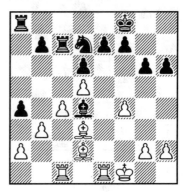

Diagram 1317
After 23. ... a4!

That's the point! Now White has an unpleasant choice: to allow Black to play ... axb3 and take over the a-file, or to play b3-b4, weakening his c-pawn.

24. b4 Rac8 25. Re4 Bb2 26. Rc2 a3!

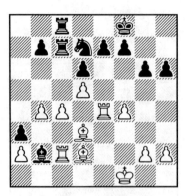

Diagram 1318
After 26. ... a3!

Black takes over the initiative and stands better. He threatens ... b7-b5 or ... Nb6.

27. Bc3 Nb6 28. Bxb2 axb2 29. Rxb2 Nxc4 30. Rf2

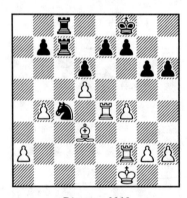

Diagram 1319

After 30. Rf2

Black is clearly better. Now pay close attention to how easily Malakhov converts his advantage.

30. ... Nb6

He prepares to invade along the first rank.

31. Rd4 Rc1+ 32. Ke2 Ra8

33. Ke3 Ra3! 34. g4

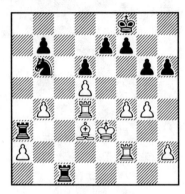

Diagram 1320
After 34. g4

White is hopelessly pinned and boxed in.

34. ... Nc4+ 35. Ke2 Rxa2+ 36. Kf3 Ra3 37. Kg2 Ne3+

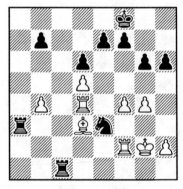

Diagram 1321
After 37. ... Ne3+

White resigns because of 38. Kf3 Nc2!.

Game Four
Maroczy Bind

FRANCISCO VALLEJO-PONS—
VLADIMIR MALAKHOV, 2003

This game illustrates how Black easily maintains equality

in an endgame considered by theory to be better for White.

1. e4 c5 2. Nf3 Nc6

Once again, note that we recommend 2. ... g6 to sidestep the Rossolimo Variation (3. Bb5).

3. d4 cxd4 4. Nxd4 g6 5. c4 Nf6 6. Nc3 d6 7. Be2

Diagram 1322
After 7. Be2

7. ... Nxd4 8. Qxd4 Bg7 9. Bg5 0–0 10. Qd2 Be6 11. Rc1

This is Variation **B**, Chapter 12, page 166.

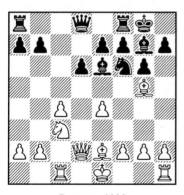

Diagram 1323
After 11. Rc1

11. ... Qa5 12. f3 Rfc8 13. b3 a6 14. Na4 Qxd2+ 15. Kxd2

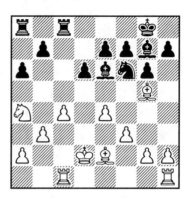

Diagram 1324
After 15. Kxd2

15. ... Rc6 16. Nc3 Kf8 17. Nd5

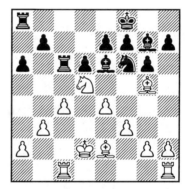

Diagram 1325
After 17. Nd5

17. ... Bxd5 18. cxd5 Rcc8

This game illustrates how Black easily maintains equality in an endgame considered by theory to be better for White.

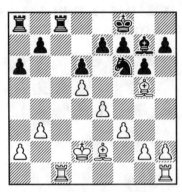

Diagram 1326
After 18. ... Rcc8

Here's where we left off on page 167, reaching one of the typical endgames of the Maroczy Bind. For a time, this ending was considered to be in White's favor because of his bishop pair and space advantage. This game proves, however, that Black has nothing to fear. GM Malakhov shows us the correct setup.

19. Be3 Nd7 20. Rxc8+ Rxc8 21. Rc1 Rxc1 22. Kxc1 Ke8

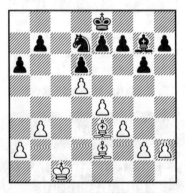

Diagram 1327
After 22. ... Ke8

Black's plan involves bringing his king to c7.

23. Kc2 Kd8 24. b4 h6

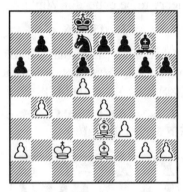

Diagram 1328
After 24. ... h6

With the idea of playing ... g5, creating a barricade to White's kingside advance.

25. g3 g5 26. a4 Nf6 27. Bd4 Kc7

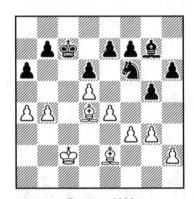

Diagram 1329
After 27. ... Kc7

Black maintains his solid position and is ready to face any advances on the kingside.

28. f4 gxf4 29. gxf4 Nh5! 30. Be3

After 30. Bxg7 Nxg7, White loses his bishop pair; Black

maintains equality easily.

30. ... Nf6 31. Bf3 Nd7

Diagram 1330
After 31. ... Nd7

It seems as if Black is simply going back and forth, waiting for White to commit, but Malakhov is preparing a powerful thrust.

32. a5 f5!

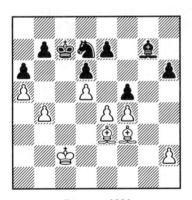

Diagram 1331
After 32. ... f5!

This pawn sacrifice is aimed at breaking up White's kingside pawns and creating a blockade.

33. exf5 Ba1 34. Bh5 b5 35. Bf7

Or 35. axb6+ Nxb6 =.

35. ... Bf6

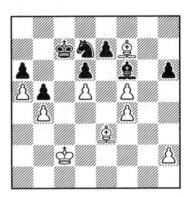

Diagram 1332
After 35. ... Bf6

Black has achieved a total blockade; White can't penetrate anywhere on the board. For the rest of the game, White tries in vain to make progress.

36. Be6 Kd8 37. Bf7 Kc7 38. Kd2 Kd8 39. Kd3 Kc7 40. Bf2 Kd8 41. Be1 Bb2 42. Be6 Kc7 43. Bd2 Nf6 44. Be3 Kb7 45. Bb6 Nh5 46. Bf7

Black has achieved a total blockade!

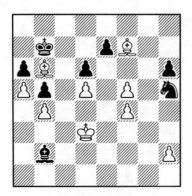

Diagram 1333
After 46. Bf7

**46. ... Nxf4+ 47. Kc2
Draw.**

Game Five

Nimzo-Indian Defense

**GLEN RUDELIS—
JOHN DONALDSON, 2002**

The following short game shows how quickly White is faced with disaster after Black's ... Qc8 in the Saemisch variation of the Nimzo-Indian.

**1. d4 Nf6 2. c4 e6 3. Nc3 Bb4
4. a3 Bxc3+ 5. bxc3 b6 6. f3**

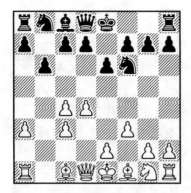

Diagram 1334
After 6. f3

We've reached a position in Chapter 21, page 260.

**6. ... Nc6 7. e4 Ba6 8. Bd3
Na5 9. e5 Ng8 10. Qa4 Qc8**

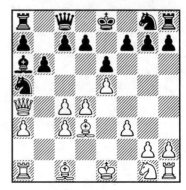

Diagram 1335
After 10. ... Qc8

Here Black's plan is to play ... c7-c5.

11. Be4?

White neglects the development of his pieces. Better is 11. Ne2 c5 12. Ng3 Qc6 13. Qxc6 dxc6 14. Ne4 cxd4 15. Nd6+

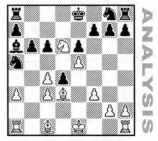

Diagram 1336
After 15. Nd6+

15. ... Ke7 16. cxd4 Nb3 17. Rb1 Nxd4 18. Be3 c5.

Diagram 1337
After 18. ... c5

The position is about equal; White has compensation for the pawn.

11. ... c6 12. c5

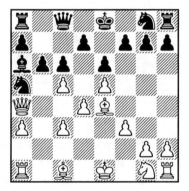

Diagram 1338
After 12. c5

12. ... f5!

Black takes over the initiative! White's position starts to collapse.

13. exf6 Nxf6 14. cxb6? axb6

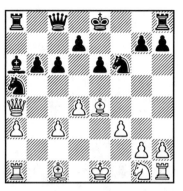

Diagram 1339
After 14. ... axb6

Now let's assess the position: White is worse on all fronts! Black is ahead in development and dominates the light squares.

15. Qc2 0–0 16. Ne2 Bc4

Preparing to put even more pressure on White with ... Qa6 and ... d7-d5.

17. 0–0?

Loses a piece, but it's hard to recommend anything for White.

17. ... Qa6 18. Re1 d5

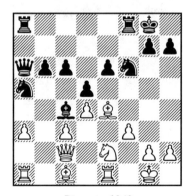

Diagram 1340
After 18. ... d5

In a few moves, **White resigns.**

Game Six

Nimzo-Indian Defense
VLADIMIR EPISHIN—
EMANUEL BERG, 2002

1. d4 e6 2. c4 Nf6 3. Nc3 Bb4 4. e3 b6 5. Ne2

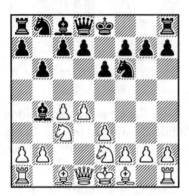

Diagram 1341
After 5. Ne2

5. ... Ba6 6. Ng3 Bxc3+ 7. bxc3 d5 8. Ba3 Bxc4 9. Bxc4 dxc4 10. e4

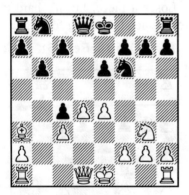

Diagram 1342
After 10. e4

We've reached Variation **B1a**, Chapter 24, page 301. In return for his pawn, White has a strong center. However, the game shows that his attacking chances on Black's king are slim. Black's plan is to transfer his queen to a6, play … Nbd7 and castle long with a very solid position.

10. ... Qd7 11. 0–0 Qb5 12. Rb1 Qa6 13. Qc1 Nbd7 14. Rd1 0–0–0 15. f3 Rhe8

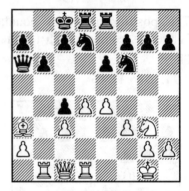

Diagram 1343
After 15. ... Rhe8

Black is in no danger and simply goes about improving his position. It's hard for White to create any threats.

16. Nf1 Nb8!

The knight is better placed on c6, where it controls the important b4-square.

17. Ne3 Nc6 18. Rd2 Qa4!

Now Black's queen is even better placed.

19. Bb4 a5 20. Ba3

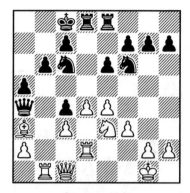

Diagram 1344
After 20. Ba3

20. ... Rd7

Here Black missed a chance to seize the initiative with 20. ... Nh5!, threatening to play ... Nf4 and break open the center with ... f5. After the likely 21. g3 f5!, Black returns the pawn, destroying White's center: 22. exf5 exf5 23. Nxf5.

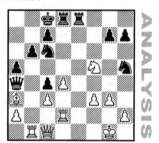

Diagram 1345
After 23. Nxf5

Black is much better. His attack on the kingside and over the e-file is unstoppable, while White's pieces are disorganized and tied up. After 20. ... Rd7, the game continued:

21. Bb2

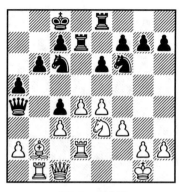

Diagram 1346
After 21. Bb2

21. ... Red8 22. Ba1 b5 23. Qc2 Qxc2 24. Rxc2 Na7 25. a4 c6

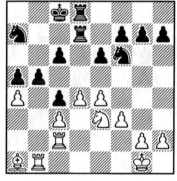

Diagram 1347
After 25. .... c6

26. Ra2 Rb7 27. axb5 cxb5 28. Rxa5 Kc7 29. Nc2 Rdb8 30. Na3 Ne8 31. Ra6 Nc6 32. Nc2 Rb6

Black's attack on the kingside is unstoppable.

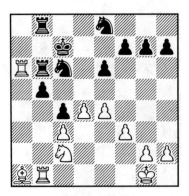

Diagram 1348
After 32. ... Rb6

33. Rxb6 Kxb6 34. Bb2 Na5 35. Bc1 Nb3 36. Be3 Ra8 37. d5+

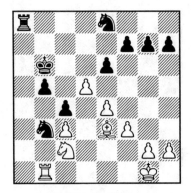

Diagram 1349
After 37. d5+

Black gets a superior position before White completes his development.

37. ... Kc7 38. Nd4 Nxd4 39. Bxd4 exd5 40. Rxb5 dxe4 41. fxe4 Nd6

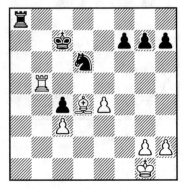

Diagram 1350
After 41. ... Nd6

42. Re5 Kd7 43. Rd5 Kc6 44. Re5 Kd7 45. Rd5

Draw.

Game Seven

Nimzo-Indian Defense

ALEXANDER GOLDIN—
ALEX YERMOLINSKY, 2002

This game illustrates Black's plan in the 4. Qc2 variation of the Nimzo-Indian (Chapter 22). Notice how quickly Black achieves a superior position before White completes his development.

1. d4 Nf6 2. c4 e6 3. Nc3 Bb4 4. Qc2 Nc6 5. Nf3 d6 6. Bd2 0–0 7. a3 Bxc3 8. Bxc3

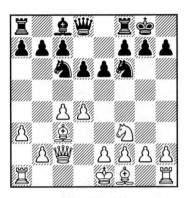

Diagram 1351
After 8. Bxc3

8. ... Qe7 9. b4 e5 10. d5 Nb8 11. e4 Nh5 12. g3 f5!

We've reached **A2**, page 274.

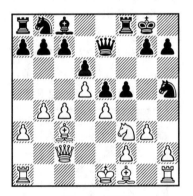

Diagram 1352
After 12. ... f5!

Black already executes his plan on the kingside while White remains behind in development.

As we have seen elsewhere (for instance, in the comments to 20. ... Rd7 on page 509), ... f5 is one of Black's handy tools in several lines of the Nimzo-Indian.

13. Be2 fxe4 14. Qxe4 Bf5 15. Qe3 Nf6 16. Nh4 Bh3

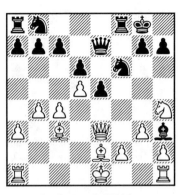

Diagram 1353
After 16. ... Bh3

Now it's difficult for White to decide what to do with his king. Castling kingside is impossible, and after 0–0–0, White's king will be easily attacked.

17. Rg1

With the idea of g3-g4.

17. ... Ng4 18. Bxg4 Bxg4

Diagram 1354
After 18. ... Bxg4

Now White's light squares become even weaker.

19. h3

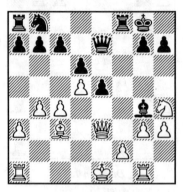

Diagram 1355
After 19. h3

White sacrifices a pawn in order to create some counter-play. After 19. f3 Bh5 20. 0–0–0 Nd7, Black is better because White's king position is vulnerable.

19. ... Bxh3 20. Rh1 Bf5 21. Nxf5 Rxf5 22. Qe4

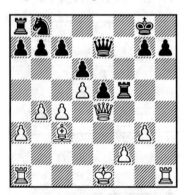

Diagram 1356
After 22. Qe4

22. ... g6 23. f4 Nd7

Black consolidates easily because White's attacking chances are illusory.

24. 0–0–0 Qf7 25. Rde1

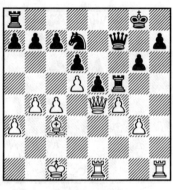

Diagram 1357
After 25. Rde1

25. ... Rf8

Not 25. ... exf4? 26. g4 Rg5 27. Qe7. After 25. ... Rf8, Black is up a pawn and clearly on top; it's hard for White to generate any play.

26. fxe5 Nxe5 27. Re2 a6?!

A quicker win is 27. ... Rf1+ 28. Rxf1 Qxf1+ 29. Kd2 Rf5!.

Diagram 1358
After 29. ... Rf5!

28. Rhe1

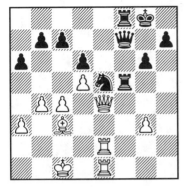

Diagram 1359
After 28. Rhe1

28. ... b5 29. c5 Nc4 30. Qd4 Re5 31. Rxe5 dxe5 32. Qe4 Qf2

Diagram 1360
After 32. ... Qf2

33. d6

A desperate attempt, but White is completely lost.

33. ... Qxg3 34. Qd5+

Diagram 1361
After 34. Qd5+

34. ... Kg7?!

Better is 34. ... Rf7, with an easy win after 35. Kc2 Qxe1! 36. Qa8+ (or 36. Bxe1 Ne3+) 36. ... Rf8. Fortunately for Black, the ensuing rook ending is also won.

35. Bxe5+ Nxe5 36. Qxe5+ Qxe5 37. Rxe5 cxd6 38. cxd6 Rd8 39. Re7+

Diagram 1362
After 39. Re7+

39. ... Kf6! 40. Rxh7 Rxd6 41. Rh1 g5

White resigns.

Game Eight

Nimzo-Indian Defense

JAN TIMMAN—
ROMAN DZINDZICHASHVILI,
1977

The following game shows the successful execution of the 9. ... Bf5 idea in the Leningrad Variation of the Nimzo-Indian. After tactical complications in the opening, Black ends up on top with a superior knight versus bishop. The resulting endgame is very instructive.

1. d4 Nf6 2. c4 e6 3. Nc3 Bb4 4. Bg5 h6 5. Bh4

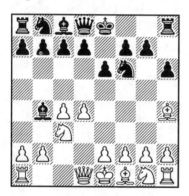

Diagram 1363
After 5. Bh4

5. ... c5 6. d5 Bxc3+ 7. bxc3 d6 8. e3 e5 9. f3

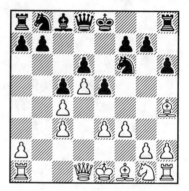

Diagram 1364
After 9. f3

9. ... Bf5! 10. Qb3 b6 11. h3 Nbd7

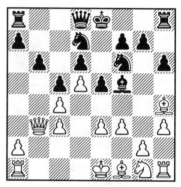

Diagram 1365
After 11. ... Nbd7

12. g4

Relatively better is 12. e4.

12. ... Bh7 13. Ne2

Even here: 13. e4!.

13. ... g5!

AFTER TACTICAL COMPLICATIONS IN THE OPENING,
BLACK ENDS UP ON TOP WITH A
SUPERIOR KNIGHT VERSUS BISHOP.

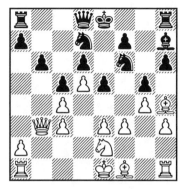

Diagram 1366
After 13. ... g5!

Black starts to seize the initiative on the kingside.

14. Bf2 h5 15. h4 e4!

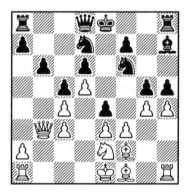

Diagram 1367
After 15. ... e4!

Unexpected but strong!

16. hxg5 exf3 17. gxf6 fxe2 18. Bxe2 Qxf6 19. Rxh5

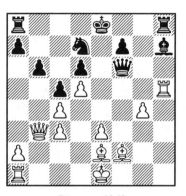

Diagram 1368
After 19. Rxh5

Black is down a pawn, but he gets sufficient compensation from his active pieces and White's broken-up pawn structure.

19. ... Bg6 20. Bh4?

Relatively better is 20. Rxh8+ Qxh8 21. 0–0–0 Qh2 22. Rf1 Ne5, with active play for Black.

20. ... Qg7

Black is down a pawn, but he gets sufficient compensation from his active pieces and White's broken-up pawn structure.

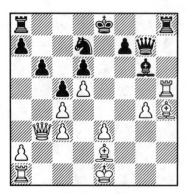

Diagram 1369
After 20. ... Qg7

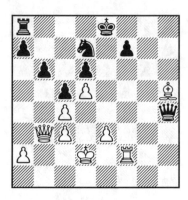

Diagram 1371
After 25. ... Qxh4

21. Kd2

White could not save the Exchange: 21. Rxh8+ Qxh8 22. Bg5 Qh1+ 23. Bf1 Bd3, and Black is winning.

21. ... Bxh5 22. gxh5 Qg2 23. Rf1 Rxh5

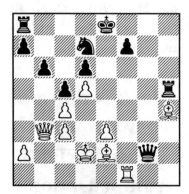

Diagram 1370
After 23. ... Rxh5

24. Rf2 Qh3

Black gives back the Exchange in return for a superior knight.

25. Bxh5 Qxh4

26. Rf5

After 26. Bxf7+ Ke7 27. Rf4 Qh2+ 28. Kc1 Ne5, Black is winning.

26. ... Ne5 27. Be2 0-0-0

Now Black's most efficient winning plan is to exchange queens and rooks in order to reach a technically won endgame.

28. a4 Rg8 29. Qb5 Qe7 30. Rh5

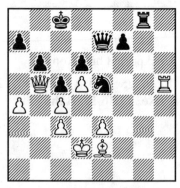

Diagram 1372
After 30. Rh5

30. ... Qd7 31. Qa6+ Qb7

32. Qb5 a6 33. Qb1 Qc7 34. Rh6 Kb7 35. Qf5 Rg6

Diagram 1373
After 35. ... Rg6

36. Rh7 Qe7 37. Qh3 Rg8 38. Kc2 Kc7 39. Bh5 Qf6 40. Kb3

Diagram 1374
After 40. Kb3

40. ... Rh8 41. Rxh8 Qxh8 42. Qf5 Qg7 43. Qe4 Qg5 44. Bd1 Qg6 45. Qc2 Qxc2+ 46. Bxc2

Black has successfully exchanged the major pieces. The endgame is very typical of the Nimzo-Indian positions: Black has a superior knight against a bad light-square bishop, and White's pawn structure is ruined.

Diagram 1375
After 46. Bxc2

46. ... Ng4 47. e4 Ne5 48. Bd1 a5

Diagram 1376
After 48. ... a5

Preventing possible counter-play with a4-a5.

49. Be2 Kd7

Now it's time to start a long king march.

50. Kc2 Ke7 51. Kd2 Kf6 52. Ke3 Kg5

Diagram 1377
After 52. ... Kg5

White is in *Zugzwang*!

53. Bd1

The alternative, 53. Bf1, loses to 53. ... Ng4+ 54. Kd2 (54. Kf3 Nh2+ 55. Kf2 Nxf1 56. Kxf1 Kf4–+) 54. ... Kf4, and White's e-pawn falls.

53. ... Nxc4+ 54. Kf3 f5 55. exf5 Kxf5 56. Ke2 Kf4 57. Bb3 Nb2 58. Kd2

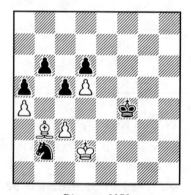

Diagram 1378
After 58. Kd2

58. ... c4 59. Ba2 Ke4 60. Kc2 Nxa4 61. Bxc4 Nc5 62. Kb2 Nd3+ 63. Ka3 Ne5 64. Ba2

Diagram 1379
After 64. Ba2

64. ... b5

White resigns.

The next two games, 9 and 10, perfectly illustrate Black's strategy in the 6. Bg2 variation of the Bogo-Indian (Chapter 30). After taking control of the key squares on the queenside, Black successfully unfolds a powerful attack on the kingside. It's instructive to notice the value of the outposts on c5 and b5.

Game Nine
Bogo-Indian Defense

SPYRIDON SKEMBRIS—
ALEX BELIAVSKY, 1994

1. d4 Nf6 2. c4 e6 3. Nf3 Bb4+ 4. Bd2 Qe7 5. g3 Nc6 6. Bg2 Bxd2+ 7. Nbxd2 d6

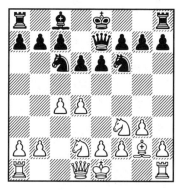

Diagram 1380
After 7. ... d6

As we point out in Chapter 30 (page 342), 7. ... 0-0 is more accurate because 7. ... d6 allows 8. Nf1, followed by Ne3, with a slight edge for White.

8. 0–0 e5 9. d5 Nb8 10. e4 a5 11. Ne1 0–0 12. Nd3 Na6

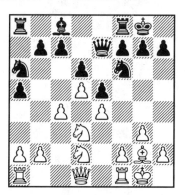

Diagram 1381
After 12. ... Na6

13. a3 Bg4 14. f3 Bd7 15. b4 c6 16. Qb3

For 16. bxa5, see Game 10.

16. ... cxd5

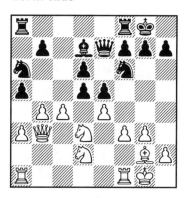

Diagram 1382
After 16. ... cxd5

17. cxd5

On 17. exd5, 17. ... b5! is strong.

Diagram 1383
After 17. ... b5!

Black's idea is to put more pressure on White's queenside pawns—for example, after 18. bxa5 Rfb8 19. Nb4 (19. Rab1 bxc4 20. Qxc4 Rc8 and ... Nc5) 19. bxc4 20. Nxc4 Nc5 21. Qe3 Bb5 22. Rfc1 Bxc4 23. Rxc4 Qd7.

BLACK'S IDEA IS TO PUT PRESSURE ON WHITE'S QUEENSIDE PAWNS.

Diagram 1384
After 23. ... Qd7

Black has a good position.

17. ... axb4 18. axb4

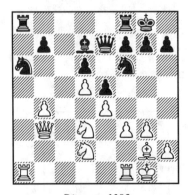

Diagram 1385
After 18. axb4

18. ... Nc7

Black takes over the b5-square.

19. Qb2

After 19. Nc4 Nb5, Black's knight heads to d4.

19. ... Bb5

If 19. ... Nb5 right away, then 20. Nb3.

20. Ra3 Rxa3 21. Qxa3 Ba6!

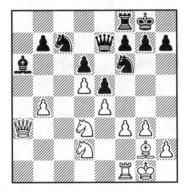

Diagram 1386
After 21. ... Ba6!

White can't stop ... Nb5 and ... Nd4.

22. Rc1 Nb5 23. Qa5 Nd4 24. Bf1 Nh5!

Diagram 1387
After 24. ... Nh5!

Now that Black's pieces are on their best squares, Beliavsky begins to play on the kingside. His plan is ... Qg5 and ... f7-f5.

25. Nf2 Be2

The bishop is joining in the attack on White's king.

26. Rc3 Qg5 27. Qa2 f5!

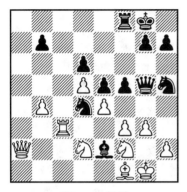

Diagram 1388
After 27. ... f5!

A complete triumph for the Black army! All of his pieces are participating in the attack.

28. exf5 Qxf5 29. Bg2 Nf6 30. Rc7?

White hasn't the stomach to wait patiently for his own destruction, and so makes an active move. Unfortunately, his choice loses the game even faster.

30. ... Bxf3

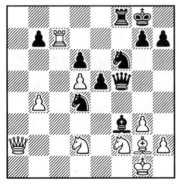

Diagram 1389
After 30. ... Bxf3

31. Rxb7 Ng4 32. Nxg4 Bxg4 33. Nf1 Ne2+ 34. Kh1 Bf3

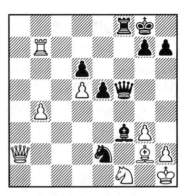

Diagram 1390
After 34. ... Bf3

35. Nd2 Nxg3+

There is no defense against mate after 36. hxg3 Qh3+.

White resigns.

White hasn't the stomach to wait patiently for his own destruction, and so makes an active move. Unfortunately, his choice loses the game even faster.

Game Ten

Bogo-Indian Defense

VLADIMIR KHOMYAKOV—
ALEXEY KOROTYLEV, 1999

Another game that shows Black's strategy in the 6. Bg2 variation of the Bogo-Indian (Chapter 30). Black sows up the queenside using the b5-outpost. Then he unleashes a powerful ... f7-f5 pawn thrust.

1. d4 Nf6 2. c4 e6 3. Nf3 Bb4+ 4. Bd2 Qe7 5. g3 Nc6 6. Bg2 Bxd2+ 7. Nbxd2 d6

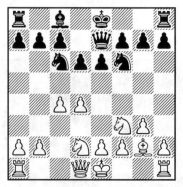

Diagram 1391
After 7. ... d6

As we've noted, it's better to castle first to prevent White from playing Nf1-e3.

8. 0–0 0–0 9. e4 e5 10. d5 Nb8 11. b4 a5 12. a3 Na6 13. Ne1

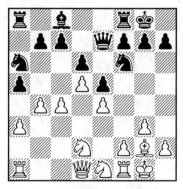

Diagram 1392
After 13. Ne1

13. ... Bg4

Black forces White to play 14. f3; 14. Qb3 loses to 14. ... Be2.

14. f3 Bd7 15. Nd3 c6 16. bxa5

Black can now control the vital c5-square. In a previous game, White played 16. Qb3 here.

16. ... Qd8 17. Nb3 cxd5 18. cxd5

On 18. exd5, Black plays 18. ... Ba4, followed by ... Nd7, taking command of the c5-outpost.

18. ... Bb5

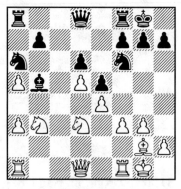

Diagram 1393
After 18. ... Bb5

Pinning White's knight and preparing ... Nd7 to fully control the outpost on c5.

19. Rf2 Nd7

Also possible is 19. ... Bxd3 20. Qxd3 Nd7 21. Rb1 Nac5 22. Qc3 Nxb3 23. Rxb3 Nc5 24. Rb5 Qd7,

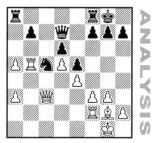

Diagram 1394
After 24. ... Qd7

with strong compensation for the pawn, as Black meets 25. Rb1 (25. Bf1 f5!) with 25. ... Qa4.

20. Nb2

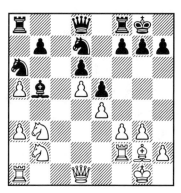

Diagram 1395
After 20. Nb2

White decides to preserve his knight, allowing Black to seize the initiative. After 20. Rb1 Black plays 20. ... Bxd3, trans-

posing to the position we looked at in the note above, with 19. ... Bxd3.

20. ... Nac5 21. a4 Ba6 22. Bh3 g6!

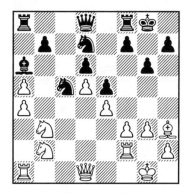

Diagram 1396
After 22. ... g6!

Black now shifts his play to the kingside, preparing the ... f7-f5 thrust.

23. Ra3 f5 24. exf5 gxf5

Black now shifts his play to the kingside, preparing the ... f7-f5 thrust.

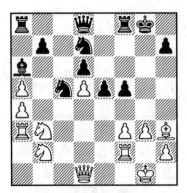

Diagram 1397
After 24. ... gxf5

White's pieces lack coordination, while Black's pieces are all well-placed.

25. Qd2?

White should worry about his king and not his a5-pawn. He had to play 25. f4 to slow down Black's play on the kingside.

25. ... Rc8 26. Bf1 Kh8

Preparing for the final assault.

27. Bb5 Nf6

Black has now mobilized all of his forces.

28. Nc1

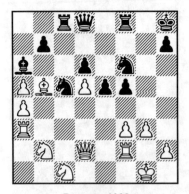

Diagram 1398
After 28. Nc1

28. ... f4!

This battering-ram of a move brings down White's position.

29. Ne2

The alternative, 29. gxf4, is met with 29. ... Nce4! 30. fxe4 Nxe4 31.Qd1 Nxf2 32. Kxf2 Rxf4+.

Diagram 1399
After 32. ... Rxf4+

Black marshals a crushing attack; he meets 33. Rf3 with 33. ... Qh4+.

29. ... Nce4!

This rips open White's king.

30. fxe4 Nxe4 31. Qe1 Nxf2 32. Qxf2 fxg3 33. Qe1

Or 33. Qg2 Qxa5, and White is hopeless.

33. ... gxh2+

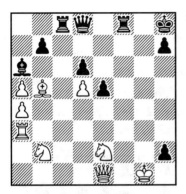

Diagram 1400
After 33. ... gxh2+

34. Kxh2

34. Kh1 loses to 34. ... Rc2 35. Nd1 Qg5, and if 36. Rg3, then 36. ... Bxb5! 37. Rxg5 Rxe2.

Diagram 1401
After 37. ... Rxe2

34. ... Rc2

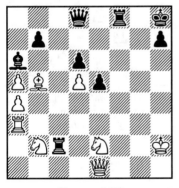

Diagram 1402
After 34. ... Rc2

35. Nd1 Qg5 36. Re3

After 36. Rc3 Bxb5! 37. Rxc2 Bxe2

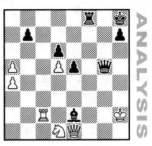

Diagram 1403
After 37. ... Bxe2

38. Rxe2 (38. Qxe2 Qh4+ 39. Kg1 Rg8+) 38. ... Rg8, mate is unstoppable.

36. ... Bxb5 37. axb5 Rg8

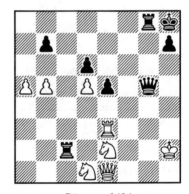

Diagram 1404
After 37. ... Rg8

38. Rg3

Or 38. Qf2 Rxe2! 39. Qxe2 Qg1+

Diagram 1405

After 39. ... Qg1+

40. Kh3 Qh1+ 41. Qh2 Qf1+ 42. Kh4 Qf6+, with mate next move.

38. ... Rxe2+

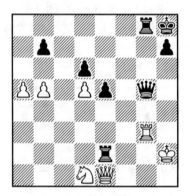

Diagram 1406

After 38. ... Rxe2+

White resigns.

Game Eleven
Bogo-Indian Defense

**BORIS AVRUKH—
RASUL IBRAHIMOV, 2001**

This game illustrates typical play in the 6. Nc3 variation of the Bogo-Indian (Chapter 31). White's play on the queenside only weakens his position and allows Black to win control of the key c5-outpost. After getting

a better game, however, Black recklessly pushes for more and, as so often happens, quickly loses the game.

1. d4 Nf6 2. c4 e6 3. Nf3 Bb4+ 4. Bd2 Qe7 5. g3 Nc6 6. Nc3 Bxc3 7. Bxc3

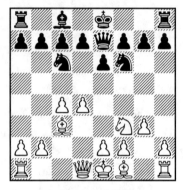

Diagram 1407

After 7. Bxc3

7. … Ne4 8. Rc1 0–0 9. Bg2 d6 10. 0–0 Nxc3 11. Rxc3 e5 12. d5 Nb8

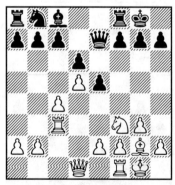

Diagram 1408

After 12. ... Nb8

13. b4 Bg4 14. Nd2 Nd7 15. Nb3

White is ready to play c4-c5.

15. ... b6

Black prepares his queenside counter-play.

16. c5 a5!

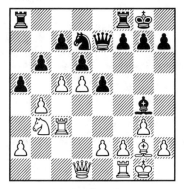

Diagram 1409
After 16. ... a5!

This move allows Black to win the c5-outpost for his knight, since White can't play 17. a3 because of 17. ... a4, when the c5-pawn falls.

17. Rc4

White improves the position of his rook before capturing on d6. After the immediate 17. cxd6 cxd6 18. bxa5 bxa5 19. Rc7 a4 20. Nc1 Qd8 21. Rc6 Nc5,

Diagram 1410
After 21. ... Nc5

it's clear that White has lost the battle on the queenside.

17. ... Nf6

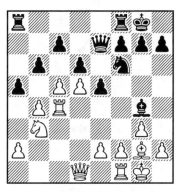

Diagram 1411
After 17. ... Nf6

18. cxd6 cxd6 19. bxa5 bxa5 20. Qd2

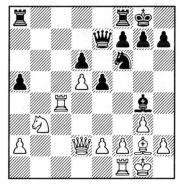

Diagram 1412
After 20. Qd2

20. ... Qb7?!

An inaccuracy. Black is better off playing 20. ... Qd7, and after 21. Rfc1 (on 21. Nxa5? Qb5!, White is lost), 21. ... a4 22. Na1 Qb5.

Diagram 1413
After 22. ... Qb5

Black is better due to White's badly placed knight and bishop.

21. Rfc1 Qb5

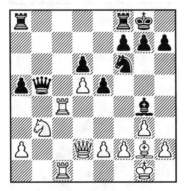

Diagram 1414
After 21. ... Qb5

22. e4 a4 23. Rb4 Qd7 24. Na1

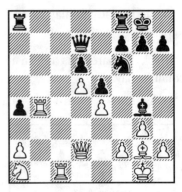

Diagram 1415
After 24. Na1

Even with his move order, Black still has a good position. White's knight on a1 is temporarily out of the game, and his bishop on g2 faces his own pawns.

24. ... Rfc8 25. Nc2 Qc7 26. Rbb1 Rab8 27. Ne3 Rxb1 28. Rxb1

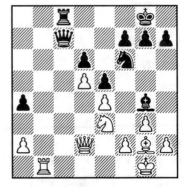

Diagram 1416
After 28. Rxb1

28. ... h5

After the modest 28. ... Bd7, the position is balanced.

29. Qb4

Worse is 29. Nxg4 hxg4, since the remaining Black knight is

Black is better due to White's badly placed knight and bishop.

much stronger than the White bishop.

29. ... Bd7 30. Bf1 h4 31. Ba6 Ra8 32. Be2

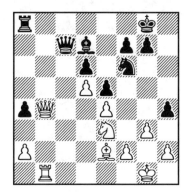

Diagram 1417
After 32. Be2

32. ... h3?

Black overestimates his chances; the attack on the king-side is not merited, since all the light squares are defended and the h3-pawn will be weak. Better is 32. ... hxg3 33. hxg3 Rc8, with the idea ... Qc5.

33. f3 a3?

Black repeats the mistake—overextending his pawns.

34. Kf2 Kh7 35. Qb7

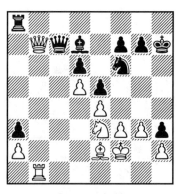

Diagram 1418
After 35. Qb7

All endgames now favor White due to Black's weak pawns.

35. ... Qa5 36. Rb4 Qc5 37. Rc4 Ra7 38. Qb8!

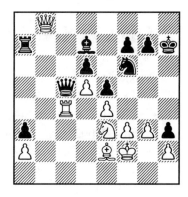

Diagram 1419
After 38. Qb8!

Now the d6-pawn is doomed.

38. ... Qa5 39. Qxd6

Black is lost.

39. ... Rb7 40. Qxe5 Rb2 41. Rc2 Qb4 42. Qc3

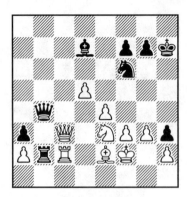

Diagram 1420
After 42. Qc3

**42. ... Qxc3 43. Rxc3 Rxa2
44. Nc2 Bg4 45. Bd3**

Black resigns.

Game Twelve

Bogo-Indian Defense

MISHO CEBALO—
VLAD JAKOVLJEVIC, 1999

This game illustrates typical plans in the 4. Nbd2 variation of the Bogo-Indian (Chapter 32). Again we see Black creating energetic counter-play on the queenside. White fights against the strong bishop on e4. The endgame is instructive: Black first equalizes, then misses a promising opportunity, and eventually even loses.

**1. d4 Nf6 2. c4 e6 3. Nf3 Bb4+
4. Nbd2 b6 5. a3 Bxd2+ 6. Bxd2
h6**

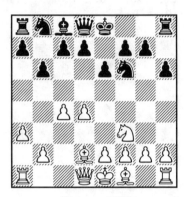

Diagram 1421
After 6. ... h6

7. g3 Bb7 8. Bg2 Be4

Black immediately takes over the e4-square. Also possible is 8. ... 0–0 9. 0–0 d6 10. b4 Nbd7 11. Bc3 Be4, transposing to the game.

**9. b4 0–0 10. 0–0 d6 11. Bc3
Nbd7 12. Re1**

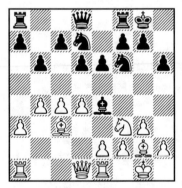

Diagram 1422
After 12. Re1

White employs a typical plan to oust Black's light-square bishop, without exchanging it for his own. His idea is to play Bf1, followed by a knight retreat and then f2-f3 and e2-e4. In the meantime, Black prepares counter-play on the queenside.

12. ... a6

Black has ... b6-b5 in mind.

13. a4 b5 14. cxb5 axb5 15. axb5 Qb8

Black's pawn sacrifice creates a strong outpost on d5 and also weakens White's light squares on the queenside.

16. Bf1

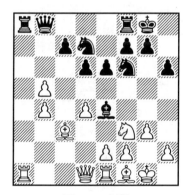

Diagram 1423
After 16. Bf1

16. ... Rxa1

Another possibility is 16. ... Nd5, with the idea of 17. Bb2 Bxf3 18. exf3 Nxb4 19. Rxa8 Qxa8,

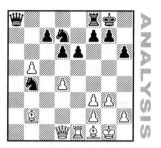

Diagram 1424
After 19. ... Qxa8

when Black has a solid position, lynch-pinned by his knight's permanent outpost on d5.

17. Qxa1 Qxb5

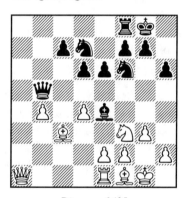

Diagram 1425
After 17. ... Qxb5

18. Nd2 Ra8 19. Qc1 Ra2

Black's pawn sac creates a strong outpost on d5.

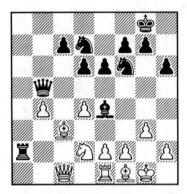

Diagram 1426
After 19. ... Ra2

White has executed his plan. He's ready to play f2-f3 and e2-e4. Meanwhile, Black's rook is wreaking havoc along White's second rank.

20. f3

The alternative, 20. Nxe4 Nxe4, benefits Black, because his knights will be more powerful than White's bishops. White's bishop on c3 is blocked in by its own pawns.

20. ... Rc2 21. Qa1 Bc6 22. e4 Qa4 23. Qxa4 Bxa4 24. Nb1 c6

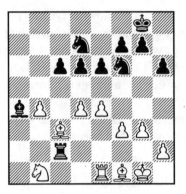

Diagram 1427
After 24. ... c6

The endgame is about equal.

25. Bd3 Ra2 26. Rc1?

White had a better choice—26. Re2. After 26. ... Rxe2 27. Bxe2 Ne8,

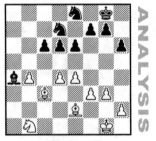

Diagram 1428
After 27. ... Ne8

with the idea of ... Nc7 and ... Bb5, the position is even.

26. ... Bb5

WHITE HAS EXECUTED HIS PLAN. MEANWHILE, BLACK'S ROOK IS WREAKING HAVOC ALONG WHITE'S SECOND RANK.

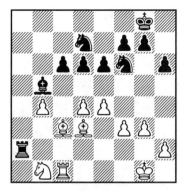

Diagram 1429
After 26. ... Bb5

**27. Bxb5 cxb5 28. Be1 Ra1
29. Bd2 Ra2 30. Bf4 e5 31. dxe5**

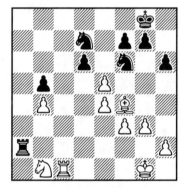

Diagram 1430
After 31. dxe5

31. ... Nxe5?

A mistake which not only gives away Black's advantage, but leads to the demise of his game. After the correct 31. ... dxe5 32. Be3 Rb2 33. Bc5?! Nxc5 34. bxc5 b4! 35. c6 Ne8,

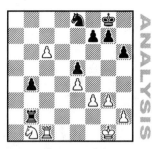

Diagram 1431
After 35. ... Ne8

White's knight is trapped, while Black threatens to ambush White's c-pawn with his king and knight. This adds up to good winning chances for Black.

**32. Bxe5 dxe5 33. Nc3 Rb2
34. Nxb5 Rxb4 35. Nd6**

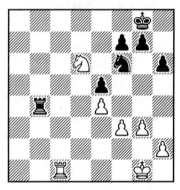

Diagram 1432
After 35. Nd6

35. ... Nd7?

It's better to play 35. ... Rb3.

**36. Rc7 Nb6 37. Nxf7 Nc4
38. Kg2 Rb2+ 39. Kh3 Ne3
40. Nxe5 Nf1 41. Kg4 Rxh2
42. Kf4 Rh3 43. g4 Nh2 44. Rc1
Kh7 45. Rc8**

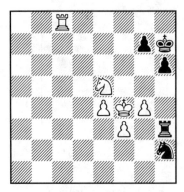

Diagram 1433
After 45. Rc8

45. ... g5+ 46. Kf5 Nxf3 47. Rc7+ Kg8 48. Nd7 Rh1 49. Kf6

Black resigns.

Game Thirteen

Torre Attack

IVAN SOKOLOV—
ANATOLY KARPOV, 1995

In this final illustrative game, we see the former world champion using our recommended system against the Torre Attack (Chapter 33).

1. d4 Nf6 2. Nf3 e6 3. Bg5 h6 4. Bh4 c5 5. e3

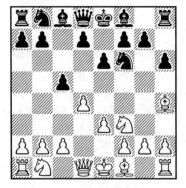

Diagram 1434
After 5. e3

5. ... cxd4 6. exd4 Be7 7. Bd3 0–0 8. c3 b6 9. Qe2 Bb7

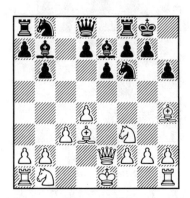

Diagram 1435
After 9. ... Bb7

10. Nbd2 Nc6 11. Bxf6!? Bxf6 12. 0–0–0

Diagram 1436
After 12. 0-0-0

Sokolov's plan is to attack on the kingside. Watch how Karpov skillfully neutralizes White's threats.

12. ... g6! 13. h4 Bg7 14. Kb1

The thrust 14. h5 is met by 14. ... g5.

14. ... Ne7!

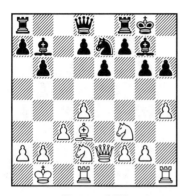

Diagram 1437
After 14. ... Ne7!

With the idea of playing ... Nd5 and ... Nf4.

15. Ne4 Nd5 16. Qd2

After 16. Bc2 Nf4 17. Qf1 f5, Black is better.

16. ... d6 17. Bc2 Rc8

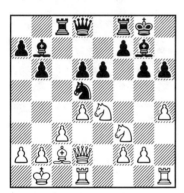

Diagram 1438
After 17. ... Rc8

Black takes over the initiative. His pieces are more active.

18. Rde1 Re8 19. Rh3 b5 20. h5 f5!

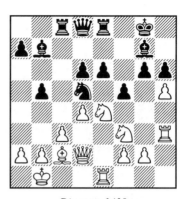

Diagram 1439
After 20. ... f5!

21. hxg6!?

Sokolov tries a piece sacrifice. No better is 21. Ng3 g5, when Black dominates the board.

21. ... fxe4 22. Bxe4 Qf6 23. Nh2

Or 23. Rxh6? Bxh6 24. Qxh6 Qg7–+.

23. ... b4

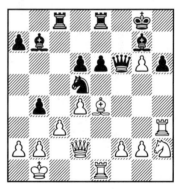

Diagram 1440
After 23. ... b4

It's Karpov's turn to attack!

24. Ng4

Or 24. cxb4 Qxd4 25. Qxd4 Bxd4 26. Rxh6

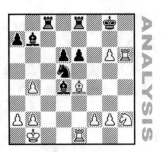

Diagram 1441
After 26. Rxh6

26. ... Bxf2 –+.

24. ... Qg5

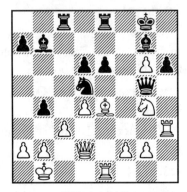

Diagram 1442
After 24. ... Qg5

25. Qxg5 hxg5 26. Nh6+

Or 26. cxb4 Rc4.

26. ... Bxh6 27. Rxh6 Bc6 28. Rh7

Or 28. Reh1 Nf6 29. Bxc6 Rxc6 –+.

28. ... a5 29. c4 Nf4!

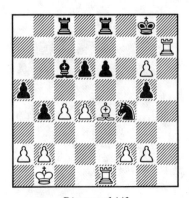

Diagram 1443
After 29. ... Nf4!

The rest is simply technique—Karpov's middle name!

30. Bxc6 Rxc6 31. b3 d5 32. cxd5 Nxd5 33. Reh1

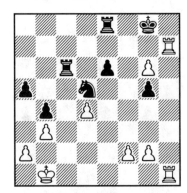

Diagram 1444
After 33. Reh1

33. ... Rec8–+ 34. g4 R8c7 35. Rh8+ Kg7 36. R1h7+

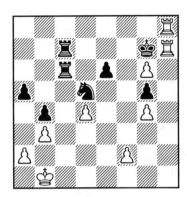

Diagram 1445
After 36. R1h7+

36. ... Kf6!

But not 36. ... Kxg6 37. Rh6+
Kf7 38. R6h7+, draw.

**37. Rh1 Nf4 38. Rf8+ Kxg6
39. Rg8+ Kf6!**

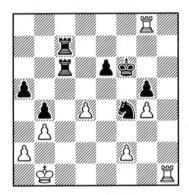

Diagram 1446
After 39. ... Kf6!

40. Rf8+

Or 40. Rh6+? Kf7 41. Rxg5
Rc1+ 42. Kb2 Nd3, checkmate.

**40. ... Kg7 41. Rfh8 Ng6 42.
Ra8 Rf7 43. Rxa5 Rf4**

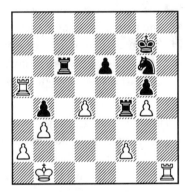

Diagram 1447
After 43. ... Rf4

44. Rd1

Or 44. Rxg5 Rxd4 –+.

44. ... Kf6 45. Rb5 Ne7!

Diagram 1448
After 45. ... Ne7!

White resigns.

**AFTER 29. ... NF4!, IT'S SIMPLY TECHNIQUE—
AND THAT'S KARPOV'S MIDDLE NAME!**

Conclusion
Afterword to a fishing lesson

This book has given you a thematically related set of defenses that will give you confidence, as well as good positions, for the rest of your chess career.

With the strategies and tactics you've learned in the Accelerated Dragon, the Maroczy, the Nimzo- and Bogo-Indians, together with the sidelines you've studied, you'll know what to do—no matter what your opponent throws at you. For, besides specific lines and theoretical novelties, you've gotten a general appreciation and feel for all major approaches in the opening.

In short, you haven't just eaten one seafood buffet; you've learned how to fish. *Chess Openings for White, Explained,* volume one of this two-book series, takes the same approach. (See page 552 to order it.)

You may have read every page in this book, but in a sense, you should never really finish it. We've designed the book to make periodic review easy. As you brush up, look especially for the blue diagrams and "call outs" (those blue boxes that draw your attention to the most important ideas). Review the "Important Points to Look For" at the beginning of each chapter. And work out the "Memory Markers," at the end of chapters, designed to make sure you've moved from the stage of rote memorization to synthesis, creating your own solutions using the information you've studied.

Use the Table of Main Lines that starts on the next page to quickly review your opening preparation before a game. Or use it any time you want quickly to find what the book tells you about a particular line or move.

Take the book to tournaments and chess club night. Refer to it before or after games. Highlight, circle, underline! Write notes in the margins. You'll learn more, and you'll keep a record of your important ideas where it does the most good—in your single reference guide to the openings.

We invite you to let us know how you liked the book and share your discoveries for the next edition by sending an email to al@outexcel.com, or by writing to GM Lev Alburt, PO Box 534, Gracie Station, NY, NY 10028.

Good luck and good chess!

Table of Main Lines

(Numbers in blue brackets refer to *Informant* classifications.
Numbers in *italics* refer to pages where lines begin.)

The Accelerated Dragon (Chapter 5)

1. e4 c5 2. Nf3 g6 3. d4 cxd4 4. Nxd4 Nc6 5. Nc3 Bg7 6. Be3 Nf6 7. Bc4 0-0 8. Bb3 a5 *(56)* [B35]

A 9. a4 Ng4 10. Qxg4 Nxd4 11. Qh4 d6 12. Nd5 Re8 13. Rd1 Nxb3 *(62)*

B 9. 0-0 d6 *(64)* [9. ... a4—p. 65; 9. ... Nxd4—p. 71]

    B1 10. Ndb5 d6 *(66)*

    B2 10. f3 Nxd4 *(66)*

    B3 10. h3 Nxd4 11. Bxd4 Bd7 12. a4 Bc6 *(67)*

        B3a 13. f4 Nd7 14. Bxg7 Kxg7 15. Qd4+ f6 TN *(68)*

        B3b 13. Qd3 Nd7 14. Bxg7 Kxg7 15. Rad1 Nc5 *(70)*

C 9. f3 d5 *(72)*

    C1 10. cxd5 Nb4 11. Nde2 a4! *(73)*

        C1a 12. Bxa4 Nfxd5 13. Bf2 Nxc3 14. Nxc3 Qxd1+ *(73)*

        C1b 12. Nxa4 Nfxd5 13. Bf2 Bf5 *(74)*

            C1b1 14. a3 Nxc2+ 15. Bxc2 Qa5+ 16. b4 *(76)*

            C1b2 14. 0-0 b5! *(77)*

    C2 10. Bxd5 Nxd5 *(77)*

        C2a 11. Nxd5 f5 *(78)*

            C2a1 12. c3 fxe4 *(78)*

            C2a2 12. Nxc6 bxc6 *(78)*

        C2b 11. exd5 Nb4 12. Nde2 e6! *(80)*

            C2b1 13. dxe6 Bxe6 14. a3 *(80)*

            C2b2 13. a3 Nxd5 14. Nxd5 exd5

                15. Bd4 Bh6! *(81)*

            C2b3 13. Qd2 exd5 *(82)*

                C2b3(I) 14. Bd4 Bxd4 *(82)*

                C2b3(II) 14. 0-0 d4! *(83)*

                C2b3(III) 14. 0-0-0 Bf5 *(83)*

    C3 10. Nxd5 Nxd5 11. exd5 *(84)*

The Accelerated Dragon—Seventh-move Sidelines
(Chapter 6) *(86)*

1. e4 c5 2. Nf3 g6 3. d4 cxd4 4. Nxd4 Nc6 5. Nc3 Bg7 6. Be3 Nf6

A 7. Nxc6 bxc6 8. e5 Ng8! *(87)* [B34]

    A1 9. Bd4 f6 10. f4 Qa5 11. Qe2 fxe5 12. Bxe5 Nf6 13. 0-0-0 0-0 *(88)*

    A2 9. f4 Nh6 10. Qd2 0-0 11. 0-0-0 d6! 12. exd6 exd6 13. h3 Nf5 *(89)*

B 7. Be2 0-0 8. 0-0 d6 9. f4 Qb6 10. Qd3 Ng4! 11. Bxg4 Bxd4 *(90)* [B73]

C 7. f3 0-0! 8. Qd2 d5 *(92)* [B34]

    C1 9. exd5 Nxd5 10. Nxc6 bxc6 11. Bd4 Bxd4 12. Qxd4 e5!

        13. Qc5 Qb6 *(93)*

    C2 9. Nxc6 bxc6 10. e5 Nd7 11. f4 e6 12. Na4? Nxe5! 13. fxe5 Qh4+ *(93)*

The Accelerated Dragon—Sixth-move Sidelines (Chapter 7)
1. e4 c5 2. Nf3 g6 3. d4 cxd4 4. Nxd4 Nc6 5. Nc3 Bg7 *(96)* [B34]
   A 6. Nde2 Nf6 7. g3 b5 8. a3 Rb8 9. Bg2 a5 *(97)*
   B 6. Nb3 Nf6 7. Be2 0-0 8. 0-0 d6 *(98)*
      B1 9. Be3 Be6 10. f4 Qc8 *(99)*
      B2 9. Bg5 Be6 *(102)*
         B2a 10. f4 b5 *(102)*
         B2b 10. Kh1 Rc8 11. f4 Na5 12. f5 Bc4 *(103)*
      B3 9. Re1 Be6 10. Bf1 a5 11. a4 Bxb3 12. cxb3 e6 13. Bg5 h6 *(104)*
         B3a 14. Bh4 Qb6 *(105)*
         B3b 14. Be3 Nb4 *(106)*
      B4 9. f4 Be6 *(107)*

Defending Against 4. Qxd4 (Chapter 8)
1. e4 c5 2. Nf3 g6 3. d4 cxd4 4. Qxd4 Nf6 *(110)* [B27]
   A 5. e5 Nc6 6. Qa4 Nd5 7. Qe4 Nb6 *(110)* [7. ... Nc7—p. 112]
      A1 8. Nc3 d5 9. exd6 Bf5 *(113)*
      A2 8. Bf4 d5! 9. exd6 Bf5 10. Qe2 Bg7 *(114)*
   B 5. Bb5 a6 6. e5 axb5 7. exf6 Nc6 *(115)*
      B1 8. Qh4 Ra4 9. fxe7 Bxe7 10. Qh6 Re4+ 11. Kf1 b4 *(115)*
      B2 8. Qe3 b4 9. 0-0 e6 10. c4 Qxf6 11. Nbd2 Bg7 12. Ne4 Qe7
         13. Rd1 d5 *(117)*
      B3 8. fxe7 Qxe7+ 9. Qe3 b4 10. 0-0 Qxe3 11. Bxe3 Bg7
         12. Re1 0-0 *(118)*
   C 5. Nc3 Nc6 6. Qa4 d6 *(119)*

The Hyper-Accelerated Dragon—Third-move Sidelines (Chapter 9)
1. e4 c5 2. Nf3 g6 *(124)* [B27]
   A 3. Bc4 Bg7 4. c3 e6 5. d4 cxd4 6. cxd4 d5 7. exd5 exd5 8. Bb5+ Bd7
      9. Bxd7+ *(126)*
      9. ... Nxd7 *(126)*
      9. ... Qxd7 *(127)*
   B 3. c3 Bg7 4. d4 cxd4 5. cxd4 d5 *(127)*
      B1 6. e5 Bg4 *(127)*
         B1a 7. Nc3 Nc6 8. Be2 Bxf3 9. Bxf3 e6 10. 0-0 Nge7
            11. Be3 0-0 *(128)*
         B1b 7. Nbd2 Nc6 8. h3 Bf5 9. Be2 f6 10. exf6 exf6 *(129)*
         B1c 7. Qb3 Qd7 8. Nc3 Nc6 9. Be3 Bxf3 10. gxf3 e6
            11. Na4 Bf8 *(130)*
      B2 6. exd5 Nf6 7. Bb5+ Nbd7 8. d6 exd6 9. Qe2+ Qe7 10. Bf4 Qxe2+
         11. Bxe2 Ke7 *(130)*

Maroczy Bind—Introduction and 7. Be3 (Chapter 10)
1. e4 c5 2. Nf3 g6 3. d4 cxd4 4. Nxd4 Nc6 5. c4 Nf6 6. Nc3 d6 7. Be3 Ng4 8. Nxc6 Nxe3
9. Nxd8 Nxd1 10. Rxd1 Kxd8. *(136)* [B36]
   A 11. e5 Bg7 12. exd6 Bxc3+ 13. bxc3 exd6 *(139)*
      A1 14. c5 Re8+ 15. Be2 b6 *(139)*
      A2 14. Rxd6+ Kc7 15. Rd4 Re8+ *(139)*
   B 11. c5 Be6 12. cxd6 exd6 13. Be2 Ke7 14. Nd5+ Bxd5 15. Rxd5 Rc8 *(139)*

Maroczy Bind—7. Be2, with Be3 and Qd2 (Chapter 11)
1. e4 c5 2. Nf3 g6 3. d4 cxd4 4. Nxd4 Nc6 5. c4 Nf6 6. Nc3 d6 7. Be2 Nxd4! 8. Qxd4 Bg7
9. Be3 0-0 10. Qd2 Be6. *(142)* [B36]

A 11. Rc1 Qa5 12. f3 Rfc8 13. b3 a6 *(144)*

A1 14. a4 Nd7 15. Nd5 Qxd2+ 16. Kxd2 Bxd5 17. exd5 *(145)*
A2 14. Nd5 Qxd2+ 15. Kxd2 Nxd5 16. cxd5 *(146)*
A3 14. Na4 Qxd2+ 15. Kxd2 Nd7 16. g4 *(147)*

A3a 16. ... f5 17. exf5 *(147)* [17. gxf5—p. 147]
A3b 16. ... Rc6 17. h3 *(148)*

B 11. 0-0 Qa5 *(149)*

B1 12. f3 Rfc8 13. Rfc1 *(149)*
B2 12. Rab1 Rfc8 *(150)*

B2a 13. Rfc1 Bxc4 *(150)*
B2b 13. b4 Qd8 *(151)*
B2c 13. b3 Ng4! *(151)*

B2c1 14. Bd4 Bxd4 *(152)*
B2c2 14. Nd5 Qxd2 *(152)*

B3 12. Rfc1 Rfc8 13. b3 Ng4 *(153)*
B4 12. Rac1 Rfc8 13. b3 a6 *(154)*

B4a 14. f3 b5! *(154)*

B4a1 15. cxb5 axb5 16. Bxb5 *(154)*
B4a2 15. Nd5 Qxd2 16. Bxd2 Nxd5 *(155)*

B4b 14. f4 b5! 15. f5! Bd7 *(156)*

B4b1 16. b4 Qxb4 *(156)*
B4b2 16. fxg6 hxg6 *(157)*

Maroczy Bind—7. Be2, with Bg5 and Qd2 (Chapter 12)
1. e4 c5 2. Nf3 g6 3. d4 cxd4 4. Nxd4 Nc6 5. c4 Nf6 6. Nc3 d6 7. Be2 Nxd4 8. Qxd4 Bg7
9. Bg5 0-0 10. Qd2 Be6 *(162)* [B36]

A 11. 0-0 Qa5 12. Rac1 Rfc8 13. b3 a6 14. f4 Rc5! *(164)*
B 11. Rc1 Qa5 12. f3 Rfc8 13. b3 a6 14. Na4 Qxd2+ 15. Kxd2 *(166)*

B1 15. ... Nd7 16. g4 f6 17. Be3 f5 *(166)*
B2 15. ... Rc6 16. Nc3 Kf8 17. Nd5 Bxd5 18. cxd5 Rcc8 *(167)*

Maroczy Bind—7. Be2 with 0-0 and Qd3 (or Qe3) (Chapter 13)
1. e4 c5 2. Nf3 g6 3. d4 cxd4 4. Nxd4 Nc6 5. c4 Nf6 6. Nc3 d6 7. Be2 Nxd4 8. Qxd4 Bg7
9. 0-0 0-0 *(170)* [B36]

A 10. Qe3 Be6 *(172)*

A1 11. Rb1 Qb6! 12. Qd3 Nd7 *(172)*
A2 11. Bd2 Qb6! 12. Qxb6 axb6 *(173)*

A2a 13. a4 Nd7 14. Ra3 Nc5 *(173)*
A2b 13. f3 Rfc8 14. b3 Nd7 *(174)*

B 10. Qd3 Be6 11. Be3 Nd7 12. Qd2 Nc5 13. f3 a5 *(175)*

Maroczy Bind—7. f3 System (Chapter 14)
1. e4 c5 2. Nf3 g6 3. d4 cxd4 4. Nxd4 Nc6 5. c4 Nf6 6. Nc3 d6 7. f3 Nxd4! 8. Qxd4 Bg7 9. Be3 0-0
10. Qd2 a5! *(178)* [B36]

Maroczy Bind—7. Nc2 (Chapter 15)
1. e4 c5 2. Nf3 g6 3. d4 cxd4 4. Nxd4 Nc6 5. c4 Nf6 6. Nc3 d6 7. Nc2 Bg7 8. Be2 0-0
9. 0-0 Nd7 10. Bd2 a5. *(184)* [B37]
    A 11. Na3 Nc5 12. Nab5 Nd4! *(186)*
    B 11. Rb1 Nc5 12. f3 f5 *(187)*
    C 11. Be3 Nc5 12. f3 a4 *(188)*
    D 11. Kh1 Nc5 12. f3 f5! *(188)*
    E 11. Qc1 Nc5 12. Bh6 Be6 *(189)*

The Closed Sicilian—2. Nc3 followed by g3 (Chapter 16)
1. e4 c5 2. Nc3 g6 3. g3 Bg7 4. Bg2 Nc6 5. d3 d6. *(192)* [B25-26]
    A 6. Nge2 Nf6 7. 0-0 0-0 8. h3 Ne8! 9. Be3 Nd4 *(194)*
    B 6. Be3 Nf6 7. h3 0-0 8. Qd2 Nd4! 9. Nd1 e5! *(196)*
    C 6. f4 Nf6 7. Nf3 Bg4! 8. 0-0 0-0 9. h3 Bxf3 10.Qxf3 Rb8 11. Be3 *(198)*

Grand Prix Attack—And a Grander Defense (Chapter 17)
1. e4 c5. *(204)*
    A 2. f4 g6 3. Nf3 Bg7 *(205)* [B21]
        A1 4. Bc4 e6 5. d4 d5! 6. Bb5+ Bd7! *(206)*
        A2 4. c3 Nc6 5. d4 cxd4 6. cxd4 d5! *(206)*
    B 2. Nc3 g6 3. f4 Bg7 4. Nf3 Nc6 *(206)* [B23]
        B1 5. Bc4 e6 *(206)*
            B1a 6. 0-0 Nge7 *(207)*
                B1a1 7. e5 d5 8. exd6 Qxd6 9. Ne4 Qc7 *(207)*
                B1a2 7. d3 d5 8. Bb3 0-0 9. Qe1 Na5
                    10. Qh4 *(208)*
            B1b 6. f5 Nge7 7. fxe6 dxe6 8. 0-0 0-0 9. d3 Na5
                10. Bb3 Nxb3 11. axb3 e5 *(209)*
        B2 5. Bb5 Nd4 *(209)*
            B2a 6. Bd3 d6 7. Nxd4 cxd4 8. Ne2 Nf6 *(210)*
                B2a1 9. Bb5+ Bd7 10. Bxd7+ Qxd7
                    11. d3 e5 12. 0-0 0-0 13. f5 *(211)*
                B2a2 9. Nxd4 Nxe4 10. Bxe4 Bxd4 11. c3 Bg7
                    12. Qf3 Qb6 *(211)*
                B2a3 9. c3 dxc3 10. dxc3 0-0 11. 0-0 b5!?
                    (212)
            B2b 6. 0-0 e6 7. d3 Ne7 8. Nxd4 cxd4 9. Ne2 0-0
                10. Ba4 *(213)*

The Alapin Variation—2. c3 and the Smith-Morra (Chapter 18)
1. e4 c5 2. c3 g6 3. d4 cxd4 4. cxd4 d5 *(218)* [B22]
    A 5. e5 Bg7 6. Nc3 Nc6 7. Bb5 f6 *(220)*
        A1 8. exf6 exf6 9. Nge2 Be6 10. Nf4 Bf7 11. 0-0 Nge7 *(220)*
        A2 8. f4 Nh6 9. Nf3 Bg4 10. Be3 0-0 11. 0-0 Nf5! *(221)*
    B 5. exd5 Nf6 *(223)*
        B1 6. Bb5+ Nbd7 7. Nc3 Bg7 8. d6 0-0 *(223)* [8. ... exd6—p. 223]
        B2 6. Nc3 Nxd5 7. Bc4 Nb6 8. Bb3 Bg7 9. Nf3 0-0 *(224)*
            B2a 10. h3 Nc6 11. Be3 Na5 *(225)*
                B2a1 12. 0-0 Nxb3 13. axb3 Be6 *(225)*
                B2a2 12. Bc2 Nac4 13. Bc1 Be6 *(226)*
            B2b 10. 0-0 Nc6 11. d5 Na5 12. Re1 Bg4 *(226)*

Wing Gambit and 2. b3 (Chapter 19)
1. e4 c5 2. b4 cxb4 *(230)* [B20]

A 3. a3 d5 4. exd5 Qxd5 5. Nf3 e5 6. axb4 Bxb4 7. c3 Bc5 8. Na3 Nf6
9. Bc4 *(232)*

B 3. d4 d5! *(235)*

    B1 4. exd5 Qxd5 5. Nf3 Nc6 6. c4 bxc3 7. Nxc3 Qa5 *(235)*

    B2 4. e5 Nc6 5. Nf3 Bg4 6. Bb2 e6 *(236)*

Nimzo-Indian Defense—Introduction and 4. a3 (Chapter 21)
1. d4 Nf6 2. c4 e6 3. Nc3 Bb4 4. a3 Bxc3+ 5. bxc3 b6 6. f3 Ba6 7. e4 Nc6 *(258)* [E24]

A 8. Bd3 Na5 9. Qe2 Qc8 10. e5 Ng8 11. f4 Ne7 12. Nf3 d5 13. cxd5 Bxd3
14. Qxd3 exd5 *(261)*

B 8. Bg5 Qc8 9. Bd3 Na5 10. Qe2 Qb7 11. d5 Nb3 12. Rb1 Nc5 *(264)*

    B1 13. Be3 Nxd3+ 14. Qxd3 exd5 15. exd5 0-0 16. Bg5 Ne8 *(266)*

    B2 13. Nh3 d6 *(266)*

C 8. e5 Ng8 9. Nh3 Na5 10. Qa4 Qc8 11. Bd3 c5 12. Ng5 Qc6 *(266)*

Nimzo-Indian Defense with 4. Qc2 (Chapter 22)
1. d4 Nf6 2. c4 e6 3. Nc3 Bb4 4. Qc2 Nc6 5. Nf3 d6 *(270)* [E33]

A 6. Bd2 0-0 7. a3 Bxc3 8. bxc3 Qe7 *(272)*

    A1 9. e4 e5 10. d5 Nb8 11. Be2 Nh5 12. Nxe5 Nf6 13. Nf3 Nxe4
14. 0-0 Nxc3 15. Qxc3 Bg4 *(273)*

    A2 9. b4 e5 10. d5 Nb8 11. e4 Nh5 12. g3 f5 *(274)*

    A3 9. e3 a5 *(274)*

        A3a 10. b3 e5 11. dxe5 dxe5 12. Be2 Bg4 *(275)*

        A3b 10. Bd3 e5 11. dxe5 dxe5 *(276)*

            A3b1 12. 0-0 Re8 13. Bf5 Bxf5 14. Qxf5 Qe6
(276)

            A3b2 12. Ng5 h6 13. Ne4 Nxe4
14. Bxe4 Nd4 *(277)*

    A4 9. g3 e5 10. d5 Nb8 11. Bg2 Ne8 *(278)*

B 6. Bg5 h6 *(278)*

    7. Bd2 0-0 *(278)*

    7. Bxf6 Qxf6 8. a3 Bxc3+ 9. Qxc3 0-0 *(278)*

C 6. e4 e5 7. d5 Bxc3+ 8. Qxc3 Ne7 9. Bd3 0-0 10. 0-0 Nh5 *(279)*

D 6. a3 Bxc3+ 7. Qxc3 a5 8. b3 0-0 9. Bb2 Re8 *(280)*

Nimzo-Indian Defense with 4. e3 and 5. Bd3 (Chapter 23)
1. d4 Nf6 2. c4 e6 3. Nc3 Bb4 4. e3 b6 5. Bd3 Bb7 *(282)* [E43]

A 6. Nf3 0-0 7. 0-0 c5 *(284)*

    A1 8. Na4 cxd4 *(284)*

        A1a 9. exd4 Re8 10. a3 Bf8 11. b4 d6 12. Bb2 Nbd7
13. Re1 Rc8 14. Nc3 a6 15. Bf1 Qc7 *(284)*

        A1b 9. a3 Bd6 10. exd4 Bxf3 11. Qxf3 Nc6 12. Be3 e5 *(287)*

    A2 8. Bd2 cxd4 9. exd4 d5 10. cxd5 Nxd5 *(289)*

        A2a 11. Qe2 Nc6 12. Rfd1 Be7 13. Rac1 Rc8 14. a3 Nxc3
15. Bxc3 Nb8 *(290)*

        A2b 11. Nxd5 Bxd2 12. Nxb6 axb6 13. Nxd2 Qxd4 *(292)*

Bogo-Indian—Introduction and 4. Bd2 with 6, Bg2 (Chapter 30)
1. d4 Nf6 2. c4 e6 3. Nf3 Bb4+ 4. Bd2 Qe7 5. g3 Nc6 6. Bg2 Bxd2+ 7. Nbxd2 0-0 8. 0-0 d6 9. e4 e5 10. d5 Nb8 *(338)* [E11]

A 11. b4 a5 12. a3 Na6 13. Qb3 c6 *(343)*

B 11. Ne1 a5 12. Nd3 Na6 *(345)*

B1 13. a3 Bg4 14. f3 Bd7 15. b4 c6 *(346)*

B2 13. f4 c6 *(347)*

B2a 14. h3 cxd5 15. cxd5 Bd7 *(347)*

B2b 14. f5 cxd5 15. exd5 e4 16. Qe2 b5! *(349)*

B2c 14. fxe5 dxe5 *(350)*

Bogo-Indian with 4. Bd2 and 6. Nc3 (Chapter 31)
1. d4 Nf6 2. c4 e6 3. Nf3 Bb4+ 4. Bd2 Qe7 5. g3 Nc6 6. Nc3 Bxc3 7. Bxc3 Ne4 *(354)* [E11]

A 8. Qc2 Nxc3 9. Qxc3 Qb4 10. Rc1 Qxc3+ 11. Rxc3 d6 12. Bg2 Bd7 *(355)*

B 8. Rc1 0-0 9. Bg2 d6 *(356)*

B1 10. d5 Nxc3 11. Rxc3 Nb8 12. dxe6 fxe6 13. Nd4 c6 14. 0-0 Nd7 *(356)*

B1a 15. e4 Nf6 *(357)*

B1a1 16. e5 dxe5 17. Nf3 e4 18. Ng5 e5 19. Nxe4 Bf5 *(357)*

B1a2 16. Rd3 e5 17. Nc2 Be6 18. Ne3 Rad8 *(358)*

B1b 15. b4 Nf6 16. b5 e5 17. Nc2 cxb5 18. cxb5 Be6 *(359)*

B2 10. 0-0 Nxc3 11. Rxc3 e5 12. d5 Nb8 *(360)*

B2a 13. c5 dxc5 14. Qc2 Na6! 15. Re3 f6 *(360)*

B2b 13. Nd2 Nd7 14. b4 f5 15. c5 e4 16. cxd6 cxd6 17. Rc7 *(360)*

B2c 13. b4 Bg4 14. Nd2 Nd7 *(361)*

Bogo-Indian with 4. Nbd2 (Chapter 32)
1. d4 Nf6 2. c4 e6 3. Nf3 Bb4+ 4. Nbd2 b6 5. a3 Bxd2+ 6. Bxd2 h6 7. e3 Bb7 8. Bd3 d6 *(364)* [E11]

Torre Attack—1. d4 Nf6 2. Nf3 e6 3. Bg5 (Chapter 33)
1. d4 Nf6 2. Nf3 e6 3. Bg5 h6 *(370)* [A46]

A 4. Bh4 c5 5. e3 cxd4 6. exd4 Be7 7. Bd3 0-0 *(371)*

A1 8. c4 b6 9. Nc3 Bb7 10. 0-0 d6 11. Re1 Nbd7 *(372)*

A2 8. c3 b6 9. Qe2 Bb7 10. Nbd2 Nc6 11. Bxf6!? *(373)*

B 4. Bxf6 Qxf6 5. e4 d6 6. Nc3 g6 7. Qd2 Bg7 8. 0-0-0 a6 *(374)*

B1 9. Bd3 Qe7 10. Rhe1 b5 11. Kb1 Bb7 *(375)*

B2 9. e5 Qe7 10. d5?! dxe5 11. Re1 Nd7 12. Bc4 exd5 13. Nxd5 Qd6 *(375)*

B3 9. Qe3 Nd7 10. h4 b5 11. Re1 Bb7 *(376)*

London System—1. d4 Nf6 2. Nf3 e6 3. Bf4 (Chapter 34)
1. d4 Nf6 2. Nf3 e6 3. Bf4 c5 4. e3 b6 5. Bd3 Bb7 6. Nbd2 Be7 7. c3 cxd4 8. exd4 0-0 9. 0-0 d6 10. Qe2 Nbd7 11. h3 Re8 *(380)* [A46]

1. d4 with 2. Nf3 and 3. g3 (Chapter 35)

1. d4 Nf6 2. Nf3 e6 3. g3 b5 4. Bg2 Bb7 5. 0-0 c5 6. Bg5 Be7 7. c3 Na6 8. Nbd2 0-0 9. Qb3 Rb8!
(386) [A46]

Colle System—1. d4 Nf6 2. Nf3 e6 3. e3 (Chapter 36)

1. d4 Nf6 2. Nf3 e6 3. e3 c5 4. Bd3 d5 *(394)* [A46]

    A 5. c3 Be7 6. Nbd2 0-0 7. 0-0 b6 *(396)*

        A1 8. Ne5 Bb7 9. f4 Ne4! 10. Nxe4 dxe4 11. Bc2 f6
        12. Ng4 Bd5 *(396)*

        A2 8. Qe2 Bb7 9. dxc5 bxc5 10. e4 Nc6 11. e5 Nfd7
        12. Re1 Re8 *(397)*

    B 5. b3 Nbd7 6. 0-0 b6 7. Bb2 Bb7 8. Ne5 Be7 9. Nd2 0-0 10. f4 Ne4! *(399)*

Veresov Opening—1. d4 Nf6 2. Nc3 d5 3. Bg5 (Chapter 37)

1. d4 Nf6 2. Nc3 d5 3. Bg5 c5!? 4. Bxf6 gxf6 5. e4 dxe4 6. dxc5 f5! *(402)* [D01]

    A 7. g4 Qc7 8. gxf5 Bg7 9. Qd5 *(404)*

    B 7. Qh5!? Nc6 8. Nh3 Bg7 9. Ng5 Bxc3+ 10. bxc3 Qd5! 11. c4 Qe5! *(405)*

    C 7. Qxd8+ Kxd8 *(406)*

        C1 8. Rd1+ Bd7 9. Bc4 e6 *(406)*

        C2 8. Nh3 Bg7 9. 0-0-0+ Bd7 10. Ne2 *(406)*

        C3 8. f3 Bg7 9. Rd1+ Bd7 10. Bc4 *(407)*

The Trompowsky—1. d4 Nf6 2. Bg5 (Chapter 38)

1. d4 Nf6 2. Bg5 c5 *(410)* [A45]

    A 3. Nc3 cxd4 4. Qxd4 Nc6 5. Qh4 Qa5! 6. 0-0-0 d6 7. e4 Be6 8. Bxf6 gxf6
    9. Kb1 f5 10. exf5 *(412)*

    B 3. d5 Ne4 4. Bf4 Qb6 *(412)*

        B1 5. Qc1 c4 6. e3 Qa5+ 7. Nd2 c3! 8. bxc3 Qxd5 *(412)*

        B2 5. Bc1 e6 6. f3 Nf6 7. c4 exd5 8. cxd5 c4 *(413)*

        B3 5. Nd2 Qxb2! 6. Nxe4 Qb4+ 7. Qd2 Qxe4 8. e3 g5 *(414)*

    C 3. Bxf6 exf6 *(415)*

        C1 4. e3 Qb6! 5. b3 d5 6. Nf3 Nc6 7. Be2 *(415)*

        C2 4. c3 d5 5. e3 Nc6 6. Nd2 Be7 7. dxc5 Bxc5 8. Nb3 Bb6
        9. Ne2 0-0 10. Nf4 *(416)*

        C3 4. d5 f5 5. Nc3 d6 6. e3 a6 7. a4 g6 8. Nf3 Bg7 9. Be2 Qa5
        10. Qd2 0-0 11. 0-0 Nd7 *(417)*

        C4 4. Nc3 d5 5. e3 Be6 6. Nf3 c4 7. Be2 Bb4 8. Qd2 0-0 9. a3 Bd6
        10. 0-0 a6 *(418)*

Blackmar-Diemer Gambit—1. d4 Nf6 2. Nc3 d5 3. e4 (Chapter 39)

1. d4 Nf6 2. Nc3 d5 3. e4 Nxe4 4. Nxe4 dxe4 *(422)* [D00]

    A 5. Be3 Bf5 6. Ne2 e6 7. Ng3 Bg6 8. h4 h5 *(424)*

    B 5. f3 Bf5 6. c3 e6 7. Be3 *(424)*

    C 5. Bc4 g6 6. f3 Bg7 7. c3 c5 8. Qb3 0-0 9. dxc5 Nd7 *(425)*

English I—Overall Review and Intro to 1. ... c5 (Chapter 40)
1. c4 c5 2. Nf3 g6 *(432)* [A30]
    A 3. d4 cxd4 4. Nxd4 Nc6 *(433)*
        A1 5. e4 Nf6 *(433)*
        A2 5. g3 Bg7 6. Nc2 Qa5+ 7. Bd2 Qc5 8. Bc3 Nf6 *(433)*
        A3 5. Nc3 Bg7 6. Nc2 Bxc3+ 7. bxc3 Qa5 8. Bd2 0-0 9. f3 d6
            (434)
    B 3. e3 Nf6 4. d4 *(434)*
    C 3. Nc3 Bg7 4. g3 Nc6 5. Bg2 e5 *(435)*

English II—White plays e3 and d4 (Chapter 41)
1. c4 c5 2. Nf3 g6 3. Nc3 Bg7 4. e3 Nf6 5. d4 cxd4 6. exd4 d5 *(438)* [A30➤B13]
    A 7. Be2 0-0 8. 0-0 dxc4 9. Bxc4 Bg4 *(440)*
    B 7. Bg5 Ne4 8. cxd5 Nxg5 9. Nxg5 0-0 *(441)*
        B1 10. Nf3 Nd7 11. Bc4 Nb6 12. Bb3 Bg4 13. 0-0 Bxf3
            14. Qxf3 Bxd4 *(442)*
        B2 10. Qd2 Nd7 11. Bc4 Qb6 12. Rd1 Qb4 13. Bb3 a5 *(442)*
    C 7. cxd5 Nxd5 8. Bc4 Nb6 9. Bb3 Nc6 10. Be3 0-0 11. d5 Na5 *(444)*
    D 7. Qb3 dxc4 8. Bxc4 0-0 9. Ne5 e6 10. Be3 Nc6 11. Nxc6 bxc6
        12. 0-0 Nd5 *(445)*

English III—Closed (Chapter 42)
1. c4 c5 2. Nc3 g6 3. g3 Bg7 4. Bg2 Nc6 *(448)* [A36-37]
    A 5. Nf3 d6 6. 0-0 e5 7. d3 Nge7 8. a3 0-0 9. Rb1 a5 10. Ne1 Be6 *(450)*
        A1 11. Nd5 Rb8 12. Nxe7+ Nxe7 13. b4 axb4 14. axb4 cxb4
            15. Rxb4 d5 *(452)*
        A2 11. Nc2 d5 12. cxd5 Nxd5 *(453)*
    B 5. a3 d6 6. Rb1 a5 7. e3 e5 8. Nge2 Nge7 9. 0-0 0-0 *(454)*
    C 5. e3 e5 6. Nge2 Nge7 7. 0-0 0-0 8. d3 d6 9. Rb1 Rb8 10. a3 a5
        11. Bd2 Be6 *(456)*
        C1 12. Nd5 b5 13. Nec3 b4 *(457)*
        C2 12. Qb3 f5 13. Nd5 Nxd5 14. cxd5 Bf7 15. Qc2 Ne7 *(458)*
    D 5. e4 d6 6. Nge2 e5 7. 0-0 Nge7 8. d3 0-0 9. a3 a5 10. Rb1 Rb8 *(458)*
        D1 11. Nd5 b5 12. cxb5 Rxb5 13. Qa4 Ba6 *(459)*
        D2 11. Be3 f5 12. exf5 gxf5 *(460)*
        D3 11. Bd2 Be6 12. f4 Qd7 13. Nd5 Bg4 *(460)*

Bird's Opening—1. f4 (Chapter 43)
1. f4 g6 2. Nf3 d5 *(466)* [A02]
    A 3. g3 Bg7 4. Bg2 Nf6 5. 0-0 0-0 6. d3 b6 7. Nc3 Bb7 *(468)*
    B 3. e3 Bg7 4. d4 Nh6 5. Be2 0-0 6. 0-0 Nf5 7. c3 Nd6 8. b3 Nd7
        9. Ne5 Nf6 *(469)*

Sokolsky—1. b4 (Chapter 44)
1. b4 e5 2. Bb2 Bxb4 3. Bxe5 Nf6 4. e3 0-0 5. Nf3 Re8 6. Be2 d5 7. 0-0 c5 8. c4 Nc6 9. Bb2 d4 10. Qb3 Ne4 11. d3 Nd6 12. e4 f5 *(474)* [A00]

The Rest—Knights-First and the Fianchettoes (Chapter 45) *(480)*
A 1. Nf3 c5 *(481)*
   A1 2. e4 g6 *(482)*
   A2 2. c4 c5 *(482)*
   A3 2. b3 d6 3. Bb2 e5 *(484)*
B 1. g3 c5 *(482)*
C 1. b3 d5 2. Bb2 Bg4*(483)* [A01]
Rare Moves *(484)* [A00]

Illustrative Games (Chapter 46)

Almasi–Kramnik   1. e4 c5 2. Nf3 Nc6 3. Nc3 g6 4. d4 cxd4
                        5. Nxd4 Bg7 6. Be3 Nf6 7. Bc4 0-0 8. Bb3 a5
                        9. a4 *(491)* Accelerated Dragon [B35]

Bauer–Malakhov   1. e4 c5 2. Nf3 Nc6 3. d4 cxd4 4. Nxd4 g6
                        5. Nc3 Bg7 6. Be3 Nf6 7. Bc4 0-0 8. Bb3 a5
                        9. f3 *(496)* Accelerated Dragon [B35]

Rowson–Malakhov   1. e4 c5 2. Nf3 Nc6 3. d4 cxd4 4. Nxd4 g6
                        5. c4 Nf6 6. Nc3 d6 7. Be2 Nxd4 8. Qxd4 Bg7
                        9. Be3 *(500)* Maroczy Bind [B36]

Vallejo–Malakhov   1. e4 c5 2. Nf3 Nc6 3. d4 cxd4 4. Nxd4 g6
                        5. c4 Nf6 6. Nc3 d6 7. Be2 Nxd4 8. Qxd4 Bg7
                        9. Bg5 *(502)* Maroczy Bind [B36]

Rudelis–Donaldson   1. d4 Nf6 2. c4 e6 3. Nc3 Bb4 4. a3 Bxc3+
                        5. bxc3 b6 *(506)* Nimzo-Indian [E24]

Epishin–Berg   1. d4 e6 2. c4 Nf6 3. Nc3 Bb4 4. e3 b6
                        5. Ne2 Ba6 *(508)* Nimzo-Indian [E45]

Goldin–Yermolinsky   1. d4 Nf6 2. c4 e6 3. Nc3 Bb4 4. Qc2 *(510)*
                        Nimzo-Indian [E33]

Timman–Dzindzichashvili   1. d4 Nf6 2. c4 e6 3. Nc3 Bb4
                        4. Bg5 *(514)* Nimzo-Indian [E31]

Skembris–Beliavsky   1. d4 Nf6 2. c4 e6 3. Nf3 Bb4+ 4. Bd2 Qe7
                        5. g3 Nc6 6. Bg2 Bxd2+ 7. Nbxd2 d6 8. 0-0 e5
                        9. d5 Nb8 10. e4 a5 11. Ne1 0-0 12. Nd3 Na6
                 ·   13. a3 Bg4 14. f3 Bd7 15. b4 c6 16. Qb3 *(518)*
                        Bogo-Indian [E11]

Khomyakov–Korotylev   1. d4 Nf6 2. c4 e6 3. Nf3 Bb4+ 4. Bd2 Qe7
                        5. g3 Nc6 6. Bg2 Bxd2+ 7. Nbxd2 d6 8. 0-0 0-0
                        9. e4 e5 10. d5 Nb8 11. b4 a5 12. a3 Na6
                        13. Ne1 Bg4 14. f3 Bd7 15. Nd3 c6 16. bxa5
                        (522) Bogo-Indian [E11]

Avrukh–Ibrahimov   1. d4 Nf6 2. c4 e6 3. Nf3 Bb4+ 4. Bd2 Qe7
                        5. g3 Nc6 6. Nc3 Bxc3 7. Bxc3 Ne4 *(526)*
                        Bogo-Indian [E11]

Cebalo–Jakovljevic   1. d4 Nf6 2. c4 e6 3. Nf3 Bb4+ 4. Nbd2 b6 *(530)*
                        Bogo-Indian [E11]

Sokolov–Karpov   1. d4 Nf6 2. Nf3 e6 3. Bg5 h6 4. Bh4 c5 *(534)*
                        Torre Attack [A46]

Three-time U.S. Champion

Lev Alburt

Grandmaster Lev Alburt was European champion, 3-time champion of the Ukraine, 3-time U.S. champion, and twice U.S. Open champion. In 2002, he was inducted into the U.S. Chess Hall of Fame. One of the few GM defectors from the Soviet Union, Alburt was mentored by world champion Mikhail Botvinnik.

Alburt is famous for providing aspiring players easy access to master-level ideas. He provides lessons through-the-mail, over-the-telephone, and face-to-face. Write to GM Lev Alburt at PO Box 534, Gracie Station, New York, NY, 10028, or call him at 212.794.8706.

Alburt and Lawrence, from opposite sides of the old "Iron Curtain," have been writing partners and friends for two decades.

Author of more than a dozen books

Al Lawrence

Al Lawrence served as Executive Director of the U.S. Chess Federation during a decade of record-breaking growth. He opened the World Chess Hall of Fame in Miami and served as its first Executive Director. He was selected as "Chess Journalist of the Year" for 2000-2001 by the Chess Journalists of America.

Lawrence is president of OutExcel! Corporation, a marketing and publishing firm. Contact him at al@outexcel.com.

www.OutExcel.com

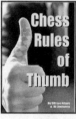

It's Easy to Order Books from Lev Alburt!

It's easy
to order!
See below!

For more information,
see page 550.

It's Easy to Order Books from Lev Alburt!

It's easy
to order!
See above!

For more information,
see page 550.